BRITAIN AND INDUSTRIAL EUROPE
1750 - 1870

BRITAIN AND INDUSTRIAL EUROPE 1750-1870

Studies in British Influence on the Industrial Revolution in Western Europe

by

W. O. HENDERSON

Reader in International Economic History in the University of Manchester

Third Edition

LEICESTER UNIVERSITY PRESS
1972

First edition 1954
(Liverpool University Press)

Second edition 1965
Third edition 1972

Printed in Great Britain by
Lowe & Brydone (Printers) Ltd, London

ISBN 0 7185 1056 9

CONTENTS

MAPS

PREFACE TO THE THIRD EDITION

THE first edition of this book, which appeared in 1954, was an early attempt to assess the significance of the role played by an advanced industrial state in promoting economic growth in relatively underdeveloped countries. Since Britain had experienced an industrial revolution well before any of her neighbours across the Channel it was natural to attempt to study the problem by examining the way in which the expansion of certain underdeveloped economies on the Continent—particularly those of France, Germany, and Belgium—had been stimulated between 1750 and 1870 by British technical knowledge and capital.

Today the attempt of the United States and the advanced industrial countries of western Europe to promote economic growth and to raise living standards in the poorer regions of the "third world" is one of the major problems of the 1970s. The conditions under which the underdeveloped countries of the modern world are trying to expand their manufactures are not the same as those which prevailed when Britain fostered the industrialization of some of her neighbours. But, although history never repeats itself, there are striking parallels that can be drawn between the efforts of a country like India to expand her industries today and the efforts of some of the states on the Continent to expand their industries in the nineteenth century. In making such comparisons the present study may perhaps prove to be useful.

W. O. HENDERSON

University of Manchester

I. INTRODUCTION

I. BRITISH INFLUENCE ON THE INDUSTRIAL DEVELOPMENT OF THE CONTINENT

It is well known that the development of modern large-scale industrial capitalism took place in Britain at an earlier period than on the Continent. A number of factors contributed to the rapid expansion of British manufactures in the second half of the eighteenth century.[1] For the development of the machine age adequate supplies of capital, raw materials and labour as well as access to suitable home and overseas markets were necessary. In Britain wealth was accumulating in the eighteenth century. Overseas trade, particularly with the colonies, was profitable and there were great landlords whose incomes from rents were sufficient to enable them to invest money in mining and manufactures. The Bank of England, the London financial houses, the country banks and the various exchanges provided the necessary financial framework within which new industrial enterprises could expand. If the typical business was still the family concern or the partnership there were also important joint stock companies operating on a large scale. As far as raw materials were concerned Britain had adequate supplies of coal and iron-ore[2] which were conveniently

[1] For the industrial revolution in Britain see Arnold Toynbee, *Lectures on the Industrial Revolution . . .* (9th edn., 1923) ; P. Mantoux, *The Industrial Revolution in the eighteenth Century* (1928) ; H. L. Beales, *The Industrial Revolution* 1750-1850 (Workers' Educational Association, 1928) ; C. R. Fay, *Great Britain from Adam Smith to the Present Day* (1928) ; L. C. A. Knowles, *The Industrial and Commercial Revolutions in Great Britain . . .* (edn of 1930); L. Brentano, *Eine Geschichte der wirtschaftlichen Entwicklung Englands*, Vol. III (in two parts, 1928-9) ; T. S. Ashton, *The Industrial Revolution* 1760-1830 (Home University Library, 1948) ; Arthur Redford, *The Economic History of England* 1760-1860 (1936) ; J. L. and Barbara Hammond, *The Rise of Modern Industry* (5th ed., 1937) ; W. Bowden, *Industrial Society in England towards the end of the Eighteenth Century* (1925); Sir Henry Trueman Wood, *Industrial England in the middle of the eighteenth Century* (1910) ; G. N. Clark, *The Idea of the Industrial Revolution* (1953) ; Sir John Clapham, *A concise Economic History of Britain to* 1750 (1949) ; S. G. E. Lythe, *British Economic History since* 1760 (1950) ; W. Hoffman, *Stadien und Typen der Industrialisierung* (1931) ; W. Hoffman, *Wachstum und Wachstumformen der englischen Industriewirtschaft* (1940) ; W. Schlote, *British Overseas Trade from* 1700 *to the* 1930's (English translation by W. O. Henderson and W. H. Chaloner, 1952).

[2] But for steel making bar-iron had to be imported from Sweden.

situated near good ports. Important industries, such as the manufacture of woollen and leather goods, had ample supplies of raw materials which were produced on farms at home. The growing population provided both the labour force for the new factories and an expanding home demand for manufacturers. The growth and importance of London was also a factor of some significance. It has been pointed out that in the 1720s Defoe "never wearied of recording how much London's greatness contributed to the prosperity of the whole country."[3] The expansion of British agriculture provided additional supplies of raw materials to certain industries as well as the extra food needed to feed a growing population. High wages in the towns led to an exodus from the countryside to the towns which helped to increase the labour force available in the new factories and workshops. Britain's favourable geographical location on world trade routes and her efficient mercantile marine gave the country relatively easy access to foreign markets.

There were also somewhat less tangible factors in the situation but their full significance can hardly be precisely evaluated. Napoleon called us a nation of shopkeepers and it may be that the habits and character of the British people were peculiarly fitted to take advantage of the industrial opportunities of the eighteenth century. And the significance of the roles played in the industrialisation of the country by such groups as the Dissenters,[4] the Scots and the Jews raises interesting speculations which cannot be discussed here.

At first sight it might appear surprising that the Continent did not become industrialised at about the same time as Britain. The Continent too, had great resources of coal, iron-ore, timber, wool and other valuable raw materials. In some respects technical knowledge on the Continent—as in mining and metallurgy—was still in advance of Britain in the middle of the eighteenth century. There was no lack of inventive genius on the European mainland. Some epoch-making machines, such as the Jacquard loom, the Seguin multitubular locomotive boiler and the Heilmann comb, were invented on the Continent. In the eighteenth century the banks of Holland and Switzerland were as important as those in Britain. And in the same period on the Continent the State itself

[3] G. D. H. Cole, *Periods and Persons* (Pelican Books, 1945), p. 63.

[4] For the influence of the Dissenters on the development of industrial capitalism in Britain see, for example, E. D. Bebb, *Nonconformity and Social and Economic Life* 1660-1800 (1934) ; Isabel Grubb, *Quakerism and Industry before 1800* (1930); W. J. Warner, *The Wesleyan Movement in the Industrial Revolution* (1930) and A. Raistrick, *Quakers in Science and Industry* (1950).

owned industrial establishments and public utilities and gave valuable financial and other assistance to private enterprise in a way that was less customary in Britain.[5] In France, for example, under the ancien régime, there were both nationalised factories and private establishments controlled and subsidised by the Crown. Moreover the Continental System shielded much of the European mainland from British competition at a critical period. Nevertheless it was some time after the Napoleonic Wars before Continental countries began to overtake the lead which Britain had secured in the industrial field.

Explanations for the relatively slow progress of industrialisation on the Continent are not far to seek. Wars and civil disturbances inevitably delayed progress. In many parts of the Continent there was a serious shortage of capital and not even the assistance offered by governments could bridge the gap between the capital needed to start new enterprises and the money available from private sources. In the eighteenth century Continental trade was hampered both by poor communications and by a fantastic multiplicity of customs duties, excises and tolls of various kinds. Gild restrictions, too, sometimes hindered the expansion of manufactures. Before 1789 there were on the Continent few changes in the agrarian economy comparable with what was occurring in Britain. Peasants on the European mainland were sometimes prepared to undertake industrial work in the towns for part of the year but they were reluctant to break all ties with the countryside by becoming full-time factory workers. Restrictive commercial policies encouraged local and regional monopolies and the absence of competition not infrequently removed an important incentive to industrial progress.

Generalisations of this kind are, however, of only limited value since conditions varied considerably in different parts of the Continent. It is necessary to examine separately the situation in individual countries in order to discover reasons for the relatively slow progress that was made in industrialisation in the second half of the eighteenth century. In Germany, for example, the existence of a large number of virtually sovereign states retarded manufacturing progress. Each of some 300 independent territories had its own system of customs and excises, currency, weights and measures. The great coalfields of the Ruhr and Upper Silesia were too far from the sea and from the main centres of population to be adequately exploited in the eighteenth century. It was not

[5] But in an earlier period—the seventeenth century—the progress of British mining, glass-works, soap manufactures, etc., had (as Hermann Levy has observed) been fostered by " privileges from the Crown, suppression of internal competition by law, and a protective trade policy " (H. Levy, *Monopoly and Competition* (1911), p. 43).

until the establishment of the Zollverein[6] and the construction of a network of railways that these difficulties could be overcome. And a comparison between the fortunes of Hamburg and Liverpool in the eighteenth century would show how the Hansa port suffered from the absence of an economically unified hinterland and the lack of both a German navy and of German overseas territories.

France, on the other hand, suffered from a shortage of coal and other important raw materials. The rigid bureaucracy of the ancien régime, the privileges of the gilds, the burden of taxation and the restrictive system of commerce and navigation (inherited from Colbert) were inimicable to industrial progress in the new age of machinery, steam power and factories. Undue concentration upon luxury industries—such as silk—was another unfavourable factor in the situation. Industrial expansion was delayed in the Belgian provinces by the closing of the Scheldt and by foreign rule and in Switzerland by lack of coal and by remoteness from populous markets.

The great expansion of British industries in the reign of George III naturally excited much interest in neighbouring countries. On the Continent both Governments and far-seeing industrialists soon realised that by developing her industries in a new way Britain was becoming both wealthy and powerful. It was clear that a significant shift in the European economic balance of power was taking place. From the European mainland envious glances were cast across the Channel and energetic efforts were soon made to wrest from Britain the secrets of industrial progress.

Technical knowledge spread from Britain to the Continent in various ways. Much information published in England was available to readers on the other side of the Channel. The *Journal of the Society of Arts*, the transactions of the Royal Society and the proceedings of the professional bodies—such as the Institution of Civil Engineers—contained details of inventions and new industrial processes. Some of this information was reprinted in technical journals on the Continent. An examination of the files of the *Annales des Mines* for example shows how assiduously foreign observers studied English periodicals which described the advances that were being made in the production of new machines.

Many foreigners visited Britain in the hope of acquiring sufficient information about recent inventions and technical processes to enable them to introduce this new technical knowledge into their own countries. Sometimes these "industrial spies" had a legitimate excuse for seeking permission to enter British factories and workshops. If they were agents of foreign customers

[6] See W. O. Henderson, *The Zollverein* (1939; new edition, 1959)

who were buying machines they might not unreasonably ask to be shown how the machinery should be handled. Other visitors however had no intention of buying machinery and they came to this country in the hope of learning some of the secrets of the new machine age. Some foreigners secured employment in British factories with the object of learning enough about the machines they handled to be able to build similar machines for themselves when they returned home. The reception accorded by British industrialists to foreign visitors varied considerably. When Faujas de Saint-Fond came to Manchester at the end of the eighteenth century he could not secure admission to a single cotton mill while at Carron he was allowed to see only the ironworks and not the cannon foundry. On the other hand many foreigners such as Gabriel Jars (1764), Marchant de la Houlière (1775), J. C. Fischer (1814-51) and Frédéric le Play (1842) appear to have had little or no difficulty in inspecting the industrial establishments in which they were interested.

Some foreigners tried to export blueprints, models and machine-parts out of England. This was not necessarily illegal. The export of some machinery was permitted and there were occasions on which the authorities issued licenses for the export of " prohibited " machines. But many models and machines were smuggled out of the country in defiance of the law. When offenders were caught they were fined or imprisoned but there can be little doubt that much smuggling escaped detection. Similarly a number of skilled artisans were enticed abroad although this was illegal until 1825. The severe punishments inflicted upon labour recruiting agents did not deter either Englishmen or foreigners from smuggling operatives and mechanics out of the country.

British industrialists in the eighteenth century made strenuous efforts to secure the enforcement of laws prohibiting the export of machinery and the emigration of skilled workers. The Home Office papers contain evidence of a duel of wits between Johan Cahman, ironfounder of Gothenburg, on the one hand, and Dr. Roebuck and Samuel Garbett of the Carron ironworks on the other. It appears that in 1763 a man named Downing induced Francis Lloyd to act as a recruiting agent for Cahman at a wage of a guinea a week. The scheme was discovered by chance but it is not clear whether the authorities succeeded in laying either Downing or Lloyd by the heels. In 1765 the scene shifted to Scotland. Here Croswell, another of Cahman's agents, persuaded Peter Duff and Thomas Lewis to leave Roebuck's employment. The two men were caught but—much to Garbett's disgust—they were released on bail. In the following year Lewis again tried to emigrate to Sweden and was again prevented from doing so.[7] Meanwhile Croswell himself had been arrested and, when he failed to surrender to his bail, he was outlawed. On November 9, 1765, Garbett reported to the Home Office that an ironworker named James Kennaway had succeeded in reaching Gothenburg. In 1767 the English chaplain at Gothenburg stated that he had interviewed James Kennaway, George Graham, Nieman Wise and Peter Clark and a youth named Bowie who were all employed by Cahman. He was unable to persuade them to return home. Garbett also drew the attention of the Home Office to the activities of a labour recruiting agent named Cotterell who persuaded three skilled workers (Groves, Craighill and Johnson) to settle in the Habsburg dominions.[8]

Heavy penalties were imposed upon those who defied the laws concerning the export of machinery and the emigration of skilled workers. In 1785 a German named Baden was fined £500 at Lancaster and in 1792 a native of Alsace named Albert was sent to prison and fined £500. Shortly afterwards an Englishman named Paul Harding, who was acting as labour recruiting agent for Lièven Bauwens, of Ghent, was fined and imprisoned. It has been stated that when James Cockerill landed in Hull in September 1802 to buy textile machinery and to engage operatives he was promptly arrested and lodged in York Castle. He succeeded in escaping however and he reached the Continent in safety.

But the authorities let many labour recruiting agents and smugglers of machinery and blueprints slip through their fingers. When one considers the numbers of British workers employed by John Holker at Rouen, by Lièven Bauwens at Ghent, by John Cockerill at Seraing, by Scipion Périer and Humphrey Edwards

[7] Thomas Lewis eventually emigrated to Sweden. In 1769 he secured permission to establish an ironfoundry " according to English methods " at Stockholm and these works were the origin of Bergsund's machine-building establishment. For an account of the influence of the Scots on the industrial development of modern Sweden see Professor Gosta Bodman's paper in *Daedalus*, 1948, (year-book of the Stockholm Museum of Technology).

[8] See J. Redington (ed.), *Calendar of Home Office Papers . . . 1760-1765* (1878) ; J. Redington (ed.), *Calendar of Home Office Papers . . . 1766-1769* (1879) ; R. A. Roberts (ed.) *Calendar of Home Office Papers 1773-1775* (1899) ; T. S. Ashton, *Iron & Steel in the Industrial Revolution* (1924), pp. 201-205 ; Professor Ashton remarks that " in view of Garbett's efforts to arouse his fellow-countrymen to a sense of the foreign peril, it is not without ironical interest to observe that his own son-in-law, Charles Gascoigne, turned apostate, took service under Catherine II, and carried skilled workmen from England to manufacture guns and shells for the armies of Russia " (*ibid.*, p. 204).

at Chaillot, by Schlumberger at Guebwiller and by Friedrich Harkort at the Wetter—to mention only a few—it is clear that the British laws prohibiting the emigration of skilled men were often successfully evaded. These establishments, and many others, contained machinery which had either been smuggled from Britain or had been constructed from British blueprints or models.

After the Napoleonic Wars there was some controversy in Britain concerning the desirability of maintaining the laws restricting the export of machinery and the emigration of skilled workers.[9] The parliamentary enquiries of 1824-5 and 1841 showed how difficult it was in practice to enforce these regulations. While many textile manufacturers and ironmasters still felt that it was in the best interests of the country to do everything possible to stop foreigners from acquiring or copying new British machines and industrial processes the representatives of the machine-building industry complained that this policy deprived them of their export markets and threatened the prosperity of a growing branch of manufacture. They argued that if foreigners could not get machinery from Britain they would get it elsewhere or invent machines of their own. Eventually both the emigration of skilled workers (1825) and the export of machinery (1842) was freed from all restrictions.

Englishmen played a significant part in the industrialisation of western Europe in three ways. First, British skilled workers installed new machinery and then instructed foreign workers how to use it. Thus in the second half of the eighteenth century British textile workers were teaching Frenchmen how to use the fly-shuttle, the waterframe and the mule-jenny, while British engineers installed steam pumps on the Continent. In the second quarter of the ninteenth century groups of English puddlers moved from one ironworks to another in Belgium and Germany instructing foreigners in their craft. A little later the English driver on the footplate of a locomotive was as familiar a figure on the Continent as the marine engineer on a river steamboat or the foreman in a cotton mill.

Secondly, there are several examples of Britons who were important as entrepreneurs and managers. In the middle years of the eighteenth century John Holker not only successfully managed a " royal manufactory " at Rouen but he supervised a

[9] The famous engineer James Nasmyth wrote in his autobiography that in his view " restriction in the communication of new ideas on mechanical subjects to foreigners of intelligence and enterprising spirit served no good purpose . . . It was better to derive the advantage of supplying them with the machines they were in quest of, than to wait until the demand was supplied by the foreigners themselves." (J. Nasmyth, *An Autobiography* (ed. S. Smiles, 1883) p. 244)

group of model textile mills in Normandy and helped to modernise the cotton industry of a whole province. In the 1830s Thomas Ainsworth exercised a similar influence in the Twente textile region in Holland. His contemporary Aaron Manby had an influence over the French engineering industry which extended far beyond the great ironworks and machine-building plants of Charenton and Le Creusot. In the middle of the nineteenth century Thomas Brassey not only built the Paris-Rouen railway and many other lines on the Continent but he showed foreigners how the complex business of constructing a railway could be efficiently organised. At the same time W. T. Mulvany not only founded the Hibernia and Shamrock coalmines in the Ruhr but he played a leading part in bringing the Ruhr coalowners and industrialists together to discuss common problems.

Thirdly, for fifty years or so after the Napoleonic wars, British investors found some of the money necessary to start important industrial enterprises on the Continent. Railway companies, river navigation companies, gasworks, waterworks, cotton and other textile mills, and engineering establishments were set up with the aid of British capital. Manby's engineering workshops at Charenton and Le Creusot, Mulvany's coalmines in the Ruhr, the Lister-Holden woolcombing establishments in France, John Douglas's cotton mill in the Vorarlberg—these and a host of other factories were started with British money. It would be rash even to guess at the actual amount of British capital involved[10] but the significance of this aspect of Britain's contribution to the industrialisation of the European mainland was undoubtedly of some importance.

Although some very able men—men who could ill be spared at home—left Britain to work on the Continent as skilled operatives, engineers and even navvies or to act as entrepreneurs, managers or foremen it should be remembered that Englishmen of a less desirable type were also to be found in Continental factories and workshops. The relatively high wages paid to Englishmen on the Continent attracted not only good but also bad workers. So while some industrialists on the Continent had reason to be grateful for the services rendered by highly skilled British managers, foremen and workers, others preferred to do without British labour. Johann Conrad Fischer, a distinguished Swiss engineer, once explained why he did not employ British workmen. " Not only

[10] John Marshall, a contemporary statistician, estimated that in 1830 £18,200,000 of British capital was invested in Europe. A. H. Imlah (*Economic History Review*, V (ii), 1952, p. 227) agrees with L. H. Jenks that this figure is too high—it " does seem to be a large sum for new investment, though not necessarily for the balance of credits earned through trade services."

do they cost a damned lot of money " he wrote in his journal on October 12, 1827, " but they are often drunkards. English workers who are both efficient and well-behaved can earn a very good living at home. It is by no means uncommon to come across English workers in foreign countries who are far from thoroughly skilled in all branches of their trade. One can expect that range of skill only from a foreman but not from the average worker. British workers seldom fulfil the sanguine expectations of their foreign employers because they are handling materials to which they are not accustomed and because they are working with different people than they would be at home."[11]

In the following chapters an attempt will be made both to sketch the activities of some of the leading British pioneers who introduced new machines, new methods and new ideas into the the chief manufacturing regions on the Continent and to survey the work of some of the foreign industrialists who brought to their own countries the new technical knowledge that was being put to such good use in Great Britain between 1750 and 1875.[12]

[11] Johann Conrad Fischer, *Tagebücher* (new edition by Karl Schib, 1951), October 12, 1827, pp. 455-456.

[12] The account given in these pages of the influence exercised by British capitalists and technical experts on the industrialisation of Western Europe has been largely confined to states on the Continent which eventually became of major importance as manufacturing countries. There were, of course, important connections in 1750-1875 between Britain and other West European countries. For the first English steam engine in Denmark see H. H. Mansa's paper to the Newcomen Society, October 14, 1953. For the Lombes and Italy see an article by W. H. Chaloner in *History Today*, November, 1953.

II. FRANCE

2. ENGLISH INFLUENCE ON THE DEVELOPMENT OF THE FRENCH TEXTILE INDUSTRIES, 1700-1850

Few aspects of the Industrial Revolution in England have received more attention than the inventions which led to the striking increase in the output of the major textile industries in the second half of the eighteenth century. These inventions soon attracted much attention abroad. Continental countries were naturally anxious to share in the wealth produced by the new machines. The English were equally anxious to keep the new machines to themselves. A number of laws were passed to prevent both the export of machinery, machine-parts, tools and blueprints and also the emigration of skilled artisans. Although from time to time severe punishments were inflicted upon foreigners who tried to smuggle machinery out of England or to recruit English mechanics for service abroad it was not possible to enforce these Acts very strictly. The result was that Continental textile manufacturers were in time able to adopt modern methods of production with the aid of British inventions and British skilled workers.

The development of the French textile industries, particularly in Normandy, owed much to British machinery and technical knowledge.[1] In the years of reconstruction that followed the wars of Louis XIV French manufacturers and officials began to visit England to study recent advances in the manufacture of textiles. Thus Daniel Scalogne of Abbeville, a woollen manufacturer of Dutch extraction, appears to have spent seven years in England.

[1] For the part played by British experts in the development of the French textile industries in the eighteenth century see Pierre Dardel, *Holker-Guillibaud & Morris, 1752-91* . . . (Rouen, 1942), André Rémond, *John Holker* . . . (1946), Camille Lion, " John Holker : un des fondateurs de l'industrie cotonnière normande " (*Bulletin de la Société Industrielle de Rouen.* July-August, 1933, pp. 253-69), Urbain Fages, " Les débuts de la grande industrie cotonnière : John Holker " (*Nouvelle Revue de Paris*, July-August, 1864, pp. 47-79), C. Ballot, *L'Introduction du machinisme dans l'industrie française* (1923), p. 747 *et seq.*, Charles Schmidt, " Le début de l'industrie cotonnière en France, 1760-1806 " (*Revue d'histoire économique et sociale*, VI (1913), pp. 261-95 and VII (1914-19), pp. 26-55), A. P. Wadsworth and J. de L. Mann, *The Cotton Trade and Industrial Lancashire 1600-1780* (1931), pp. 193-208, 449-71 and 503-6, G. Martin, *La grande industrie en France sous le règne de Louis XV* (1900), pp. 185-193. It is not always possible to ascertain the correct spelling of the names of English artisans who settled in France. The French form of an English name sometimes differs considerably from the original. Thus Elias Barnes was known as " Barnetz " in France, MacCloud as " Maclow," O'Flanagan as " Offlanegan " and Clark(e) as " Lecler(c)."

Marc Morel and Jubié, two factory inspectors, visited England to study the organisation of the textile industries—the former in 1738, the latter in 1747.[2]

Soon after the signing of the Treaty of Utrecht skilled English textile artisans were to be found in France.[3] In 1718 an English woolcomber named Townsend was reported to have settled in the Calais district.[4] In 1725 Elias Barnes—a former employee of the English Board of Trade and Plantations—asked the French authorities for a grant in return for introducing an improved wheel for spinning cotton and a machine for opening and mixing wool. Barnes's spinning wheel was used at the S. Sulpice charity industrial school in Paris.[5] In 1730 the brothers Havard were engaged in the cotton industry at Rouen.[6] In the following year the Commissioners for Trade and Plantations succeeded in securing the return to this country of a woolcomber named Glyn who had established himself at Lille.[7]

By the middle years of the eighteenth century the trickle of skilled English textile workers migrating to France had assumed greater proportions. In 1747 John Kay, the inventor of the fly shuttle,[8] settled in France to be followed by his son Robert, the inventor of the drop box. In 1748 Badger, a calenderer, was engaged in the Lyons silk industry. In 1750 John Holker began

[2] Vincent de Gournay, who was appointed Intendant of Commerce in 1751, had travelled in England and—at the suggestion of the elder Trudaine—he had translated Sir Josiah Child's *Brief Observations concerning Trade and Interest* (1668) into French (*Traités sur le commerce et sur les avantages qui résultant de la réduction d'interest de l'argent* (Amsterdam and Berlin, 1755)). See A. R. J. Turgot, " L'Eloge de Gournay " (in Du Pont de Nemours, *Oeuvres de Turgot*, III (1808)).

[3] Some thirty years earlier it had been stated that " for want of employment many of our weavers go over into France " (J. B. *An Account of the French Usurpation upon the Trade of England* (1697), p. 12, quoted by E. Lipson, *The Economic History of England*, III (1931), p. 48. In the early seventeenth century William Lee attempted to introduce the stocking frame to Normandy (Rouen).

[4] *Journal of the Commissioners for Trade and Plantations 1714-5 to 1718* (1924), Oct. 21, 1718 : statement by George Cape of Spitalfields (p. 441).

[5] A. P. Wadsworth and J. de L. Mann, *op cit*., pp. 123-4. Elias Barnes also established a factory at the Hague where the labour of paupers and orphans was used. For Barnes see also *Journal of the Commissioners for Trade and Plantations, 1718-1722* (1925) p. 253, p. 286 and p. 397, and *Journal of the Commissioners for Trade and Plantations, 1722-1728* (1928), p. 70, p. 132, p. 152, p. 179 and p. 193.

[6] A. Rémond, *John Holker* . . . (1946), p. 49 and p. 65 (note 153).

[7] *Journal of the Commissioners for Trade and Plantations 1728-9 to 1734* (1928), Oct. 27-29, 1730 (pp. 156-7) and July 8, 1731 (p. 217) ; A. P. Wadsworth and J. de L. Mann, *op cit*., p. 196.

[8] For the eighteenth century textile inventions in England see Bennett Woodcroft, *Brief Biographies of Inventors of Machines for the manufacture of Textile Fabrics* (1863).

his eventful career as a textile manufacturer in Rouen. Shortly afterwards he introduced a number of skilled workers into the newly established royal manufactury at Saint Sever and to Haristoy's cloth works at Darnétal.[9] In 1753 Wilson was brought to Rouen by Inspector Morel to curry leather for textile cards. In 1757 Davis, Morrison and Porter were engaged in clothmaking at Bourges.[10] At about the same time a dyer named MacCarthy was active in the woollen industry in Picardy and founded a school for woollen weavers at Aumale ; the brothers Thomas and Matthew Kelly helped to develop the cloth industry at Reims ; MacAuliffe established a cloth manufactory at Rennes ;[11] Michael Alcock set up factories at Saint Omer and Saint Etienne to make shears for clothmakers ; while Bettingen of Manchester manufactured textile cards at Nantes.

The careers of two of these pioneers—Kay and Holker—merit closer examination. John Kay paid his first visit to France in 1745.[12] The most probable motive for the journey was his dissatisfaction at failing to maintain in England the patent rights of his fly shuttle.[13] Kay's next visit was in 1747. He secured employment with Scalogne, a Dutchman who had settled in Abbeville where his famous countryman Josse van Robais had

[9] Saint Sever was a suburb of Rouen while Darnétal was a village near Rouen.

[10] The following other British workers are mentioned as having been at Bourges between 1758 and 1763 : Robert Balfe (an Irishman who was also employed by Maurice Chedrean of Tours) ; Thomas Kelly, Matthew Kelly and Mrs. Kelly (who subsequently worked at Amiens) ; Richard Smith, Edward Casey, Mrs. Casey, Joseph Cusack, William Bradley, Robert O'Connor, Margaret Ryan and Thomas Lecler(c) (? Clark(e)) : see A. Rémond, *op cit.*, p. 37 (note 40). For the industrial development of Bourges and Amiens see H. Boyer, *Histoire de l'industrie et du commerce Bourges* (Memoires de la Société historique . . . du Cher: Bourges, 1884) and P. Dubois, "Les industries amiénoises de la laine et du coton sous le règne de Louis XV " (Bulletin de la Société des Antiquaires de Picardie, 1935, pp. 249-81).

[11] For MacAuliffe see H. Sée, " Etudes sur l'industrie en Bretagne " " (i) La draperie au xviiie siècle " in J. Hayem (ed), *Memoires et Documents pour servir à l'histoire du commerce et de l'industrie en France*, X (1926), pp. 91-3. In the 1770s MacAuliffe had thirteen looms and employed fifty-two operatives. His annual output was seven hundred pieces of cloth valued at seventy thousand livres. A number of Irishmen settled in the French Atlantic ports—for example at Nantes—in the eighteenth century. Most of them were engaged in commerce and shipping. For MacCarthy see A. Rémond (*op cit.*, p. 10) who refers to him as a man who " played a very important part in the development of French industry."

[12] The date is given by A. Rémond, p. 36.

[13] Wadsworth and Mann point out that " the story that Kay was driven from Leeds in 1745 and from Bury in 1753 does not appear until the nineteenth century and the suggestion that the riots were the cause of his flight is not borne out by contemporary evidence " (p. 456).

established the manufacture of cloth in Colbert's day. Scalogne put Kay in touch with the authorities and before long Kay was making shuttles in Paris and teaching French weavers how to use them.[14]

In 1749 Kay came to a new arrangement with the French Government. In return for a grant of three thousand livres and an annual salary of 2,500 livres he agreed to visit various textile centres in Normandy to instruct weavers in the use of the fly shuttle. Three of Kay's sons made shuttles in Paris. But the success of this early attempt to introduce the fly shuttle into France was short-lived. By 1790 the French Government was again trying to interest manufacturers in this appliance.

John Kay also invented a machine to make cards for the textile industries.[15] In 1754 he built two such machines and his son Robert made some improvements to this invention. Owing to disputes with the French Government concerning the payment to be made for the invention John Kay more than once returned to England but he always went back to France. In the early 1770s he spent much of his time at Daniel Hall's cotton mill at Sens.[16] He died in about 1779.[17]

[14] On November 29, 1747, Kay and Scalogne were granted a patent in respect of two fly shuttles. See P. Bonnassieux (ed), *Conseil de Commerce et Bureau du Commerce, 1700-91* (1900), p. 353.

[15] " Cards are instruments which serve to disentangle the fibres of wool, cotton and other analogous bodies, to arrange them in an orderly lap or fleece, and thereby prepare them for being spun into uniform threads . . . Cards are formed for a sheet . . . of leather pierced with a multitude of small holes, in which are implanted small staples of wire with bent projecting ends called teeth. . . . The leather is afterwards applied to a flat or cylindrical surface of wood or metal, and the co-operation of two or more such surfaces constitute a card." (Andrew Ure, *Dictionary of Arts . . .* (1840), pp. 259-60).

[16] Sens lies in the Yonne Department. Holker wrote of this town : " Sens est la plus belle ville du monde pour faire des filatures et des fabriques, de telle nature que ce puisse estre, et il y a dans cette ville une espèce d'hôpital, où l'on avoit commencé la filerie à filer du coton, et où il y a vingt à vingt-cinq enfants qui y filent, et environ vingt-six métiers à faire des bas tant en soye que laine et cotton. Cette ville est aussy la plus commode pour faire une blanchirie, tant en toille, que toille de cotton, fil, et fil de cotton, parce qu'elle est environnée de très belles prairies et parties de terres, que l'on peut facilement couvrir d'eau trois ou quatre fois par jour ; par ce moyen, les marchandises se trouveront mouillées egallement, sans aucun dérangement par ce que l'on peut facilement se servir de la façon des Anglois, qui ont des picquets à crochets pour arrester et bander la toille qui ne peut être dérangée que par la grande force du vent, par cette façon les marchandises blanchissent egallement et beaucoup plus vite, estant meilleur que celle usitée en France." (A. Rémond p. 152).

[17] " His career in France exhibits the French Government in a very favourable light. In spite of his quarrels with its officials, they fully recognised his talent and treated him with astonishing patience " (Wadsworth and Mann, p. 464).

John Holker[18] was born in 1719. His father, a Stretford blacksmith, died shortly afterwards. On his mother's death in about 1740 John Holker went to Manchester where he learned the trade of a calenderer and then he went into partnership with Peter Moss. Holker gained a considerable knowledge of the cotton industry and—but for the Forty Five—he might well have become one of Lancashire's leading manufacturers.

Holker's career, however, was profoundly affected by the Jacobite rising of 1745. He was a Catholic and a Jacobite and when the Young Pretender's forces reached Lancashire John Holker and Peter Moss joined Colonel Townley's Manchester Regiment. Holker was commissioned as a lieutenant. Holker and Moss were captured on December 30, 1745 when the Carlisle garrison surrendered. But before they were brought to trial they both escaped from Newgate in June 1746 and eventually reached France in safety. They were fortunate to escape since members of the Manchester Regiment were punished with great severity. Nearly all the officers and sergeants were hanged while the men were transported.

Holker then joined David Ogilvy's Regiment of Scotch Infantry with the rank of captain and served in the Flanders campaign (battle of Lawfeld) of 1747. He is stated to have accompanied the Young Pretender on a secret mission to England in 1750.[19]

[18] For John Holker (the elder) see Roland de la Platière, *L'Art du fabricant de velours de coton* . . . (written 1776, published 1780) ; Brown (probable author), *Lettre d'un citoyen de Villefranche à M. Roland de la Platière*, 1781 (a reply to Roland de la Platière's attack on Holker) ; Roland de la Platière, *Réponse à la lettre d'un soi-disant citoyen de Villefranche*, 1781 ; D. Bailliere and Roland de la Platière, *Lettres imprimèes a Rouen en octobre 1781* (six letters of which two were by Balliere and four by Roland de la Platière) ; A. O. O'Connor and M. F. Arago, *Oeuvres de Condorcet* (12 vols., 1847-9), II, p. 580 ; L. Lelong's introduction and appendix to *Conseil de Commerce et Bureau du Commerce* . . . (ed. by P. Bonnassieux, 1900) ; C. Perroud, *Lettres de Mme Roland* (2 vols., 1902), II, Appendix G (ii), pp. 672-41 ; and A. Rémond, *John Holker* . . . (1946).

[19] The accounts of his youth given by John Holker (the elder) in later life contained some inaccuracies. He claimed to have been a yeoman (the *Dictionary of National Biography* states that his father was a yeoman) if not a country gentleman (A. Rémond accepts this story). Actually his father was a blacksmith. For John Holker's early years see T. H. Crofton, *A History of Stretford* . . . (3 vols., 1899-1903), III (Chetham Society, New Series, Vol. 51), p. 42. Holker led his family to believe that in the Forty Five he was at Falkirk and Culloden and this story was accepted by some contemporaries (see, for example, *Oeuvres de Condorcet*, II, p. 580) and is repeated by A. Rémond. Actually all Holker's service with the Young Pretender's army was in England : see Sir Bruce Gordon Seaton and Jean Gordon Arnot, *Prisoners of the* '45 (Scottish Historical Society, third series, XIII to XV, Edinburgh, 1929), II, p. 288 and the article on John Holker in the *Dictionary of National Biography*). It has been observed that, through no fault of its own, the Jacobite Manchester Regiment in which Holker served " had no glorious history : no crowded hour of glorious life " (Seaton and Arnot, I, p. 325).

In the following year Holker left the army although he did not resign his commission until 1755 when he was granted a pension of 600 livres a year.[20] Holker settled in Rouen in 1751. At that time the Normandy capital was the centre of a small-scale domestic textile industry.[21] The manufacture of linen and lace appears to have been more important than the production of woollen or cotton cloth in those days. A few Rouen master-craftsmen, who had accumulated a little capital, gave out materials to be spun and woven by domestic workers living in the suburbs and adjacent villages.[22] Holker made the acquaintance of Marc Morel, Inspector of Cloths at Rouen (1741-63), and accompanied him on some of his visits to textile workshops in the district. Holker soon realised the potentialities of the Normandy region as a textile centre if factories were established and English machinery were introducted. Morel was impressed with Holker's ambitious plans which he passed on to his superiors—Daniel Charles Trudaine and Louis Charles de Machault[23]—in Paris.

[20] Some years elapsed before Holker was awarded the Cross of St. Louis in recognition of his military services.

[21] For the development of the Normandy cotton industry see Vicomte R. d'Estaintot, *Recherches sur l'industrie de la filature mécanique du coton dans la Haute-Normandie* (Rouen, 1865) ; P. S. Lelong, "Aperçus historiques . . . sur l'industrie cotonnière dans le Département de la Seine-Inférieure " (*Bulletin de la Societé . . . pour le commerce et l'industrie de la Seine-Inférieure*, Rouen, 1834) E. Perrée, *Les origines de la filature mécanique du coton en Normandie* (Précis des travaux de l'Academie de Rouen, 1922) ; G. Beaumont, *L'Industrie cotonnière en Normandie* (1901) ; J. Levaineville, *Rouen : étude d'une agglomération urbaine* (1913) ; Pierre Dardel, *Histoire de Bolbec des origines à la Révolution*, II (Rouen, 1913) (includes chapter on the origins of the Rouen cotton industry). For the Normandy textile industries at the end of the seventeenth century see G. Dubois, " La Normandie économique à la fin du xviie siècle . . . " (*Revue d'histoire économique et sociale*, XXI, 1933, pp. 336-88). For the development of French rural industries see Evgeny Viktorovich Tarle, *L'Industrie dans les campagnes en France à la fin de l'ancien régime* (1910).

[22] To such an extent had the manufacture of cloths developed in the villages around Rouen that the master clothmakers (*maîtres toiliers*) of Rouen protested to the local chamber of commerce. See J. Hayem (ed.), *Mémoires et Documents pour servir à l'histoire du commerce et l'industrie en France*, X (1926), essay by Henri Sée on " Quelques documents sur l'industrie de la région Rouennaise . . . " (pp. 231-8).

[23] D. C. Trudaine was Councillor to the Parlement (1721), Master of Requests (1727), Intendant at Riom (1730), Intendant of Finances (1734), Councillor of State (1744), and member of the Bureau of Commerce. Voltaire wrote of Trudaine (the elder) : " Je n'ai connu d'esprit plus juste et plus aimable." For Trudaine and his son see E. Choullier, *Les Trudaine* (Arcis sur Aube, 1884 : reprinted from the *Revue de Champagne de la Brie*) and (le Capitaine) Andrieux, *Trudaine : sa vie, son oeuvre, ses idées* (Clermond-Ferrand 1922). L. C. Machault (d'Arnouville) was Master of Requests (1694), Intendant of Commerce (1722), and chairman of the Bureau of Commerce from 1744 until his death (1750) at the age of eighty three.

Trudaine was a Commissioner while Machault was President of the Bureau of Commerce.

In March 1750 Holker went to Paris where he was introduced to Trudaine and Machault by David Ogilvy, his former commanding officer. He submitted a memorandum[24] which set forth his suggestions for the modernisation of the French textile industries. Holker's proposals were accepted and early in October 1751 he sailed from Dunkirk to secure textile machinery and to engage skilled artisans. This was obviously a dangerous enterprise for an escaped rebel to undertake. He stayed in England for three months and, with the help of his relatives, he succeeded in smuggling some skilled workers across the Channel to Normandy. The export of the machinery that he required was arranged in co-operation with a London agent named Singleton. Shortly before Christmas 1751 Holker reached Ostend on his way back to France. The expenses of the journey were over 7,000 livres. In March 1752 the English workers engaged by Holker were established at Pierre d'Haristoy's clothworks at Darnétal near Rouen.[25]

A few months later a privileged royal textile factory was set up at Saint Sever, a suburb of Rouen. The capital was provided by Pierre d'Haristoy of Darnétal, Louis Paynet and Robert Dugard of Rouen and Claude Torrent of Paris. Holker at first provided no capital but—in return for acting as director and technical adviser of the establishment—he was entitled to one fifth of the profits. The Government provided a small annual subsidy of 1,200 livres. The Saint Sever factory was engaged in the weaving and finishing of cloth manufactured mainly—though not exclusively—from wool and cotton. The spinning was, for the most part, done by hand in neighbouring villages. Only machinery of the English type was used at Saint Sever and skilled craftsmen were secured from England. An official return of October 1754 showed that out of 86 skilled artisans 20 were British—John Holker himself, the head foreman (Daniel Hall) and his deputy

[24] This memorandum was translated into French by Mignot de Montigny who should not be confused with Trudaine de Montigny (son of D. C. Trudaine). A. Rémond states (p. 69, note 86) that he has been unable to trace the original of this report to which several writers refer (e.g. Urbain Fages in the *Nouvelle Revue de Paris*, II, 1864 and Camille Lion in the *Bulletin de la Société Industrielle de Rouen*, July-August, 1933).

[25] These British workers included D. Hall and P. Anson (foremen)—who soon afterwards served under J. Holker at the royal cloth factory at Saint Sever—James Wild (joiner), Robert Mathenson (carpenter), Robert Toyra, William Pattington, John Knowles (calenderers), and James Archer (interpreter).

(James Anson),[26] two cutters (*coupeurs*), one shearer (*tondeur*), six weavers, a dyer, four calenderers and three mechanics to erect and service the machinery.[27]

The Saint Sever establishment was not only a successful business enterprise but it was also the main centre for the diffusion of English cotton inventions throughout the French textile districts. The British cotton machinery installed at Saint Sever was copied and set up in other factories. Some of the workers employed at Saint Sever received a specialised instruction while others received a more general training which later enabled them to secure appointments as foremen. Both types of workers proved to be a great asset to the French cotton industry not only in Normandy but in other textile regions. Three British mechanics employed at Saint Sever and Darnétal—the two Wills (father and son) and Richard Smith—did valuable work as pioneer builders of textile machinery. Their influence extended far beyond Normandy into other French industrial centres. Some of the more enterprising of John Holker's British and French workers eventually set up factories of their own—for example Daniel Hall and Philémon-Martin Guillibaud at Sens, James Morris at Rouen, Pierre Fouquier at Bevnay and Thomas Leclerc at Bourges.

The progress of the Saint Sever cloth works owed much not only to John Holker himself but also to his two British foremen. Their exceptional technical knowledge, business acumen, administrative skill and ability to handle both English and French workers were invaluable to the directors of the royal manufactory. The quick success of the Saint Sever undertaking soon led to the establishment of new—though small—privileged interprises at Vernon, Elbeuf and Pont de l'Arche. But at various times John Holker had to face serious difficulties. His ambitious schemes were sometimes opposed by his more cautious associates who had put up the capital for the enterprise. Changes in fashion sometimes adversely affected the sales of certain types of cloth with

[26] Daniel Hall was also known as Guy Hutin while Anson (or Andson) was also known as Leatherbarrow. Hall, Anson and Wild appear to have been the three key British experts at Saint Sever in the early days of the new factory. All three were mentioned by name in one of the two royal decrees of September 19, 1752 establishing the factory.

[27] See " Etat et dénombrement des ouvriers travaillant aux manufactures et calandres royales au faubourg Saint Sever les Rouen, par arrêt du Conseil de 19 septembre 1752 " (A. Rémond, pp. 161-3). The factory was situated between the rue d'Elbeuf and not—as stated by Rémond—in the rue Pavée. John Holker later established a chemical factory in the rue Pavée. The two decrees of the Council of State—both issued on September 19, 1753—establishing the royal manufactory at Saint Sever are reprinted by Pierre Dardel, *Etudes d'histoire économiques*, III, *Holker-Guillibaud & Morris, 1752-91* (Rouen, 1942), pp. 36-52.

which Holker was experimenting and eventually the factory concentrated to a considerable extent upon the production of cotton velveteen. During the Seven Years War the British blockade reduced supplies of raw materials and jealous rivals took advantage of rising French national feeling to try to discredit Holker with the Government. But the production of the Saint Sever factory continued to expand even during the war—the output of cloth was 21,000 pieces in 1755 as compared with 16,666 pieces in the previous year—and Holker retained the confidence of the Director of Commerce. The number of looms rose from 37 in 1753 to 200 in the 1780s. By 1763 the Saint Sever enterprise had grown to such an extent that it was divided into two separate factories. One was a factory for the manufacture of cotton velveteen which was run by John Holker and the second was a calendering establishment run by his cousin James Morris. The calendering works received the title of " royal manufactory " in 1766. The works for which Holker was responsible were a very profitable enterprise but no evidence survives concerning the financial results achieved by Morris's factory.

Only eighteen months or so after the opening of the Saint Sever works John Holker—never lacking in self-confidence—submitted a memorandum to his superiors in which he boldly suggested a vast extension of his activities and responsibilities.[28] Holker proposed that the Government should inaugurate a comprehensive scheme for the modernisation of the French textile industries. Factories would replace domestic workshops while British machinery—in charge of workers trained by skilled English artisans—would replace old-fashioned hand appliances. He considered that a start should be made by extending to other towns in Normandy—and later into other provinces—the practices already successfully introduced into the Saint Sever weaving sheds and calendering establishment. Later the same methods might be used to modernise the lace and woollen industries.

John Holker criticised the methods hitherto employed to encourage the modernisation of French industries. He condemned the payment of premiums and the granting of exclusive privileges to Frenchmen who claimed to have invented machines that were as efficient as those already working in British factories. Not infrequently these machines did not come up to expectations and then the money paid by the Government was wasted while the concession granted to the promotor of the scheme might hinder other inventors from producing a better machine.

[28] The copy of this memorandum that survives (printed by P. Boissonnade in the *Revue d'histoire économique et sociale*, VI (1913), pp. 68-77 and by A. Rémond, pp. 150-6) is unsigned and undated but internal evidence clearly establishes both its authorship and the approximate date.

In the circumstances Holker believed that the Government should encourage the modernisation of French textile industries by introducing British machines that had already proved their worth. It would not be necessary to go to the expense of smuggling a large number of machines into France. A few would be quite sufficient since many machines could be copied from a single model. Similarly there was no need to employ large numbers of British textile workers. It would be necessary only to secure the services of a few highly skilled British artisans who could train French workers to handle the new machines.

Holker discussed the means by which the English laws prohibiting the export of machinery and the emigration of skilled artisans might be circumvented. He suggested that owing to the considerable volume of shipping using the port of London the officials could not exercise the same vigilance there as was possible in the provinces. He thought that it was from London that machinery could be shipped with least danger of detection—particularly if it were sent by way of Rotterdam since vessels destined for Dutch ports were usually not so strictly searched as those bound for France. With regard to skilled artisans Holker suggested that Catholics should be recruited rather than Protestants and unmarried rather than married workers. He pointed out that some British artisans could be secured from Scottish and Irish regiments stationed in France. Those who had enlisted under the impression that they were going to work in French factories and not to serve in the army would obviously welcome any opportunity to leave their regiments.

Holker boldly suggested that the French Government would find no better way of attracting British artisans than by conferring some signal honour upon Holker himself. If Holker received a well paid post under the Government the news would soon reach England. Men who had formerly been associated with him in Lancashire would be glad to join Holker when they realised what opportunities for advancement existed in France. And Holker's judgement was not at fault. Some years later a Mr. Cramond, in a letter to the Home Office (July 22, 1772) expressed some concern lest the encouragement given to Holker by the French Government would tempt other British artisans to follow his example.[29]

Holker's application was successful. On April 15, 1755 Moreau de Séchelles appointed John Holker to the post of Inspector General of Factories. He was instructed to confine his attention principally to those factories employing foreign

[29] R. A. Roberts (ed.), *Calendar of Home Office Papers . . . 1770-72* (1881), p. 525.

workers.[30] Holker's salary was 8,000 livres a year and this was later (1764) raised to 12,000 livres. Normally inspectors of factories were not allowed to engage in industrial work themselves. An exception to this rule, however, was made in Holker's favour. Despite his official appointment he received permission to continue to be responsible for the running of the royal factory at Saint Sever. In practice much of the day to day work of the undertaking was now left in Guillibaud's hands.

For just over thirty years (1756-86) Holker played an important part in fostering the industrial development of France. He frequently visited D. C. Trudaine in Paris and at his country home (Montigny-Leucoup) and he enjoyed the confidence of ministers and senior officials responsible for commercial affairs. Trudaine appreciated Holker's technical skill and administrative gifts. So long as Trudaine was in office Holker knew that he could rely upon his support.

It was largely owing to the elder Trudaine's influence that Holker's son (John Holker Junior) received an excellent scientific training from some of the leading French scholars of the day. In 1768 the younger Holker received an official appointment under his father. In the following year D. C. Trudaine died. His son, Trudaine de Montigny,[31] took over his father's duties and the contacts between the Trudaine and Holker families were maintained.

The elder Holker adhered to the policy laid down in his memorandum of 1754. His tour of Champagne, the Lyonnais, Beaujolais and Forez in 1755-6—which was undertaken shortly after his appointment as Inspector General—was the first of many journeys covering the length and breadth of the country. He inspected one industrial establishment after another and made suggestions for their improvement. He made arrangements for installing modern machinery and for securing the services of skilled artisans. He secured samples of English cloth for French

[30] The number of French Inspectors General of Manufactures had been fixed at four. The establishment was increased to five when John Holker was appointed. For the French factory inspectors in the eighteenth century see J. Hayem, *Mémoires et Documents pour servir à l'histoire du commerce et de l'industrie en France*, XI (1927) : essay by F. Bacquié on " Les inspecteurs des manufactures sous l'ancien régime."

[31] Jean Charles Philibert Trudaine de Montigny (1733-77) was a Councillor of the Parlement and Commissioner of Requests (1751). Master of Requests (1754), assistant to his father (in the office of Intendant of Finances) and a member of the Bureau of Commerce (1759), He was appointed Councillor of State in 1768 and in the following year he took over the duties formerly carried out by his father.

manufacturers to copy. He distributed to manufacturers pamphlets on technical subjects.[32] Between 1764 and 1770 the two Holkers were in the Bourgogne, Auvergne, Languedoc and Picardy. In 1765 the Languedoc Estates voted Holker a considerable sum to cover the expenses of his tour in that province.

British manufacturers and artisans in France found a good friend in the Inspector General. Holker was in close touch with the English colony in the textile centre of Bourges (Davis, Porter and Morrison). He secured subsidies for them and encouraged other British artisans—such as MacCarthy, Garrity, Lecler(c) and the Kellys—to join them. It was at Holker's suggestion that Badger of Lyons was granted a new subsidy to pay for the training of workers in the finishing processes of the manufacture of heavy woollen cloths. After the Kellys moved to Amiens they were given new cloth-pressing machinery. Holker helped several of the men who had worked with him at Saint Sever to start their own factories.

His cousin Morris took charge of the calendering works at Saint Sever. Jane Law and Miss Hayes came to France in about 1760 and travelled in Normandy and other provinces to teach new spinning methods to local workers. Miss Law (Mme Robion) was later in charge of a mill at Montigny-Leucoup while her husband looked after a dozen looms. When Holker's son brought a jenny to France in 1771-2 the services of Miss O'Flanagan were secured to teach spinners how to use the new machine. She visited Albi and the districts of Velay and Vivarais and set up a training institute at Bayeux.[33] Morgan, who had a factory at Amiens, made some improvements to the jenny in 1755.[34] John Holker not only introduced the jenny into his works at Saint Sever and Oissel but set up an establishment to manufacture this machine for other textile factories. Nevertheless the jenny did not come into very general use in France at this time. Tolozan (Intendant of Commerce) estimated in 1790 that there were only about 900 jennies in the country. John MacCloud (Maclow) was sent by Holker to Amiens, Abbeville and Sens to set up machines for the manufacture of muslins. Thomas Lecler(c) established clothworks at

[32] (*a*) John Holker, *Memoir instructif sur la fabrique, les apprêts, dégraissage et blanchissage des bayettes et autres lainages anglais* (Paris, Imp. royale, 1764) ; (*b*) *Observations de M. Holker pour améliorer les bêtes à laine et les pâturages* (no date) ; (*c*) Holker's translation (*Essai sur le blanchiment des toiles*, 1762) of Francis Home, *Experiments on Bleaching* (Edinburgh, 1756).

[33] G. Martin, *La grande industrie en France sous le règne de Louis XV* (1900), p. 290.

[34] A. Rémond, *op cit.*, p. 41 (note 81).

Bas-Limousin and later went into partnership with the Milnes to set up a cotton mill at Brive.

Two other families with whom John Holker was connected—the Halls and the Milnes—helped to introduce Arkwright's machinery into France. Daniel Hall had been Holker's senior foreman at Saint Sever. In July 1760—in association with Richard le Jeune—he took charge of a new royal cloth factory at Sens. Over 600 workers were employed in this factory in 1776.[35] Hall not only manufactured cloth but built textile machinery. His brother William brought one of Arkwright's machines to France in 1779 but it did not give satisfactory results. In the same year Holker was in touch with the Milne family who came from Lancashire. John Milne and his sons (John, James and Thomas) smuggled one of Arkwright's machines into France and successfully erected it at Oissel.[36] Foxlow,[37] Milne's son-in-law, became one of the leading cotton manufacturers in Orleans where he set up a steam engine.[38] In the year VIII he claimed that his factory was the biggest of its kind on the Continent.

Although Holker is remembered mainly for his efforts to modernise the French textile manufactures he was also active in promoting the advance of a number of other industries such as the manufacture of iron, armaments, pottery, glassware and chemicals. In the 1760s he established a factory at Rouen to make sulphuric acid. His association with the Alcocks showed his interest in the progress of the iron and armament industries. As early as 1756 Holker had reported gloomily to Trudaine on the backwardness of the Saint Etienne ironworks. He encouraged an Englishman named Michael Alcock to introduce up to date metalworking at Saint Etienne, Roanne and La Charité sur Loire. In 1758 Alcock claimed that he could turn Saint Etienne and La Charité into " the Birminghams of France." Some years later Holker drew up the instructions given by Trudaine to Gabriel Jars when he visited England to examine ironworks and collieries.

During his long career in France Holker inevitably had to face many difficulties. It was unfortunate for Holker that war

[35] Official report of July 13, 1776 reprinted by A. Rémond, *op cit.*, p. 161.

[36] The Oissel works (south of Rouen) had been established in 1776 by the same capitalists who owned the Saint Sever muslin factory. It may be added that roller-spinning machinery was introduced into cotton mills at Louviers by John Wood (or Flint) and by John Hill (or Theakson) who had both previously worked in Arkwright's factory at Cromford.

[37] When in Manchester Foxlow had been a member of the Committee for the Protection of Manufacturers and of the Literary and Philosophical Society.

[38] C. Ballot, *L'introduction du machinisme dans l'industrie française* (1923), p. 137.

should have broken out between Britain and France in 1756. The newly appointed Inspector General faced a situation very different from what he had envisaged when he applied for the post. The Government threatened to expel some English artisans and Holker interceded successfully with d'Argenson on their behalf. The war seriously interfered with Holker's plans for a rapid extension of the French textile industries. The British blockade restricted the supply of raw cotton and so—for a time—Holker directed his attention particularly to the woollen industry which used a raw material produced in France itself. Moreover the French now had to export their surplus woollen and cotton goods largely through Spanish ports and they tried to open up new markets in North and South America to replace the Levant trade which was declining. Holker was by no means unsuccessful in his efforts to overcome the difficulties caused by the war of 1756-63.

The position of a foreign expert is seldom an easy one. The French authorities fully appreciated the value of his services but Holker sometimes suffered from those who were envious of the emoluments and privileges that he enjoyed. The fact that Holker was both a manufacturer and a public official invited criticism although Holker does not seem to have taken any unfair advantage of his dual position. While Holker was generally well received in districts that were far from his own home he was sometimes less warmly welcomed in Normandy cloth factories where he was regarded as a competitor—the manager of the Saint Sever factory—rather than as a colleague. Indeed some of the Normandy mill-owners refused Holker admission to their works.[39]

The antipathy towards Holker culminated in a lively controversy in the 1780s concerning the value of Holker's services to his adopted country. Holker's enemies, led by Roland de la Platière—himself an Inspector of Factories at Amiens—denounced him as a shady character of dubious antecedents who had emerged from the slums of Manchester to make a fortune for himself and his Lancashire friends. He was alleged to have concerned himself much more with feathering his own nest than with promoting the welfare of the French economy. Holker and his English colleagues earned higher salaries than most French workers and this led to some bad feeling between English and French textile artisans.

Holker's closing years were clouded by these attacks upon his character and abilities. He suffered serious financial losses owing to his son's rash speculations and he was disappointed at the failure of his son's commercial mission to the United States.

[39] In 1773, for example, Price—an English employee—refused to admit Holker to certain workshops in Martin and Flesselle's factory at Amiens.

The elder Holker remained in office until his death but he realised that his opinions no longer carried as much weight as they did when he had the confidence of the elder Trudaine. In view of these disappointments he must have appreciated the honours that he received. In 1775, for example, he was elevated to the nobility and in 1780 he was honoured by the Academy of Sciences. His fame spread far beyond the frontiers of France and in July 1785 (shortly before his death) he enjoyed a visit from Benjamin Franklin.[40] Holker died on April 27, 1786.

Although Holker's personal influence had declined in his later years his policy of fostering the modernisation of the French textile industries survived his death. In the years 1788 and 1789 alone there are several references in the records of the Conseil de Commerce[41] to the activities of skilled British textile workers in France. Thus Wright and Jones and other English artisans installed carding and spinning machinery in a cotton mill at Melun. John Berry received a grant for having assisted in establishing cotton works at Neuville sur Saône. Leturc, a hosiery manufacturer of Popincourt, applied for a subsidy to cover the cost of engaging a skilled artisan named Thomas and of bringing over two machines from England. Peton and Decrétot recovered from the *Conseil de Commerce* the payments they had made to two Irishmen who had erected machinery at a spinning mill at Louviers. The Sub-Inspector of Factories at Abbeville asked the *Conseil de Commerce* to authorise Lord and MacCloud (Maclow) to Amiens[42] to construct various machines for spinning combed wool. MacCloud proceeded to open up a quilting manufactory at Troyes. In 1789 Morgan and Massey received a grant of 12,000 livres in respect of a mule-jenny which they had

[40] A. H. Smith (ed.), *The Writings of Benjamin Franklin*, X (1907) pp. 466-7 (extract from Franklin's diary) ; Georges Dubosc, " Benjamin Franklin à Rouen " (*Journal de Rouen*, May, 1906). M. Pierre Dardel of Boos (Seine-Inf.) has kindly supplied me with an extract from Dubosc's article. Dubosc remarks that the younger Holker " au commencement du xixe siècle, devait découvrir, pour la fabrication d'acide sulfurique ' la combustion continue du soufre dans les chambres de plomb ' et fonder avec Chaptal et d'Arcet le grand établissement de Nanterre." It may be added that the elder Holker's country seat was at Montigny about 5 kilometres from Rouen and not—as Rémond (*op cit.*, p. 118) states—at " Montigny en Roumois." The Roumois district lies to the south of the River Seine about 20 kilometres distant from Rouen.

[41] P. Bonnassieux, *Conseil de Commerce et Bureau de Commerce 1700-91* (1900), pp. 455, 460, 465, 470, 472, 481 and 482.

[42] For the development of the textile industries of Amiens see P. Dubois, " Les industries amiénoises de la laine et du coton sous le règne de Louis XV " (*Bulletin de la Société des Antiquaires de Picardie*, 1935, p. 249 *et seq.*).

constructed at Amiens.[43] In 1787-8 Lecler(c) visited England to secure skilled artisans and new textile machinery for his factory at Brive-le-Gaillard. An Englishman named Pickford installed a mule in this mill. Pickford then set up works in the rue de Charenton in Paris for the construction of textile machinery. At the time of the Directory he returned to England and founded a similar establishment in London. He maintained his contacts with France and appears to have been involved in the smuggling of English textile machinery to the Continent.

In 1791 Charles Albert, a native of Alsace, visited England on behalf of a Toulouse manufacturer to secure textile machinery and skilled artisans. He was caught in 1792 and sentenced to twelve months imprisonment and a fine of £500. As he was unable to pay the fine he remained in prison until 1796. On his return he directed from Paris an agency for the importation into France of smuggled English machines.[44]

When the French overran the Austrian Netherlands, efforts were made to foster the cotton industry at Ghent. Lièven Bauwens, who was well acquainted with the English textile districts, was largely responsible for the success of these plans. In 1798 he went to England with a certain Paul Harding to secure men and machinery. Harding's first consignment of machine parts—which had been stored in Pickford's warehouse in London

[43] John Macgregor, *Commercial Statistics*, Vol. I (1844), p. 404. In the same year (November 16, 1789) Thomas Milne approached the Duke of Orleans with a view to establishing a cotton mill in the Duke's castle at Honfleur (*Archives Nationales* F 7. 4385[1]). In 1789 one of John Milne's sons went to the United States and tried to persuade George Washington to foster the expansion of the cotton industry. Washington in a letter to Jefferson (February 13, 1789) remarked that his visitor's father was in charge of a cotton mill " at the royal chateau of Muette in Passy " (J. Sparks (ed.), *The Life and Writings of George Washington* (12 volumes, 1837-55), vol. IX, p. 470).

[44] The Lancaster City Library possesses a photograph of a print showing Lancaster Castle in the 1790's. It bears the following inscription :

> " Fs Charles Ls Albert, after five years confinement was restored to liberty thro the generous exertions of Jno Higgin Esqr, the humanity of the Manchester gentlemen, and the cares of the Relations of Elizabeth Johnson-Albert. Justice à qui elle est due."

For Charles Albert see the *Manchester Mercury*, March 13 and 20, 1792 ; August 21 and 28, 1792 ; and November 8, 1796 ; C. Schmidt " Les débuts de l'industrie cotonnière en France, 1760-1806," Part II : 1786-1806 (*Revue d'Histoire économique et sociale*, VII, 1914) ; and Paul Leuilliot, " Activités économiques et financières en Alsace au début du xixe siècle " (*ibid.*, XXIX (1951), p. 42). Albert showed several machines at the Paris industrial exhibition of 1806 : see E. Levasseur, *Histoire des classes ouvrières et de l'industrie en France de 1789 à 1870* Vol. I (edn. of 1903), p. 415. See also below pp. 46-47.

—was seized by customs officials. Harding was arrested, fined and imprisoned. Bauwens was more fortunate. It is true that he had to leave some machinery and some artisans behind and that other workers deserted him at Hamburg. But eventually he reached Paris with some machinery and five skilled artisans. By 1800-1 he was able to start his new enterprise at Ghent. A few years later it was reported that Bauwens had secured 40 skilled artisans and 17 mules (16,000 spindles) from England.[45]

During the period of the revolutionary and Napoleonic wars there were obvious difficulties in securing English machinery and skilled workers. On at least one occasion the French Government turned to the United States. Two Americans—Reynaud and Ford—received a grant of 6,000 livres in the Year VI to establish a modern cloth factory. But the venture appears to have been unsuccessful.[46] At this time skilled English cotton operatives were still engaged in French factories. In the Year VI La Rochefoucauld-Liancourt was employing an Englishman named Gibson and four Irish prisoners of war at his cotton mill at Cire des Mello. A few years later other English workers were employed in this factory. At the same time an English artisan who had been found working near Brussels, was sent by the French authorities to Dunkirk to give instructions to local operatives. During the period of the Revolution Henry Sykes set up a spinning mill at St. Remy sur Aire (Eure Department) which later passed into the hands of another English family (the Waddingtons). The Tarare muslin industry benefitted from the skill of an Irish prisoner of war who, in 1794, chanced to visit a weaving shed there. He explained that he had once worked in a Glasgow factory where broader pieces of muslin were woven on a loom that was an improvement upon the machine commonly used in Tarare. He showed a local joiner how to make the improved machine which came to be generally adopted in the district.[47]

English influence was not so important in the development of

[45] Arthur Redford, *Labour Migration in England 1800-50* (1926), p. 153. For Bauwens see Napoléon de Pauw, *Lievén-Bauwens son expedition en Angleterre et son procès, 1798-99.* (Ghent, 1903).

[46] E. Levasseur, *Histoire des classes ouvrières et de l'industrie en France de 1789 à 1870.* Vol. I (edn. of 1903), p. 273.

[47] M. R. Louis Reybaud, *Le Coton* . . . (1863), pp. 134-5. It may be added that shortly after the Napoleonic wars William Cockerill (junior)—the eldest son of William Cockerill (senior) who had played an important part in developing modern textile industries in Verviers (Belgium)—ran a cloth factory at Sedan before migrating to Guben in the Lower Lausitz (Brandenburg) : see F. Redlich, *History of American Business Leaders*, Vol. I (Ann Arbor, Michigan, 1940), p. 42.

the cotton industry in Alsace[48] as it had been in Normandy. Nevertheless the activities of two Manchester men—Heywood and Dixon—deserve a mention. The former had some share in introducing powerloom weaving while the latter was a pioneer builder of textile machinery in Alsace.

In 1806 John Heywood smuggled drawings of the mule and power loom to Strassburg where—in association with an army contractor named Malapert—he established a small cotton mill at the Metzgertor. Hand jennies appear to have been used in this workshop. Before long the partners moved to the foothills of the Vosges in the valley of the River Breusch where waterpower was available and labour was cheaper than in Strassburg. They built a small cotton mill at Schirmeck. In a nearby smithy Heywood himself constructed a mule and a power loom. Subsequently he built looms for sale to local mills. They were known as "Schirmeck looms."

The first factory set up by Heywood and Malapert was soon enlarged. By 1819 it was of sufficient importance to be marked on a town plan of Schirmeck as " Manufactures de Mrs. Heywood & Malapert." In the following year Heywood's agreement with Malapert expired. Heywood now gave up his interest in the Schirmeck mill and built a weaving shed in the adjacent town of Vorbruck. In 1828 he introduced the power loom into these works. Other manufacturers in the Breusch valley followed his example and by 1840 handspinning and handweaving had virtually disappeared in this corner of Alsace. In 1836 the firm of Seillière, Heywood & Cie was established. Largely owing to the enterprise of a third partner named Scheidecker a larger mill of 1,500 spindles was erected at Lützelhausen and this was run in conjunction with a weaving shed of 400 looms at Mühlbach.[49]

Water-power and steam-power to drive mules and looms was adopted more quickly in Alsace than in other French cotton districts. In 1819 the cotton spinning firm of Dollfus-Mieg & Cie replaced its first 10 h.p. steam engine (of 1812) with an English machine of 30 to 40 h.p. By 1831 it was reported that virtually all spinning in Alsace was done by steam power or water power. And Alsace had 18,000 power looms at a time when the first such

[48] For the development of the cotton industry in Alsace see H. Herkner, *Die oberelsässische Baumwollindustrie . . .* (1887) ; R. Lévy, *Histoire économique de l'industrie cotonnière en Alsace* (1912) ; L. Laufenburger " L'industrie cotonnière en Haut-Rhin . . ." (*Revue politique et parlementaire*, CXXV (1925), pp. 319-30) ; and *Histoire documentaire de l'industrie à Mulhouse* (Société industrielle de Mulhouse, 2 vols., 1902).

[49] J. Klein, *Die Baumwollindustrie im Breuschtal* (1905), ch. 1. Benoit-Aimé Seillière was Heywood's son-in-law.

machine was installed at Roubaix, the great cotton centre of the Nord Department.[50] The self-acting mule—invented in England in 1825-30—was not adopted in France as promptly as might have been expected. In 1842 the first Roberts self-actors were introduced from England into Motte-Bossut's spinning mill at Roubaix.[51]

Job Dixon was an English engineer who was one of the earliest machine builders in Alsace. This industry first developed to meet the requirements of the local textile industries and later expanded to serve a wider demand for a variety of machines and steam engines. In 1818 he was engaged by Nicholas Schlumberger—the well known cotton spinner of Guebwiller—to build spinning machinery.[52] In 1820 he became a partner of Risler Brothers of Cernay. This firm (founded 1817), built not only steam-driven machinery but also locomotives and it became a large undertaking of considerable importance. But it gave credit too generously, ran into serious difficulties during the business crisis of 1827 and collapsed in 1832. Both Schlumberger and Risler Brothers employed a number of English designers, foremen and skilled workers as did Jourdain of Altkirch and André Koechlin of Mülhausen.[53] Richard Roberts—the inventor of

[50] This was erected by Dobson & Barlow of Manchester for the Roubaix firm of Toulemonde-Destombe. See C. Fohlen, " Esquisse d'une évolution industrielle, Roubaix au xixe siècle " (*Revue du Nord,* XXXIII, April-September, 1951, p. 100) For the development of the cotton industry in the Nord Department see J. Houdoy, *Le filature du coton dans le Nord de la France* (1912).

[51] In 1856 Alsace had only 108,176 self-acting spindles but by 1864 the number had increased to 706,368. De Jong, a native of Alsace, who was part-proprietor of a cotton·mill in Warrington, had invented a self-acting mule in 1827 but it failed to work satisfactorily either in Warrington or in Nicholas Schlumberger's establishment at Guebwiller (Alsace). In 1825 Richard Roberts patented a self-acting mule which was improved in 1830 by the invention of the winding quadrant. The patent for the self-actor was extended in 1839 and expired in 1846. See A. Ure, *A Dictionary of Arts . . .* (ed. of 1840), p. 370. L. Reybaud, *Le Coton . . .* (1863) ; (Anon), *Motte-Bossut : un homme, une famille, une firme* (Tourcoing, 1944) ; article on Richard Roberts in the *Dictionary of National Biography* XLVIII p. 393 and H. W. Dickinson, " Richard Roberts, his Life and Inventions " (*Newcomen Society Transactions,* XXV, 1945-7, pp. 123-137).

[52] Between 1818 and 1820 half a dozen skilled English operatives were employed by Nicholas Schlumburger at his Guebwiller cotton mill. One of them—a Manchester carder named Adam Young—subsequently gave an account of his experiences before a parliamentary committee. He had earned three guineas a week in Alsace but had been far from happy. He was glad to return home. See *Fifth Report of the Select Committee on Artisans and Machinery* (1824), pp. 579-82.

[53] P. Leuilliot, " Activités économiques et financières en Alsace au début du xixe siècle " (*Revue d'Histoire Economique et Sociale,* XIX, 1951, pp. 43-4) and *Histoire documentaire de l'industrie à Mulhouse,* pp. 664-5

the self-acting mule—was in Alsace for two years to plan and arrange the machinery for a new factory which André Koechlin et Cie were constructing.[54]

Even the art of printing textile cloths—the oldest branch of the Alsace cotton industry—owed something to the skill of Lancashire experts. In about 1825 a small number of Manchester printers went to France for a couple of years or so to give instruction to local engravers. An English observer subsequently stated that French workers were " actually able to engrave the same sort of things better than we do ourselves."[55]

English and Scottish technical skill also influenced the finishing branch of the cotton industry in France. A century after Holker had introduced improved methods of calendering into Normandy a Scot named MacCulloch set up a large factory at Tarare for bleaching and finishing muslins by methods already successfully used in Scotland. Eventually he virtually monopolised the finishing of muslins in this district.[56]

The expansion of the French lace industry was partly due to English inventions and the skill of English artisans. In the early 1790s a new piece of apparatus called a " pin-machine " was introduced into the Nottingham district to produce a particular type of fine lace. The demand for this lace in England eventually ceased and in 1841 it was reported that the pin-machine had been forgotten in Nottingham. But it had found its way to France where it was being extensively used to manufacture the net called *tulle*.[57] In 1809 Heathcote patented his bobbinet frame and two years later Clark and Mart invented the bobbinet " pusher machine." John Lindley showed how bobbinet machinery could be worked by steampower.[58] In 1816 Thomassin, with the connivance of an English manufacturer, introduced bobbinet

[54] H. W. Dickinson writes of Roberts in Alsace : " We should have liked to have known his reactions to his new surroundings as well as details of the actual work he did, but we have no record " (*Newcomen Society Transactions* XXV 1945-7, p. 128).

[55] Evidence of T. Lockett before the *Select Committee on Designs*, 1840, Qn. 8819. He added that he was referring to Alsace " where all the best prints are produced . . . " (Qn. 8820).

[56] Louis Reybaud, *op cit.*, pp. 143-5.

[57] *First Report from the Select Committee on the Exportation of Machinery*, 1841 : evidence of W. Felkin, Qn. 2359. Felkin was the author of a book on the *History of the Machine-wrought Hosiery and Lace Manufacture* (1867).

[58] J. R. McCulloch, *A Dictionary of Commerce* . . . (edn. of 1847), Vol. II, p. 762. A. Ure in his *Dictionary of Arts* . . . (1840), p. 735 mentions six different types of bobbinet machines. The expiry of Heathcote's patent in 1823 was followed by a spectacular boom in the Nottingham lace trade which lasted some three years.

machinery into Douai.[59] Similar machines were erected in Calais by Webster in 1817[60] and by Clark in 1820. Shortly afterwards there were said to be 35 bobbinet looms in the district. French engineers were soon able to build bobbinet lace machinery.[61] A number of English lace workers settled in Calais in the 1820s.[62] In 1824 the British vice-consul at Boulogne asked the police authorities at Calais for particulars of English skilled workers who had recently arrived at that port. He stated that the British Government was concerned at the number of skilled artisans who were leaving the country.[63] Some twenty years later English lace workers were still to be found in France. Richard Birkin told a parliamentary enquiry that he had visited groups of such workers at Calais and Lille. He remarked : " They have small clubs amongst themselves to provide for one another when they are out of work, and if they think there is any imposition practised upon them, they maintain each other, in order to get their grievances redressed."[64] As late as 1863 Louis Reybaud declared that Saint-Pierre-les-Calais still resembled "a suburb of Nottingham."[65]

The French woollen industry adopted new machinery rather later than the cotton industry. Some of the English cotton machinery which had been introduced into France in the eighteenth century could be adapted to the needs of the manufacturers of woollens. In the early nineteenth century two Englishmen—William Douglas and John Collier—made significant contributions to the progress

[59] Louis Reybaud, *Le Coton* . . . (1863), p. 206.

[60] L. Reybaud, *op cit.*, p. 207.

[61] *First Report from the Select Committee on the Exportation of Machinery*, 1841 : evidence of Grenville Withers (Qn. 999) and W. Felkin (Qn. 2101).

[62] When certain Nottingham lace workers were agitating for an eight hour day in 1825 they sent a copy of the resolutions passed at one of their meetings " to the Bobbinet Committee at Calais, Lille, and St. Quentin": see H. Bourgin and G. Bourgin (editors), *Le régime de l'industrie en France de 1814 à 1830* (recueil de textes), Vol. III (1941), p. 121 (citing the *Nottingham Mercury*, September 23, 1825).

[63] H. and G. Bourgin (ed.), *op cit.*, II (1921), p. 220. In the same year (1824) a Mr. Alexander told the Select Committee on Artisans and Machinery that 16,000 workers had migrated to France in 1822-3. This was almost certainly an exaggeration. A writer in the *Quarterly Review* (XXXI, 1824-5, p. 392) estimated that there were only about 1,300 or 1,400 English skilled workers in France at that time.

[64] *First Report from the Select Committee on the Exportation of Machinery*, 1841 : evidence of R. Birkin, Qn. 2473. English lace workers in Calais, Lille and Cambrai were then receiving wages of thirty to fifty shillings per week (Qns. 2565-6).

[65] L. Reybaud, op cit., p. 207. See also H. Hénon, *L'industrie des tulles et dentelles mécaniques dans le département du Pas de Calais, 1815-1900* (Calais, 1900).

of the woollen industry. Douglas was brought over to France by Chaptal, Napoleon's Minister of the Interior. He was placed in charge of a factory at l'Ile des Cygnes in Paris (which had cost 144,000 francs to erect) and received a State subsidy of 20,000 francs. William Douglas introduced a number of the newest appliances —particularly carding and spinning machinery into the manufacture of woollens. His methods soon became so well known that some of the manufacturers of the Midi district sent their wool to Douglas to be spun. Ternaux[66] and Decrétot were among the first woollen manufacturers to adopt Douglas's methods. Within a short time he had sold 340 machines to French cloth makers.[67]

John Collier was an English engineer who settled in France. In 1824 he was reported to be constructing cloth-shearing machines in Paris.[68] In 1825 he bought a wool-combing machine which had recently been invented by Godart of Amiens. Collier took the machine to Manchester where it was much improved. This combing machine was successfully used in England and was later exported to France.[69]

Although it was the genius of Philippe de Girard[70] that contributed greatly to the improvement of modern flax-spinning and flax-carding machinery it was mainly from England that these machines were secured by French linen manufacturers. The first

[66] G.L. Ternaux, one of the leading French manufacturers in the early nineteenth century, had factories at Louviers, Sedan, Elbeuf, Rouen and elsewhere.

[67] Jean-Antoine Chaptal (Comte de Chanteloup), *De l'industrie françoise* (two vols. 1819), Vol. II, p. 16 ; Jean-Antoine Chaptal, *Mes souvenirs sur Napoléon* (edited by A. Chaptal, 1893), p. 99. For Chaptal see Jean Pigeire, *La vie et l'œuvre de Chaptal* III (1932). Douglas was reported to have introduced two steam engines into Rouen in 1817: see E. Levasseur, *op cit.*, Vol. I, p. 627. On November 22, 1823 the Comité consultatif des arts et manufactures reported :

> " nous avons commencé, il y a dix ou douze ans, l'établissement de machines de Douglas; leur apparition occasiona quelque trouble dans le midi ; aujourd'hui elles sont généralement adoptées, elles fonctionnent paisiblement et l'on en demande dans les provinces les plus pauvres, afin d'y revivifier l'industrie."

(see G. and H. Bourgin (editors), *op cit.*, Vol. II (1921), p. 210). John MacGregor stated that it was in 1803 that Douglas first introduced machinery for carding and spinning woollens into France (John MacGregor, *Commercial Statistics*, Col. I (1844), p. 399). See also E. Levasseur, *op cit.*, Vol. I, p. 414.

[68] *First Report of the Select Committee on Artisans and Machinery*, 1824 ; evidence of A. Galloway, p. 21.

[69] *First Report of the Select Committee on the Exportation of Machinery*, 1841 ; evidence of Grenville Withers, Qn. 996.

[70] C. Ballot, " Philippe de Girard et l'invention de la filature mécanique du lin " (*Revue d'histoire économique et sociale*, VII (1914-19), pp. 135-195). For the French linen industry see Alfred Renouard, *Histoire de l'industrie linière* (three volumes 1879).

flax-spinning machine was invented in England by John Kendrew and Thomas Porthouse and was set up at their Low Mill works on the River Skerne near Darlington in about 1787. James Aytoun was one of the first to introduce this machine into Fifeshire.[71] In 1797 an Englishman named William Robinson imported an early flax-spinning machine into France and in the same year a Frenchman named Demaurey patented a similar machine of his own invention. In 1798 Robinson secured a licence to import English flax-spinning machinery into France and he set up a flax-spinning mill in Paris. His partner Fournier showed samples of this machinery at the Paris industrial exhibitions of 1802 and 1806. At about the same time Bauwens, assisted by an Englishman named Wilson, introduced English flax-spinning machines into factories at Ghent.[72]

Between 1810 and 1815 Philippe de Girard considerably improved the Kendrew-Porthouse type of machine. But unfavourable factors—such as lack of capital, the hostility of the hand-spinners, and the political uncertainties of the last months of Napoleon's regime—prevented de Girard's machine from being adopted in France. Then John Marshall and Horace Hall obtained particulars of the machine from one of de Girard's colleagues and when de Girard visited England in 1826-7 he was chagrined to find that his machine had fostered the development of a new flax-spinning industry in Leeds.

In 1847 J. R. McCulloch remarked that "the increase in the exportation of (British) linens and linen yarn (to France) since 1833 has been quite extraordinary."[73] In view of this English competition French flax-spinners made every effort in the 1830s to obtain—even at some risk and considerable expense—English machinery largely of French invention which they could have secured without difficulty over twenty years before. Scrive worked in England as an artisan for two years to learn the secrets of flax-spinning by machinery and he then opened a modern

[71] A. J. Warden, *The Linen Trade . . .* (1864), pp. 690-2.

[72] Several English inventors took out patents in France at this time for flax-spinning machines—for example: Foulton, Mrs. Clarke, John Madden, Patrick O'Neal, Milne and Collier. See C. Ballot, "Philippe de Girard . . ." (*Revue d'histoire économique et sociale*, VII (1914-19), p. 139). On May 7, 1810 Napoleon offered a prize of a million francs for the invention of a flax-spinning machine (A. Blanqui, *Cours d'économie industrielle 1838-9* (Paris, 1839), p. 6).

[73] J. R. McCulloch, *A Dictionary of Commerce . . .* (edn. of 1846), Vol. I, p. 655. In 1830-37 French imports of British linen yarn rose from a mere 3,049 kgm. to 3,199,917 kgm. (Blanqui, *op cit*., p. 8). Cf. article by C. Coquelin in the *Revue des deux mondes*, July 1, 1839, p. 71.

flax-spinning mill in Lille (1834-5). He also introduced J. C. Dyer's card-making machine into France.[74]

In 1835 Pierre André Decoster—who had visited English flax-spinning mills in 1834—set up two establishments in Paris for building flax-spinning machinery.[75] In 1838 a joint stock company for constructing flax machinery was set up at Amiens. An Englishman (John Maberley) was the principal director. Machinery worth £30,000 was purchased from Thomas Marsden of Salford and 100 English mechanics were sent to France to erect the machinery.[76] By this time there were in France eight flax-spinning mills in which modern machinery had been installed. Three of them were using smuggled English machinery while five used machines built by Decoster. In about 1840 Schlumberger of Guebwiller began to construct flax-spinning machinery from models obtained from Peter Fairbairn of Leeds.[77] The number of mechanical flax spindles in France rose from 14,800 in 1838 to 120,000 in 1845.[78]

[74] This was an English improvement—patented in 1810—of a machine invented by Whittemore of New York. J. C. Dyer's sons established themselves at Gamaches (Somme Department) as manufacturers of (i) their father's card-making machinery, (ii) their father's patent tube roving-frames (also originally an American invention), and (iii) other machinery. Dyer Frères also ran a cotton mill. See *First Report of the Select Committee on the Exportation of Machinery*, 1841 : evidence of Matthew Curtis, Qns. 1554-65.

[75] When J. MacGregor visited Decoster's works he saw " rooms filled with parts of machinery then recently imported by various directions from England " (*Commercial Statistics*, Vol. I (1844), p. 423). For Decoster see Émile Eude, *Histoire . . . de la mécanique française* . . . (1902), p. 256.

[76] Thomas Marsden—in evidence before the Select Committee on the Exportation of Machinery, 1841—stated that there were five establishments in France which made flax machinery. He said : " They have purchased excellent tools of all descriptions from Manchester and Leeds, and (they have) purchased one specimen of the best models of machines from the different machine makers in Leeds and other parts of the country, and have established works for the purpose of making machines ; (and) they have taken over the cleverest Englishmen they could get . . . giving very enormous salaries . . . and . . . they have been able to make machines . . . quite equal to any that I have seen in England " (*First Report of the Select Committee on the Exportation of Machinery*, 1841, Qn. 1160). It may be added that in March, 1837, Hogwood of Belfast was making enquiries at Dunkirk with regard to the possibility of setting up a flax-spinning mill (Archives nationales, F 12. 2307).

[77] *First Report from the Select Committee on the Exportation of Machinery*, 1841 : evidence of P. Fairbairn (Qn. 3119).

[78] Some years later Mr. Barrow, British consul at Nantes, reported that " for a number of years past many spinners and other operatives have gone from Britain to France, where they are employed in almost every town where linen manufactures . . . are carried on " (quoted by A. J. Warden, *The Linen Trade* (1864), p. 316).

Flax carding machinery was also introduced into France from England. The first such machine had been invented by Thomas Porthouse in 1805. It was however much improved by Philippe de Girard. Once more this inventor was unlucky. Decoster, his dishonest associate, sold the English rights of de Girard's invention to an English merchant named Evans who had a machine building works in Warsaw. Evans had the new carding machine built by Sharp & Roberts of Manchester. It was a success and—as with the flax-spinning machines—French manufacturers eventually had to smuggle from England a machine which owed much to a French inventor.[79]

The establishment of the jute industry in France owed something to English and Scottish technical skill. The brothers Baxter set up the first jute spinning mill in France at Ailly-sur-Somme near Amiens in 1845 and placed James Carmichel in charge of it. Jute spinning was introduced into the Dunkirk district by David Dickson, a partner in the flax-spinning and sail making firm of Malo-Dickson et Cie.[80]

Since France secured new English textile machinery at an early date and had the benefit of the experience of skilled English artisans it might have been expected that the French textile industries would have made more substantial progress than in fact they did in the years between 1700 and 1850.[81] In 1835 Edward Baines, in his well-known account of the British cotton industry, drew attention to various adverse factors which had long hindered the more rapid development of the French cotton

[79] It is interesting to note that the same thing happened with regard to Louis Robert's machine for manufacturing paper. This French invention of 1799 was exploited in England and was not used in France until after 1815.

[80] Information kindly supplied by M. Claude Fohlen of the University of Lille There is evidence that the firm of Malo-Dickson was active in Dunkirk in 1842 (Archives nationales F 12. 6889) and earlier (C. Ballot, " Philippe de Girard . . . " in the *Revue d'histoire économique et sociale*, VII (1914-19), pp. 139-195). See also *Expositions des Produits de l'industrie française en 1844 : rapport du jury central*, Vol. II, p. 409 where the high quality of the linen sails produced by Malo-Dickson was praised.

[81] For the economic development of France in 1815-48 see A. Blanqui, *Histoire d'exposition des produits de l'industrie française en* (1827) ; A. de Colmont, *Histoire des expositions de l'industrie française* (1855); Paul Poiré, *La France industrielle* (1875); E. Levasseur, *Histoire des classes ouvrières et de l'industrie en France de 1789 à 1870* (two volumes, edition of 1903); Henri Sée, *La vie économique de la France sous la monarchie censitaire, 1815-48* (1927) ; Henri Sée, *Histoire économique de la France: les temps modernes 1789-1914* (1951); A. L. Dunham, *La révolution industrielle en France* (1953); David S. Landes, " French entrepreneurship and industrial growth in the nineteenth Century," *Journal of Economic History*, 1949, pp. 45-61.

industry.[82] Several of his comments were of a general character and applied also to other French manufacturers.

Baines pointed out that English cotton workers were generally more efficient than French operatives. One reason for this was that (except for a certain number of handloom weavers) the English cotton operatives were normally full-time factory workers while the French spinners and weavers were to a great extent still only part-time textile workers. In the summer they often returned to the land for the harvest or the vintage.

Secondly, " the political state of France is unfavourable. Wars, invasions and revolutions, and the liability to their recurrence, have shaken credit, and prevented the manufacturing establishments from gaining that duration and firmness which are needed to the full development of mercantile enterprise."

Thirdly, France was short of coal. In Paris, for example, factories drew their coal from Mons and paid about ten times more for it than did their Manchester rivals. Fourthly, " the artificial state into which French manufacturing industry has been been brought, from being propped up on every side with protections, and therefore incapable of free movement, greatly aggravates the natural disadvantages of the country." Coal and iron might be imported far more cheaply than they can be raised in France, but duties nearly prohibitory are levied upon those articles when imported, to protect the domestic iron and coal proprietors." " Of course, these duties fall directly upon machinery, which is in consequence double the price in France that it is in England."[83] Fifthly, the French textile factories and workshops were small in size and they were scattered in many parts of the country. " Each spinner and manufacturer is obliged to make a variety of articles to suit his customers." " It is a necessary consequence of this state of things, that the attention both of the manufacturer and of his workmen is divided among several kinds of work, and they are prevented from acquiring excellence in any."

Finally Baines commented upon the relatively high cost of transport (owing to a defective system of roads and inland waterways) ; the import duty levied upon raw cotton (which was two per cent higher than the duty levied in Britain at that time) ; and the shortage of capital.

[82] E. Baines (the younger), *History of the Cotton Manufacture of Great Britain* (1835). See also G. Villiers and Dr. John Bowring, *First Report on the Commercial Relations between France and Great Britain* (1834).

[83] J. R. McCulloch expressed the same point of view. He wrote : " The truth is, that until the French Government reduces or repeals the duties on raw cotton and on other articles indispensable to the cheap construction of cotton factories it were idle to suppose that the French should be formidable competitors in the production of cottons " (*A Dictionary of Commerce* . . . (edn. of 1847), Vol. I, p. 440).

More recent enquiries by modern scholars[84] have elaborated this brief analysis of the causes of the relatively slow pace of the Industrial Revolution in France, but Baines's discussion of the problem showed that informed contemporaries[85] fully appreciated the main factors which were retarding French industrial developments in the first half of the nineteenth century.

[84] See Henri Sée, " L'influence de la Révolution sur l'évolution industrielle de la France " (reprinted from the *Volume commemorative in onore del Prof. G. Prato* : Institute superiore di scienze economische e commerciale. Turin) ; A. L. Dunham, " A new Perspective on the Industrial Revolution in France " (*Michigan Alumnus Review*, LVII, 1951, pp. 148-159) ; Paul Leuilliot, " La révolution industrielle en France " (*Annales* . . . , VI, 1951, p. 401) ; S. B. Clough, " Retardative factors in French economic development in the nineteenth and twentieth centuries " (*Journal of Economic History*, Supplement VI, 1946, pp. 91-102) ; and G. Duveau, *La vie ouvrière en France sous le second Empire* (1946), pp. 124-139. See also Léon Cohen, " L'enrichissement de la France sous la Restauration " (*Revue d'histoire moderne*, 1920) and Bertrand Gille, "La concentration industrielle en France au début du second empire" in the *Bulletin de la Société d'Histoire Moderne*, eleventh series, IV, Nov.-Dec., 1952, pp. 11-16.

[85] Louis Reybaud for example in his *Le Coton* . . . (1863), pp. 261-4, quotes some passages from an interesting memorandum of 1787—attributed to a lawyer named Thouret—which compares Lancashire and Normandy as textile districts and gives reasons for Lancashire's superiority. Reybaud remarks that Thouret's views were by no means out of date eighty years later. See also an extract from Thouret's memorandum in A. Rémond, *op cit.*, p. 45 note 128.

3. ENGLISH INFLUENCE ON THE GROWTH OF THE FRENCH IRON ENGINEERING AND TRANSPORT INDUSTRIES, 1750-1850

DURING the hundred years between 1750 and 1850 Britain not only became the leading manufacturing country in the world but her inventors, skilled mechanics and entrepreneurs exercised a profound influence upon the industrialisation of the Continent and the United States of America. The laws prohibiting the export of many machines and blueprints and the emigration of skilled artisans did not seriously check the movement of capital and technical knowledge from Britain to the Continent. The way in which the "workshop of the world" assisted the industrial development of less advanced countries may be illustrated by examining English influence on the growth of certain basic French industries—particularly iron and steel, engineering, machine building and transport.

In the eighteenth century the iron industry of France was backward when compared with those of England and Germany.[1] French ironmasters relied too much upon native iron ores which were not of the best quality. The great Lorraine ironfield was hardly exploited except at Hayange and the extent of its vast resources was not known. Absence of foreign competition—owing to prohibitions and high tariffs—gave French ironmasters a monopoly of the home market and there were few incentives to adopt improved methods of production. Even between French ironmasters themselves there was relatively little competition. Most of them had their own little local markets into which rival products hardly penetrated owing to the poor state of communications. France had an unwelcome reminder of the backwardness of her iron industry during the Seven Years War when the performance of her naval cannon was markedly inferior to that of the British cannon.

In the circumstances it was natural that the rapid progress of the British iron and steel industry in the eighteenth century should have aroused considerable interest in France. The Government was particularly anxious to promote the efficiency of the armaments branch of the iron industry while progressive manufacturers—such as John Holker the Lancashire Jacobite

[1] For the early development of the modern French iron industry see Bertrand Gille, *Les origines de la grande industrie métallurgique en France* (1947).

refugee who did so much to modernise the Normandy cotton industry—realised that France would continue to depend upon England for new textile machinery so long as the French iron and engineering industries were in a backward condition.

John Holker gave every encouragement to Michael Alcock, an English metalworker who had settled at Saint Omer in the early 1750's. Shortly afterwards Alcock moved to La Charité-sur-Loire where—in partnership with a Miss Willoughby—he set up new metal works (1757). On May 12, 1758 he wrote to D. C. Trudaine (Intendant of Finances) that Saint Etienne and La Charité could be turned into the Birmingham of France.[2] Both Miss Willoughby and Mrs. Alcock went to England to recruit skilled workers for the French metal industries. Alcock received 2,400 livres from the Government for placing eight English mechanics in an armaments factory at Saint Etienne. In 1762 he established new engineering works at Roanne and in 1767 he set up steelworks at Villefay-en-Charolais.[3] For some thirty years—between about 1750 and 1780—Alcock was one of the leading entrepreneurs in the French metalworking, engineering and machine-building industries. In 1771, at the request of the French Government, he visited England to see Matthew Boulton and other English experts with a view to securing information concerning recent progress in the British engineering industry.[4]

On July 3, 1764, Gabriel Jars, a young scientist from Lyons, was sent to England and Scotland by the French Government to study modern methods of iron production.[5] His abilities had been recognised by D. C. Trudaine and he had been trained as a chemist at the Ecole des Ponts et Chaussées. He had already visited mines and ironworks in Germany and Austria. The instructions which Jars received for his new journey had been drawn up by John Holker.

Jars was cordially received in England and he was elected a

[2] André Rémond, *John Holker . . .* (1946), p. 37 (note 33).

[3] G. Martin, *La grande industrie en France sous le règne de Louis XV* (1900), p. 190 ; A. Rémond, *op. cit.*, p. 18.

[4] Jean Bouchary, *L'Eau à Paris à la fin du xviiie siècle. La Compagnie des Eaux à Paris . . .* (1946), p. 43.

[5] Gabriel Jars, *Voyages métallurgiques . . .* (3 vols., 1774-81 : German translation—*Metallurgische Reisen . . .* edited by A. C. Gerhard in four volumes, 1777-85). For Jars see obituary notice in the *Histoire de l'Académie des Sciences,* 1769, pp. 173-9; C. Ballot, "La révolution technique et les débuts de la grande exploitation dans la métallurgie française" (*Revue d'Histoire des Doctrines Economiques et Sociales,* V (1912), pp. 29- 62); L. Beck, *Die Geschichte des Eisens,* III (1897), pp. 305-8.

member of the Society of Arts. Ballot has commented upon " the extreme liberality with which English manufacturers threw open the doors of their factories and allowed him to undertake a detailed examination of their processes." Jars toured the collieries of the Newcastle-upon-Tyne district. He observed the new tramways for conveying coal and he was impressed by the Newcomen engine at the Walker colliery. In Sheffield he studied the Huntsman process of making cast steel. In Scotland he examined the blast furnaces which Roebuck had erected in the Carron ironworks in 1760. In Cumberland he visited the Clifton furnace between Cockermouth and Whitehaven.

On his return Jars endeavoured to make use of the information that he had secured in Britain by introducing into France improvements in the smelting of iron and the manufacture of steel. He set up works for the manufacture of steel in the Paris suburb of St. Antoine while his brother M. G. Jars tried to smelt iron with coke at ironworks at Sain Bel. On August 30, 1768, Gabriel Jars was instructed by the Government to tour the French provinces and to advise ironmasters on improved methods of production. He visited the Hayange foundry in Lorraine in January, 1769, and advised François Ignace de Wendel—a son of the proprietor—to study on the spot recent progress in metallurgy in Germany and Austria. The promising collaboration between Jars and the de Wendels soon came to an end for Jars died in August, 1769.

The de Wendels now turned their attention to the attempts to smelt iron with coke that had recently been made by Count William Stuart at Sulzbach in the neighbouring territory of the Saar which was then part of the Duchy of Nassau. In 1773 the French scientist de Gensanne supervised the erection of a furnace at Hayange and tried to smelt iron with coke on the lines suggested by Stuart and his associates. But he was unsuccessful. Stuart and his friend Kesling continued their experiments at Neunkirchen in the Saar. In August, 1775, the Stuart Company was founded in France by Stuart, Kesling, Milleville de Bergère and Roettiers de la Tour with the object of making coke and using it to smelt iron.

In the same year that de Genssane had worked with the de Wendels at Hayange he had also conducted ironsmelting experiments at Alais for Marchant de la Houlière. This ironmaster decided to visit England to investigate the latest methods of smelting iron. In January, 1775, he obtained a travelling grant from the Languedoc Estates and he subsequently secured the full support of the Government for his project. The French ambassador in London gave him several letters of introduction and placed Mr. MacDermott—one of the Embassy chaplains—at his disposal as a travelling companion. Marchant de la Houlière informed the French Government[6] that he proposed " to investigate whether the superior quality of English coal and the peculiar nature of English iron ores constituted the reason why they were used together, with such a great measure of success, in that country to make cast and wrought iron ; to see the methods used for the purpose and to become acquainted with the preparatory treatment given to these minerals, what substances were added to them in order to facilitate smelting and lastly the construction of furnaces and bellows."

In August, 1775, Marchant de la Houlière inspected several ironworks in the Midlands and in the north-east of England. He visited the ironworks of Richard Jesson and John Wright at West Bromwich where malleable iron was made, not by puddling but, by the " stamping and potting " process ; John Wood's collieries and ironworks at Wednesbury where many steam pumps were used ; John Wilkinson's foundry at Broseley ; the Coalbrookdale ironworks where the Darbys had first smelted iron with coke ; William Reynolds' blast furnaces at Ketley ; William Wilkinson's forges and foundries at Bersham ; as well as ironworks with large reverberatory furnaces at Newcastle-upon-Tyne. Marchant de la Houlière's visits to Broseley and Bersham had two results. In the first place the French ambassador in London asked the British authorities whether Garvay, a Rouen merchant, might be allowed to import eight cannon made by the Wilkinsons.[7] Secondly, William Wilkinson was invited to go to France to establish a royal cannon foundry at Indret.

In 1777 William Wilkinson migrated to France[8] where he received an annual salary of 12,000 livres from the Government. He was entrusted with the erection and management of a new royal cannon foundry on the island of Indret which lies in the

[6] Marchant de la Houlière's report is preserved in the *Archives Nationales* in Paris (F. 12/1300 and 14/4261). There is a photostat copy in the Birmingham Public Library. Dr. W. H. Chaloner has printed a translation of the report in the *Edgar Allen News* (Sheffield), December 1948 and January 1949. It may be added that the Home Office papers for 1773-5 contain a letter from Major Watson to Mr. Robinson in which it was stated that a Frenchman had come to England to engage ironfounders for a new foundry on the Languedoc Canal (see R. A. Roberts (ed.), *Calendar of Home Office Papers . . . 1773-5* (1899), No. 1157, p. 414).

[7] Le Cte. de Guines to Lord Weymouth, December 23, 1775, printed by T. S. Ashton, *Iron and Steel in the Industrial Revolution* (1924), p. 46.

[8] Jean Chevalier states (in " François Ignace de Wendel " in the *Annuaire de la Société d'histoire et d'Archéologie de la Lorraine*, XLVII (1938), p. 13) that William Wilkinson arrived in France in November, 1775. This visit lasted for only a short time since there is evidence from William Wilkinson's correspondence that he was in England for part of 1776.

River Loire ten kilometres from Nantes. The first buildings were quickly erected. Furnaces and cannon-boring machinery were installed and by 1779 the first cannon were produced. The works were extended with the assistance of the able French engineer Pierre Toufaire[9] to include shops for carpenters and fitters; works for forging, casting and drilling by water power; buildings for the display of models and pieces of artillery ; and proving grounds for the cannon. The more important workshops were linked by iron tramways.[10] The output of the foundry was, however, limited since virtually only scrap-metal—worn-out pieces of artillery—was used to manufacture new cannon. The French Government realised that increased supplies of suitable pig-iron must be secured if an adequate supply of naval cannon were to be obtained from the Indret foundry.

The Minister of Marine decided in 1779 to send François Ignace de Wendel to Indret to inspect the foundry and to suggest methods of increasing its output. De Wendel stayed at Indret for two months[11] and on April 7, 1780, he was granted a lease of the foundry for fifteen years. William Wilkinson left Indret in December, 1780, to examine possible sites for the establishment of new modern blast furnaces to produce iron for the Indret cannon foundry. He recommended that the old established iron-works at Le Creusot—where coal and iron ore were near at hand—should be acquired for this purpose. Le Creusot, of course, was some distance from Indret but it was hoped that with the eventual completion of the Charolais Canal (now Canal du Centre) joining the Loire and the Rhône, cheap communication between the two centres would be established. Wilkinson was asked to stay in France to undertake the construction of the blast furnaces. His annual salary was raised to 60,000 livres and he received expenses at the rate of 1,000 livres a month. The project was delayed by two difficulties—inability to raise the necessary capital and disputes concerning the ownership of the mines and other property at Le Creusot. Eventually the necessary capital was

[9] William Wilkinson's first French colleagues were the naval officers de Serval and Magin. They did not work well with Wilkinson and were replaced by Pierre Toufaire. For Toufaire see Philippe Rondeau, " Un grand ingénieur au xviiie siècle, Pierre Toufaire . . . " (*Bulletin de la Société des Archives Historiques de la Saintonge et de l'Aunis*, Vol. IV, January 1883-April 1884).

[10] P. M. J. Conturie, *Histoire de la fonderie nationale de Ruelle . . . et des anciennes fonderies des canons de fer de la marine*, Part I : *1750-1855* (1951), ch. 4 ; Bertrand Gille, *Les origines de la grande industrie métallurgique en France* (1947), pp. 193-6.

[11] De Wendel's report on the Indret naval foundry to the Minister of Marine has been printed by G. Bourgin, "Deux documents sur Indret" (*Bulletin d'histoire économique de la Révolution*, 1917-19, p. 468).

secured from Jacques Constantin Perier (founder of the first modern Paris waterworks company) and from Nicolas Bettinger ; the legal difficulties were settled so that de Wendel secured effective control over the land that he desired to use. De Wendel also came to an arrangement with François de la Chaise for a regular supply of coal from the Montcenis mines.

William Wilkinson, de Wendel and Toufaire now went ahead with the building of new blast furnaces in which coke should be used instead of charcoal. While Wilkinson presumably laid down the main principles upon which the furnaces were to be built it is doubtful to what extent he actually supervised the process of construction. William Wilkinson was a notoriously difficult colleague to get on with—his brother John was to discover this before long—and it appears that William Wilkinson was at Le Creusot for no more than six months during the three years that the new ironworks were under construction. The main burden of the supervision of the building of the furnaces fell on Toufaire. It may be that Wilkinson had qualms about assisting in building up the French armament industry at a time when France was allied with the American colonists fighting for their independence. It may be that he quarrelled with de Wendel and spent his time in Paris intriguing against his colleagues. He was not at Le Creusot when (on December 5, 1785)[12] the new furnace—the first on the Continent to use coke successfully—was fired by de Wendel.[13] The furnace was tapped on December 11. Furnaces of this type,

[12] See Wendel, Perier, Dulubre, " Journal de mise à feu de la fonderie royale de Creusot " printed by Bertrand Gille, *op. cit.*, pp. 207-9.

[13] The commencement of the building of this furnace is commemorated at Le Creusot by a plaque with the following inscription : L'an de l'ére chrétienne 1782. Le 8e du règne de Louis seize. Pendant le ministere de M. de la Croix-Castries, M. Ignace Wendel, Commissaire du Roi, M. Pierre Toufaire, ingénieur, cette fonderie, la prèmiere de ce genre en France, a été construite pour y fondre de la mine de fer au coke, suivant la méthode apportée d'Angleterre et mise en pratique par M. William Wilkinson. See Pierre Benaerts, *Les origines de la grande industrie en Allemagne* (1933), p. 452. Baron de Dietrich wrote in an official report (1794) : " Four furnaces, 39 feet high, form at Mont Cenis the ironwork, with coal free from sulphur ; four reverberatory furnaces are erected there, capable of making 12,000 lbs. weight at a single cast, and in a state to be refined with coke . . . " (Harry Scrivenor, *History of the Iron Trade* (new edn., 1854), p. 178). For the Wilkinsons see W. H. Chaloner, " John Wilkinson, Ironmaster " (*History Today*, May, 1951). For the Le Creusot ironworks see Napoleon Vadot, *Le Creusot* (Le Creusot, 1875) H. Chazelle, *Le Creusot, histoire générale* (Dôle, 1936) ; Jean Chevalier, *Le Creusot. Berceau de la grande industrie française* (new edn., 1946) ; and Bertrand Gille, *op cit.*, pp. 197-9. William Wilkinson wrote a short account of the French iron industry in the early 1780s (dated February 5th, 1787) which is preserved in the Boulton & Watt Collection (Birmingham Public Library).

were twice the size of the furnaces hitherto normally used in France. William Wilkinson returned to England and when he next visited the Continent in 1788-9 it was with the object of studying iron production in the Scandinavian states. He went to the Friedrichsgrube in Silesia where he succeeded in smelting lead ore with coke.

François Ignace de Wendel directed the modernised Le Creusot ironworks until the early years of the French Revolution. In about 1789 Johann Jakob Ferber, a Prussian mining engineer, visited Le Creusot and reported that four blast furnaces were in action.[14] This suggests that de Wendel had survived the critical situation that had faced French ironmasters when they first began to feel the effects of English competition after the Anglo-French commercial treaty of 1786 came into force. But de Wendel did not survive the storms of the French Revolution. During the Reign of Terror he fled to the little Thuringian town of Ilmenau in the Duchy of Saxe-Weimar. Here he lived in exile for two years. He made the acquaintance of Goethe and pointed out to him how primitive were the methods still employed by the local ironmasters. De Wendel continued his experiments on the smelting of iron with coke.[15] He died by his own hand in 1795 at the age of fifty-four.[16]

The introduction into France of steam pumps and steam engines to drive machinery was another step on the road to industrialisation. Once again it was from Britain that these new machines were obtained. In 1726 a Newcomen engine[17] was set up at Passy, near Paris, to pump water and in 1732 a similar pump was

[14] J. J. Ferber, *Mineralogische und metallurgische Bemerkungen in Neuchâtel, Franche Comté und Bourgogne* (1789), Ferber (p. 49) was mistaken in supposing that William Wilkinson's ironworks were in Bedfordshire. L. Beck, *op. cit.*, III, p. 1033 repeats the error.

[15] *Goethes Werke* (Weimar edition, 1892), XXXV (" Tag-´und Jahres-Hefte . . . 1749-1806 "), pp. 57-9 and LIII (" Uber die verschiedenen Zweige der hiesigen Tätigkeit "), p. 189. Goethe wrote as follows concerning de Wendel's experiments: " In der technologischen Chemie wird es interessant sein, die Versuche eines ausgewanderten Franzosen in Ilmenau, Eisen durch Reverberir-Feuer zu schmelzen, näher kennen zu lernen : die ersten Versuche sind, man darf sagen, zu gut gerathen, indem nicht allein der Ofen sondern auch die Esse glühend wurden " (LIII, p. 189).

[16] Goethe wrote on de Wendel's death (*op. cit.*, XXXV, p. 59) : " Weit entfernt von seinem Vaterlande, in einem stillen Winkel des Thüringer Waldes fiel auch er ein Opfer der gränzenlosen Umwälzung."

[17] For the steam engine see Boulton and Watt, *Directions for erecting and working . . . Steam Engines* (reprinted as an appendix in H. W. Dickinson and Rhys Jenkins, *James Watt and the Steam Engine* (1927)) ; R. H. Thurston, *A History of the Growth of the Steam Engine* (1878) ; Theodor Beck, *Beiträge zur Geschichte des Maschinenbaues* (1900) ; Conrad Matschoss, *Geschichte der Dampfmaschine* (2 vols., 1908); H. W. Dickinson, *A short History of the Steam Engine* (1938) and *James Watt* (1935).

erected at a colliery at Fresnes near Condé sur l'Escaut.[18] But engines of this type do not seem to have been widely used in France and they were still sufficiently novel in 1765 for Gabriel Jars to include—in his account of his journey to England—a careful description of the Newcomen pump which he saw at the Walker colliery at Newcastle-upon-Tyne.

The brothers Jacques Constantin Perier and Auguste Charles Perier played an important part in introducing James Watt's steam engine into France. In February, 1777, the Periers secured a concession from the municipal authorities to supply Paris with water from the Seine.[19] Constantin Perier went to England in that year and—without approaching Boulton and Watt—he tried to persuade John Wilkinson to build him a steam engine. Wilkinson very properly refused to construct an engine without Watt's permission and Perier went away empty handed.

Boulton and Watt now decided to patent the steam engine in France. When the Comte d'Heronville ordered a steam engine to drain a marsh near Dunkirk, Boulton and Watt agreed to supply one provided that the Count would use his influence with the French Government to secure a patent. On April 14, 1778, James Watt secured a patent for fifteen years provided that he submitted one of his engines for trial at Dunkirk or Paris and proved that it was more efficient than the older types of engines. But nothing came of the Count's drainage scheme. Then Jary, who ran a colliery near Nantes, secured for Watt an amended French patent under which the trial of an engine could be made at Nantes. Boulton and Watt supplied Jary with specifications and machine parts—for which he never made any payment—and the first Watt engine to be erected on the Continent was set up at Jary's coalmine.[20] In January, 1779, Constantin Perier was in England again. This time he dealt directly with Boulton and Watt and secured the right to make Watt steam engines in France from specifications supplied from the Soho foundry.[21] Two payments of 24,000 livres

[18] For a description of the Newcomen engine at Fresnes see Bernard Forest de Bélidor, *Architecture Hydraulique* (1739), II, pp. 308-338. Other contemporary accounts in French of Newcomen engines are to be found in R. P. Pézenas's translation (1751) of Desaguliers, *Experimental Philosophy* (English editions 1734, 1744 and 1763) and in Perronet's article on the steam engine in the *Grande Encyclopédie*, VI (1766), pp. 602-9.

[19] For these waterworks see Jean Bouchary, *op. cit.* For J. C. Perier and the steam engine see his book *Sur les machines à vapeur* (1810).

[20] Another Boulton and Watt engine was erected near Nantes in 1791-2 to drive a corn mill. Richard Dayus, who went to France with the machine, commented unfavourably upon the skill of the French workmen employed on the erection of the engine : see H. W. Dickinson and Rhys Jenkins, *James Watt and the Steam Engine* (1927), p. 260 and p. 283.

[21] H. W. Dickinson, *James Watt* (1935), pp. 99-100. Constantin Perier's name is also spelt "Perrier".

each were made to Boulton and Watt by the Perier brothers in 1779 and 1783.

The Periers built their waterworks at Chaillot and two steam engines were erected.[22] The first was set to work on August 8, 1781. In the same year it was reported that two steam engines were being used at Nimes to drive a corn mill. The Periers established engineering works at Chaillot and built steam engines. When Boulton and Watt went to Paris at the invitation of the French Government in 1786 they visited the Perier's establishment. Watt wrote that Constantin Perier had " erected a most magnificent and commodious manufactory for steam engines where he executes all the part(s) exceedingly well. He is a man of abilities and would be very estimable if he were a little more just or more honest."[23] In 1788 at the request of the French Government the Periers supplied steam engines to work corn mills on the Ile de Cygnes (Paris). During the wars of the French Revolution the Periers reorganised their works to produce armaments.[24]

James Watt's rotative steam engine was introduced into France by François Ignace de Wendel. When he visited England in January, 1784, he learned that Watt had improved his original steam engine so that it could now be used not only to work pumps but also to drive machinery. One of the earliest rotative steam engines to be built was supplied to de Wendel and was used at the Le Creusot ironworks. In 1784 five English steam engines were

[22] Chaillot was a suburb of Paris. It became part of the Paris municipal area in 1786. It is said that Brunel—then a schoolboy—once saw some large iron castings being landed at the harbour of Rouen. On enquiry he learned that they were parts of a steam pump which had been ordered for the Paris waterworks.

[23] H. W. Dickinson and Rhys Jenkins, *James Watt and the Steam Engine* (1927), p. 66. The French Academy elected James Watt a correspondent in 1808 and a foreign associate in 1814.

[24] Gilbert Gilpin wrote to William Wilkinson on March 23rd, 1797, that he had recently met a Mr. Armfield who had been employed in France in the large pottery works which Christopher Potter (Member of Parliament for Colchester, 1784-90) had set up at Chantilly. Gilpin wrote: "Armfield knows the Periers very well. (He) saw their work(s) at Paris lately. They were then casting and finishing eight brass guns per day. They had bored and turned two engines on B(oulton) and W(att)'s plan, of their own manufacture. The yard is full of church bells and brass saints etc. These are mixed with copper brought from a mine near Rouen, which mine is worked by Welsh miners, at the head of whom is one Powell . . . " (see *Birmingham Weekly Post*, October 19th, 1895). That French interest in English technical advances in the iron industry continued during the period of the wars of the French Revolution may be seen from Charles Cocquebert's article on Henry Cort's process in the *Journal des Mines*, I (1794), No. 6, pp. 27-37.

working at Le Creusot.[25] French industrialists were, however, slow to follow the example set by the Periers and de Wendel. In 1810 Perier stated that there were only two hundred steam engines in France as compared with five thousand in England.[26]

Although between 1793 and 1815 Britain and France were at war, with one short interval, the French continued to secure new machines from England. The activities of F. C. L. Albert[27] show how French manufacturers were able to make use of English technical knowledge even in time of war. Charles Albert, who was born in Strassburg, travelled in his youth in Italy, Germany, Hungary and England. Then the Toulouse firm of Boyer-Fonfrede and Le Comte[28] sent him to England to secure cotton machinery and skilled operatives. Albert went to Lancashire and was arrested in December, 1791. In the following August at the Lancaster assizes he was sentenced to a year's imprisonment and a fine of £500 for trying to entice abroad a cotton operative named Geoffrey Scholes. He was unable to pay the fine and despite the efforts of the French authorities to secure his release he remained in prison for five years. He was eventually released in 1796 on condition that he left England and did not return.[29]

[25] In 1784 Baron de Dietrich, in an official report stated that " five (steam) engines are actively employed at the foundry of Le Creusot. They serve at the same time to raise from the bosom of the earth the coals which are consumed, (to) furnish blast to the furnaces, and also to work the immense forge-hammers." Quoted by Harry Scrivenor, *History of the Iron Trade* . . . (new edn., 1854), p. 178.

[26] See J. Chevalier, " François Ignace de Wendel " (*op. cit*., p. 22). J. Burat, *Exposition de l'industrie francaise* : *année 1844* (1844), estimated that in 1818 there were only between 150 and 200 steam engines in France of which fifty had been made in France. Werner Sombart suggests that France had only about a dozen steam engines in 1815 (*Der moderne Kapitalismus*, II (2), p. 1067) but this is obviously too low an estimate.

[27] For Albert see Paul Leuilliot, " Contribution à l'histoire de l'introduction du machinisme en France : La Biographie industrielle de F. C. L. Albert " (*Annales Historiques de la Révolution française*, September-October, 1952) which makes use of Albert's " Biographie industrielle " preserved in the Archives Départementales du Bas-Rhin.

[28] Both partners had themselves previously visited England and had in 1791 established in Toulouse a cotton spinning mill in which some English workers were employed.

[29] See the *Manchester Mercury*, March 13th, March 20th, August 2nd and August 28th, 1792 and November 8th, 1796. How suspicious Manchester cotton manufacturers were of foreign visitors at this time may be seen from the following extract from B. Faujas de Saint-Fond, *Voyage en Angleterre* . . . (2 vols., 1797), Vol. II, p. 304 : " Cependant, malgré le désir qu'on avoit de nous obliger, il ne nous fut jamais possible devoir la moindre chose en ce genre ; toute tentative eût été vaine ; car la vigilance des fabricans avoit redoublée depuis qu'ils s'étoient persuadés qu'un colonel françois, venu quelque tems auparavant dans cette ville, avoit eu le projet de se procurer des plans de ces machines pour les faire éxecuter en France. Nul étranger, depuis cette époque, nul citoyen de la ville un peu éclairé ne peut avoir accès dans ces sortes de manufactures." At Carron this traveller was allowed to see the ironworks but not the cannon foundry (*ibid*., Vol. I, p. 210).

On his return to France Albert set up in 1799 a spinning mill (run by water power) at Coye-la-Forêt with the help of some of the skilled English artisans—for example James Collier of Manchester—with whom he had formerly worked at Toulouse. In 1803 he established a factory in Paris for the construction of textile machines, particularly mules, and was awarded a gold medal at the Paris industrial exhibition of 1806 for his spinning machines. Albert now turned his attention to the construction of steam engines. In 1807 he was awarded a medal by the Société d' encouragement pour l'industrie nationale for a model of a steam-engine and in the following year Albert and Martin patented a steam engine which, he claimed, was the first in France to be used for driving cotton spinning machinery. The economic depression of the last years of Napoleon's rule led to the collapse of Albert's business undertakings. After 1815 Albert was associated for a few years with Humphrey Edwards, an English engineer who had settled in Paris. But Edwards (at that time) wanted to import English machines rather than to build them in France, whilst Albert proposed to construct machinery in France. Albert gave up his connection with Edwards but in the end devoted himself after all to the importation of English—and also American—machines and not to the manufacture of machinery.[30] His Paris importing agency was particularly active between 1822 and 1831.[31]

At the end of the Napoleonic wars a number of French iron-masters and mining officials visited England to study modern methods of iron and steel production.[32] François de Wendel of Hayange, Calla of Paris, de Gallois-Lachapelle of Saint Etienne, and Dufaud of Grossource were among the French ironmasters and engineers who came to England soon after Waterloo to learn something of recent technical progress in the iron industry. Among the mining officials who visited Britain in the early years of

[30] A few examples may be given. In 1823 Albert imported a machine invented by S. W. Wright of London to make pins. In 1826-9 he imported a number of machines used in the manufacture of cloth—including those invented by John Jones of Leeds, Joseph Rayner of London and John Goulding of Massachusetts—for Victor Grandin's cloth factory at Elbeuf. In 1827 Albert procured for a recently-established saltworks at Dieuze machines invented by Furnival of Anderton (Cheshire).

[31] Albert retired to Strassburg. He died in 1853. For a portrait of Albert see *Histoire documentaire de l'industrie de Mulhouse* (2 vols., 1902), II, p. 336.

[32] Soon after the conclusion of the Napoleonic Wars a Paris coachmaker named Belvallette (senior) sent his two sons to England to serve as apprentices. During the second Empire the sons owned two large establishments at Paris and Boulogne for the construction of carriages such as landaus. See Georges Duveau, *La vie ouvrière en France sous le second Empire* (1946), p. 126. See also Ethel Jones, *Voyageurs français en Angleterre de* 1815 *à* 30 (1930).

the nineteenth century mention may be made of de Bonnard, Defrénoy, Coste and Le Play.

At the time of the Peace of Amiens (1802-3) Auguste Henri de Bonnard made a tour of the ironworks of Merthyr Tydfil, Coalbrookdale and the Black Country, paying particular attention to the coke-smelting and puddling processes.[33] Dufrénoy and Beaumont—of the French Department of Mines—visited English iron districts in 1827[34] and their investigations were supplemented shortly afterwards by those of Léon Coste.[35] Dufrénoy came to England and Scotland a few years later and studied Neilson's hot blast process.[36] Lady Charlotte Guest—wife of the well known Dowlais iron-master—translated this memoir into English in 1836.[37] It has been suggested that it was through this pamphlet—rather than through Neilson's own brief report to the Institution of Civil Engineers[38]—that English ironmasters became familiar with the hot blast process. An Englishman introduced Neilson's invention into France even before the publication of Dufrénoy's report.

Frédéric Le Play visited Sheffield in 1842. Like Gabriel Jars

[33] Auguste Henri de Bonnard, a Government mining engineer, wrote a " Mémoire sur les procèdes employés en Angleterre pour le traitement du fer par le moyen de la houille " in the *Journal des Mines*, XVII, 1804-5, pp. 245-96. This article was also printed (with useful notes by R. O'Reilly) in the *Annales des Arts et Manufactures*, XIII, 1805, pp. 225-254 and XIV, 1806, pp. 44-62. It appears that de Bonnard's investigations were carried out in association with the Swedish metallurgist E. T. Svedenstiernja.

[34] Pierre Armand Dufrénoy et Elie de Beaumont, *Voyage métallurgique en Angleterre* . . . (two vols., 1827, second edition 1837-9) : see also Dufrénoy et de Beaumont; " Fabrication de la fonte du fer en Angleterre . . . " (*Annales des Mines*, second series, I (1827), pp. 353 and II (1827), pp. 3-52 and 177-238).

[35] Léon Coste, *Mémoires métallurgiques sur le traitement des minerais de fer, d'etain et de plomb en Angleterre, faisant suite au Voyage métallurgique de MM Dufrénoy et Elie de Beaumont* (1830).

[36] Pierre Armand Dufrénoy, *Rapport à M le directeur général des ponts et des mines sur l'emploi de l'air chaud dans les usines à fer de l'Angleterre* (1834) and article in the *Annales des Mines*, third series, IV (1833), pp. 431-508.

[37] Pierre Armand Dufrenoy, *On the Use of Hot Air in the Ironworks of England* (translated from a report made to the Director General of Mines in France by M. Dufrénoy in 1834) (London, 1836 : British Museum library 538.c.30). Lady Charlotte Guest (later Schreiber) wrote in her journal on December 3, 1834 : " I . . . have been all the afternoon translating for Edward a French pamphlet on the advantage of using hot air in the manufacture of iron. It is full of technicalities and will take me a long time . . . " (Earl of Bessborough (ed.), *Lady Charlotte Guest : Extracts from her Journal*, 1833-52 (1950), p. 57). See also Alan Birch, " The Blast Furnace in the early nineteenth Century " (*Engineering*, May 23, 1952, pp. 657-8).

[38] J. B. Neilson, " On the Hot Air Blast " (*Transactions of the Institution of Civil Engineers*, I (1836), pp. 81-3).

many years before, Le Play paid particular attention to the Huntsman process of making cast steel. Indeed by emphasising the significance of Huntsman's invention in his report he did something to rescue Huntsman's name from undeserved oblivion. Le Play pointed out that the development of the French steel industry was hindered because the Sheffield manufacturers had secured a virtual monopoly of the raw material (bar iron) from Sweden. He considered that Valenciennes was well suited to develop into an important centre of steel production.[39]

The introduction into France of the various new techniques of iron and steel production was greatly facilitated by the work of a number of English engineers who either settled in France permanently or at any rate lived and worked there for many years. The Manbys were one of the most important English families who helped to foster the industrial development of France in the first half of the nineteenth century. They were prominent in the iron and engineering industries ; they established gasworks and they were pioneers in introducing iron steamships on to the French rivers. It is true that their giant engineering concern—with one foot in Paris and another in central France—lasted for only a few years but Aaron Manby and his sons gave a great impetus to the French iron and engineering industries in the difficult years of reconstruction that followed the downfall of Napoleon.

Aaron Manby was born at Albrighton in Shropshire in 1776. Very little information is available concerning his activities up to the age of thirty-five or so. It is believed that he gained some commercial experience in his early days as an employee of a bank in the Isle of Wight—his eldest son was born at West Cowes in 1804—but nothing seems to be known of how or where he acquired the skill which he later showed as ironmaster and engineer. In 1813 Aaron Manby took charge of some ironworks at Horseley by Tipton (south Staffordshire) in the heart of the Black Country.[40] There is no evidence to support the assertion

[39] Pierre Guillaume Frédéric Le Play, " Mémoire sur la fabrication de l'acier en Yorkshire . . . " (*Annales des Mines*, fourth series III (1843), pp. 538-714) and " Mémoire sur la fabrication et le commerce des fers à acier dans le nord de l'Europe . . . " (*ibid.*, fourth series, IX (1846), pp. 113-208 and 209-306). Le Play also investigated the Welsh copper industry : see P. G. F. Le Play, *Description des Procédés métallurgiques employés dans le Pays de Galles pour la fabrication du cuivre* . . . (1848). Le Play was professor of metallurgy at the Paris Mining College (Ecole des Mines) between 1840 and 1848. Dorothy Herbertson in her *Life of Frédéric Le Play* (1950) deals only very briefly with Le Play's activities as a mining engineer. See Louis Thomas, *Frédéric le Play 1806-1882* (1943).

[40] *The Engineer*, CXXXV, June 15, 1923, p. 641 : the article gives a brief summary of a brochure issued by the Horseley Bridge and Engineering Company Ltd.

that he founded these ironworks.[41] In the same year Aaron Manby took out a patent (No. 3705 of 1813) for a process for making bricks out of refuse slag from blast furnaces. In 1815 a Leeds ironmaster—Thomas Butler of Kirkstall—visited Horseley where he saw two furnaces in blast. He noted in his diary that these " well managed works " were in charge of Aaron Manby[42] whom he described as a partner in the firm of Harrison, Kitely & Smith.[43] When Joshua Field visited the Horseley establishment six years later he saw three furnaces in blast.[44]

It was at the Horseley ironworks that Aaron Manby and his son Charles built the first iron steamship to sail in the open sea. In 1821 Aaron Manby took out patents in England and France for a marine engine with oscillating cylinders.[45] Shortly afterwards the prefabricated wrought iron steamship *Aaron Manby* was constructed at Horseley. The vessel was transported to London in sections and was assembled at the Surrey Canal Dock. It was 120 feet long and, when laden, it drew three feet six inches

[41] The article on Aaron Manby in the *Dictionary of National Biography*, XXXVI, pp. 14-15 and the obituary notices of his son Charles in the *Proceedings of the Institution of Civil Engineers*, LXXXI, 1884-5 (Part iii) and in the *Tablettes Biographiques*, IX (1884) all refer to Aaron Manby as the founder of the Horseley ironworks. It is uncertain when these ironworks were established but it may have been as early as the 1780s. The undertaking appears to have started by mining coal and producing pig iron. Later—perhaps when Aaron Manby joined the firm—a foundry and an engineering works were added to the original establishemnt. For Aaron Manby see also a paper by W. O. Henderson and W. H. Chaloner, " Aaron Manby, builder of the first Iron Steamship "read to the Newcomen Society on February 10, 1954.

[42] Thomas Butler, (MS) *Journal of a Tour amongst the Ironworks of Staffordshire* . . . August 29, 1815 (extracts from this manuscript diary—now in the possession of Mr. R. F. Butler, great grandson of Thomas Butler—have been printed by Alan Birch in the *Edgar Allen News* (Sheffield), XXXI, No. 362, August 1952, p. 210).

[43] Thomas Butler, *op. cit.*, Appendix.

[44] " Joshua Field's Diary of a Tour in 1821 through the Midlands " (*Transactions of the Newcomen Society*, VI (1925-6), pp. 1-41): the manuscript of the diary is in the Science Museum, South Kensington.

[45] *Patent Specification and Drawing of Aaron Manby's oscillation Engine* (1821 : copy in the library of the Institution of Civil Engineers). The idea of constructing an engine of this type was not a novel one. Both W. Murdock (1785) and R. Witty (1811) had anticipated Aaron Manby's invention but Aaron and Charles Manby were the first to build such an engine for actual commercial use. The English patent was No. 4558 of July 9, 1821. It included the use of an intermediate heating agent (oil) for getting up steam. These two inventions represented a great advance upon the old high pressure steam engine. The French patent included specifications of (i) an oscillating marine engine, and (ii) an iron ship.

water. It was propelled by paddle wheels worked by a single engine.[46]

The *Aaron Manby* was launched in May, 1822.[47] The recent successful voyages of the wooden steamships *Defiance* (1816) and *Caledonia* (1817) across the North Sea and up the Rhine to Cologne had opened up the possibility of securing direct links by steamship between English ports and inland harbours on the Continent. In June, 1822, the *Aaron Manby* crossed the Channel and sailed up the Seine to Rouen and Paris. It left Rouen at 8 a.m. on June 6 and arrived in the French capital on the evening of June 10.[48] Captain Charles Napier—who later distinguished himself in the Portuguese civil war and at Beyrouth—was in command of the ship while young Charles Manby was in charge of the engine. This was the first iron steamship to sail on the high seas and it was the first vessel of any kind to make the direct voyage from the port of London to Paris. If Aaron Manby hoped to demonstrate to the French the superior qualities of British shipbuilding he did not succeed because a rival French vessel—the *Duc de Bordeaux*—easily outdistanced the *Aaron Manby* as it steamed up the Seine. And Manby may also have been disappointed that his epoch-making voyage failed to stir the imagination of the public on either side of the Channel.[49]

Nevertheless Aaron Manby pushed ahead with his scheme to establish a cargo steamer service on the Seine. In a prospectus dated January 1, 1823, Manby's company announced that the

[46] For the iron steamship *Aaron Manby* see " Joshua Field's Diary of a Tour in 1821 through the Midlands " (with introduction and notes by J. W. Hall) (*Transactions of the Newcomen Society*, VI, (1925-26), pp. 1-41) and Sir John Rennie's presidential address to the Institution of Civil Engineers on January 20, 1846. (*Proceedings of the Institution of Civil Engineers*, V (1846)), p. 96. Cf. *The Courier* newspaper, May 15th, 1822.

[47] *Morning Chronicle*, May 14, 1822. A. W. Kirkaldy, *British Shipping* (1914) p. 45 gives the date of the construction of the *Aaron Manby* as 1820.

[48] The *Dictionary of National Biography* (article on Aaron Manby) gives the date of the arrival of the *Aaron Manby* in Paris as Tuesday, June 11, but it is clear from statements in the French press (for example the *Constitutionnel*, June 13, 1822) that the *Aaron Manby* reached St. Cloud on the morning of Monday, June 10 and Paris (Port Saint Nicolas) at about 8 p.m. on the same day. The rival French ship, the *Duc de Bordeaux*, had left Rouen at 4 a.m. on June 6 and had reached Paris at 5.30 p.m. on Sunday June 9. The French vessel returned to Saint Cloud and on the morning of June 10 the two ships left St. Cloud together. The *Duc de Bordeaux* reached Paris 45 minutes before the *Aaron Manby*. The engine of the *Duc de Bordeaux* had been made at the Horseley works.

[49] Sir John Clapham, *An Economic History of Modern Britain*, I (1928), p. 439, wrote : " This feat might have been expected to fire imagination in two countries : but it did not."

Aaron Manby would sail regularly between Paris and Le Havre without discharging cargo at Rouen. Under normal weather conditions it was estimated that the voyage downstream would take three days and the voyage up-stream would take five days. Cargoes for London or Southampton would be accepted in Paris and would be transhipped at Le Havre.[50] This service was maintained by the *Aaron Manby* for twenty years or so.[51] A second iron steamship was built in sections at the Horseley iron-works and was put together at Manby and Wilson's engineering establishment at Charenton.[52] This vessel, too, plied on the Seine. In 1824 it was reported that Aaron Manby had " established iron steamboats on almost every river in France "—and practically all the marine engines had been built in England.[53]

In about 1822 Aaron Manby founded an important ironworks and engineering establishment at the junction of the Seine and the Marne at Charenton near Paris.[54] He placed Daniel Wilson in charge as manager and took him into partnership.[55] The firm was

[50] A copy of this prospectus of the *Compagnie des bateaux à vapeur* is in the possession of Mr. John Manby. The prospectus was issued from 367 rue St. Honoré. Business was also transacted at sub-offices in Paris (129 rue Montmartre and at the Quai d'Orsay) and at Le Havre (rue de la Gaffe).

[51] Sir John Rennie stated in 1846 that " the hull is yet in existence and is still used with new engines on board " (*Proceedings of the Institution of Civil Engineers*, V (1846), p. 96). The high quality of Aaron Manby's workmanship may be seen from the fact that an iron steamship built at Horseley plied on the Shannon for a quarter of a century : see A. W. Kirkaldy, *British Shipping* (1914), pp. 45-6 and G. R. Porter, *The Progress of the Nation* (revised edition, 1851), p. 575.

[52] W. S. Lindsay, *History of Merchant Shipping* (4 vols., 1874-6), IV. p. 86.

[53] *First Report of the Select Committee on Artisans and Machinery*, 1824 : evidence of J. Martineau, p. 8.

[54] *The Dictionary of National Biography* (article on Aaron Manby, Vol. XXXVI, p. 14) states that the Charenton engineering works were established in 1819. But A. M. Héron de Villefosse (*Annales des Mines*, second series, II (1827), p. 513 and 523) and E. Pelouze (*L'Art du Maitre des Forges* . . . (1827), I, pp. vi-vii) who both wrote in 1827 stated that at that time the Charenton works had been open for only four or five years. L. Beck, *op. cit.*, IV, pp. 328-9 stated that the Charenton ironworks were founded in 1822. Daniel Wilson stated that the works were opened at the end of 1822 (*Enquête sur les fers*, 1828). Cf. *Report of the Select Committee on Artisans and Machinery*, 1824 p. 110.

[55] Daniel Wilson was born in Glasgow in 1790 and worked in Dublin as an industrial chemist before he was associated with Aaron Manby in various enterprises. See the *Minutes of the Proceedings of the Institution of Civil Engineers*, IX, 1849-50, p. 10. His son Daniel Wilson (junior) appears to have squandered his inheritance. He was the central figure in the *affaire des décorations* which led to the resignation as President of his father in law Jules Grévy (1887). The younger Daniel Wilson's sister became Mme. Pelouze and acquired the famous chateau of Chenonceaux.

known as Manby, Wilson et Cie.[56] The partners undertook not only the remelting, puddling, and rolling of iron but also the manufacture of machinery, iron ships and steam engines. In 1824 Manby's engineering works supplied a 50 h.p. auxiliary engine for the wooden schooner *Galibi* which had been launched at Rouen in the previous year. The engines ran satisfactorily on trials held in July, 1824. The vessel was transferred to the French navy and was renamed the *Caroline*. It sailed for Cayenne at the end of 1824 and returned in August, 1827. This was the second ship to use steam—in addition to sail—on a voyage across the Atlantic from east to west. By the end of 1827 she had been under steam for 9,000 hours but her machinery was still in good condition. This is evidence of the high quality of the workmanship of Manby's engineering establishment.[57]

Within a few years Manby and Wilson's plant included fourteen furnaces and it had a weekly output of 80,000 kgm. of cast iron and 70,000 kgm. of rolled iron.[58] Power was supplied by five steam engines. Some four or five hundred men were employed of whom about half were Englishmen.[59] Manby and Wilson were awarded gold medals by the *Société de l'encouragement pour l'industrie nationale*[60] and by the judges at the Paris industrial exhibition of 1827.[61]

Edmond Pelouze, writing in 1827, described with enthusiasm the meteoric rise of the firm of Manby and Wilson and he drew attention to the great influence which the establishment had already had upon the expansion of the French engineering

[56] When Daniel Wilson (senior) took over the management of the Manby-Wilson gasworks in Paris Aaron Manby's son Charles was—for a time—in charge of the engineering workshops at Charenton.

[57] H. Philip Spratt, " The Origin of Transatlantic Steam Navigation " in the *Transactions of the Newcomen Society*, XXVI, 1947-9, pp. 135-6.

[58] L. Beck, *op. cit.*, IV, p. 239 and table on p. 334. The firm was later known as Manby, Wilson, Henry et Cie.

[59] Estimates of the number of men employed by Manby and Wilson at Charenton in 1824-5 varied considerably. Chaptal, in a speech to the Conseil Supérieur de Commerce et des Colonies on August 29, 1825, stated that only three hundred men were employed (G. Bourgin and H. Bourgin, *Le Régime de l'industrie en France de 1814 à 1830 : recueil de textes*, III (1941), p. 83). In 1826 however the editor of *Annales de l'industrie nationale et étrangère*, (XXV (1826) p. 16) stated that 700 men were employed by Manby & Wilson—350 British and 350 French.

[60] *Bulletin de la Société d'encouragement pour l'industrie nationale*, XXIV (1825), p. 123.

[61] A. M. Héron de Villefosse, " Des métaux en France : rapport fait au jury central de l'exposition des produits de l'industrie française de l'anne 1827 sur les objets relatifs à la métallurgie " (*Annales des Mines*, second series, II (1827), pp. 513, 532 and 592).

industry. He wrote : " In an old tumble-down convent—which French manufacturers considered incapable of holding the smallest factory—there arose, as if by magic, a unique enterprise. It included forges for rolling iron, foundries with large and complicated plant machines capable of exerting very great power. These works were thrown open to the inspection of (French) manufacturers and were a model for others to copy. It is not surprising that various machines and methods used (at Charenton) quickly found imitators." Pelouze went on to refer to " the extraordinary influence exercised by the Charenton ironworks upon all—or nearly all—the many manufacturers who, in the short period of four years, have decided to establish forges of the English type."[62] By 1825 Manby and Wilson had fitted out ironworks or engineering establishments for the Duke of Ragusa (Marshal Marmont) at Châtillon-sur-Seine, for Muel & Doublet at Abainville (Meuse Department) ; for Renaux et Cie at Raismes, for Débladis at Imphy (Nièvre Department), for Saglio, Humann et Cie at Audincourt (Doubs Department)[63] and for Debuyère at La Chaudeau (Haute Saône). The firm of Manby & Wilson was also responsible for installing heating by hot water pipes in the new Paris bourse.[64]

In the initial stages of the enterprise most of the plant installed at the Charenton works came from England. Witnesses before the Select Committee on Artisans and Machinery (1824) complained that Aaron Manby had broken the law not merely by smuggling machine parts from England to France but also by enticing skilled mechanics to Paris. It may be estimated that in 1824-5 Manby & Wilson were probably employing between 200 and 250 Englishmen at Charenton. The fact that Aaron Manby had been prosecuted for seducing English artisans abroad does not seem to have prevented him from continuing to secure English workers. The evidence given before the Select Committee on Artisans and Machinery indicated clearly the alarm caused among

[62] Edmond Pelouze, *L'Art du Maître de Forges* . . . (2 vols. in one, I (1827) II (1828)), I, pp. vi-vii.

[63] See J. C. Fischer, *Tagebücher* (Schaffhausen, 1951), p. 202.

[64] For Manby & Wilson's Charenton ironworks and engineering works see also the following articles in the *Bulletin de la Société d'Encouragement pour l'industrie nationale* : (i) " Rapport sur les fonderies et établissement d'industrie de MM. Manby et Wilson, à Charenton, près Paris " (XXIV, 1825, pp. 123-6) (by the younger Molard) ; (ii) " Description d'une grave en fonte de fer, employée aux fonderies de MM. Manby et Wilson . . . " (XXV, 1826, pp. 295-9 ; (iii) " Notice sur le chauffage par le moyen de la vapeur, et application de ce procédé au chauffage de la . . . nouvelle Bourse " (XXVII, 1828, pp. 202-8). See also A. Ferry " Notice sur les fonderies, forges, et ateliers de MM. Manby et Wilson à Charenton " (*Annales de l'industrie nationale et étrangère*, XXIII, 1826, pp. 5-16 and S. Berard, *Observations sur Manby & Wilson* (1825).

English ironmasters and engineers at Manby's success in forestalling them in the French market.[65] Richard Harrison complained bitterly that Aaron Manby—who had once been "a partner in our concern"—had taken an unfair advantage of his intimate knowledge of the Horseley ironworks to entice their mechanics to Paris "in a very improper and most dishonourable manner."[66]

Manby and Wilson also played a leading part in introducing gas lighting to Paris.[67] Frederick Albert Winsor—a German who had lived in England for most of his life[68]—had obtained permission in December, 1815, to set up gasworks in Paris but beyond installing gas lamps in the Passage des Panoramas (January, 1817) and the Odeon arcade the company which he established achieved little and soon went into liquidation. Two other Paris gas companies also failed. On May 12, 1821, Aaron Manby, Daniel Wilson and a colleague named Henry took out a French patent for the manufacture of gas. A year later the three associates established the Compagnie d'éclairage par le gaz hydrogène—popularly known as the English Company—to light Paris by gas. Many difficulties had to be surmounted—tiresome litigation with the rival "Royal Company,"[69] strenuous opposition to gas lighting from the indefatigable Charles Nodier, and finally

[65] *Report from the Select Committee on Artisans and Machinery*, 1824: see, in particular, the evidence of John Martineau (pp. 6-8), Bryan Donkin (p. 36), William Turner (pp. 109-113: Turner had been employed at Charenton for a year fitting steam engines; his wages had been two guineas a week compared with 27/- to 30/- in England); Thomas Lester (pp. 113-116: Lester had erected three engines for Manby; he had been employed at the Charenton works for a year); W. Yates (pp. 116-123); S. Walker (pp. 120-6) and R. Harrison (pp. 123-7). William Brunton stated in evidence on March 26, 1824: "I know that even the celebrated Aaron Manby was in London within these three months and carried off twelve men in the inside and on the top of a coach, out of Gracechurch Street" (p. 325).

[66] *Ibid.*, Evidence of R. Harrison, p. 125.

[67] See Maxime du Camp, "L'Eclairage à Paris" (*Revue des deux Mondes*, June 1873, pp. 766-92).

[68] See article on Frederick Albert Winsor in the *Dictionary of National Biography* (Vol. LXII, p. 204). Winsor was born in Brunswick in 1763. In 1799 he had settled in England. He set up a company to light London by gas which issued a prospectus in 1807. The company failed. Winsor died in France in 1830 and was buried in the Père Lachaise cemetery in Paris.

[69] *Au Roi, au Conseil d'état: les sieurs Manby, Henry et Wilson, formant le Compagnie d'éclairage par le gaz hydrogène, contre les sieurs Bourenne, Caret et Chaptal formant le compagnie, dite Royale, d'éclairage par le gaz hydrogène (1822)*: copy in the library of the Institution of Civil Engineers.

the inexperience of the French labourers engaged to lay the pipes. The task of actually erecting the gas works and supervising the laying of pipes was entrusted to Aaron Manby's son Charles. At last on December 31, 1829 the English Company successfully lit the Rue de la Paix by gas. In the 1830's Manby's company went ahead and the undertaking remained in English hands until 1847 when all the Paris gas companies were amalgamated by Dubuchet. By that time Paris had some 8,000 gas lamps. Meanwhile Aaron Manby had extended his interests in the gas industry. In association with Barlow he had founded the Imperial Continental Gas Association (1825) which set up gasworks in a number of Continental countries. One of Manby's sons—Joseph Lane Manby—was, for a time, the manager of the French concerns of the Continental Gas Association.

Aaron Manby's most grandiose but least successful venture was his attempt to absorb into his industrial empire the famous Le Creusot ironworks—the scene of William Wilkinson's labours forty years before. Had he been able to unite permanently the ironworks of Le Creusot and Charenton he might have dominated the whole French engineering industry. On January 11, 1826, Aaron Manby, Daniel Wilson and A. J. F. Regny—acting on behalf of the firm of Manby & Wilson—acquired an interest in the Le Creusot concern from the Chagot family.[70] Manby & Wilson paid the Chagots 620,000 francs for 31 of their 80 shares in a great " mixed " enterprise which included collieries, iron ore mines, William Wilkinson's blast furnaces, a foundry, a forge, rolling mills, a machine building workshop, landed property and forests.[71] Manby and Wilson were in control of the management of the Le Creusot concern. The two establishments in which they were interested were united in May, 1828, when the *Société anonyme des Mines, Forges et Fonderies du Creusot et de Charenton* was founded.[72] In addition to the 620,000 francs paid for 31 shares

[70] The contract for the purchase of 31 shares in the Le Creusot concern was between (i) Aaron Manby, Daniel Wilson and A. J. F. Regny (jointly represented Manby, Wilson et Cie) and (ii) J. M. F. Chagot, L. J. Chagot, M. A. de Cheptainville, Madame Alexandrine Pauline Chagot and A. C. de Gournay (in his own name and on behalf of his wife Mme. Palmire Chagot). Mr. John Manby has kindly shown me a copy of the contract.

[71] The first five payments—for 31 shares at 20,000 francs each—were 100,000 francs each while the sixth and last payment was the balance of 120,000 francs.

[72] For a detailed description of the Le Creusot concern in 1828 see *Rapport sur les Etablissements du Creusot adressé par les Membres du Conseil d'Administration à Messieurs les Membres du Conseil Extraordinaire dans la Séance du 24 Octobre, 1828* (copy in the library of the Institution of Civil Engineers : Pamphlets (quarto), VI, No. 10). The Charenton

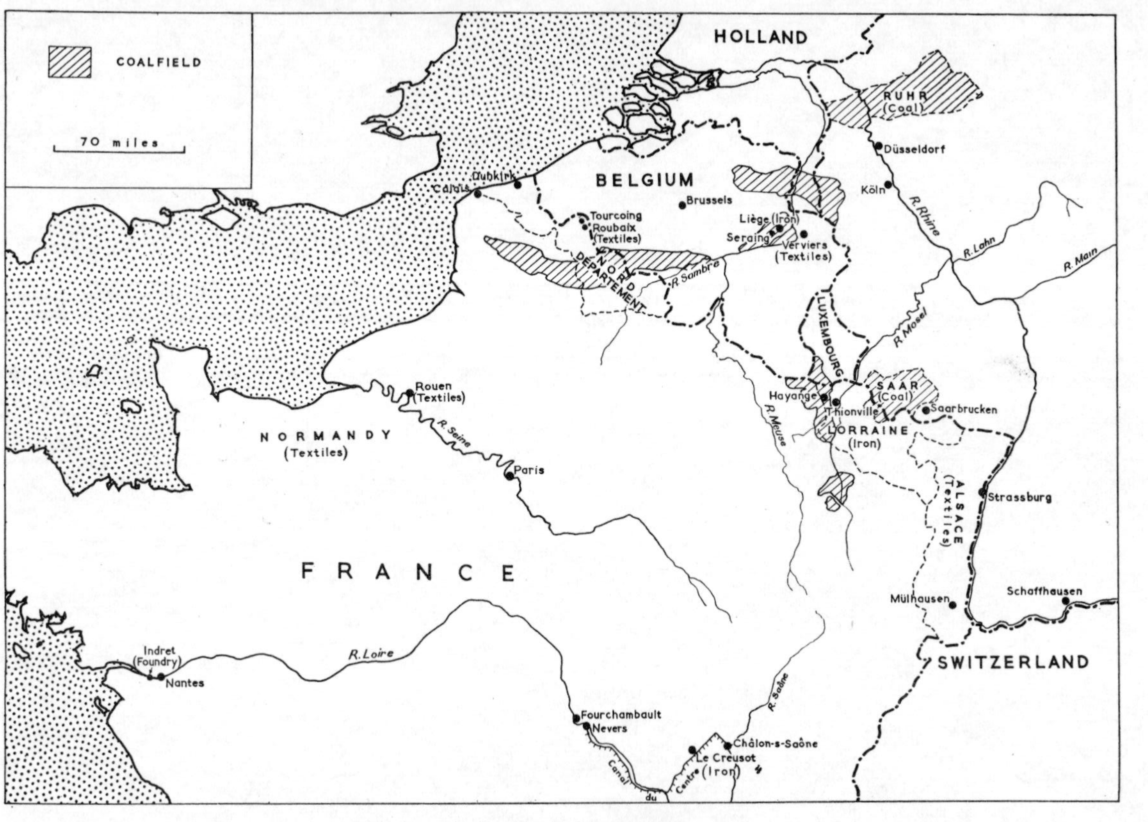

INDUSTRIAL REGIONS OF FRANCE, BELGIUM and N.W. GERMANY IN THE MIDDLE OF THE NINETEENTH CENTURY

Manby and Wilson laid out large additional sums in order to modernise the Le Creusot ironworks. New forges and rolling mills were erected. Much new plant—made at Charenton—was installed at Le Creusot and the iron and steel and engineering establishments were entirely reorganised. In 1827 Le Creusot had 16 puddling furnaces, eight refineries and three rolling mills. New shafts had been sunk to increase the output of the Le Creusot coalmines. Although the firm was successful in securing some important orders—such as one from Seguin frères, Biot et Cie for materials for the Saint Etienne-Lyons railway—the returns were on the whole inadequate in view of the large initial outlay. The commercial crisis of 1830 was the death-blow to Manby's hopes. Two efforts to secure a Government loan failed and on June 25, 1833, the company went into liquidation. On December 21, 1836, the firm's creditors sold the Le Creusot ironworks to Adolphe and Eugène Schneider who were financed by the Seillière banking firm.[73]

Aaron Manby returned to England in about 1840 and lived in retirement until his death in the Isle of Wight in 1850. His four sons were all civil engineers and all of them were active on the Continent as well as in England.[74] It has been seen that Charles

works were closed in 1829 and the machinery was transferred to Le Creusot. It may be added that the brief account of the work of the Manbys in France given by L. H. Jenks in *The Migration of British Capital* (New York and London, 1927), pp. 180-1, is misleading since Charles Manby is given the sole credit for several activities for which Aaron Manby was mainly responsible.

[73] Jean Chevalier, *Le Creusot* . . . (1946), p. 159. See also N. Vadot, *Le Creusot* . . . (1875) and H. Chazelle, *Le Creusot* . . . (1936).

[74] Aaron Manby had one son (Charles) by his first wife and three sons by his second wife : (i) For Charles Manby, 1804-84, who was secretary of the Institution of Civil Engineers between 1839 and 1856, see the *Dictionary of National Biography*, XXXVI, p. 16 and obituaries in the *Minutes of the Proceedings of the Institution of Civil Engineers*, LXXI, 1884-5 (part iii), pp. 327-34 (photograph of Charles Manby as frontispiece to this volume) and in the *Tablettes Biographiques, mémorial universel*, IX (1884). Charles Manby was employed both at the Charenton and the Le Creusot ironworks for a time and he also held the post of chief engineer to the Tobacco Department of the French Government. He was a member of the international commission which investigated the possibility of constructing the Suez canal. Charles Manby's generosity may be illustrated by mentioning the help that he gave to George Hudson when the dethroned and impoverished " Railway King " was living in exile in France. See R. S. Lambert, *The Railway King* (1934), pp. 295-6. (ii) For John Richard Manby, 1813-69, see the *Minutes of the Proceedings of the Institution of Civil Engineers*, XXX (1869-70), p. 446. (iii) For Joseph Lane Manby, 1814-62, see the *Minutes of the Proceedings of the Institution of Civil Engineers*, XXII (1862-3), pp. 629-30. (iv) For Edward Oliver Manby, 1816-64, see the *Minutes of the Proceedings of the Institution of Civil Engineers*, XXIV (1864-5), pp. 533-4.

Manby was associated with his father in expanding the French iron industry, in introducing iron steamships on the River Seine and in providing Paris with gas light while Joseph Lane Manby held a senior appointment in France under the Continental Gas Association. John Richard Manby worked at Charenton for a time and he was subsequently responsible for the construction of the Cette-Montpellier railway. He—and his brother Edward Oliver—planned to establish the Languin ironworks near Nantes.[75]

Several other English engineers were active in Paris in the 1820's and 1830's. Humphrey Edwards deserves mention since he introduced the compound engine into France and elsewhere on the Continent at a time when this type of engine had almost been forgotten in England. Edwards was a Lambeth millwright who had worked with Arthur Woolf on improving Watt's steam engine. The partnership came to an end in 1811 and a few years later Edwards migrated to Paris where he patented the Woolf compound engine in a modified form (1815). In 1826 he introduced a further improvement by using wrought iron instead of cast iron in the manufacture of his boilers. Edwards became manager and partner in the well known foundry and engineering works which the Perier brothers had established at Chaillot. When Jacques Constantin Perier died in 1818 the works were purchased by Scipion Périer[76] (who was not related to the founders of the firm). Scipion Périer went into partnership with Edwards and Chappert. It appears that in the course of his career Edwards made about three hundred Woolf compound engines—one hundred in London and two hundred in Paris. He also imported " Cornwall " and other types of steam pumps and steam engines and set them up where required.[77] In 1824 the Chaillot works employed some five hundred men. In that year J. Martineau complained to the Select Committee on Artisans and Machinery that some of his best mechanics had recently been enticed to Chaillot.[78]

[75] E. O. Manby and J. Manby, *Notes of a Survey and Estimate of the proposed Ironworks at Languin* (London, 1841 : copy in the library of the Institution of Civil Engineers : Tracts (octavo), LVI).

[76] Scipion Périer was the brother of Casimir Périer (prime minister in 1832). For Scipion Périer see the obituary notice by Baron Gevando in the *Bulletin de la Société pour l'encouragement de l'industrie nationale*, XX (1821), pp. 117-126. Edwards was assisted by his son Henry and by Jennings.

[77] H. W. Dickinson, *A short History of the Steam Engine* (1938), pp. 99-100 and p. 126. It has been seen that during the early part of his career in Paris Humphrey Edwards was associated for a time with F. C. L. Albert : see Paul Leuilliot, " Contribution à l'histoire de l'introduction du machinisme en France. La ' Biographie industrielle ' de F. C. L. Albert " *Annales Historiques de la Révolution Française*, Sept.-Oct. 1952), p. 16.

[78] *First Report of the Select Committee on Artisans and Machinery* 1824 : evidence of J. Martineau, pp. 9-10.

Another Englishman named Steele managed some engineering works in Paris in the early nineteenth century[79] while his compatriot Radcliffe established a foundry in the rue Saint Ambroise in 1823.[80] At the same time John Collier manufactured cloth-shearing—and other textile—machinery in Paris.[81] Between 1810 and 1812 William Cockerill (junior) and James Cockerill (brothers of the well known John Cockerill of Liège) were installing machinery for a number of French woollen cloth manufacturers. At that time James Cockerill had both a workshop and a dwelling house in Paris while William Cockerill (junior) had his headquarters first at Reims and then at Sedan. James Cockerill erected new machines in a number of centres of the woollen cloth industry including Elbeuf, Louviers, Limoux, Chalabre and Crest.[82] Etienne Calla, the head of well known engineering works in Paris, had visited England to study new methods of production before setting up a foundry in 1815.[83]

In the French provinces English technical knowledge influenced the development of the important iron and steel centres of Hayange in Lorraine and of Le Creusot and Saint Etienne in the Midi. François de Wendel of Hayange—who had in 1803 purchased the ironworks lost by his father (François Ignace de Wendel) during the Revolution—studied new methods of iron-working in England. In 1818 he erected at Hayange the second French blast furnace to smelt iron with coke instead of charcoal. He also introduced Cort's puddling process into his works. At

[79] Mr. Alexander told the *Select Committee on Artisans and Machinery*, 1824 (*Third Report*, p. 103) that Messrs. Steele and Atkins had recently built a steamboat " for the post office at Calais."

[80] A. M. Héron de Villefosse, *op cit.*, pp. 518-9 wrote of Radcliffe : " Four years ago this skilful foreigner established a foundry in a small shed in Paris. Today his establishment makes the most difficult pieces (of iron work) up to thirty metric quintals in weight."

[81] *First Report of the Select Committee on Artisans and Machinery*, 1824 : evidence of Alexander Galloway, p. 21.

[82] E. Mahaim, " Les débuts de l'établissements John Cockerill à Seraing " (*Vierteljahrschrift für Sozial und Wirtschafts-Geschichte*, III, 1905; see pp. 647-8).

[83] *Exposition des Produits de l'industrie française en 1839* : *rapport du jury central* (three volumes, 1839), I, p. 381. Calla's works were in the rue Faubourg-Poissonnière. Alexander Galloway, in evidence before the *Select Committee on Artisans and Machinery*, 1824, mentioned Calla as a very able French engineer who made cotton machinery. But Calla's factory cannot have been a very large one since only about fifty workers were employed there in 1825 : see statement by Count Saint Cricq before the Conseil supérieur du Commerce et des Colonies on August 29, 1825 (G. Bourgin and H. Bourgin, *Le Régime de l'industrie en France de 1814 à 1830*, III (1941), p. 73). For Etienne Calla (1760-1835) see Emile Eude, *Histoire documentaire de la mécanique française* (1902), p. 236.

about the same time Gabriel de Gallois-Lachapelle paid a long visit to England to study the most up-to-date methods of producing iron. On his return to France he founded the Compagnie des mines de fer de Saint Etienne (1819).[84] In his new ironworks he set up three modern blast furnaces and he introduced puddling and rolling plants. His machinery was imported from England.[85] Dufaud, after visiting English ironworks, introduced modern puddling furnaces and rolling mills for the production of wrought iron at the works which he managed at Grossource near Nevers. But no great progress was made. In 1822, however, Dufaud's son became a partner in some neighbouring ironworks at Fourchambault and here English methods of producing iron were introduced with much greater success.[86] It has been seen, too, that in 1826 Aaron Manby and Daniel Wilson acquired an interest in the Le Creusot ironworks and modernised their plant.

At about the same time James Jackson established near Saint Etienne one of the first large plants in France for the production of cast steel by Huntsman's process.[87] Swedish ore was used. Progress was rather slow at first but after James Jackson's death in 1829 his sons William, John and Charles—joined later by James (jnr.)—acquired new works at Assailly (1830) where they were soon employing some 230 men. To their original works the Jacksons had added those founded by Beaunier (Inspector General in the royal corps of mines) as well as factory at Hérimcourt (Doubs Department)—on the Swiss frontier—for the production of files and other tools. The Jacksons were awarded gold medals at the Paris industrial exhibitions of 1827, 1834 and 1844.[88] By the 1850s the Jacksons

[84] Andrew Ure, in *A Dictionary of Arts, Manufactures and Mines . . .* (second edition, 1840) wrote : " Since the peace, many French engineers and ironmasters have exerted themselves in naturalising in France this species of industry ; and M. de Gallois (-Lachapelle), in particular, after a long residence in Great Britain, where he was admitted to see deliberately and minutely every department of the iron trade, returned with ample details, and erected at Saint Etienne, a large establishment entirely on the English model " (p. 686).

[85] L. Beck, *op cit.*, IV, p. 330, note ii. Harry Scrivenor stated that de Gallois-Lachapelle's blast furnace " had not at first that success which he expected, and his premature death is attributed to the grief and trouble which this enterprise occasioned him " (*op. cit.*, p. 180).

[86] Sir John Clapham, *Economic Development of France and Germany 1815-1914* (1928), p. 60.

[87] Sanche produced cast steel at Amboise in the 1780s. In 1819 J. C. Fischer of Schaffhausen had established in France — for F. Japy—a plant for the manufacture of crucible cast steel.

[88] *Exposition des Produits de l'industrie française en 1839 : rapport du jury central* (three volumes, 1839), Vol. I, pp. 387-8. This report stated : " This steel enjoys the highest commercial reputation. It should not be

and their associates controlled an important iron and steel combine which comprised eight major ironworks and engineering establishments. The concern employed about 2,500 workers and had a large annual output of iron and steel. In 1861 William Fritz Jackson, a grandson of the founder of the firm, was the first to introduce the Bessemer process into France.[89]

Other British ironworking and engineering establishments in France in the 1820s and 1830s included the Waddington brothers of Saint-Rémi-sur-Aire (Eure), and Saint-Lubin des Joucherets (Eure-et-Loire Department);[90] Thomas, Holland and Stanhope of Château-la-Vallière (by Tours); Thomas Hughes and Co. of Basse-Indre (by Nantes); and Hims, Higgs and Co. of St. Julien (by St. Chamond).[91] In 1820 the Manchester engineering firm of Galloway and Bowman erected two cornmills at Lille and in 1824 it "received an order for some large boilers, engines and pumps for the French Government" to be erected at Dunkirk.[92] In October

forgotten that it was the Jacksons who first set up in France a plant of any size for the manufacture of cast steel." See also Jules Burat, *Exposition de l'industrie française : année* 1844, Vol. I, pp. 34-5 and p. 39 and L. Beck, *op. cit.*, IV, p. 677. It was no doubt with the Jacksons in mind that Le Play wrote in 1846 in the *Annales des Mines* (fourth series, IX, p. 260) that "the only cast steel made in France which has so far competed successfully with high-class British steel is that made in the Loire Department from Swedish iron. The significant expansion of this industry dates only from 1838." For the Jacksons see L.-J. Gras, *Histoire économique de la métallurgie* (St. Etienne, 1908) and *Histoire économique de la Loire* (Saint Etienne, 1908) and W. F. Jackson, *James Jackson et ses fils* . . . (1893).

[89] L. Beck, *op. cit.*, IV, pp. 970-1. For the introduction of the Bessemer converter into France see Roger Gourmelon, "Reactions d'entrepreneurs en face d'une invention. L'introduction du convertisseur Bessemer en France" (*Techniques et Civilisations*, II, 1952, Numbers iii and iv, pp. 96-99).

[90] The Waddingtons were cotton manufacturers and makers of textile machinery. William Henry Waddington (born at Saint-Rémy-sur-Avre in 1826), a member of this family, was a distinguished French statesman. He held office as Minister of Education (1876-7), Foreign Minister (1877), President of the Council (1879) and French ambassador in London (1883-1892). His younger brother Richard (born in 1838) was a leading Rouen cotton spinner : he was elected deputy for Rouen in 1876. For William Henry Waddington see G. Perrot, *Vie et travaux de Henry Waddington* (1909).

[91] See list of French puddling works and rolling mills in the early 1820s in E. Pelouze, *op. cit.*, I, pp. vii-ix and L. Beck, *op. cit.*, IV, p. 334.

[92] *Recollections of John Galloway, 1804-94* (typescript in the Manchester Central Reference Library, MS 926.2 Gl), p. 27 and p. 29. This John Galloway was a son of William Galloway one of the founders of the firm of Galloway and Bowman. A French passport (visa) allowing James Bowman to visit St. Quentin in 1822 is preserved in the Galloway MSS in the possession of Col. J. G. Riddick of Mobberley, Cheshire.

1830 an Englishman named M. T. Roper who ran a workshop in the Avenue de Neuilly in Paris for the manufacture of tools had to close his factory owing to labour unrest among his English workers.[93] In 1831 Philip Taylor introduced the Neilson hot blast into ironworks at Vienne (Isère Department) and at Voulte (Ardèche Department).[94] Three years later he received an award at the Paris industrial exhibition for making an apparatus to introduce the hot blast into a smelting furnace.[95] James Nasmyth's steam hammer was actually in use in France before it was adopted by English engineers. The inventor states in his autobiography that Schneider, the owner of the Le Creusot ironworks, was shown drawings of the steam hammer by Nasmyth's partner. When Nasmyth was at Le Creusot in 1842 he was shown a steam hammer made from his own drawings and he suggested ways in which it might be improved. It was only after he returned to England that Nasmyth took out a patent for his invention. The jury's report on exhibits shown at the exhibition of 1844 commented favourably upon the Chartreux railway workshops of Allcard and Buddicom at Petit-Quevilly (by Rouen)[96] where some six hundred men were employed ; the ironworks of Harding and Cocker at Lille and Tourcoing ; the Rouen machine-building works of John Hall, Powell and Scott;[97] and the well-established factory of Applegarth and Cowper for building steam printing presses.[98] In 1849 Allcard and Buddicom opened a new factory for building locomotives at La Bastide (by Bordeaux). In the 1850s it was reported that John Masterman was mining coal and smelting iron at Aubin (by Decazeville) ;[99] that W. B. Buddicom, Brassey and Blount were directors of the Meng de colliery near Marseilles ; and that a British firm was building iron steamships at Marseilles.

[93] *Archives Nationales* (Paris), F/12 : 2223.

[94] L. Beck, *op. cit.*, IV, p. 674.

[95] Jules Burat, *op. cit.*, historical introduction. A. L. Dunham in *La révolution industrielle en France 1815-48* (1953) p. 108 states that the introduction of the hot air blast has been attributed to a certain Charles Taylor of Beaugrenelle, Paris (1834).

[96] The Chartreux works of Allcard and Buddicom at Petit-Quevilly were closed in 1845 when new workshops for the building of locomotives were built adjoining the firm's repair workshops at Sotteville (Rouen).

[97] This firm had been commended at the industrial exhibition of 1839 for making improvements to a fulling machine. In 1844 the firm received a bronze medal.

[98] *Exposition des Produits de l'industrie française en 1844 : rapport du jury central* (three volumes, 1844), II, pp. 171-2, 205, 210 and 232.

[99] *The Times*, July 12, 1852 and April 7, 1856 ; L. H. Jenks, *op. cit.*, p. 181.

James Nasmyth's Bridgewater Foundry supplied many machine tools to the French naval dockyards at Cherbourg.

British engineers who specialised in the construction of textile machinery included Collier, Douglas, Heywood, Dixon, Roberts and the brothers Dyer. Early in the nineteenth century John Collier established a factory at 20 rue Richer, Paris, to make textile machines. His output was considerable and the high quality of his products gained him medals at the Paris industrial exhibitions of 1819, 1823 and 1827. The *Société de l'encouragement pour l'industrie nationale* presented John Collier with its highest award in May 1828.[100] William Douglas, who settled in France at the invitation of the French government in the Year X, was a pioneer in the manufacture of modern carding and spinning machinery for the making of woollen cloth. He invented a gig-mill which was improved by John Collier. By 1810 William Douglas had supplied 949 machines to a hundred factories. John Heywood, who introduced power-driven cotton machinery into the Breusch valley in Alsace, built so-called "Schirmeck Looms" for other cotton manufacturers in the district. Job Dixon worked for Nicholas Schlumberger at Guebwiller (Alsace) in 1818 and later became a partner in the machine-building firm of Risler frères of Cernay (Sennheim) near Mülhausen (1820). In 1824 it was stated that Dixon was employing twenty English workers. Richard Roberts, the inventor of the self-actor, planned the layout of a new cotton mill for André Koechlin of Mülhausen. In the 1830s the brothers Dyer of Gamaches (Somme Department) were making various types of textile machinery including the card-making machines and tube roving frames invented by their father.[101] Mention may also be made of John Maberley who was the managing director

[100]For the Platt-Collier woolcombing machine see Andrew Ure, *Dictionary of Arts* . . . (second edition, 1840), p. 1310.

[101]For John Collier see C. Mollet, "Rapport sur les ateliers de construction de machines, fondés à Paris par M. John Collier" (*Bullet de la Société d'Encouragement pour l'industrie nationale*, XXVII (1828), pp. 167-170); for Douglas see J. A. C. Chaptal (Napoleon's Minister of the Interior), *De l'industrie françoise* (two vols., 1819), I, p. 16 and R. J. Lenoir, "Les Etrangérs et la Formation du Capitalisme en Belgique" (*Revue d'histoire économique et sociale*, XX (1932), pp. 301 and 316: Lenoir points out that Douglas's machines were to be found in Brussels and Verviers as well as in France): for Heywood (who went to France in 1806) see J. Klein, *Die Baumwollindustrie im Breuschtal* (1905), ch. 1: for Dixon see the *Fifth Report from the Select Committee on Artisans and Machinery*, 1824: evidence of Adam Young, pp. 597-82: for Roberts see article by H. W. Dickinson in the *Newcomen Society Transactions*, XXV (1945-7), p. 123 *et seq*; for J. C. Dyer and his sons see the *First Report from the Select Committee on the Exportation of Machinery*, 1841: evidence of Matthew Curtis, questions 1533-64.

of a large factory established in 1838 at Amiens to build flax-spinning machinery. The contract for supplying and erecting the necessary machinery was given to Thomas Marsden of Salford. About a hundred English mechanics went to Amiens to erect the equipment.[102]

British capital, technical knowlege and skilled labour were of considerable significance in the early development of French railways.[103] Towards the end of the eighteenth century wooden and cast-iron tramways were laid down to serve the coal-mines of Montcenis (Le Creusot) and Anzin, the royal cannon foundry on the island of Indret, the copper mines of Poullaouen, and a few other industrial establishments. The first modern railways were short lines serving the coal districts of central France.[104]

[102]*First Report from the Select Committee on the Exportation of Machinery*, 1841 : evidence of T. Marsden, questions 1146-51. See also L. H. Jenks, *op. cit.*, p. 180. The firm of John Maberley & Co. had been engaged in the manufacture of linen in England and Scotland and also in banking in Scotland. The Company became insolvent in 1832 : see A. J. Warden, *The Linen Trade* (1864), pp. 67, 541 and 711 and A. W. Kerr, *History of Banking in Scotland* (1902), pp. 187, 202, 211 and 213.

[103]The French showed considerable interest in the development of the early colliery tramways and other " railways " in England. See for example the following articles in the *Annales des Arts* : (i) " Sur l'emploi des chemins de fer pour le transport des minérais et des charbons " (IX, 1801) ; (ii) " Sur les avantages et sur la construction des chemins de fer " (XI, 1803) ; (iii) " Description de deux nouvelles espèces de chemins de fer " (XII, 1804) ; (iv) " Note sur les Rail-Ways ou chemins de fer " (1817). Copies of these volumes of the *Annales des Arts* are in the Patent Office Library (London). See also Lunier's article on railways in the *Dictionnaire des Sciences et des Arts* (1805) ; de Gallois, " Des chemins de fer en Angleterre . . . ", (*Annales des Mines*, 1818) ; H. de Villefosse, *De la richesse minérale* (3 vols. 1819), II, pp. 534,59 ; and J. Dutens, *Mémoires sur les travaux publics de l'Angleterre* (1819).

[104]For the early development of the French railway network see, for example: P. C. Laurent de Villedeuil, *Bibliographie des chemins de fer* (1903); Tarbé de Vauxclass, *Dictionnaire des travaux publics . . .* (1835) ; article on " chemins de fer "; Marc Seguin, *De l'influence des chemins de fer . . .* (1839) ; Michel Chevalier, " Chemins de fer " (article in Coquelin and Guillaumin, *Dictionnaire de l'Economie politique*, 2 vols., 1854, Vol. I, pp. 337-63) ; Coste and Perdonnet, " Les chemins à ornières en fer " (*Annales des Mines*, second series, 1829, p. 205 *et seq.*) : A. Audiganne, *Les Chemins de fer aujourd'hui et dans cent ans . . .* (2 vols., 1858-62) and " Les chemins de fer sous le gouvernement de Juillet " (*Revue des deux Mondes*, February 15, 1855, pp. 825-36) ; Auguste Perdonnet, *Notions générales sur les chemins de fer . . .* (1879) ; Isaac Pereire, *La question des chemins de fer* (1879) ; Alfred Picard, *Les chemins de fer français* (six volumes, 1884-5 : standard work on railway legislation) ; Deghliage, *Origine de la locomotive* (1886) ; E. Charles, *Les chemins de fer en France pendant le regne de Louis Philippe* (1896) ; Richard von Kaufmann, *Die Eisenpolitik Frankreichs* (2 vols., 1896 : French translation, 1900) ; L. Lamotte, *Histoire de réseau des chemins de fer de France* (Issoudon,

After visiting England in 1825 and 1826-7[105] to consult the Stephensons and to inspect the Stockton and Darlington railway the French engineer Marc Seguin built the single track eighteen kilometre line joining Saint Etienne and Andrézieux (July 1827). Then Marc Seguin and his brother built a 58 km line from Saint Etienne to Lyons (1830). In February 1833 the Andrézieux-Roanne line (67 km)—a continuation of the first French railway—was completed. At about the same time a 27 km line was opened between Epinac on the Le Creusot coalfield and the Burgundy canal.

In 1828 Marc Seguin bought two locomotives from Robert Stephenson & Co.[106] for £550 each. The French Government allowed them to be imported duty free. One of them was sent to the engineering workshops of the Saint Etienne—Lyons railway at Perrache while the other was delivered at Alexis Hallette's establishment at Arras. These railway engines were not put into service but were used as models for the first twelve locomotives built by

1904) ; M. Wallon, " Les saint-simoniens et les chemins de fer " (*Annales de l'Ecole des Sciences Politiques*, 1905) ; H. Lambert, *Le réseau du Nord* (1909) ; (Anon) *Hommes et Choses du P. L. M.* (1910) ; Meinordier, *Le réseau du P. L. M.*; G. Lefranc, " Die Begründung des franzosischen Eisenbahnnetzes . . . " (*Zeitschrift für die Gesamte Staatswissenschaft*, LXXXVI) and " The French Railroads 1823-42 " (*Journal of Economic and Business History*, II (1929-30), p. 298) ; L.-J. Gras, *Histoire des premiers chemins de fer français et du premier tramway de France* (Saint Etienne, 1924) ; Marcel Blanchard, " La politique ferroviaire du second empire " (*Annales d'Histoire économique et sociale*, VI (1934), pp. 528-45) " Aux origines de nos chemins de fer : saint simoniens et banquiers " (*ibid.*, X (1938), pp. 97-115), " Les premiers chemins de fer autour d'Orléans " (*Revue d'Histoire economique et sociale*, XXII, 1934-5, pp. 375-401) and Louis Girard, *La politique des travaux publics du second Empire* (1951).

105 J. G. H. Warren, *A Century of Locomotive Building by Robert Stephenson & Co., 1823-1923* (1923), p. 135, states that Marc Seguin was in England from December, 1827 to February, 1828. This is incorrect. This visit took place a year earlier from December, 1826 to February, 1827.

106 The partners in the firm of Robert Stephenson & Co. were George Stephenson, his son Robert, Edward Pease, Thomas Richardson and Michael Longridge. The works of the firm were in Forth Street, Newcastle upon Tyne. J. G. H. Warren (*op. cit.*, p. 93) states that " through his work in France Robert Stephenson became intimate with Paulin Talabot, whose friendship afterwards proved of great benefit to the Newcastle firm. Talabot, who was born in 1799, had been warmly welcomed by George Stephenson when visiting England as a young man to study its railways ; he became with Seguin, his senior, one of the leading railway engineers in France, and by his efforts did much to make up for the comparatively tardy adoption of railways in that country : he was engineer for the Alais and Beaucaire, and Marseilles to Avignon lines for which, among others in France, numerous locomotives were built by Robert Stephenson & Co."

Marc Seguin.[107] The first train in France to be drawn by a locomotive ran between Saint Etienne and Lyons in May 1831. In the following year (August 5, 1832) a train drawn by one of Robert Stephenson's engines ran from Feurs to Balbigny and back.

The Minister of Public Works set up a commission in 1833 to study future French railway routes and engineers were sent to Britain and to the United States to examine recent railway developments in those countries. It was not until August 1837 that the first Paris railway was opened. This was the 19 km line to St Germain which was built by a company of which the leading directors were Emile Pereire and Baron James de Rothschild. One of the first engine drivers on this line was an Englishman named John English. The Paris-Versailles line, running along the right bank of the Seine—a second Pereire-Rothschild venture—was completed in 1837 while the rival line on the left bank of the river was opened in 1840. In Alsace the cotton manufacturer Nicholas Koechlin constructed at his own expense a line from Mülhausen to Tann (1839). All these were short lines which were of local rather than of national significance. The opening of three longer and more important lines in the early 1840s marked the real beginning of the construction of France's network of main line railways. These were the lines between Paris and Rouen, Paris and Orleans and Strassburg and Basel. The Paris-Rouen line was of particular significance since it greatly improved communications between Paris and London. For this reason English capitalists were interested in the scheme.

The Paris banking firm of Laffitte and Blount took the initiative in promoting the Paris-Rouen railway. The partners had access to influencial circles in France. Charles Laffitte was a nephew of the banker Jacques Laffitte who had been President of the Council in Louis Philippe's first ministry. Edward Blount was a young man who had been an attaché at the British

[107] J. G. H. Warren, *A Century of Locomotive Building by Robert Stephenson & Co., 1823-1923* (1923), ch. 8 and Ferdinand Achard, " The first British Locomotives of the Saint Etienne-Lyon Railway " (*Transactions of the Newcomen Society*, VII (1926-7), pp. 68-80). It is probable (though not certain) that one of the locomotives purchased by Marc Seguin from Robert Stephenson & Co. had previously seen service on the Stockton and Darlington railway. A model of one of these locomotives is exhibited in the Conservatoire National des Arts et Métiers in Paris. It may be added that on February 22, 1828, Marc Seguin patented in France a multitubular boiler. Robert Stephenson and Henry Booth—working quite independently of Seguin—also invented a multitubular boiler which was patented in England in 1828. See Ferdinand Achard and Laurent Seguin, " Marc Seguin and the Invention of the Tubular Boiler " (*Transactions of the Newcomen Society*, VII (1926-7), pp. 97-116).

embassy in Paris and he had useful contacts both with English bankers and with members of the English aristocracy living in France. Blount devoted most of his life to the promotion of Anglo-French financial enterprises and he was connected with a number of French railways. He began his banking career in Paris, with the help of his father, by founding the firm of Edward Blount, Père et Fils. Then he went into partnership with Charles Laffitte. Blount was ruined by losses incurred during the Revolution of 1848 and the partnership with Laffitte was dissolved. In 1852 Brassey and Buddicom helped to find the capital to start Blount in business again as a banker. The new firm—a limited liability company—was called Edward Blount et Cie and it was a flourishing concern in the 1850s and 1860s. The business was absorbed by the Société Générale of Paris in 1870. In the critical days of June 1848 Blount drove an engine from Paris to Amiens to carry dispatches from General Cavaignac to the military authorities at Amiens ordering them to send troops to relieve the capital which was in danger of falling into the hands of armed workers. Blount organised the transport of the troops which arrived in Paris within 24 hours and helped to put down the rising. In 1870 Blount stayed in Paris during the siege and acted as British consul. Subseqently he took a leading part in founding the British Chamber of Commerce in Paris.[108]

After discussing the question of the constructing of a railway between Paris and Rouen with Dufaure, the Minister of Public Works, Blount visited London, Liverpool and Manchester in an effort to raise some of the funds necessary to cover the cost of building the line. He secured the support of William Chaplin, the chairman of the London and Southampton Railway—the directors of which were naturally interested in the project—and he obtained the money he needed. Joseph Locke[109] (one of George Stephenson's pupils who had made a name for himself as chief engineer of the Grand Junction Railway) reported favourably on the route to be followed by the proposed railway.[110]

Blount also approached Count Jaubert, the new Minister of

[108] For Sir Edward Blount see S. J. Reid (ed.), *Memoirs of Sir Edward Blount* (1902) and article in the *Dictionary of National Biography*, second supplement Vol. I pp. 184-6

[109] For Joseph Locke see J. Devey, *The Life of Joseph Locke . . .* (1862) and obituary notice in the *Minutes of the Proceedings of the Institution of Civil Engineers*, XX (1860-1), pp. 141-8.

[110] The route followed the valley of the River Seine. In 1836 a company had been formed to build a railway from Paris to Rouen across the plateaus of Pontoise and Gisors (see prospectus in the *Times*, August 13, 1836) but nothing came of this scheme.

Public Works, to secure the necessary concession for the Paris-Rouen railway. When a hitch occurred in the negotiations a small group of English financiers, headed by Sir John Easthope,[111] approached Guizot, the French ambassador in London. Guizot hoped that Anglo-French relations—which were strained owing to the Mehemet Ali crisis—might be improved by co-operation in economic affairs. So he asked Jaubert to try to meet the views of the English investors in the railway. This was done and the Chamber of Deputies approved a State loan for the railway in the summer of 1840. The concession was for 99 years. The municipality of Southampton marked the occasion by inviting Guizot as the guest of honour to a banquet which was held on June 20 in a marquee on the sea shore.[112] The Paris-Rouen railway company, registered in Paris under French law, was now able to go ahead with its plans. The board included both English and French members[113] and Charles Laffitte was elected chairman. About one third of the initial capital of the company was subscribed by English investors, one third was raised through a French bank and one third (fourteen million francs) was lent to the company by the French Government.

The British directors secured the right to nominate the engineers and they appointed Joseph Locke and Newman. The directors advertised for tenders for the first ten miles of the railway. Thomas Brassey[114] and William Mackenzie offered to do the work for £157,000 which was so much cheaper than the lowest tender from a French contractor that Brassey and Mackenzie were asked to go over their calculations again. They confirmed their original estimate which was accepted. The contract was later extended to cover the whole line.

Building commenced in 1841. Tools, rails and many other materials for the construction of the line were brought from

[111]Sir John Easthope, a stockbroker, was one of the owners of the influential Whig *Morning Chronicle.*

[112]F. P. G. Guizot, *Mémoires pour servir à l'histoire de mon temps,* Vol. V (1862), pp. 118-9 and 434-8. An English translation of the Law of July 15, 1840, authorising the State loan to assist in the construction of the Paris-Rouen railway is printed in the *Memoirs of Sir Edward Blount* (1902), pp. 54-7.

[113]The arrangement was that eight of the directors should reside in France and four in England. But one of the directors residing in France was to be an Englishman (William Reed, the former Secretary of the South Western Railway in England).

[114]For Thomas Brassey see Arthur Helps, *Life and Labours of Mr. Brassey, 1805-70* (1872) and the obituary notice in the *Minutes of the Proceedings of the Institution of Civil Engineers,* XXXIII (1871-2), pp. 246-51.

England.[115] Some ten thousand foreign workers—including about five thousand Englishmen and Irishmen—were engaged as miners, navvies, platelayers and bricklayers.[116] William Reed, a director of the railway company, stated that " the English were chiefly navigators ; a great many of them miners ; we had some long tunnels."[117] They were billeted in various villages in the Seine valley. The Englishmen in charge of the enterprise had to exercise considerable tact in maintaining discipline in a cosmopolitan labour force in which ten different languages were spoken and in establishing good relations with their French colleagues and with the local inhabitants who viewed this unexpected " invasion of Normandy " with some alarm. Some of the French workers, who were said to be " more respectable " than the English navvies,[118] not unnaturally resented the presence of so many foreign workers who received higher wages than they could earn.[119] The tendency of English and Irish navvies to drink more cheap brandy than was good for them was only one of the problems that confronted the contractors.

Faced with the difficulty of securing sufficient locomotives Joseph Locke persuaded William Barber Buddicom and William Allcard[120] to establish works in France for the construction of railway engines and rolling stock. Thomas Brassey gave the scheme financial support. With the help of the Martin family—

[115] Arthur Helps observed that " the French used wooden spades. Their barrow was of a bad form and they had very inferior pickaxes " (*op. cit.*, p. 80).

[116] Thomas Brassey's son declared in 1877 : " I cannot but remember that when my father went over to France, as the pioneer of the business of the railway contractor in that country, he owed his success, in a great measure, to the superior qualities of a body of five thousand English workmen who followed him to the Continent " (Thomas Brassey (junior), *Lectures on the Labour Question* (third edn., 1878), p. 229).

[117] *Report from the Select Committee on Railway Labourers*, 1846 : evidence of William Reed, Qn. 331.

[118] *Ibid.*, evidence of W. Reed, Qn. 373 : " A French labourer is a much more independent person than an English one, and a much more respectable one."

[119] Thomas Brassey told the *Select Committee on Railway Acts Enactment*, 1846, that the average earnings of English labourers on the Paris-Rouen railway had been 4.50 francs per day in the summer and 4.25 francs in the winter while French workers had earned 3.50 francs in the summer and 3 francs in the winter. This was for a ten hour day. It may be added that there was a longstanding link between Normandy and England owing to the presence of skilled English operatives in the cotton mills of the Rouen district. In 1840 J. McGregor told the *Select Committee on Import Duties*, 1840, that in France " the principal foremen at Rouen and in the cotton factories are from Lancashire " (Qn. 1046).

[120] For William Allcard see the obituary notice in the *Minutes of the Proceedings of the Institution of Civil Engineers*, XXI, 1861-2, pp. 550-2.

relatives of Buddicom who owned old-established engineering works at Rouen—Allcard and Buddicom were able to rent temporary premises at Petit-Queville from Corbran and Lemarchand. Here the two English engineers built " Buddicom " (or " Crewe ") locomotives as designed by Allan, Locke and Buddicom for the Grand Junction Railway.[121] One of these locomotives was the only railway engine shown at the Paris industrial exhibition of 1844. Allcard and Buddicom secured a contract to supply the Paris-Rouen railway company (at fixed rates per mile) with all the locomotives, rolling stock, engine drivers and mechanics that it required.[122] At first all the engine drivers on the Paris-Rouen railway were Englishmen,[123] about fifty of them having formerly been employed on the lines which were later amalgamated to form the London and North Western Railway. Later Allcard and Buddicom secured contracts to supply railway engines, carriages, waggons and drivers on lines linking Paris with the Channel at Dieppe, Fécamp, Le Havre and Cherbourg.[124] In 1843-4 Allcard and Buddicom erected the largest railway workshops in France at Sotteville-les-Rouen to replace the temporary establishment at Petit-Queville.

The contractors completed the construction of the Paris-Rouen line within the stipulated time[125] and made a handsome

[121] The first three " Buddicom " (or " Crewe ") engines to be built in England were constructed by Messrs. Tayleur & Co. at the Vulcan Foundry near Warrington and they were called *Aeolus*, *Sunbeam* and *Tartarus*. For Alexander Allan's claim to have invented this type of locomotive see his letter to the *Crewe Guardian*, October 17, 1882, and his statement in *The Engineer*, May 25, 1885, as well as articles in the *Railway Magazine* by C. E. Lee (May, 1951) and W. H. Chaloner (June, 1951).

[122] Thomas Brassey stated that Allcard and Buddicom were paid at the rate of 1/6d. per mile for locomotive power and one eighth of a penny per mile for each goods waggon in transit.

[123] Henry Dove, for example, who had once been an office boy in Robert Stephenson's employment, went to France in 1843 and worked on the Paris-Rouen railway. He was still in Rouen in December, 1870 when the German invaders approached the town. He succeeded in getting away 52 trains filled with refugees between 7 a.m. and 1 p.m. on December 5. For Dove's own account of his railway service in France see the *Memoirs of Sir Edward Blount* (1902), pp. 75-82.

[124] These large workshops were taken over by the railway company in 1864 when the firm of Buddicom et Cie was wound up. Allcard had died in 1861 having retired from active participation in the affairs of the firm between 1847 and 1851.

[125] Celebrations to mark the completion of the line began on March 25, 1843, with the roasting of an ox at a feast given to the workers who had built the Tourville tunnel. A few weeks later the mayor of Vernon attended a feast given to French and English railway workers in the Vernon and Aubevoye district. See Jean Vidalenc, *Le Département de l'Eure sous la monarchie constitutionnelle 1814-1848* (1952), p. 542.

profit. The works included fifteen stations, the terminus at Rouen, a goods yard of fourteen hectares at Batignolles, five bridges over the Seine and four tunnels. It was not necessary to build a station in Paris since for the first few miles to Asnières the Paris-St Germain line was used. The official opening on May 3, 1843[126] took place on the day after the opening of the line from Paris to Orleans. The successful completion of this great enterprise established the reputations of the contractors and the engineers. It marked the start of some twenty years of English activity in railway building not only in France but also in several other countries on the Continent.

The Paris-Rouen railway was soon extended to Le Havre with the aid of a Government subsidy of eight million francs. The same engineers and contractors were employed as on the Paris-Rouen line. The 84 kilometre Rouen-Le Havre line was not an easy one to construct since the undertaking involved the building of a large bridge over the Seine and several viaducts, cuttings, and embankments. The whole scheme might have failed when the Barentin viaduct suddenly collapsed in 1846. This was a brick structure 100 feet high consisting of 27 arches of 50 feet span. But Brassey was equal to the emergency and within six months he had rebuilt the viaduct at his own expense. The railway was completed in time and was opened in 1847.

The English engineers, contractors and locomotive builders who had been responsible for the successful completion of the Paris-Rouen-Le Havre lines were later entrusted with the construction of several other lines in the north west of France. The most important were those between Rouen and Dieppe,[127] Mantes and Caen,[128] and Caen and Cherbourg.[129] On these lines English and other foreign labourers were no longer employed on the scale that had been found necessary on the Paris-Rouen line.[130] But

[126] For the Paris-Rouen railway see *Times*, June 5, 1840 (prospectus) ; the evidence of various witnesses before the Select Committee on Railway Acts Enactment of 1846 (see particularly T. Brassey's evidence, *Second Report*, Questions 816-990) ; A. Helps, *op. cit.*, chap. 4 ; J. Devey, *op. cit.* ; L. H. Jenks, *op. cit.* ; and P. Dauzet, *op. cit.*, ch. 10.

[127] The contract for the Rouen-Dieppe line was secured by Thomas Brassey and W. Mackenzie in 1847 : the engineers were Newman and Murton.

[128] The contract for the Mantes-Caen line was secured by Thomas Brassey in 1852 : Joseph Locke was one of the engineers.

[129] The Caen-Cherbourg line was built by Thomas Brassey. The contract was secured in 1853. The engineers were Joseph Locke and W. Locke.

[130] Many of the English and other foreign workers engaged on the Paris-Rouen line returned to their homes when the railway was completed. But some stayed in France. Arthur Helps (*op. cit.*, p. 93) states that some English navvies, formerly employed on the Paris-Rouen railway, subsequently worked on the Paris fortifications.

the services of skilled English workers—particularly platelayers—and mechanics continued to be used for some time. As late as 1860 Brassey and Buddicom were entrusted with the task of doubling the track of the Rouen-Dieppe railway. In view of the important part played by British financiers and technicians in building the main lines in the north west of France it was appropriate that when these lines were amalgamated in 1855 as the *Compagnie du l'Ouest* Edward Blount should have been elected chairman of the board of directors of the new company. He retained this office until 1894.

English promoters and contractors were also active in other parts of France. The attempt of the London and South Eastern Railway to emulate the London and Southampton Railway by financing lines from Lille to Calais and Boulogne—thus opening up a quicker route between London and Paris—was not successful. In 1843 a party of English railway projectors visited northern France and Robert Stephenson subsequently reported favourably on the financial prospects of railways in that part of the country. The report encouraged French promoters to push ahead with schemes of their own. Eventually English influence was virtually limited to the short line between Amiens and Boulogne. Owing to the efforts of Charles Laffitte and Edward Blount part of the capital for this railway was raised in England. Charles Laffitte was the chairman of the board of directors. The line was built in 1844 by Thomas Brassey and Messrs. W. and E. Mackenzie and one of the engineers (William Cubitt) was an Englishman. The Northern Railway from Paris to Amiens, Lille and Calais was largely constructed by the French Government but was then acquired by a company formed by Baron James de Rothschild and the Pereire brothers. English investors, however, held some of the shares of the Northern Railway. The locomotive invented by the English engineer T. R. Crampton was used on the Northern Railway. About 300 locomotives of this type were constructed between 1849 and 1854 at Chaillot by the firm of Deresne & Cail.[131]

Greater success attended the efforts of the English promoters in central France. In 1842—while the construction of the Paris-Rouen line was still in progress—Thomas Brassey and Messrs. W. and E. Mackenzie secured an important new contract. The Paris-Orleans line (which had many English shareholders but was built by French engineers and contractors) was nearing completion and Brassey and W. Mackenzie were asked to extend the line to Tours. The work was done under the supervision of a French

[131] Pierre Dauzet, *op. cit.* pp. 143-5 and F. Gaise, *Die Crampton Lokomotive* (1909).

RAILWAYS CONSTRUCTED BY THOMAS BRASSEY ON THE CONTINENT

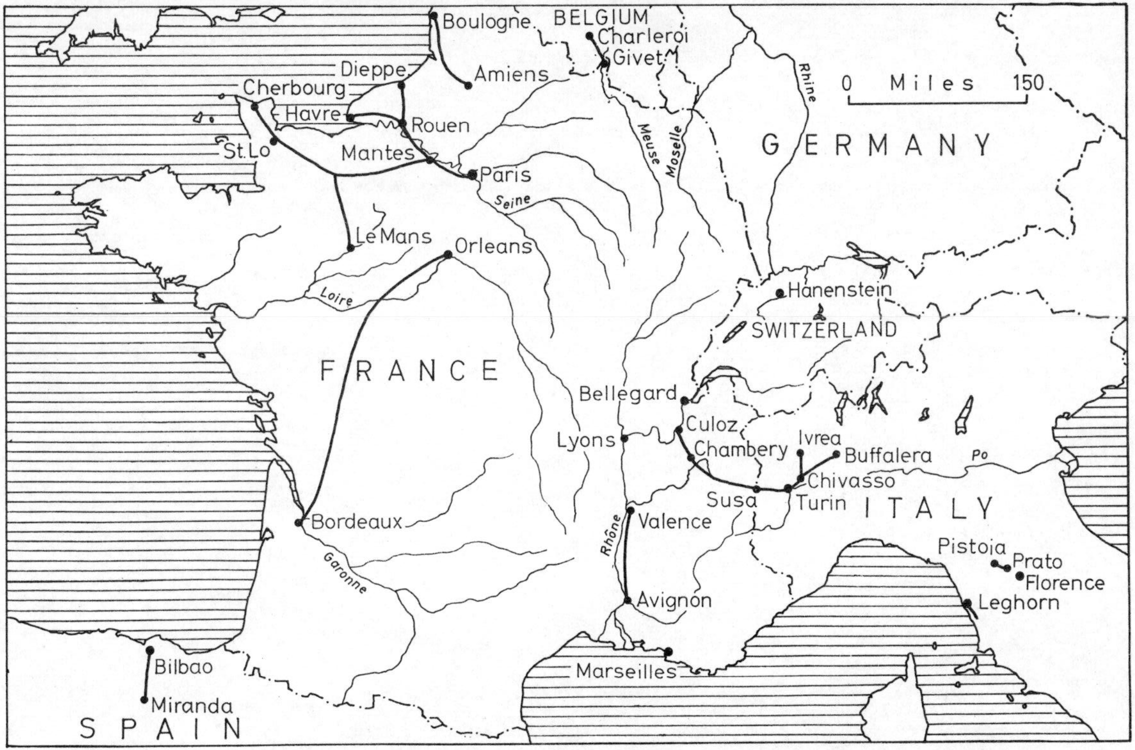

From Arthur Helps, *Life and Labours of Mr Brassey, 1805-70* (1872)

engineer. American excavating machinery was used and the line was ready by March 1846. The contractors were responsible for supplying the necessary locomotives and rolling stock. They bought thirty engines in England and the rest were built by Allcard and Buddicom.

The main lines from Tours westwards to Nantes and southwards to Bordeaux were also partly financed and built by Englishmen. In 1846 it was reported that 70,000 out of 130,000 shares of the Orleans-Bordeaux railway company were in the hands of 715 English investors In 1849 Allcard and Buddicom established at La Bastide (near Bordeaux) a factory for the construction and maintenance of locomotives and railway stock. In the 1850s Thomas Brassey was responsible for the construction of the Le Mans-Mézidon line,[132] the Lyons-Avignon line, [133] and the Sambre and Meuse railway[134] as well as the Mantes-Caen line. In 1854 Brassey and Buddicom (in association with a Belgian firm) built the 4,000-metre Bellegarde tunnel on the Lyons-Geneva railway. Benjamin Piercy was the chief engineer of the Tours-Sables d'Olonne railway; John Richard Manby was associated with the construction of the Montpellier-Cette railway; while H. H. Edwards (son of Humphrey Edwards) was appointed chief engineer of the Paris-Strassburg line in 1847. Masterman, Laing and Hutchinson had a financial interest in the short lived Grand Central Railway which was promoted by Count Morny. The confidence of French investors in English railway promoters may be seen from the following incident. When the Paris-Lyons railway company was unable to raise enough capital Allcard and Buddicom agreed to accept shares instead of cash in payment for locomotives to be supplied to the line. When this became known French investors quickly found the necessary money. As Allcard and Buddicom had many orders in hand they released the Paris-Lyons railway company from their obligation to buy their locomotives from the Sotteville works.

The French Government appreciated the value of the services rendered to the French railways by British financiers, contractors, and engineers. Several of the Englishmen who played a leading part in the building of railways received high honours. There were, however, some Frenchmen who viewed with considerable alarm the great influence which Englishmen exercised on the

[132]The contract for the Le Mans-Mézidon line was obtained by Thomas Brassey in 1852 : J. Locke was one of the engineers.

[133]The Lyons-Avignon railway was built by Brassey, Peto and Betts : the contract was secured in 1852.

[134]The Sambre and Meuse railway was built by T. Brassey : the contract was obtained in 1853.

French railways in the middle years of the nineteenth century. Two incidents in the late 1840s may serve as illustrations. At a meeting of shareholders of the Amiens-Boulogne line in October 1847 there were protests when English shareholders tried to address the meeting in English. And in the following year one of the demands of the French strikers on the railways was the dismissal of English engine drivers.[135]

English capital and technical knowledge also contributed to the development of steam navigation on the French inland waterways. It has been seen that Aaron Manby built an iron steamship which was the first vessel of its type to make the direct voyage from London to Paris. In 1823 he established a regular steamship cargo service on the Seine, within a few years his ships were plying on most of the navigable rivers of France. River steamships—whether owned by French or English companies—were generally fitted with English marine engines which were in charge of English engineers. Withers told the Select Committee on the Exportation of Machinery in 1841. "I was on board twenty boats on the Saône, the Rhône and the Mediterranean and I never found one Frenchman as manager : the stoker was a Frenchman but the engineer was invariably an Englishman."[136] By the 1840s however French steamships were competing successfully with English-built vessels on the French rivers. Thus an English attempt to establish a service on the Loire—in competition with Gâches' steamboats—failed. On the Saône the *Gondole*, built by the Schneiders of Le Creusot in 1839, was able to steam up the river between Trevoux and Lyons while English steamtugs had to be assisted by horses on this difficult stretch of the river. Similarly on the Rhône the 60 h.p. steamers *Le Crocodile* and *Le Marsouin* (also built at Le Creusot in 1839) gave better service than the English-built ships plying on the river.[137] Jules Burat, writing in 1844, claimed that English shipbuilders had failed to appreciate that steamships which would render satisfactory service on the Mersey or the Thames would not be suitable for the Rhône or the Garonne. He declared that "enormous losses" had been suffered

[135] P. L. Laurent de Villedeuil, *Oeuvres de Emile et Isaac Pereire*, Section G, Vol. III (1913), p. 2347 *et seq.* and p. 2612 *et seq.* A number of English engine drivers employed on the Paris-Rouen line returned to England in 1848 after mobs had attacked railway stations and burned down railway bridges in the Paris district (*Memoirs of Sir Edward Blount*, p. 80).

[136] *Select Committee on the Exportation of Machinery* (1841) : evidence of G. Withers, Qn. 1119.

[137] *Exposition des Produits de l'industrie française en 1844 : rapport du jury central* (three volumes, 1844), II, p. 368.

by those who had invested their money in English steamships plying on the French rivers.[138]

It is clear that between 1750 and 1850 the industrial revolution in France was fostered by English inventions and English capital and by services of English entrepreneurs, contractors and skilled workers.[139] Throughout these hundred years however the expansion of French manufactures was on a very modest scale when compared with that of English industries. The steam pump and the rotative steam engine were introduced into France not long after they had been invented but for thirty or forty years very few French mines or factories installed these engines. William Wilkinson helped to introduce iron smelting by coke at Le Creusot in 1785 but well into the mineteenth century hundreds of French ironmasters were still smelting wtih charcoal. The French railway network was constructed far more slowly than those of Britain, Belgium or Germany. In the textile industries many important inventions such as the mule, the powerloom and self-actor, were adopted very slowly.

Various factors contributed to the slow development of the basic French industries. Lack of adequate supplies of coal and iron ore; lack of sufficient capital resources; excessive regulation of various branches of industry ; a mistaken commercial policy of prohibitions and high tariffs which gave many manufacturers a virtual monopoly of the home market and removed the salutary incentive of foreign competition ; the reluctance of those who worked on the land to migrate to the towns and become full-time workers in industry ; the failure to construct promptly a really adequate network of roads, railways and canals ; the undue predominance in the industrial economy of a few great manufactures which produced luxury goods for a few wealthy customers—these were some of the reasons which help to explain why the industrial revolution in France proceeded at so leisurely a pace between 1750 and 1850.[140]

[138] Jules Burat, *Exposition de l'industrie française : année 1844* (1844), II, p. 27.

[139] It may be added that several French engineers visited England to study MacAdam's method of making roads and this technique was widely adopted in France. But Trésaguet's methods of road construction, so successfully employed in Languedoc in Turgot's day, were neglected.

[140] For the industrial revolution in France see A. L. Dunham, *La révolution industrielle en France* 1815-48 (1953). For French industry in 1849 see M. D. Wyatt, *A Report on the eleventh French Exposition of the Products of Industry* (1849).

4. TWO YORKSHIRE PIONEERS IN THE FRENCH WOOLCOMBING INDUSTRY IN THE REIGN OF NAPOLEON III[1]

WHEN Samuel Cunliffe Lister and Isaac Holden set up a woolcombing factory near Paris in 1848-9 they were following in the footsteps of a number of British entrepreneurs and skilled workers who had for a century fostered the development of the French textile industries. In the middle of the eighteenth century the exiled Lancashire Jacobite John Holker had introduced modern machinery into a royal cloth factory at Rouen. He became an Inspector General of Factories and travelled throughout the country to encourage the use of technical improvements in French textile establishments.

At the time of the Consulate and Empire French manufacturers of woollen cloth were able to secure several machines based upon recent English models from the Cockerills, William Douglas and John Collier. At the end of the eighteenth century the elder William Cockerill had established himself in the Belgian provinces as a builder of machinery for the spinning of woollen yarn

[1] (i) S. C. LISTER. See Lister's autobiography *Lord Masham's Inventions written by himself* (1905), the obituary in *The Times*, February 3, 1906, and an article in the second supplement (1901-11) of the *Dictionary of National Biography*, II, pp. 469-71.
(ii) ISAAC HOLDEN. Holden's business records are preserved in the Brotherton Library (University of Leeds). Some of Holden's business correspondence has been printed by F. Byles and A. J. Best in the *Holden-Illingworth Letters* (P. Lund, Humphries & Co., Bradford, 1927). See also the obituary in *The Times*, August 14, 1897 and an article in the first supplement of the *Dictionary of National Biography*, II, pp. 434-6.
(iii) WOOLLEN AND WORSTED INDUSTRIES. For the development of these industries in England and France in the nineteenth century see : James Bischoff, *A comprehensive History of the Woollen and Worsted Manufactures* . . . (2 vols., 1842) ; John James, *History of the Worsted Manufacture in England* (1857) ; H. Forbes, " The worsted manufacture " in *Lectures on the Results of the Great Exhibition of 1851* (Society of Arts), second series (1853), No. 21 ; A. Lohren, *Die Kamm-Maschinen* . . . (Stuttgart, 1875) ; M. R. Louis Reybaud, *La Laine* . . . (1867) ; W. Cudworth, *Worstedopolis. A sketch of the History of . . . Bradford* . . . (Bradford, 1888) ; James Burnley, *History of Wool and Woolcombing* (1889) ; L. Dechesne, *L'évolution économique et sociale de l'industrie de la laine en Angleterre* (1900) ; Willy Senkel, *Wollproduktion und Wollhandel im 19en Jahrhundert* . . . (*Zeitschrift für die Gesamte Staatswissenschaft*, Ergänzungsheft II, 1901) ; J. H. Clapham, *The Woollen and Worsted Industries* (1907) ; E. Lipson, *The History of the Woollen and Worsted Industries* (1921) and E. M. Sigsworth's essay on Bradford in C. R. Fay, *Round about Industrial Britain, 1830-60* (University of Toronto Press, 1952), pp. 114-131.

and in 1810-13 about half of his output of machinery was sold in France. His son William managed cloth factories at Rheims and Sedan before migrating to Prussia. William Douglas and John Collier had textile machine building establishments in Paris. The former imported an excellent gig-mill from the west of England while the latter invented an apparatus for shearing broad cloth. During and immediately after the Napoleonic régime the cotton industry in Alsace profited from the activities of three Manchester men. John Heywood introduced a mechanical loom to Schirmeck in the Breusch valley. Job Dixon became a partner in the textile machine building firm of Risler Brothers while Richard Roberts (the famous inventor of the self-actor) installed new cotton machinery into André Koechlin's works at Mülhausen. Thus by the middle of the nineteenth century many links had been forged between the English and the French textile industries.

Isaac Holden was born at Hurlet where his father had settled on migrating to Scotland from Cumberland[2] to work at a colliery at Nitshill near Paisley. Subsequently the family moved to Kilbarchan. Isaac's schooling was interrupted when he was a boy by spells of illness[3] and when he was a youth by periods of employment as an apprentice to handloom weavers and as an assistant to a joiner. But he pursued his studies in the evenings[4] and made sufficient progress to secure an appointment under John Kennedy, a Paisley schoolmaster, whom he later described as "one of the best mathematicians in the west of Scotland."

At the age of 19 Isaac Holden left Scotland for England where he pursued his scholastic career as an usher in private schools for four years.[5] A breakdown in health caused him to give up teaching and to return to Scotland. In November 1830 he secured an appointment as book-keeper with Townsend Brothers of Cullingworth (Bingley) who were then the largest manufacturers of heald

[2] He had been a leadminer in Alston.

[3] Isaac Holden stated : "I could never go to school in winter ; a puny little unthriving child" (quoted by Joseph Constantine, *Sir Isaac Holden* . . . (1898), p. 14).

[4] Isaac Holden to his brother George, October 19, 1860 : "From ten to twelve years of age I was a draw-boy and from twelve to fifteen with occasional intervals at school, I worked as a piecer in cotton mills, from fifteen to sixteen and a half I was a weaver. During a great part of this time I went to evening schools where I got the greater part of my education" (*The Holden-Illingworth Letters*, p. 323).

[5] He held appointments in 1826-30 at Mr. Sigston's academy at Queen Square, Leeds ; at Lingard's grammar school at Slaithwaite in the West Riding ; and at Castle Street School at Reading. He subsequently stated that while teaching at Reading he had invented the lucifer match but did not take out a patent for it : see his evidence before the *Select Committee on Letters Patent*, 1871, Qn. 1938 and his speech of December 30, 1893, quoted by J. Constantine, *op cit.*, pp. 126-8.

and genappe yarns in England.[6] Although originally engaged in a clerical capacity Holden soon took an active part in the technical side of the firm's activities.[7]

By the early 1840s Isaac Holden was enjoying a small share of the profits of the business.[8] In his spare time he was acting as a textile engineering consultant and it was in this way that he came into contact with the Illingworths who were among the leading woolspinners of Bradford. They owned the Prospect Mill, the Hope Street Mill, and the Providence Mill. The families of Holden and Illingworth came to be linked not only by ties of common business interests but also by marriage.[9]

From 1843 onwards Isaac Holden was becoming unsettled at the Cullingworth works. The causes of his first disputes with his employers are uncertain. It appears, however, that in the summer of 1845 some of Townsend Brothers' customers were complaining of the poor quality of the yarn supplied by the firm. The partners held Holden responsible for this. Holden replied that the fault lay with colleagues over whom he had no authority. Moreover Holden was working on new machines and processes such as the square motion comb, a carding process and a new method of manufacturing genappe yarns. He was disappointed when Townsend Brothers declined to support him by patenting these inventions.[10]

Nothing came of Holden's suggestion that he should be made a partner and in 1846, at the age of 39, he left Townsend Brothers and set up a small worsted spinning mill in Pit Lane, Bradford.

[6] The " heald " is a part of a loom (eyed or hooked threads through which the warp passes) and " heald yarn " is a type of worsted yarn. " Genappe " is a worsted yarn or cord used in the manufacture of braids, fringes, etc. : its smoothness enables it to be combined with silk.

[7] Evidence of Isaac Holden before the *Select Committee on Letters Patent*, 1871, Qn. 1939. It may be added that shortly after joining Townsend Brothers Holden married Marion Love of Paisley.

[8] An undated draft memorandum (probably 1839 or 1840) initialled by the three Townsend brothers and by Isaac Holden assured Holden 7½% of the firm's profits (*The Holden-Illingworth Letters*, p. 82).

[9] Isaac Holden's son Angus married Margaret, daughter of Daniel Illingworth (1860) while Isaac Holden's daughters Mary and Margaret married Henry Illingworth (1860) and Alfred Illingworth (1866) respectively.

[10] Isaac Holden told the *Select Committee on Letters Patent, 1871*, that " the reason why I left the house (of Townsend) was that they would not agree to take out patents; they were opposed . . . on general principle to patents at all, and it was on that ground that I left that house " (Qn. 1939).

The worsted trade was slack at this time[11]—though less depressed than some other industries—and Holden was soon in difficulties. The Bradford Banking Company was pressing him to reduce his overdraft and he owed friends money on which he could not pay interest. Early in 1848 he stopped production.[12] He had lost his capital (£4,000) and for some time he was burdened by debts.

Isaac Holden fortunately found a partner who was willing to provide the capital for a new enterprise. This was Samuel Cunliffe Lister who owned the Mill Street and the Manningham worsted mills at Bradford. Lister had never had to face the difficulties that Holden had had to overcome. His father was a landowner who lived at Calverley Hall near Bradford and was Bradford's first member of Parliament after the passing of the Reform Act of 1832. He had enough capital to build the Manningham mill for his sons John and Samuel. The partnership between the brothers lasted until 1845 when the death of an older brother made John his father's heir. When his brother retired from business Samuel Lister went into partnership with J. Ambler and later with J. Warburton.

Lister and Holden were drawn together by a common interest in the production of an efficient woolcombing machine. Many efforts had been made since Cartwright's day to construct such a machine[13]—and the great Bradford hand-combers strike of

[11] J. James, *op cit.*, stated that 1845, 1846 and 1847 were " three unprosperous years " but he added that worsted manufacturers suffered less than some other branches of industry. The Leeds woollen industry, for example, was more depressed than the Bradford worsted industry in 1848. In that year " exports of woollen cloth had fallen to their lowest level for ten years with the exception of 1842 " (E. M. Sigsworth, " The West Riding Wool Textile Industry and the Great Exhibition " in the *Yorkshire Bulletin of Economic and Social Research*, IV (i), January 1952, p. 25).

[12] Isaac Holden to John Ward, November 20, 1847 (in the Holden MSS): Holden gave his landlord six months notice.

[13] Early woolcombing machines included those of Edmund Cartwright (first patent 1789, second and third patents—the most important—in 1790, and fourth patent 1792), Popple (1792), William Toplis (1793), Wright and Hawkesley. Cartwright's woolcombing machine—called " Big Ben " after a popular prizefighter—combed only very coarse wools. In the worsted branch of the wool textile industry the object of combing is to separate the long wool (tops) from the short wool (noils) and to lay the wool fibres left in the " top " as nearly parallel as possible. The tops are then drawn and spun while the noils are used in the woollen branch of the industry. For Cartwright's mechanical comb see W. H. Chaloner, " The Cartwright Brothers . . ." (*Wool Knowledge*, summer 1953, pp. 15-21). In 1801 it was stated that Hawkesley & Davison of Arnold (Notts.) had saved £6,600 annually by using six sets of Cartwright's mechanical comb (*Journals of the House of Commons*, LVI, p. 272, April 13, 1801).

1825[14] had stimulated inventors—but the mechanical combs on the market were only partially successful so that even in the early 1840s most wool was still combed by hand. In the Bradford district alone there were probably some ten thousand hand-combers in 1845. Of the many mechanical combs that had appeared between 1800 and 1840 the most important were those of James Collier (1814) ; John Platt and John Collier (1827) ;[15] James Noble (1834) ;[16] and George Edmund Donisthorpe and Henry Rawson (1835).

Samuel Lister now came into the scene[17] Not only did he possess abilities as an inventor himself but he had the knack of recognising the possibilities of new machines which were as yet in an early stage of development. He was prepared to lay out capital judiciously to maintain impecunious inventors who were trying to improve machines which had not quite achieved the

[14] The Bradford woolcombers' strike of 1825 was a failure. These skilled artisans—their fathers had been " gentlemen combers " who drank their ale apart from other workers in public houses—complained to their Bradford employers in 1840: " Our homes, which were not many years ago the abodes of comfort and domestic enjoyment have now—in consequence of the frequent reductions in wages and other alterations in the sorts—become the dwelling places of misery and receptacles of wretchedness ". For the decline of the West Riding hand-woolcombers see James Burnley, *The History of Wool and Woolcombing* (1889), ch. 7 and J. L. and Barbara Hammond, *The Skilled Labourer, 1760-1832* (1927).

[15] The mechanical comb patented by John Platt of Salford in 1827 was an improvement of a French machine (invented by Godart) which John Collier, a well known English engineer and machine-builder who had settled in Paris—not to be confused with James Collier—had brought over to Manchester.

[16] For the early (1825) mechanical comb invented by James Noble of Halifax see Andrew Ure, *Dictionary of Arts . . .* (second edition, 1840), p. 1310. For the later improved Noble machine see J. Burnley, *op. cit.*, ch. 14. Noble's first patent had been taken out as early as 1805. The Noble mechanical comb was eventually improved by S. G. Donisthorpe in 1853. J. Burnley, *op. cit.*, p. 379 wrote: " Noble's principle . . . became only of real importance for machine-combing after the introduction of the peculiar feed apparatus introduced in 1856 by Tavernier, Donisthorpe and Crofts and by its admirable construction by the firm of Taylor, Wordsworth & Co. of Leeds. In this shape . . . it was largely adopted . . ."

[17] In his old age S. C. Lister (then Baron Masham) commented on the fact that it took many inventors half a century to produce efficient woolcombing machines. He wrote: " There is nothing like it recorded in the history of any invention. Indeed I doubt if the steam engine, the locomotive, the spinning frame and the power loom all put together have occupied so many minds and taken as much effort, time, and expenditure as the woolcombing problem; and yet, at the end of more than fifty years after Cartwright's great invention no one had succeeded and it appeared almost hopeless to think that anyone would " (*Lord Masham's Inventions* (1905), p. 9).

efficiency necessary to secure complete success.[18] He had both the money and the foresight to buy up patents which might stand in the way of the success of the machines in which he was interested.

Lister was concerned with two types of mechanical combs. These were the nip machine and the square motion machine. In the early 1840s Lister and Donisthorpe worked together at the Manningham factory on the Donisthorpe machine. By 1845 they had greatly improved this comb which was used not only in Lister's own works but also in other spinning establishments. Many years later Lister boasted that in the three years 1843-5 he had accomplished " what the whole trade and a host of inventors had failed to do in fifty and what looked to be at the time almost impossible."[19]

A further improvement in the Donisthorpe-Lister machine was made in 1850-1 by the introduction of the nip principle. The new nip machine became popular after it had been shown—still under Donisthorpe's name—at the Great Exhibition at the Crystal Palace.[20] Unfortunately for Lister this machine had certain features which the French inventor Josué Heilmann had already used in a mechanical comb invented in Alsace in 1845 and patented in England in 1846. The Heilmann machine was originally constructed for use by the cotton industry but it was adapted to the combing of wool in 1848. Probably both Heilmann and Lister hit upon the same idea independently of each other. Nicholas Schlumburger et Cie of Guebwiller in Alsace, the owners of Heilmann's mechanical comb, prosecuted Lister in the English courts in 1852 and won their case. Lister then acquired the English patent of the Heilmann machine for £30,000,[21] so as to

[18] Isaac Holden told the Select Committee on Letters Patent, 1871, that S. C. Lister had " become very celebrated as, if not an inventor himself, at all events an encourager of inventors " (Qn. 1942).

[19] *Lord Masham's Inventions*, p. 14.

[20] At the Great Exhibition (1851) G. E. Donisthorpe was awarded a Council medal for his woolcombing machine. Queen Victoria wrote in her journal: " There is a new invention by Mr. Donisthorpe of Bradford for cleansing and combing our cotton which is so important that he got £25,000 for selling only the fourth of the patent ". The Queen appears to have been misinformed since S. C. Lister subsequently stated that he had paid Donisthorpe only £2,000 for half of the patent rights and later £10,000 for the other half. See C. R. Fay, *Palace of Industry, 1851* (1951), p. 59.

[21] Josué Heilmann had originally invented his comb for use in the cotton industry. It had been successfully modified for the combing of short wool. The inventor died in 1848. The firm of N. Schlumberger et Cie owned the patent rights of the Heilmann woolcombing machine. Schlumberger sold the *English* patent rights to Akroyd and Titus Salt for £30,000 and they disposed of the patent to S. C. Lister for the same sum on condition that

suppress it in this country and to leave the field clear for the nip machine on which spinners were paying him a handsome royalty of £1,000 on each mechanical comb.[22] In 1857 it was stated that " by far the greater proportion of all the wool of whatever kind, now combed is combed by Lister's machines.[23]

Meanwhile S. C. Lister had also been concerned with the invention of the square motion combing machine. In the late 1840s both Lister and Holden were working on this type of mechanical comb. There was later a long and acrimonious controversy between the two inventors concerning the origin of this machine.[24] Although the first two patents for square motion machines—taken out in 1846 and 1848—were in Lister's name[25] it is uncertain who really invented the square motion principle. There can however be little doubt that Isaac Holden is entitled to

they might use this comb in their own works without paying him any royalty. For the Heilmann mechanical comb see Michael Alcan, *Rapport tendant à accorder à M. Josué Heilmann, inventeur de la peigneuse mécanique la prix fondé par M. le Marquis d'Argenteuil* (Société d'encouragement pour l'industrie nationale, 1857). The prize to which Michael Alcan referred was awarded posthumously. Alcan stated in his report that whereas formerly imperfect hand-woolcombing had cost 2 fr 50 centimes per kgm the Heilmann machine combed the same quantity of wool more efficiently for only one franc per kgm. For Heilmann see A. A. Ernouf, *Histoire de quatre inventeurs français* . . . (1884) pp. 76-141.

[22] S. C. Lister monopolised the construction of nip woolcombing machines. They cost him only £200 each to build and they were in such demand that he was able to sell them to spinners for £1,200 each. See *Lord Masham's Inventions*, p. 46. S. C. Lister purchased woolcombing patents from (i) Schlumberger (Heilmann machine), (ii) Donisthorpe, (iii) Noble. In cross examination during the Heilmann case Lister agreed that he had purchased 23 patent rights.

[23] J. James, *op cit*., p. 537.

[24] The Holden-Lister correspondence of 1872-86 in the *Bradford Observer* and *Leeds Mercury* was reprinted in a pamphlet entitled *The Square Motion Combing Machine: its Origin* (1886). Holden's claim to be the inventor of the square motion machine was also put forward in a manuscript entitled " Retrospective Notes " which was consulted by J. Burnley when he was writing his history of wool and woolcombing. These " Retrospective Notes " are preserved in the Holden MSS. Lister stated his point of view in a pamphlet entitled *Sir Isaac Holden and the ' Square Motion '* and in his autobiography entitled *Lord Masham's Inventions* (1905). One of the first occasions on which Isaac Holden claimed a share of the credit of inventing the square motion comb was in a letter to Lister dated December 25, 1851 which was printed in *Lord Masham's Inventions*, pp. 21-22.

[25] James Burnley in his *History of Wool and Woolcombing* (1889) wrongly stated that " the first patent in which the square motion principle was brought forward was dated the 19th October 1848 " (p. 303). Burnley failed to mention that Lister had taken out a patent for a square motion mechanical comb in 1846. Lister sued the author and Burnley eventually agreed to withdraw the book from circulation. Holden wrote to Lister on February 5, 1858: " It is true that you took the patent for the square motion but you should have put my name to it " (Holden MSS).

the credit of turning an imperfect machine into an efficient mechanical comb since he alone was responsible for important improvements which were patented in England in 1856-7.[26] Holden later claimed that when " using our combing machine for certain wools one woman can now do the actual combing work in quantity which was done by 200 men previously."[27]

In 1848, after having co-operated as inventors for some months, S. C. Lister and Isaac Holden went into partnership and set up a woolcombing establishment in France.[28] Lister provided the capital while Holden undertook the management of the concern. After five per cent interest had been paid on the capital two thirds of the profits were to go to Lister and one third to Holden.

It was a somewhat hazardous undertaking upon which Lister and Holden had embarked. Neither partner had first-hand knowledge of woolcombing in France where the industry differed in many respects from that of Bradford. Holden's knowledge of France was restricted to a visit to the Paris industrial exhibition in 1834. Moreover the political situation in France was obviously very uncertain in 1848. The establishment of the second Republic in February had been followed by riots which had caused the destruction of valuable railway property. In June a rising of workers in Paris had been suppressed by Cavaignac with heavy loss of life. Nevertheless Isaac Holden—confident that the Providence which watches over the affairs of devout Wesleyan businessmen was directing his steps to France[29]—went with Samuel Lister to Paris in the autumn of 1848 to find suitable

[26] In 1871 Isaac Holden in evidence before the *Select Committee on Letters Patent*, stated that he had spent at least £50,000 on his experiments (Qn. 1944).

[27] Isaac Holden in evidence before the *Select Committee on Letters Patent*, 1871, (Qn. 1966).

[28] Many years later Lister gave the following account of his first meeting with Holden: " A Mr. Bentham first introduced him to me in 1847. At that time he was very poor, having lost the bit of money that he had saved whilst at Messrs. Townsends at Cullingworth, and as I was then taking out a patent for some trifling improvements in combing (and patents were then expensive) he asked me to let him join and put something in about improvements in genappe yarns. Townsends were makers of such yarns, and he got his ideas from them: But I was careful to get a deed drawn up and signed, that everything relating to combing was altogether mine, and that he had nothing to do with it " (*Sir Isaac Holden and the 'Square Motion'* (1904), p. 1). Isaac Holden however, in his " Retrospective Notes " states that he was introduced to Lister by Mr. Ambler (Lister's partner).

[29] Isaac Holden to Mrs. Holden, January 10, 1851: " Providence I believe has called me to be here. As a man of business I enter into the most inviting openings that Providence places before me and there remain, with contented mind, till Providence again directs my path into a course more desirable " (*The Holden-Illingworth Letters*, p. 161).

factory premises. They secured the assistance of Ferdinand Tavernier[30] who claimed to have some knowledge of the woolcombing business in France. A building was rented at St. Denis near Paris. In 1852 Lister and Holden opened new factories at Croix (near Roubaix) and at Reims so as to be closer to their customers.[31]

One of the earliest decisions that Lister and Holden had to make concerned the type of combing machine to be used in their French factory. In 1849 the nip machine had not yet been perfected so Donisthorpe-Lister machines of the type then used at the Manningham works were installed at St. Denis. Holden was not only dissatisfied with the performance of the Donisthorpe-Lister machine but he realised the danger of using mechanical combs which might infringe the Heilmann patent. So he replaced the Donisthorpe-Lister machines with square motion combs. These too were as yet imperfect and their use was abandoned for a time. But Holden made every effort to improve the square motion mechanical comb and this machine was introduced first into the St. Denis factory and subsequently into all the other woolcombing establishments owned or managed by Holden in France and England. The use of the square motion machine eventually spread in France—though Heilmann, Noble, Hübner and other mechanical combs were used as well[32]—while in

[30] Tavernier had been agent for Baron Dufourment, a well-known French wool-spinner.

[31] It is a little puzzling that St. Denis should have been chosen by Lister & Holden for their first factory. Later experience showed that the location was not a very satisfactory one. To a great extent the partners were in Tavernier's hands in this matter and they followed his advice. It may have been that the premises at St. Denis were the only ones that Tavernier could find at that time. For the French woollen and worsted industries at the time of the second Empire see Michael Alcan, *Fabrication des étoffes . . .* (two volumes, 1866); M. R. Louis Reybaud, *La Laine . . .* (1867); the official *Enquête parlementaire sur le régime économique en France* (two volumes, 1870), Vol. 2 (wool); and A. L. Dunham, *The Anglo-French Treaty of Commerce of* 1860 . . . (University of Michigan Press, 1930), ch. 11. See also C. Fohlen, "Esquisse d'une révolution industrielle, Roubaix au xixe siècle" (in the *Revue du Nord*, xxxiii April—September 1951) pp. 92-102 and Julien Turgan, *Les grandes usines . . .* (Paris, 1866-89), Vol. 8 (1871), pp. 102-108.

[32] For example in Alsace the firm of N. Schlumberger (Guebwiller) used the Heilmann comb and Dollfus Mieg et Cie used the Hübner comb (constructed by André Koechlin et Cie at Mülhausen). At Amiens Thuillier-Gellee used the Noble machine and at Roubaix Amedée Prouvouste also used this comb. In 1870 at Reims all the machine combers (except Isaac Holden) used the Heilmann machine for combing. According to Julien Turgan (*Les grandes usines . . .* VIII (1871), p. 70) the Heilmann mechanical comb was adopted at Reims by Lachapelle & Levarlet in 1850, by Walbaum et Cie in 1851, by Villeminot-Huard & Victor Rogelet in 1860 and by Fortel & Villeminot in 1865.

Britain the nip machine was generally used and in Germany the Heilmann machine was most popular.

The fact that Isaac Holden soon replaced the Donisthorpe-Lister by the square motion comb did not save him from vexatious and expensive litigation. The Donisthorpe-Lister machine had been used at St. Denis and Nicholas Schlumberger et Cie claimed that their rights had been infringed. To settle the matter Isaac Holden eventually purchased the Heilmann patent in France (1857-8) just as Samuel Lister had bought the same patent in England.[33] Schlumberger continued to manufacture Heilmann machines under licence from Holden. Isaac Holden was also involved in litigation with French competitors—such as Vigoroux & Nottelet and Duriez fils who tried to copy his machinery[34]—and with Messrs. Donisthorpe & Co. who sold Noble machines in France for a short time (1857).[35]

The introduction of mechanical woolcombing led to an important change in the organisation of the worsted industry. There had been some commission-woolcombing in the days of the hand-combers[36] but the significant development of large-scale specialised woolcombing undertakings was associated

[33] Isaac Holden to S. C. Lister, June 19, 1857: "I returned from Guebwiller on Wednesday. I at length agreed with MM. Schlumberger & Co. I sent for Defilice and got a good contract drawn or rather three contracts. It was an awfully difficult affair. I cut off the negotiations several times. We were minute and they equally so, so that it should be well prepared to avoid future litigation. The main thing is we buy all patents for £35,000 ..." (*Holden-Illingworth Letters*, p. 218). The sum paid by Holden seems to have been a large one since Schlumberger's patent was due to fall into the *domaine publique* in November 1860: see Angus Holden to Isaac Holden, March 17, 1859 in the *Holden-Illingworth Letters*, pp. 260-2. See also " Original papers by I(saac) H(olden) of the Contract Schlumberger and the copy of their first proposal " in the Holden MSS.

[34] See Isaac Crothers to Isaac Holden, April 26, 1858 in the Holden MSS and July 12, 1858 in the *Holden-Illingworth Letters*, pp. 254-5 and " Arguments in Process Vigoroux " in the Holden MSS.

[35] Isaac Holden claimed that this action infringed the rights regarding the Heilmann machine which he had purchased from Schlumberger. The firm of Donisthorpe, Tavernier & Crofts went into liquidation in 1858 and Lister & Holden purchased (i) their machinery, and (ii) their French patent rights in the Noble machine. The original agreement is in the Holden MSS. Holden later allowed Mercier of Louviers to manufacture Noble machines under licence: see Julien Turgan, *Les grandes usines* . . . Vol. 8 (1871), p. 102.

[36] In 1846 Robert Clough of Keighley was having his wool combed by William Baxter of Grassington who was an employer of handcombers (Clough MSS in the Brotherton Library). I am indebted to Mr. E. M. Sigsworth for this reference.

with the production of really efficient woolcombing machines. Much wool was no longer combed by the spinners but was handled by firms which devoted themselves entirely to the combing branch of the trade. On the Continent the three French establishments of Lister and Holden were among the earliest and most important of these works which combed wool on a commission basis. Lister and Holden did not own the wool that they combed. They handled wool which belonged to spinners and was returned to them after combing. This development in the organisation of the worsted industry involved the establishment of new trade customs. Commission woolcombers had to organise the work of their factories in such a way as to ensure that each customer's wool was treated separately. It was necessary to make certain that every spinner received back the same wool—and the whole of the wool—that he had entrusted to the woolcomber. The inadvertent mixing of wools belonging to different clients had obviously to be avoided at all costs.[37]. Spinners had also to be satisfied that they were getting back the noils left over after combing.[38] The time that might reasonably be taken by a woolcomber to comb a given quantity of wool was another matter on which combers and spinners had to reach agreement. The price to be charged by the machine woolcomber also raised difficulties. Normally the comber charged different rates for handling different types of wool but sometimes a large customer would secure a quotation for combing all his wool for a particular period at a uniform rate—even though several types of wool were involved. It was largely owing to the efficiency with which Isaac Holden and his colleagues planned the work of the woolcombing factories at St. Denis, Reims and Croix that these difficulties were overcome with a minimum of friction with the customers. French spinners soon recognised Holden's efficiency and integrity. Orders flowed into his French works and in the summer of 1856 he was

[37] J. Burnley remarked that in Isaac Holden's factories " the arrangements for securing economy of working and the prevention of the mixing of the wool of different clients was as good as it was new ". (*The History of Wool and Woolcombing* (1889), p. 322).

[38] In the " Memoir of Isaac Holden " printed in the *Holden-Illingworth Letters*, Appendix 5, it is stated that when Lister and Holden first established themselves at St. Denis " the business of commission woolcombing was quite new in France. Trade customs and satisfactory working conditions between the owner and comber of the wool had not yet been established. It was only natural therefore that some disputes should arise, and one of these, concerned with the disposal of the waste wool, led to a tedious and highly vexatious lawsuit, in which Holden's character was seriously impugned. He was, however, completely vindicated by the court " (p. 785).

lionised on the Mülhausen exchange as " the first comber of Europe ".[39]

It was no mean achievement for a foreigner—who had been in business in France for only seven years—to be recognised as the leading woolcomber in the country. The success of the woolcombing establishments owned by S. C. Lister and Isaac Holden had been largely due to the efficiency and energy not only of Holden himself but also of a small group of Englishmen who held responsible positions in the factories. Thus Jonathan Holden, a young nephew of Isaac Holden, was placed in charge of the combing department of the St Denis factory although he appears to have had little previous experience of this type of work. In 1853 he was appointed manager of the new branch establishment at Reims. He held this post for many years and it was not until 1880 that he resigned so as to set up a rival woolcombing business of his own in the " eastern suburb " of Reims. Even in 1914 Holden's original Reims factory—the *Vieux Anglais*—was managed by two Englishmen (John Lewthwaite and John Hodgson) while other Englishmen, such as Tom Whitaker and Rayner Smith, were on the staff. Another of Isaac Holden's nephews—Isaac Holden Crothers—was first the bookkeeper of the St. Denis establishment and then the manager of the branch factory at Croix (Roubaix). Other members of Isaac Holden's family who worked in the French woolcombing establishments were his brother George and his sons Edward and Angus. Isaac Holden's sons do not appear to have inherited their father's exceptional business abilities. Isaac Holden wrote to Angus on May 12th, 1859 : " I fear much whether ever you (will) acquire those minutious and careful, painstaking habits which are necessary in a manufacturing business ; and as to Edward I fear he will not only be seriously wanting in this respect but also in constancy and perseverance."[40] And in the same letter he implied that Edward Holden was at least partly responsible for the recent decline in the fortunes of the St. Denis factory.[41]

[39] Isaac Holden to Mrs. Holden, July 16, 1856 (Mülhausen): " I have been lionised today on the exchange (this being market day) as the first comber of Europe. One after the other most of the principal houses of Alsace were introduced to me, till I got quite enough of their beer and coffee " (*Holden-Illingworth Letters*, p. 216).

[40] Isaac Holden to Angus Holden, March 12, 1859 in *The Holden-Illingworth Letters*, p. 258.

[41] Isaac Holden wrote: " It is astonishing how the best business may be the means of sinking a fortune, and that soon, by mismanagement . . ." " Edward is very wishful to do his best but wants a spirit of strict economy, a calm judgement and perseverance " (*ibid.*, pp. 258-9). A few months later (December 22, 1859) Isaac Holden wrote to Angus Holden: " You

It was not only in the management of the woolcombing factories that the services of Englishmen were required. In the early days of the enterprise French skilled artisans were not available in sufficient numbers. Isaac Holden had been warned of this difficulty by Jonas Sugden, his future brother in law, who wrote on August 3rd, 1849 that he had recently met " a French worsted spinner . . . who has had long experience in the French trade and he estimates the character of the French tradespeople at a very low rate."[42] Consequently a number of skilled operatives had to be brought over to France from Yorkshire. There are a few references to these men in Isaac Holden's correspondence. Early in 1860 for example it was stated that a mechanic named John Craig wished to be transferred from the St. Denis factory—which was closing down—to the Reims works.[43] Two years later a foreman named Walters arrived at Reims from England.[44] In 1866 Isaac Crothers wrote to his uncle : " I have taken Jemmy Leach from his allegiance to Rawson's place at Amiens and have set him here over raw wool and washing in both of which departments he is perfect."[45] After the first World War—during which the Reims factory was destroyed by German gunfire—a local newspaper paid a warm tribute to the " English colony " which had for so many years played a prominent part in the industrial and social life of the town.[46]

have been drawing money very briskly the last month or two. I do not know how you spend so much but I hope you will be able to explain it to me. I beg you not to form expensive habits at least till you are worth something " (*ibid.*, p. 279).

[42] Jonas Sugden to Isaac Holden, August 3, 1849. Sugden was a worsted manufacturer at Dockroyd by Keighley. In the spring of 1850 Isaac Holden married for the second time. His bride was Sugden's sister Sarah.

[43] Jonathan Holden to Isaac Holden, April 24, 1860 in *The Holden-Illingworth Letters*, p. 327. Jonathan Holden mentioned that the wages of a skilled mechanic at the Reims woolcombing factory at this time were forty-six shillings a week. A 12-hour day was worked and overtime was paid extra. According to G. Duveau, *La vie ouvrière en France sous le second empire* (1946), p. 313 piecework rates for woolcombing at Holden's factory at Reims varied (in 1868) from 80 centimes to 1 franc, 25 centimes per kgm.

[44] Isaac Holden to Mrs. Holden, February 20, 1862 in *The Holden-Illingworth Letters*, pp. 349-350.

[45] Isaac Crothers to Isaac Holden, January 22, 1866 in *The Holden-Illingworth Letters*, p. 403.

[46] *La Dépêche* (Reims), October 12, 1922. An English translation of the article is printed in *The Holden-Illingworth Letters*, pp. 815-821. The article mentions the following names of English families connected with Holden's woolcombing factory at Reims: Craig, Foster, Smith, Bentley, Crossley, Mitchell, Cox, Whittaker, Hodgson and Lewthwaite (p. 817).

Despite many difficulties a number of French workers were eventually trained for the various operations carried out in the woolcombing factories. At Reims there was a shortage of labour in the 1850s and Jonathan Holden supported a scheme to build model dwellings to attract skilled workers to the town.[47] Eventually the firm built a canteen, a lecture hall, a recreation room and a communal wash-house for the workers and their families.

Isaac Holden would have been in a happier position had he been able to secure the services of an experienced and competent French colleague. Unfortunately Ferdinand Tavernier, who had been associated with Lister and Holden from the start of the enterprise, seems to have been an unreliable and inefficient colleague. He had an office in Paris and acted as commercial manager. But some of the orders that he secured in the early days of the enterprise were far from profitable. For a time Tavernier played off one partner against the other with some success. He secured Lister's support against Holden who appears to have distrusted Tavernier almost from the first. Eventually Lister realised that Tavernier was not only incompetent but something of a rogue as well. Tavernier brought an action against Lister and Holden claiming that he was entitled to a partnership. In this he failed though the court awarded him some compensation.

Numerous quarrels with his partner S. C. Lister increased Isaac Holden's difficulties. The partners were both strong-willed and they wished to pursue divergent policies with regard to their French undertakings. Lister had many irons in the fire. In addition to his substantial financial interests in the three French woolcombing factories he owned—or was a partner in—five Yorkshire mills at Bradford, Manningham, Leeds, Halifax and Addingham and he also had a factory in Germany.[48] He was

[47] Jonathan Holden to Isaac Holden, October 30, 1860 in *The Holden-Illingworth Letters*, p. 328. Jonathan Holden informed his uncle that he had joined a committee which was planning the erection of a *cité ouvrière*. He added: " We begin to feel a great need of hands in Reims and this might be a way of drawing workpeople, for houses are very scarce and unhealthy here ". In August 1858 Jonathan Holden had complained that shortage of labour prevented him from starting night work (*ibid.*, p. 255). It is possible that this development of a *cité ouvrière* was suggested by the example of Titus Salt at Saltaire.

[48] Isaac Holden, in evidence before the *Select Committee on Letters Patent*, 1871, stated that " Mr. Lister established a house in Germany in order to derive some benefit from some of his inventions, which are different from mine, but for the same purpose; and he found it so unprofitable that he has abandoned it altogether " (Qn. 1952).

at the head of nine establishments and had six working partners.[49] Although he must have been receiving large sums annually in royalties from his nip woolcombing machine he often appears to have been short of money and he was somewhat unreasonable in his demands for quick financial returns from the French establishments to support his other activities. Although he had heavy business responsibilities Lister devoted much time and money to new textile inventions. Indeed in the early 1850's these inventions became almost an obsession with Lister. In the year 1855 alone he took out twelve patents for textile processes. It was presumably to finance his inventions that S. C. Lister continually pressed Isaac Holden for profits from the French concerns.

Isaac Holden on the other hand had in the 1850's no business interests beyond the three French factories. He lived in France until 1860 and he devoted the whole of his time to building up a prosperous commission woolcombing business. He was continually improving his machinery and he introduced important changes in the preliminary washing processes by passing the wool through two successive baths and then through rollers. Holden wanted to plough profits back into the French concern so as to build up a reserve to extend and improve the plant. Moreover Lister pressed Holden strongly to introduce the nip machine into the French factories.[50] Holden considered that the nip machine was less efficient than the square motion machine and he foresaw the difficulties that would arise with Schlumberger if he continued to use the nip machine. It has been seen too that for a time the partners failed to agree on how to deal with the troublesome Tavernier.

In a letter to his wife in 1852 Isaac Holden confidently asserted that he was quite capable of handling his partner. " Be easy. I know him full well and know how to manage him. I am his

[49] Statement by S. C. Lister in *The Square Motion Combing Machine: its origin*, p. 26. Sir John Clapham writes: " Within a few years Lister dominated the industry. He sold machines to spinners for a royalty of £1,000 each. By 1855 he had five English, three French and one German mill combing on commission for spinners. Never before had a factory industry been more quickly born, once the long gestation was over; nor did one ever grow more quickly " (*An Economic History of Modern Britain, II,* (1932), p. 31).

[50] S. C. Lister to Isaac Holden, November 18, 1856: " I have to request and insist . . . that you do not mount another square motion machine of any kind, as I am quite certain I can mount better machines ". Shortly afterwards (December 17, 1856) Lister wrote: " I have no doubt every square motion will be broken up for old iron, or my opinion is worth nothing " (quoted in *The Square Motion Combing Machine: its origin*, pp. 20-21).

master and shall make him do as I want . . ."[51] As early as the end of 1851 Lister was already threatening to start a new woolcombing business at Lille with another partner.[52] Differences of opinion between Holden and Lister culminated in an action by Lister in October, 1855, before a French court to dissolve the partnership. The court however decided that it was not competent to deal with the matter[53]

The financial crisis of 1857 brought matters to a head. Lister's Halifax establishment failed and he was in serious difficulties. He appears to have drawn £30,000 from the French business in 1857 and 1858.[54] After long negotiations the partnership between S. C. Lister and Isaac Holden was dissolved in November, 1858.[55] Rather than see the French business involved in the Halifax crash Holden paid £74,000 for Lister's share in the French woolcombing factories. That he could raise so large a sum shortly after paying £35,000 for Schlumberger's (French) patent of the Heilmann mechanical comb suggests that commission woolcombing in France in the 1850s had yielded handsome profits.

Isaac Holden took his sons Angus and Edward into partnership and the firm was henceforth known as Isaac Holden et fils. Subsequently Holden's two nephews Jonathan Holden and Isaac Crothers—and also Thomas Craig—became partners. The leading members of the Holden family, however, were not united in their views on the future policy of the business. As early as 1854 Angus Holden was trying to persuade his father to return to England. He wrote : " Do try and let us be out of the way of Tavernier and the whole bundle ".[56] In 1859 Angus was arguing that woolcombing in France was a highly speculative

[51] Isaac Holden to Mrs. Holden, June 21, 1852 in *The Holden-Illingworth Letters*, p. 174.

[52] Note by Isaac Holden in the Holden MSS (Brotherton Library): "I remonstrated that it would be a violation of deed of partnership and also reminded him ' that my square motion had saved the concern from ruin '."

[53] Isaac Holden stated that in 1855 Lister " had actually made a sale of the whole concern without my consent, which sale, needless to say, was rescinded " (*The Square Motion Combing Machine*: *its origin*, p. 17).

[54] Statement by Isaac Holden in *The Square Motion Combing Machine*: *its origin*, p. 17.

[55] In March 1858 Donisthorpe and Crofts had joined Lister and Holden as partners in the French woolcombing enterprise but this agreement was cancelled a few months later when the partnership between Lister and Holden was dissolved.

[56] Angus Holden to Isaac Holden, March 1, 1854 in *The Holden-Illingworth Letters*, p. 183.

business—a " bubble " enterprise—the success of which depended very largely upon the maintenance of a semi-monopoly of good machines. Angus felt that the firm was fighting a losing battle against those who tried to pirate their mechanical combs and he argued that as patents expired so competition would grow more severe. He pined for a safe snug little business in the West Riding.[57] Isaac Holden was made of sterner stuff. He had fought for his patents before and he could do so again. He was confident that mechanical woolcombing in France would long remain a profitable enterprise.

Isaac Holden's correspondence illustrates the progress of a single group of machine woolcombing establishments in France at the time of the second Empire. As early as December, 1849 Isaac Holden wrote that he was very busy getting the factory mounted with machinery. " The demand for our work is also very great so that we have the mill running day and night ".[58] This suggests that the French worsted industry—famed for its high class all-wool (merino and *de laine*) worsted cloths—was recovering quickly from the depression of 1848. In the autumn of 1851 Isaac Holden reported that he could not comb all the wool that was offered to him. So he visited Lille, Roubaix, Douai and Reims in search of new premises for a branch factory and he extended the plant at St. Denis. On November 1st, 1851 Isaac Holden wrote to his wife that he was " making several changes ". " I have bought another steam engine of 20 horses power which is to be put down and we are also setting about making more machinery and buying more ". " I went this week on Thursday to near Rouen to buy two carding engines "[59] He added that the " business is a great good to France and is profitable to us ". It was in this year that—in the words of the jury—French merino cloths maintained their " unquestionable superiority " at the Great Exhibition in London. In 1852 new factories were being built by Lister and Holden at Croix (by Roubaix) and at Reims. They were opened in 1853. In that year Isaac Holden remarked that it would be difficult to get a business in England " anything like as good " as the one he had built up in France.[60] The woolcombing trade was brisk in the early part of 1853 but rather slack in the second half of the year. Night work was abandoned and the need for additional capital

[57] Angus Holden to Isaac Holden, March 17, 1859 in *The Holden-Illingworth Letters*, pp. 260-3.

[58] Isaac Holden to Eliza Townsend, December 19, 1849 in *The Holden-Illingworth Letters*, p. 138.

[59] Isaac Holden to Mrs. Holden, October 28, 1851 (*ibid.*, p. 164).

[60] Isaac Holden to Mrs. Holden, November 1, 1851 (*ibid.*, p. 165).

to complete the new branch factories and to provide for the all too rapid depreciation of machinery caused both partners some concern.

The year 1854 was a very satisfactory one from the point of view of machine-woolcombing. In December of that year Isaac Holden was able to inform his banker that he proposed to deposit £1,000 every month.[61] In 1855 trade was still good and profits high. On March 26th Jonathan Holden wrote to his uncle that the Reims factory was " well employed running long hours as we well can without commencing night work again ".[62] But at the end of the year Isaac Holden told his wife that the St. Denis works had been closed for a week. " The wool merchants are expecting a change in the wool duties. We are likely to be very slack for some time which is very trying for our poor workers ".[63] At Reims, however, Jonathan Holden was still busy. On January 20th, 1856 he wrote to his uncle: " I am happy to inform you that we are pretty well supplied with wool; we run thirteen hours per day and still continue to receive from all parties ".[64] To such an extent did French all-wool worsteds dominate the world market at this time that a delegation of the Bradford Chamber of Commerce visited France in 1855 to try to discover the secret of French success in this branch of the industry.[65] Between 1849 and the end of 1856 Lister and Holden made a profit of £170,000.[66] The year 1857 was one of business depression but the woolcombing factories of Lister and Holden in France do not seem to have suffered. In 1858 Isaac Holden purchased S. C. Lister's share in the French woolcombing factories and became their sole owner.

[61] Isaac Holden to Mrs. Holden, August 24, 1853 (*ibid.*, p. 180). Isaac Holden to S. Laycock, 16 December, 1854 in the Holden MSS.

[62] Jonathan Holden to Isaac Holden, March 26, 1855 in *The Holden-Illingworth Letters*, p. 195.

[63] Isaac Holden to Mrs. Holden, December 18, 1855 (*ibid.*, p. 204). Between 1853 and 1855 numerous French import duties were reduced by decree. The Government's policy was confirmed by the legislature in 1856. See Percy Ashley, *Modern Tariff History* (1904), p. 299.

[64] Jonathan Holden to Isaac Holden, January 20, 1856 in *The Holden-Illingworth Letters*, p. 212.

[65] Bradford, on the other hand, concentrated on the production of cheap mixed (cotton warp and wool weft) worsteds. Henry Forbes remarked that the policy of the Bradford worsted manufacturers was: " Rather produce a large quantity at a small profit than a small quantity at a greater percentage " (*Lectures on the Results of the Great Exhibition of 1851*, second series, XXI (1853), p. 325.)

[66] Statement by S. C. Lister in *The Square Motion Combing Machine: its Origin*, p. 38.

In 1859 and 1860 new dangers appeared to threaten the future prosperity of Isaac Holden's business in France. In September, 1859 Isaac Holden, writing from St. Denis, declared : " Business has been very bad and I have had a great deal of care and trouble to get on. My business is too large and too risky for peace of mind and spiritual prosperity."[67] The St. Denis factory was now running at a loss[68] and it was closed down in 1860, the machinery being moved to Croix and Reims.[69] At the same time (November 1860) Schlumberger's patent rights over the Heilmann mechanical comb expired and there was reason to fear that Holden would have to face unwelcome competition from the many Heilmann combs that might be expected to spread from Alsace to other wool textile centres.[70] Moreover, in 1860 the signing of the Anglo-French (Cobden-Chevalier) commercial treaty—and its supplementary conventions—provided for reductions in the French import duties on English wool textiles. There was naturally some apprehension among French woollen and worsted manufacturers lest they should now have to face strong competition from the West Riding in the French home market. Isaac Holden wrote to a correspondent in October, 1860 : " I am persuaded combing will be one of the worst businesses existing in France before six months pass . . . It would be sheer madness

[67] Isaac Holden to his sister Mrs. Cockrane, September 1, 1859 in *The Holden-Illingworth Letters*, p. 273. Over a year before (March 1858) Isaac Holden had written to his wife that he would like to settle in Yorkshire and leave his sons and nephews to manage his French factories (*ibid.*, p. 235).

[68] Isaac Holden to Angus Holden, March 12, 1859: " The last half year while Jonathan (Holden at Reims) has cleared £18,000, St. Denis has made a loss of £3,400 " (*The Holden-Illingworth Letters*, p. 258).

[69] Isaac Holden to Margaret Holden, March 29, 1860: " We have decided to leave St. Denis and the mill will be stopped in a week or two to remove the machinery to Reims and Croix " (*The Holden-Illingworth Letters*, p. 294). See also Isaac Holden to Margaret Holden, April 23, 1860 (*ibid.*, p. 308). On November 16, 1860 Isaac Holden wrote that the removal was nearly completed (*ibid.*, p. 323). There is a reference in a letter from Angus Holden to his father, April 11, 1860, to complaints from Paris clients at the closing of the St. Denis factory (*ibid.*, p. 301).

[70] Angus Holden to Isaac Holden, March 17, 1859: ". . . When Schlumberger's patent falls into the *domaine publique* . . . I expect there will be a complete revolution in combing. Don't let us deceive ourselves. Concerns will be mounted without end on the different systems . . ." (*The Holden-Illingworth Letters*, pp. 261-2). But only three years later Angus Holden stated that Schlumberger's (Heilmann) mechanical comb was making no progress and that combers who had it installed wanted to be rid of it. Angus Holden criticised the author of the catalogue of the Paris Exhibition of 1862 for ascribing the recent expansion of the French worsted industry solely to *la peigneuse Schlumberger*. See Angus Holden to Isaac Holden, September 16, 1862 in *The Holden-Illingworth Letters*, pp. 353-5.

for anyone to lay out good capital on a combing establishment in France. Better by a hundred times to do it in England which will be benefitted soon by the treaty of commerce by which the French worsted trade will undoubtedly suffer ".[71]

Despite these adverse factors Isaac Holden's woolcombing establishments in France flourished in the years following the commercial crisis of 1857.[72] In August, 1858 Jonathan Holden told his uncle that at Reims " we are more and more pressed by our customers . . . Still we cannot satisfy the demand. Our magazine (warehouse) is full and the yard covered. We should commence night work but cannot get hands sufficient as yet ".[73] A year later (September 1859) Isaac Crothers reported from Croix: " We never had better prospects : to all appearances we shall be kept going very busily night and day with the three rooms all this year and very possibly far into the next half year. We are positively worried by our customers who all want to have their wool combed at once ". In two and a half years 90,000 francs had been spent in extending and improving the Croix factory.[74] In the middle of 1860 both the Reims and Croix establishments were very busy. Edward Holden wrote to his father on June 22nd, 1860 : " Reims is so busy now that they cannot do one half sufficient work, both new and old magazines are filled up outside to the top of the mill nearly. They are in the same mess at Croix and I think we have never been so busy since we came to France ".[75] In October, 1860 Isaac Crothers reported that

[71] Isaac Holden to Mr. Bentham, October 9, 1860 in *The Holden-Illingworth Letters*, pp. 324-5.

[72] Isaac Holden appears to have weathered the storm in 1857 without difficulty. He wrote to his wife on March 14, 1858: " Mr. Leon Vallais has failed. He owes us about 60.000 francs—say £2,000. This is the largest bad debt (in fact almost the only one) we ever made. He will pay 15/- in the £ " (*The Holden-Illingworth Letters*, p. 233).

[73] Jonathan Holden (Reims) to Isaac Holden, August 9, 1858 in *The Holden-Illingworth Letters*, p. 255. A few months previously Jonathan Holden had been complaining of lack of work. On April 24, 1858 he wrote: " We stopt today at noon for want of wool and though it is market day I have not got a kilogram " (Holden MSS).

[74] Isaac Crothers (Croix) to Isaac Holden, September 3. 1859 in *The Holden-Illingworth Letters*, pp. 270-2. At the same time (September 12, 1859) Angus Holden wrote: " Trade is very brisk in Bradford " (*ibid.*, p. 274). In the previous year (November 1858) Isaac Crothers had reported that he was combing 5,000 kgm of wool per day (Holden MSS).

[75] Edward Holden to Isaac Holden, June 22, 1860 in *The Holden-Illingworth Letters*, pp. 313-4. A temporary cause of good trade was that " though the import duty on wool was removed in the spring the drawback on stuff goods and yarns was continued till September " (Isaac Holden to Mr. Bentham October 9, 1860 in *The Holden-Illingworth Letters*, p. 325).

at Croix they were " always head over ears in work ".[76] In April, 1861 Isaac Holden visited Reims and informed his wife that " business is pretty good here ".[77] In the same month Isaac Crothers reported that at Croix " our position is improving although " the Roubaix combers are very slack and (are) combing at very low prices ".[78] The main reason for the depression in the woollen and worsted industries in the Nord Department in 1861 was the increased English competition that followed the Anglo-French commercial treaty.[79] In Tourcoing only 2,776,000 kgm of wool were delivered in the month of November, 1861 as compared with 4,500,000 kgm in November, 1860. It has been stated that in the Nord Department " in 1860 the principal combing mills were working night and day ". " In 1861 not merely did night work stop, but most factories only worked intermittently and lived from day to day ".[80]

By the autumn of 1861 the slackness of trade already apparent at Roubaix was also noticed at Reims. For some years wool had been pouring into the Reims factory but in August, 1861 Jonathan Holden found it necessary to visit his customers in Paris and the Nord Department to solicit fresh orders.[81] The depression in the French woollen and worsted industries continued in 1862 when the president of the Tourcoing chamber of commerce complained that " the activity of Bradford contrasts with the distress of our spinning mills ". " In all our mills some machinery is stopped ".[82] But for Isaac Holden's wool-

[76] Isaac Crothers (Croix) to Isaac Holden, October 13, 1860 in *The Holden-Illingworth Letters*, p. 327.

[77] Isaac Holden to Mrs. Holden, April 29, 1861 in *The Holden-Illingworth Letters*, p. 330.

[78] Isaac Crothers to Isaac Holden, April 15, 1861 in *The Holden-Illingworth Letters*, p. 345. Crothers added: " I find that other combers have had and (still) have a systematic mode of bribing commission agents and head men in firms or rather—not to use the word " bribing "—they make them a systematic allowance. It has been going on for years. We shall get on all the better for not descending to such dirty work; as it will only tend to spur us on to greater excellence in work " (*ibid.*, p. 346).

[79] For the expansion of the West Riding woollen and worsted exports when the Anglo-French commercial treaty of 1860 came into force see J. Watts, *Facts of the Cotton Famine* (1866), p. 400.

[80] P. Morazé " The Treaty of 1860 and the Industry of the Department of the North " in the *Economic History Review*, X, 1939-40, p. 19.

[81] Jonathan Holden to Isaac Holden, August 17, 1861 in *The Holden-Illingworth Letters*, p. 347. He wrote: ". . . We shall soon need wool to keep us going. We have stopped night work. Trade here is much the same only darker: we must hope for better days ".

[82] Quoted by P. Morazé, " The Treaty of 1860 and the Industry of the Department of the North " in the *Economic History Review*, X, 1939-40, p. 19.

combing establishments the recession of 1861 was only of a temporary character. When Isaac Holden visited his factory at Reims in February, 1862 he found that the works were as busy as ever. He wrote : " The mill is running full time . . . night and day with a good supply of wool to go on with ".[83] In September of the same year Isaac Holden's woolcombing works both at Reims and at Croix appear to have had plenty of orders.[84] The revival of the French woollen and worsted industries in 1863 may be attributed partly to ample supplies of cheap overseas wool and partly to an increased demand for wool textiles owing to the shortage of cotton goods at the time of the Cotton Famine.[85] In May, 1864 it was stated that Isaac Holden's factory at Reims was " still very busy and full up with wool and all still running night and day ".[86] One of the rare occasions on which Jonathan Holden had trouble with his operatives occurred in July, 1864. In an attempt to stop absenteeism on Monday mornings the management proposed to fine workers who failed to report for duty after the weekend. The operatives went on strike. Jonathan Holden withdrew the proposed fines and the operatives promised to come to work regularly on Mondays.[87] In 1865 Isaac Crothers wrote from Croix : " We are improving here continually in combing fine wools and are growing in favour. Our customers here say that—although they ought not to tell us—we are the only combers who know how to deal with fine wools. I am expecting a roaring business ".[88] And in December, 1865 he boasted that the Croix factory was " at the head of the trade in fine and intermediate wools ".[89] In January, 1866 he

[83] Isaac Holden to Mrs. Holden, February 20, 1862 in *The Holden-Illingworth Letters*, p. 349-50.

[84] Angus Holden to Isaac Holden, September 22, 1862 in *The Holden-Illingworth Letters*, p. 358.

[85] In England the West Riding woollen and worsted industries flourished in the early 1860s. E. Baines stated: " Whilst one half of the machinery of Lancashire was for three years idle, every spindle and every loom in Yorkshire was increasingly busy; the absence of cotton increased the demand for woollen and worsted goods . . . (quoted by J. Watts, *Facts of the Cotton Famine* (1866), p. 393). The total exports of British woollen and worsted manufactures rose from £11,118,692 in 1861 to £18,566,078 in 1864 (i.e. by 67%): see J. Watts, *op cit.*, p. 400.

[86] Angus Holden to Isaac Holden, May 27, 1864 in *The Holden-Illingworth Letters*, p. 368.

[87] G. Duveau *La vie ouvrière en France sous le second Empire* (1946), pp. 245-6.

[88] Isaac Crothers to Isaac Holden, May 5, 1865 in *The Holden-Illingworth Letters*, p. 377.

[89] Isaac Crothers to Isaac Holden, December 29, 1865 in *The Holden-Illingworth Letters*, p. 387.

reported that " work is rolling in upon us again ".[90] Jonathan Holden, on the other hand, was not so satisfied with the state of trade at Reims. While he was " busy as usual " in December, 1865 he was " short on the French and low wools which are very scarce and dear ".[91]

In a letter to his uncle dated May, 5th, 1866 Isaac Crothers made an interesting comparison between the work of Holden's woolcombing establishments at Reims and at Croix (Roubaix). He pointed out that at Reims " they have a regular trade, the merino trade varying very little all the year round and varying little from one year to another . . . " Roubaix, on the other hand, " is more American and altogether different. It is either a great calm or a furious tempest. In 1860, 1861 and 1862 they gave themselves up for dead, but towards 1863 perceiving their error there began to be vigorous life and now began the rage for increase ".[92] But in 1867 the failure of Pollet's bank led to the immediate collapse of seven Roubaix woollen manufacturers. There was severe unemployment and an attempt to make weavers manage two looms instead of one led to disturbances in Roubaix in the spring of 1867.[93]

Both in the spring and in the autumn of 1867 Jonathan Holden reported that the Reims factory was very busy but he was worried about a possible trade depression owing to the uncertain international situation.[94] In the summer of the following year (1868) Angus Holden expressed the view that " both at Reims and Croix our extensions have been too rapid and both he (i.e. Isaac Crothers) and Jonathan (Holden) have felt during last year that the production was ahead of the market, instead of it being the reverse, so that they have been compelled to take almost anything to keep the machinery going, and durst not say anything about the price from the fear of being cut off in supplies. However our position is much more favourable now . . . "[95]

In June, 1869 Angus Holden informed his father that " we are very busy at both Reims and Croix ". At Reims three of

[90] Isaac Crothers to Isaac Holden, January 22, 1866 in *The Holden-Illingworth Letters*, p. 403.

[91] Jonathan Holden to Isaac Holden, December 30, 1865 in *The Holden-Illingworth Letters*, pp. 388-9.

[92] Isaac Crothers to Isaac Holden, May 5, 1866 in *The Holden-Illingworth Letters*, p. 404 *et seq.*

[93] C. Fohlen, " Crise textile et troubles sociaux: le Nord à la fin du second Empire " (*Revue du Nord*, XXXV, No. 138, April-June 1953, pp. 109-123).

[94] Jonathan Holden to Isaac Holden, May 18 and November 19, 1867 in *The Holden-Illingworth Letters*, pp. 411-12.

[95] Angus Holden to Mrs. Holden, July 13, 1868 in *The Holden-Illingworth Letters*, p. 413.

Holden's chief competitors—Villeminot-Huard,[96] Pierrab Parpuite and the successor to Vigoroux's business—had given up combing. The efficiency of Holden's establishment at Reims may be judged from the fact that in 1870 this factory was able to comb 100 kgm of wool in thirteen hours whereas rival firms in the town combed only 33 kgm in the same time.[97]

By 1870 Isaac Holden had been living in England again for nine years. When the St. Denis factory closed (1860) he settled in Yorkshire (1861). With his two sons he ran the small Penny Oaks mill at Bradford from 1861 until 1864—with Thomas Craig as manager—and he then founded the much larger Alston woolcombing works which were situated in Thornton Road, Bradford. The Alston establishment flourished and for many years Isaac Holden controlled "the largest machine combing concern in the world".[98] He became a very wealthy man and in the 1880s a newspaper correspondent credited him with an income of £200,000 a year. The size of Isaac Holden's two French undertakings may be gathered from information supplied in 1874 by his nephews. Jonathan Holden stated that the Reims works covered "20,337 (square) metres of flooring all included, houses as well". The machinery included "16 boilers of about 1,400 horse power in three engines working constantly and two engines standing of 200 h.p." The daily output of "top" amounted to 15,000 kgm. "We employ 1,100 hands and pay 37,000 francs per fortnight in wages, this inclusive of managers and clerks to whom we pay about 6,000 francs per month". Isaac Crothers stated at the same time that the floor-space of the Croix mill buildings was 39,000 square metres. He added:

[96] The firm of Villeminot-Huard, Victor Rogelet et Cie had been founded in 1852. Next to Holden's factory this was the most important house in the Reims worsted industry.

[97] Appendix to evidence submitted by Dauphinot on behalf of the Reims chamber of commerce to the *Enquête parlemantaire sur le régime économique* (2 volumes, 1870), Vol. 2, p. 159. It may be added that the floorspace of Holden's woolcombing factory at Reims was 11,000 sq. m. in 1868 as compared with only 1,500 sq. m. in 1852: See G. Duveau, *La vie ouvrière en France sous le second Empire* (1946), p. 168.

[98] C. R. Fay, *Great Britain from Adam Smith to the Present Day* (1928), p. 296. Samuel Lister (later Baron Masham), who had once played so important a rôle in machine woolcombing, had now turned his attention to the spinning of silk waste. Sir John Clapham wrote: "Manningham mill became one of the giant factories of Europe sending silk sewing thread all over the world, making velvets and softly draping silks fitted to the taste of the eighties, with imitation sealskins and furs very popular indeed" (*An Economic History of Modern Britain,* II (1932), p. 88). Lister commemorated his woolcombing inventions by presenting the Cartwright statue and the Cartwright memorial hall to the city of Bradford.

"We have besides 160,000 square metres of land on which there are no buildings except dwelling houses". "We have 33 boilers of 3,988 horse power (and) 11 engines of 1,180 indicated H.P. We have 1,785 workpeople and we pay £3,000 fortnightly in wages. We have consumed—with grease works—nearly 100 tons of coal per day but we have pared this down to a much more modest figure".[99]

James Burnley declared in 1889 that for the last twenty-five years Isaac Holden's woolcombing factories in Bradford and France "have carried on with ever increasing success". "At their three establishments they have a combined area of flooring of over forty acres and . . . they comb an average of 31,166,666 fleeces annually, consisting almost entirely of merino wool".[100] Isaac Holden visited his French factories from time to time but his main interests now lay in England. He devoted much of his time to politics and sat as Liberal member of parliament for Knaresborough (1865-8), the north west division of the West Riding (1882-4) and Keighley (1885-95).[101] He was created a baronet in 1893 and he died in 1897.

In the period of the second Empire Isaac Holden had played an important part in the expansion of commission woolcombing in the north east textile districts of France. In 1848 woolcombing in France had been done almost entirely by hand. In those days it was the main industry at Tourcoing. In 1870, on the other hand, there were a number of large machine woolcombing establishments in Roubaix,[102] Tourcoing and Croix. It was

[99] Jonathan Holden to Isaac Holden, June 23, 1874 and Isaac Crothers to Isaac Holden, July 6, 1874, in *The Holden-Illingworth Letters*, pp. 497-99. In 1871 Julien Turgan described Holden's woolcombing establishment at Reims as the largest in the world. He wrote: "L'usine consomme annuellement 12,000 tonnes de houille pour chauffage, et 600 tonnes de charbon à gaz ; le travail manuel représente plus de 1,000 ouvriers, et la puissance de production est par an, de plus de 3,000,000 kilogrammes de laine peignée, dont les prix de façon varient de 0 fr. 80 c. à 1 fr. 25 c. le kilogramme." See J. Turgan *Les Grandes Usines* . . . , VIII (1871), pp. 102-8).

[100] J. Burnley, *The History of Wool and Woolcombing* (1889), p. 323.

[101] Angus Holden, too, was interested both in local government (being Mayor of Bradford in 1878-80 and in 1886) and in national politics. He represented East Bradford in parliament in 1885-6 and he was returned in 1892 for Buckrose Division which he represented for eight years. He succeeded to his father's baronetcy in 1897 and he was created Baron Holden of Alston in 1908.

[102] The first large mechanical woolcombing establishment at Roubaix—the firm of Allart-Rousseau—was founded shortly after the revolution of 1848. A year or two later the woolcombing establishment of Amédee-Prouvost was set up. Roubaix is stated to have had eleven woolcombing factories in 1860 and thirteen in 1871. See C. Fohlen, "Esquisse d'une évolution industrielle. Roubaix au xixe siècle" in the *Revue du Nord*, XXXIII, April-September, 1951, p. 99.

estimated that they combed annually 48,000,000 kgm of wool worth between 140,000,000 and 150,000,000 francs. One third of the wool combed by machinery in this district was spun locally while two-thirds was spun else-where in France or abroad.[103] At the same time ten machine-combing firms were active in Reims. There were 295 combing machines in the town.[104] And whereas formerly French and English wool had been used, the French combers were now handling many types of wool from overseas.

Many factors promoted the development of machine-combing in France between 1848 and 1870. The building of railways, the founding of credit banks, and the reform of the tariff deserve mention. So does the invention of the Heilmann mechanical comb in Alsace which was used by Schlumberger and several other firms. But it is a mistake to give the whole credit for the progress of machine combing in Napoleon III's reign to Heilmann and Schlumberger.[105] The work of Samuel Lister, Isaac Holden and other Englishmen at St. Denis, Croix and Reims should not be forgotten.[106] These Yorkshire pioneers introduced commission woolcombing into France and they greatly fostered the expansion of this important branch of the worsted industry in France.[107]

[103]Evidence submitted by Jules Decroix on behalf of the Lille chamber of commerce to the *Enquête parlementaire sur le régime économique* (2 vols., 1870), Vol. 2, p. 312.

[104]Appendix to evidence submitted by Dauphinot on behalf of the Reims chamber of commerce to the *Enquête parlementaire sur le régime économique* (2 vols., 1870), Vol. 2, p. 159.

[105]See for example the point of view expressed in A. L. Dunham, *The Anglo-French Treaty of Commerce of 1860 . . .* (University of Michigan Press, 1930), p. 220.

[106]It may be added that English entrepreneurs and skilled operatives fostered the development of other branches of the French textile industry. In the middle years of the nineteenth century, for example, there was an English colony of lace workers at Calais while workers from Scotland were pioneers in the development of the jute industry at David Dickson's factory at Dunkirk. See above, p. 30.

[107]I thank Mr. E. H. Illingworth for the loan of a copy of *The Holden Illingworth Letters* and for permission to quote from this privately printed correspondence.

III. BELGIUM

5. THE INFLUENCE OF BRITISH ENTREPRENEURS ON THE INDUSTRIAL REVOLUTION IN BELGIUM, 1750-1850

BELGIUM was the first Continental country to experience an industrial revolution comparable with that of Britain. The introduction of new machines, the adoption of steam power, the development of the factory system, the growth of great manufacturing cities, the construction of a network of canals and railways and the establishment of joint-stock companies and banks took place sooner and more rapidly in Belgium than in France or Germany. Factors which promoted the early industrialisation of Belgium included a favourable location, the existence of long established domestic textile and metal industries, the possession of the great port of Antwerp, the presence of important raw materials such as timber, coal, iron ore and hides, and an industrious population ready to take advantage of these favourable circumstances. Foreigners played an important part in fostering the industrialisation of Belgium. Much of the country had been ruled successively by the Spaniards, the Austrians, the French and the Dutch before independence was secured[2]

[1] Robert J. Lemoine, " Les étrangers et la formation du capitalisme en Belgique " (*Revue d'Histoire économique et sociale*, XX, 1932, pp. 252-336).

[2] In the late eighteenth century and in the early part of the nineteenth century several territorial changes occurred in the Low Countries. In the eighteenth century there were three main territories in this area : (*a*) United Netherlands (including part of Limburg) ; (*b*) Austrian Netherlands (which included the duchies of Flanders, Hainault, Brabant, Namur, Luxemburg and part of Limburg) ; (*c*) Principality of Liège (ruled by the Prince-Bishops of Liège) which stretched across the southern Low Countries from the Dutch to the French frontier, dividing Luxemburg and Austrian Limburg from the rest of the Habsburg territories.

The French victories of 1794-6 were followed by the establishment of the Batavian Republic (which Napoleon later turned into the Kingdom of Holland and then annexed to France) while the Austrian Netherlands (including Luxemburg) and the Principality of Liège were incorporated into France.

The former Austrian Netherlands and Liège (to which were added some Dutch territories on the Scheldt and Meuse) were divided into the following Departments : Jemappes (capital Mons) ; Dyle (Brussels) ; Deux Nèthes (Antwerp) ; Scheldt (Ghent) ; Lys (Bruges) ; Meuse Inférieur (Maestricht) ; Ourthe (Liège) ; Forêts (Luxemburg) ; Sambre and Meuse (Namur).

In 1814-15 the northern and southern parts of the Low Countries were joined to form the Kingdom of the United Netherlands. The former and all contributed something to the future industrial greatness of Belgium. In the eighteenth century the Prince-Bishops of the virtually independent ecclesiastical territory of Liège were active in fostering the economic development of their coal and iron resources at a time when the Habsburgs were losing interest in their possessions in the Low Countries. The English and Germans were neighbours of Belgium and they had a share in promoting the modern economic development of the country. The activities of the Lombard financiers in Bruges and Ghent as far back as the middle ages also deserves mention.[3]

British influence upon the industrialisation of Belgium was particularly significant since in the early days of the industrial revolution it was only from Britain that the most modern machinery and information concerning the most recent advances in technical knowledge could be secured. In the eighteenth century and in the early nineteenth century the emigration of skilled artisans and the export of many types of machines, models and blueprints from Britain was forbidden. Nevertheless a number of British workers did make their way to the Low Countries and some British machinery was sent to Belgium.

For hundreds of years there had been close commercial links between Britain and the territories which were later known as " Belgium." The significance of Flanders for the English trade in wool and cloth in the middle ages—and later—is well known.[4]

Departments of the Belgian provinces survived under different names. Lys became East Flanders ; Scheldt became West Flanders ; the Belgian part of Deux Nèthes became Antwerp; Dyle became Brabant Méridional; Sambre and Meuse became Namur ; Ourthe became Liège ; Meuse Infèrieur became Limburg and Forêts became Luxemburg. The Grand Duchy of Luxemburg (a member of the German Confederation) was in personal union with the Kingdom of the Netherlands and was represented in the legislative assembly at The Hague. The fortress of Luxemburg was garrisoned by Prussian troops on behalf of the German Confederation.

Belgium secured her independence in 1830 but the frontiers of the new state were not finally settled until 1839 when Limburg and Luxemburg were partitioned between Holland and Belgium. The Meuse formed the new frontier between Dutch Limburg and Belgian Limburg. Luxemburg was divided so that the French speaking (Walloon) districts fell to Belgium while the German speaking districts remained independent. The personal union between Holland and the new Luxemburg survived until the death of William III of the Netherlands.

[3] G. Bigwood, *Le régime juridique et économique de l'argent dans la Belgique du Moyen Age* (Brussels, 1920).

[4] O. de Smedt, " De Engelsche handel te Antwerpen in de Jaaren 1305-15 " (*Bijdragen tot de Geschiednis*, XV, 1923) ; H. L. Gray, " The Production and Export of English Woollens in the Fourteenth Century " (*English Historical Review*, XXXIV, 1924) ; Eileen Power, *The Wool Trade in English Medieval History* (1941) ; van Werveke, " Essor et déclin de la

When Antwerp became one of the chief financial centres on the Continent there were many contacts between that city and London. Stephen Vaughan was the financial agent of the English Crown at Antwerp in 1544-45 while in Elizabeth's reign Sir Thomas Gresham was so frequently in Antwerp both on the Queen's business and on his own that he purchased a house in the Lange Nieuwstrasse.[5]

In the eighteenth century British merchants, bankers and company promoters were to be found in the Austrian Netherlands. James Dormer was a typical commercial adventurer of the period. He established himself first at Ostend (1728) and then at Antwerp. He married twice and two dowries laid the foundations of his fortune. Dormer dealt in wines, textiles, tobacco, tea, butter and herrings. He exported Dutch paintings to England. He acted as financial agent for the English armies in Flanders and he lent money to various public authorities. In 1754 he founded a privileged insurance company (la Société Royale et Impériale d'Assurances) which was run by two English employees named Thompson and Hollis. Dormer died in London in 1758. His son took over the family business. Dormer's private bank was liquidated in 1771 while the insurance company was wound up in 1780. Another financier who had some influence upon the economic development of the Austrian Netherlands in the second half of the eighteenth century was the banker Herries, a Scot who carried on business in London and Ostend. He helped to devise an early form of letter of credit on the Continent and he established his own countrymen (G. Keith, T. Ray, W. Boyd and J. G. Kerr) as his correspondents in Brussels, Bruges, Ostend and Ghent.

A few English manufacturers and skilled workers were to be found in the Austrian Netherlands and in the Principality of Liège in the middle years of the eighteenth century. In 1720-1 an Irishman named O'Kelly introduced a new pumping machine into Liège. In 1759-61 a certain Thomas Murray received financial assistance from the government to establish a factory just north of Brussels for the manufacture of sulphuric acid. At about the same time an Englishman named Brown secured subsidies from

Flandre" (*Studi in onore di Gino Luzzatto*, Milan, 1949, p. 158); E. M. Carus-Wilson, "Trends in the Export of English Woollens in the Fourteenth Century" (*Economic History Review*, New Series, III, 1950-1, pp. 162-179); Florence Edler, "Winchcombe Kerseys in Antwerp, 1538-44" (*Economic History Review*, VII, 1936-7, pp. 57-62); G. Schanz *Englische Handelspolitik* . . . (2 vols., 1881), I, Part i.

[5] For Gresham see W. Burgon, *The Life and Times of Sir Thomas Gresham* (1839); an article in the *Dictionary of National Biography*, XXIII, p. 142; and Richard Ehrenberg, *Capital and Finance in the Age of the Renaissance* (abridged English translation, 1928), pp. 252-5.

the administration for the works in which he manufactured mixed textile stuffs. At Ostend in 1784 Peter MacDonald was registered as a ship's carpenter while two Englishmen were registered as cordwainers.[6] Mention may also be made of a visit paid by one of the Wilkinsons to the Saint Michel ironworks at Saint Hubert in Luxemburg. He told the owner (Dom Nicholas Spirlet, abbot of Saint Hubert) that the best way to cast iron was in a reverberatory furnace and he strongly advised the use of coal instead of charcoal in such furnaces.[7]

The most important piece of English machinery introduced into the Low Countries in the middle years of the eighteenth century was the Newcomen engine. These pumping engines were working at Londelinsard (Charleroi) in 1721, at Sars (Charleroi) and Namur in 1743 and at the Haut Flénu colliery in 1753. In the 1750s and 1760s a number of Newcomen engines—usually built in the Austrian Netherlands or in the Principality of Liège—were introduced into the Hainult district.[8] When John Wilkinson visited the Liège region early in 1782 he commented unfavourably upon the quality of the casting of the cylinders of the Newcomen engines which he had inspected. He considered that the Belgian

[6] R. L. Lemoine, *op cit.*, pp. 276-314. For the economic development of the Austrian Netherlands and the Principality of Liège in the last years of Habsburg rule see H. van Houtte, *Histoire économique de la Belgique à la fin de l'ancien régime* (Ghent, 1920).

[7] Dom Nicolas Spirlet wrote on 9 September, 1782; " Puisque vous voules couler les canons, je vous félicite d'y employer des fourneaux à réverbère, car c'est la seul façon de les réussir, ainsi que me l'a assuré Mr. Wilkinson, qui est venu ici et qui a trouvé excellente la fonte de mon fourneau ; il a aussi examiné le fourneau à réverbère que j'ai dans mon abbaye pour y fondre les cloches et il le trouve très bien construit ; il m'a seulement faire observer qu'il me coûterait cher d'y fondre au bois, puisqu'il y faut 12 heures, tandis qu'à la houille la fonte se fait en 3 heures. J'ai cru devoir vous dire ceci pour votre direction " (Belgian State Archives at Arlon : Correspondence of the abbots of Saint Hubert : Register 25, folio 280). M. René Evrard has drawn my attention to this letter. There is evidence in a letter (written from Brussels on January 16, 1782) from John Wilkinson to Matthew Boulton (preserved in the Assay Office at Birmingham) that both John Wilkinson and his brother William had just visited the Liège district to inspect ironworks. John Wilkinson stated that he proposed to go on to the Hainault area. It is uncertain whether it was John Wilkinson or William Wilkinson (or both) who visited the Saint Michel ironworks. William Wilkinson visited the Continent on several occasions and he played an important part in modernising the French iron industry (at the Indret cannon foundry and at the Le Creusot ironworks). For the Saint Michel ironworks at Saint Hubert see René Evrard, *Dom Nicolas Spirlet* (Liège, 1952).

[8] H. W. Dickinson wrote : " An engine is stated to have been erected in a coalmine at Jemappe-sur-Meuse near Liège, prior to 1725 and to have been followed by others, but details are lacking " (*A Short History of the Steam Engine* (1938), p. 50).

pumps were no better than those used in England twenty years previously.[9]

Few English families can have played a greater part than the Cockerills in introducing machinery into Belgium—and also into neighbouring countries—in the early years of the nineteenth century. The elder William Cockerill, his sons and his son-in-law were largely responsible for reorganising on modern lines the carding and spinning of wool and the weaving of woollen cloth in Belgium. John Cockerill—in association first with his brother James and then with his nephew Conrad Gustav Pastor—guided the fortunes of the famous ironworks at Seraing which was the largest integrated engineering concern in the world in the 1830s. It was one of the first establishments in which the production of coal, pig iron, machinery, steam engines, river steamboats, locomotives, railway rolling stock, rails and armaments as well as many other engineering products were all controlled by one management. John Cockerill's business interests extended beyond the frontiers of Belguim into Holland, France, Germany, Spain, Poland and Russia[10] His brothers James and William eventually settled in Prussia where they established successful textile and machine-building businesses.

The achievements of the elder William Cockerill as a constructor of textile machinery can hardly be compared with those of his youngest son John as an ironmaster and engineer. Nevertheless the career of the founder of the family fortunes is by no means devoid of interest.[11] Less than justice has sometimes been done to the work of the elder William Cockerill. Henri Pirenne,

[9] John Wilkinson to Matthew Boulton, January 16, 1782 (Assay Office, Birmingham).

[10] It is stated in B. T. Barton, *History of the Borough of Bury* . . . (1874), pp. 233-7 that the elder William Cockerill and his sons went to Russia at the invitation of the Empress Catherine before going to Sweden. No authority is given for this statement. Barton also states that in September, 1802, James Cockerill returned to England to secure new machinery and skilled mechanics. He was arrested at Hull and imprisoned in York Castle. He escaped to friends in Lancashire and was later able to rejoin his father in Belgium.

[11] For the elder William Cockerill's career and for the expansion of the woollen cloth industry at Verviers in the late eighteenth and early nineteenth centuries see an article by Edouard Morren in the (Belgian) *Biographie Nationale*, IV (1872), cols. 229-30 ; Jean Simon Renier, " Histoire de l'industrie drapière au Pays de Liège " (*Mémoires de la Société libre d'Emulation de Liège*, second series, VI, 1881, ch. 4 and 5) ; Théodore Gobert, " Conditions de l'industrie du tissage à la fin de l'Ancien Régime. Les Cockerill à leur début " (*Bulletin de l'Institut archéologique liègeois*, LXI (ii), 1911, pp. 155-186) ; Pierre Lebrun, *L'Industrie de laine à Verviers pendant le xviiie siècle et le début de xixe siècle* (Bibliothèque de la Faculté de Philosophie et Lettres de l'Université de Liège, fascicule CXIV, 1948), pp. 334-40.

for example, when discussing the expansion of the Verviers cloth industry between 1797 and 1810 mentions only John Cockerill and ignores his father.[12] But John was only a boy during the period when William Cockerill (senior) introduced modern textile machinery into Verviers.

Little is known of the activities of the elder William Cockerill as a young man. The place and the date of his birth are unknown.[13] The register of the parish church at Bury shows that in 1779 he was living at Haslingden and that his occupation was that of a joiner. On Christmas Day of that year he married Elizabeth (Betty) Charles of Bury. In 1791 he was described as a maker of jennies.

Accompanied by his sons William and James the elder William Cockerill left England in 1797—a year of unemployment and distress—in the hope of establishing himself in Sweden as a constructor of machinery for the carding and spinning of wool. When this project failed he turned his attention to the timber trade. He was again unsuccessful and left Sweden for Hamburg where he chanced to meet a Belgian named Mali—the representative of the Verviers firm of Simonis & Biolley who had come to Germany to buy wool.[14] The elder William Cockerill agreed to go to Verviers and to construct machinery exclusively for Simonis & Biolley who were at that time one of the largest cloth manufacturers in the district.[15] Verviers was just recovering from the serious dislocation of trade caused by the two French invasions of a few years before—when business had been stagnant and many spinners and weavers had been out of work.[16]

[12] H. Pirenne, *Histoire de Belgique*, VI (1926), p. 173.

[13] P. Lebrun, *op cit.*, p. 234 gives the date of the elder William Cockerill's birth as 1759. There appears to be no evidence in support of assertions that William Cockerill (senior) was either a Scot (E. F. Heckscher, *The Continental System* (1922), p. 585) or an Irishman (J. S. Renier, *op cit.*, p. 165). In 1839 J. C. Symons described the elder William Cockerill as " a common blacksmith " who " could neither write not read (I believe) " : *Reports from Assistant Handloom Commissioners*, Part I (1839), p. 157 (report by J. C. Symons on Belgium).

[14] J. S. Renier, *op cit.*, p. 165, states that his account of the elder William Cockerill's engagement by Simonis & Biolley was derived from Mali himself.

[15] The exact date of the arrival of the elder William Cockerill at Verviers is uncertain. The years 1798, 1799 and 1800 have all been suggested by various authorities. William Cockerill (senior) himself (in a report to the Prefect of the Ourthe Department printed by T. Gobert, *op cit.*, pp. 180-3) stated that he had " arrived in France during the month of October, 1799."

[16] In November, 1794, an officer in the French army of occupation had reported on the Verviers district : " It is difficult to describe the unhappy situation of the people of this commune of 13,000 inhabitants most of whom lack both work and bread " (T. Gobert, *op cit.*, p. 163).

Having no resources of his own the elder William Cockerill had to rely upon his Belgian sponsors to put up the capital to erect a machine-building shop for him and also to supply him with the tools and raw materials that he needed. In 1800 he delivered twelve machines for carding and spinning wool—costing 12,000 francs each—to Simonis & Biolley who soon found that they were saving time and labour by using the new equipment.[17] Rival woollen manufacturers in the district, envious of the way in which Simonis & Biolley were forging ahead, asked the elder William Cockerill to supply them with the new machines but he did not do so as he was bound by his contract to work only for Simonis & Biolley.

In 1802 when he was in England to bring his wife and his youngest son John[18] to Verviers the elder William Cockerill persuaded James Hodson, a young Nottingham mechanic who had established a small machine building establishment in London, to join him in Belgium. Hodson married Cockerill's daughter Nancy.[19] It has been suggested that the elder William Cockerill brought Hodson to Verviers to build machines for other textile manufacturers than Simonis & Biolley. Hodson was not restricted by any contract with this firm. It seems clear, however, from the documents examined by Gobert and by Lebrun that there is no foundation for this allegation. The circumstances leading to the

[17] Grenville Withers wrote in 1839 that in Verviers wool was still being " carded upon the old-fashioned single swift engine, which was first introduced in Belgium in the year 1800 by the father of the present John Cockerill, and the first carding engine ever made here is still at work in the factory of Messrs. J. Biolly & fils at Verviers " (*Reports from Assistant Handloom Weavers' Commissioners*, Part I, 1839 : report by J. C. Symons on Belgium—appendix by Grenville Withers, p. 162).

[18] The elder William Cockerill's sons had been born at Haslingden in Lancashire :

(*a*) William Cockerill (junior) in 1784 ;
(*b*) Charles James Cockerill (usually known simply as "James") in 1787;
(*c*) John Cockerill in 1790.

Three other children of the elder William Cockerill died in infancy. See Thomas Woodcock, *William Cockerill and his Family* (reprinted from the *Haslingden Observer*, 1927: copies in the British Museum Library and in the Manchester University Library). E. Mahaim in an article in the *Vierteljahrschrift fur Sozial- und Wirtschafts-Geschichte*, III, 1905, p. 629 (n) states that John Cockerill was born on April 12, 1789, and was a year older than he himself supposed. But this John Cockerill died in infancy in 1789. John Cockerill (of Seraing) was baptised on October 2, 1790 : the exact date of his birth is uncertain. In 1884 Sadoine (director general of the Société Anonyme Cockerill) stated that John Cockerill had been born on August 3, 1790.

[19] Nancy Cockerill, daughter of the elder William Cockerill, was born at Haslingden in 1782. Her daughter Adele Hodson married Conrad Gustav Pastor who was appointed managing director of John Cockerill's iron-works at Seraing in 1829.

collapse of the local monopoly of the Cockerill textile machines hitherto enjoyed by Simonis & Biolley reflect no discredit upon the elder William Cockerill. In May 1803 the Cockerills and Hodson were in Dunkirk—probably because the authorities of the Ourthe Department were threatening to intern English civilians—and only the younger William Cockerill remained at Verviers. William Cockerill (junior) did not consider himself bound by his father's contract with Simonis & Biolley and he now began to make machines for other woollen manufacturers in Verviers. When Hodson returned from Dunkirk he joined the younger William Cockerill in making machines for several manufacturers. He too felt quite free to do this[20]

Before long Hodson had a machine-building business of his own and he had enough capital to offer generous credit to his customers. In November 1807 for example he agreed to supply 15,777 francs worth of machinery to a client who promised to make a deposit of 1,185 fr. and to pay off the balance in six annual instalments. Hodson's ledger for 1811-13[21] shows that his capital rose from 547.000 fr. to 798.000 fr. in these years. In 1813 he engaged a skilled English mechanic named William Watson. Subsequently Hodson extended his activities from building textile machinery to the mechanical spinning of woollen yarn. He employed about 100 workers in his spinning mill. The introduction into Verviers of modern textile machinery of the English type by the Cockerills and by Hodson brought prosperity to the town. In 1810 it was reported that there were 86 cloth manufacturers in Verviers and that they employed 25,000 workers. In 1827 when Friedrich von Motz, Finance Minister of Prussia, visited Verviers he commented on the high standard of living enjoyed by the wealthy local manufacturers as a result of the continued prosperity of the cloth industry.

Little is known of the elder William Cockerill's activities between 1803 and 1806. Possibly he was in England for at least part of the time. In 1807 he established himself at Liège which was the centre of a rapidly expanding industrial district.[22] Since

[20] To the complaints of Simonis and Biolley the younger William Cockerill retorted : " Having never entered into any contract with Simonis Brothers & Biolley I am surprised that I am now accused of having broken such an engagement. The only contracts that I have made have been with Lecoup & Meunier, Godar, and Jean Nicolas David " (quoted by T. Gobert, *op cit.*, pp. 175-6).

[21] Hodson's ledger for 1811-13 is preserved in the archives of Société Anonyme John Cockerill.

[22] For the early development of the iron and metal industries of the Liège district see A. Godin and A. Warzée, " Faire l'histoire des progrès de la fabrication du fer dans la province de Liège " (*Mémoires de la Société libre d'Emulation de Liège*, new series, I, 1860, pp. 293-538 : Part I by

the annexation of the Austrian Netherlands and the Principality of Liège by the French a great new market had been opened up for the textile and engineering products—including armaments[23]—of the manufacturing regions of Flanders, Hainault and the valleys of the Meuse and Sambre.[24] The elder William Cockerill set up his first workshop at Liège at the Pont des Arches but he soon moved to larger premises at the Pont des Jésuites (later the Rue de Régence). With his three sons he made carding and spinning machines and mechanical looms for the manufacture of woollen cloth. In 1809 it was stated that he was employing 144 adult workers in his machine shops[25] and 100 children in a workshop in which textile cards were manufactured. It has been stated that he constructed textile machinery to a total value of three million francs in seven years. Although the elder William Cockerill's main workshops for the construction of textile machinery were now at Liège he continued to use his old factory at Verviers and he also had a similar establishment in France at Reims[26] which was managed by his son William.

Early in 1809 an attempt was made to place the elder William Cockerill under police surveillance as he was still a British subject. Micoud d'Umons (the Prefect of the Ourthe Department) wrote

Godin, Part II by Warzée) ; Ludwig Beck, *Die Geschichte des Eisens*, III (1897), pp. 990-993 ; and P. Harsin, " Etudes sur l'histoire économique de la Principauté de Liège . . . au xviie siècle " (*Bulletin de l'Institut archéologique liègeois*, LXII, pp. 60-161). See also the books and articles listed in the bibliography of R. Evrard and A. Descy, *Histoire de l'usine des Vennes . . . 1548-1948* (Liège, 1948). The iron industry and metal working manufactures of the Principality of Liège had been among the most advanced on the continent in the seventeenth and eighteenth centuries. Skilled Walloon craftsmen carried their expert knowledge to Britain (e.g. Godefrey Box's foundry at Dartford and the Walloon cutlers at Sheffield in the seventeenth century) and Sweden (e.g. Louis de Geer of Liège who brought some three hundred Walloon ironworkers to Sweden in about 1616). In July, 1764, it was stated that the son of Samuel Garbett, the well known Birmingham ironmaster, was on his way to the Low Countries to examine " the methods of working in the famous iron-works there " (*Calendar of Home Office Papers, 1760-65* (1878), No. 1358, pp. 420-21).

[23] For the development of the Liège armaments industry see Maurice Anziaux, *L'industrie armurière liègeoise* (Brussels, 1899).

[24] For the economic development of the Belgian provinces in the period of the Consulate and Empire, see, for example, H. Pirenne, *Histoire de Belgique*, VI (1926), pp. 150-197 and P. Verhaegen, *La Belgique sous la domination française, 1792-1814* (two volumes, 1923-24).

[25] i.e. 80 carpenters, 14 blacksmiths (*forgerons*), and 50 locksmiths (*serruriers*) and tool-makers (*limeurs*). These figures do not include the foundry workers : see T. Gobert, *op cit.*, p. 182.

[26] Jules Burat, *Exposition de l'industrie française* : *année 1844*, historical introduction, p. 4.

on January 16, 1809 to the police authorities that " William Cockerill lived for many years in Verviers where he rendered inestimable services to the cloth industry which is of great importance in that town. He constructed many machines from English models at Verviers and he did this long before people had heard of Douglas who now claims to have invented these machines."[27] In a letter to the Prefect of the Ourthe Department, dated May 9, 1809, the elder William Cockerill gave some particulars of his business career at Verviers and Liège. He gave the following list of the firms (other than Simonis and Biolley) to whom he had supplied textile machinery: André de Heuflize fils (Sedan), Bernhard Scheibler (Montjoie), Frostorff (Montjoie), Ignace van Houtem (Aachen), Pranghe Hompt (Aachen), P. H. Pastor (Aachen), E. J. Kelleter (Aachen), Brass frères (Aachen), Fey frères (Aachen), Grand' Ry (Néaux), Maas (Néaux), Euffler (Néaux), Ponsardin fils (Reims), Derode, père et fils (Reims), Dillen Putmans (Louvain), Sauvage (Francomont), Angenot Homps (Verviers), Damzeaux (Verviers), Comblen et Dehasse (Liège).[28]

William Cockerill's youngest son John—although only nineteen years of age in 1809—was already showing those remarkable powers of organising and of administration that were soon to bring him to the fore as one of the leading entrepreneurs on the Continent. The elder William Cockerill gradually gave greater responsibilities to John and to his older brothers and the great extension of the family machine-building business at Liège between 1809 and 1814 owed much to their initiative and energy.

The Government recognised the value of the elder William Cockerill's services as an industrialist by granting him French citizenship in 1810. In the same year William Cockerill (senior) was a candidate for a Government prize awarded to inventors of outstanding ability. The prize was won by William Douglas, a Scottish engineer who had been brought over to France by Chaptal (Napoleon's Minister of the Interior) to construct modern machinery for the manufacture of woollen cloth. The elder William Cockerill, who regarded Douglas as one of his most

[27] Quoted by T. Gobert, *op cit.*, pp. 177-8.

[28] The elder William Cockerill's list included details of the number of sets of machines supplied to each customer. One set of machines for spinning fine yarn (à filer fin) consisted of " une machine à drousser, une machine à carder, une machine à l'avant filature (ou machine à bondins), (et) quatre machines à filer fin." One set of machines to spin coarser yarn (à filer gros) consisted of " une machine qui drousse et qui carde la laine en même temps, (et) deux machines à filer." The elder William Cockerill's letter of May 9, 1809 is printed by T. Gobert, *op cit.*, p. 177 *et seq.*

serious rivals, protested that his machines were as good as those made by Douglas. The jury responsible for awarding the prize examined samples of the elder William Cockerill's work and recommended that he too should receive a prize.[29]

Some information concerning the extent of the elder William Cockerill's activities at the height of his career may be gathered from the letters of his firm and also from Thomassin's industrial statistics of the Ourthe Department.[30] According to Thomassin the Cockerills were by far the most important builders of machinery in the Department. They made carding machines, spinning machines and looms as well as machines for shearing and pressing broad cloths. They were employing some 2,000 workers in 1812 and the value of their output of textile machinery was estimated to be two and a half million francs a year. The firm was also making textile cards to the value of over 80,000 francs a year. At this time the Cockerills owned or controlled factories not only at Liège but also at Verviers, Spa, Eupen, Ensival and Reims. They imported their first Watt engine in 1813 and this no doubt served as a model for the steam engines which they themselves were soon constructing.

The correspondence of James Cockerill between 1810 and 1812 shows how the Cockerills were pushing the sale of their textile machinery in France in the heyday of the Napoleonic régime. It has been estimated that about half their output was sold in France at this time. In September 1810 James Cockerill was at Elbeuf where he sold machines to Flavigny and Godet (two leading woollen manufacturers in the district) and to Pley of St. Omer. After meeting his father in Paris (October 1810) James Cockerill went on to Crest in the Drôme Department where he complained. "I am in a strange country to set up machines in. They know nothing of manufacturing and to teach them is useless."

In April 1811 he was back in Paris and forwarded to his father some money that he had received from customers in Lyons. In the following month James Cockerill was erecting machinery for manufacturers at Louviers. By the autumn of 1811 he was in Crest again and he also visited Chalabre, Limoux and Carcassonne. In a letter of November 15, 1811 he rejoiced over the discomfiture of his rivals. He wrote that "Douglas has four sets returned. Spineux is ruined. They offer their machines at credit for a year at 6,000 francs and yet nobody will have them. Collier can't

[29] T. Gobert, *op cit.*, p. 184 and Count de Becdelièvre, *Biographie liègeoise ...* (two vols., 1836-7), Vol. II (appendix), pp. 792-8.

[30] L. F. Thomassin, *Mémoire statistique du département de l'Ourthe* (Liège, 1879).

work."[31] His brother, the younger William Cockerill, was also active in France at this time. He ran a cloth factory at Reims which was destroyed by Russian troops at the end of the Napoleonic war. William Cockerill (junior) eventually settled in Guben in Prussia.

In Liège the former joiner of Higher Lane, Haslingden, might well survey with some satisfaction the ramifications of his far-flung industrial dominions. Having amassed a considerable fortune the elder William Cockerill retired from the family business in 1813 after the double wedding of his sons James and John to two sisters, the daughters of Phillipp Heinrich Pastor who owned large wool-spinning mills at Aachen and Burtscheid.[32] William Cockerill (senior) lived to see his son John become the guiding spirit of the largest and most efficient ironworks and engineering plant in Belgium. He died at Behrensberg near Aachen—the home of his son James—in 1832.

The Cockerills were not the only Englishmen who helped to modernise the Belgian textile industries in the late eighteenth and early nineteenth centuries. It has been seen that James Hodson of Verviers established works for the construction of textile machinery in 1802. Ten years later Thomassin estimated that the value of the machines made by Hodson and his partner Dejardin was about 57,000 francs a year. At about the same time Mather was making textile cards at Mons and probably ran a spinning mill as well. William Douglas—a former Manchester manufacturer who had been established in France by Napoleon's government—assisted in the development of the Belgian woollen industry since he supplied new machines to such leading manufacturers as Engler & Co. (Verviers), Simonis & Biolley (Verviers) and van Diest (Brussels). Several English skilled workers—Farrer,[33] Kenyon, Smith, Swainson, Thomas and others—were

[31] E. Mahaim, " Les débuts de l'établissement John Cockerill à Seraing " (*Vierteljahrschrift fur Sozial- und Wirtschafts-Geschichte*, III, 1905, pp. 627-48).

[32] James Cockerill married Caroline Pastor while John Cockerill married Jeanette Frederique Pastor. For Philipp Heinrich Pastor (1787-1844) and his family see H. F. Macco, *Geschichte . . . der Familie Pastor* (Aachen, 1905) and Albert Huyskens, *125 Jahre Industrie- und Handelskammer zu Aachen*, Vol. I (Aachen, 1929), p. 17 (portrait of P. H. Pastor) and p. 150 *et seq.* P. H. Pastor's sons manufactured needles at Aachen. William Cockerill (junior) married twice. His first wife (1810) was Ernestine Henriette, daughter of Bernhard Scheibler, who was a leading manufacturer of woollen cloth at Eupen and Montjoie. His second wife was Henriette Wilhelmine, daughter of Karl Georg von Maassen, the Prussian Director General of Taxes (1818-30) and Finance Minister (1830-4).

[33] This may be the same Farrer who later built textile machinery at Mons and was awarded a prize by the French Government in the Year X.

brought to Ghent by Lièven Bauwens in about 1800.[34] Subsequently John Collier of Paris introduced new machinery for shearing broad cloths to Verviers (1819) ; Topham brought new cloth-pressing machinery to Belgium (1825) ; Powell, Evans and James Ensor erected bobbinet looms at Ghent (1824-5) ; while Gibson and Thomas Wilson established at Brussels modern works for bleaching and printing calicoes.[35] Subsequently he set up a similar establishment at Harlem. Wood installed up-to-date equipment for bleaching into a factory at Antwerp (1825) while James Stuck showed how flax-waste could be used to the best advantage (1823). At about the same time J. Maertens-Smith of Tournai established works for the construction of textile machinery.[36]

On the collapse of Napoleon's empire the Low Countries ceased to be part of France. The Dutch and Belgian provinces were joined to form the United Netherlands. This change led to temporary but serious economic dislocation in the Belgian provinces[37] since the erection of new tariff barriers greatly restricted the former flow of Belgian manufactured articles into France and the Rhenish territories. Moreover when the Continental System ended Belgian manufacturers had to face severe competition from Britain. Eventually the Belgian industrialists gained some compensation by securing access to new markets in the Dutch colonies. But the cessation of hostilities in the Belgian provinces was followed by a period of unemployment and high prices which caused great distress. Thousands of unemployed roamed the countryside raiding farms and bakers' shops. Those out of work in Liège alone were said to number 17,000.

Under the energetic leadership of King William I the government took prompt measures to revive the economy of the country.

[34] E. F. Heckscher, *The Continental System* (1922), p. 281 states that Bauwens "started his machine spinning mills with the help of five foremen whom he had virtually kidnapped from England and whom he detained half with their consent and half by violence." It may be added that a certain Paul Harding was associated with Bauwens in bringing textile workers from Britain to Flanders. Harding, however, was caught, imprisoned and fined. Napoleon himself visited Bauwens' works in 1810.

[35] In 1827—when his output was reported to be 1,000 pieces of cloth a week—Wilson visited England and improved his methods on his return to Brussels.

[36] In 1823 Smith received a Government loan of 30,000 gulden (florins), repayable in five instalments : see R. Demoulin, *Guillaume Ier et le transformation économique des Provinces Belges 1815-30* (1938), p. 164.

[37] For documents on Dutch history between 1813 and 1815 see H. T. Colenbrander, *Gedenstukken der algemeene geschiednis van Nederland 1813-15* (The Hague, 1914).

The finances of the state were brought into order ; the tariffs of 1816 and 1821-2 provided a modest measure of protection for native manufacturers ;[38] a sum of 1,300,000 florins was set aside for loans and grants to industry (1821) ; the Netherlands Bank was refounded as a bank of issue ; a new bank—the *Société Générale des Pays-Bas pour favoriser l'industrie nationale*—was set up in Brussels with a nominal capital of fifty million florins to provide credit for manufacturers ;[39] the *Nederlandsche Handels-matschappij* was established with a capital of twelve million florins to foster the export trade ;[40] communications were improved by the building of some important canals ;[41] industrial exhibitions were held ;[42] and every encouragement was given to entrepreneurs to establish new undertakings.[43]

[38] W. L. Groeneveld-Meyer, *De tariefwetgeving van het Koninkrijk der Nederlanden* 1816-19 (Rotterdam, 1924). See also Franz Haumer, *Die Handelspolitik der Niederlande* 1830-1930 (1936). Although the general level of import duties was only 8 to 10 per cent. some imports were prohibited while subsidies were granted to encourage certain exports. Additional differential duties were introduced in the tariffs of 1821 and 1822.

[39] J. Malon, *Notice historique sur la Société Générale de la Belgique* (Brussels, 1863) and a centenary volume entitled *La Société Générale de la Belgique 1822-1922* (Brussels, 1922). The initial capital consisted of 30 million florins in shares (six thousand shares of five hundred florins each) and 20 million florins in State domain lands. By the middle of 1823 however, only 31,226 shares had been taken up—the King himself having purchased 25,800 shares. For Belgian banking see B. S. Chlepner, *La Banque en Belge*, Vol. I : *Le marché financière belge avant 1850* (Brussels, 1926).

[40] W. M. Mansvelt, *Geschiednis van de Nederlandsche Handelmaatschappij* (Haarlem, 1924). William I personally guaranteed the shareholders four and a half per cent. interest.

[41] Canals constructed in the Belgian provinces in this period included : the Brussels-Charleroi canal, 1827 ; the Pommeroeul-Antoing canal, 1823-6 ; a section of the Maestricht-Hertogenbosch (i.e. Meuse lateral) canal : this incorporated the completed part of Napoleon's Scheldt-Meuse canal ; the Ghent-Terneuzen canal, 1825-7. In 1830 Belgium had about a thousand miles of inland waterways of which very nearly two thirds were owned by the provinces. For Belgian waterways see W. H. Lindley, *Report on the Waterways of France, Belgium, Germany and Holland* (Cd. 4841 of 1909), pp. 41-54 ; the British Admiralty Geographical Handbook on Belgium (1944), pp. 504-537 and O. Teubert, *Die Binnenschiffahrt . . .* (second edn., 1932), Part ii.

[42] e.g. Ghent 1820 : Brussels 1830.

[43] For the economic development of the Belgian provinces in the years 1814-30 see Robert Demoulin, *Guillaume Ier et la transformation économique des provinces belges* (Bibliotheque de la Faculté de Philosophie et Lettres de l'Université de Liège, fascicule LXXX, 1938) ; C. Terlinden, " La politique économique de Guillaume 1er roi des Pays Bas en Belgique 1814-30 " (*Revue Historique*, Year 47, Vol. 139, January-April, 1922, pp. 1-40) : Rudolf Häpke, " Die wirtschaftliche Politik im Königreich

Few of the industrial concerns that benefitted from the King's enlightened economic policy ultimately enjoyed a greater measure of success than the engineering establishments of the Cockerills.[44] Already in 1815 William Cockerill's works at Liège were turning out steam engines and hydraulic presses. Already the reputation of the Cockerill family stood so high on the Continent that the elder William Cockerill's sons were extending their activities as

Niederlanden 1815-30" (*Vierteljahrschrift für Sozial- und Wirtschafts-Geschichte*, XVII, 1923-4, pp. 152-5) ; M. G. De Boer, " Guillaume 1er et les débuts de l'industrie metallurgique en Belgique " (*Revue belge de philologie et d'histoire*, III, July-September, 1924, p. 527 *et seq*) ; H. Pirenne, *Histoire de Belgique*, VI (1926), pp. 336-49 ; and Paul D. Evans, " King Willem I and Belgian Sericulture " (*Economisch-Historisch Jaarboek*, XIX, 1935, pp. 64-74). For the industrial revolution in Belgium see Gachard, *Rapport du Juri sur les produits de l'industrie belge exposés à Bruxelles : 1835* (Brussels, 1836) ; Natalis Briavoinne, *Mémoire sur l'état de la population, des fabriques, des manufactures et du commerce dans les Pays-Bas* (Mémoire couronné par l'Academie des sciences et belles lettres, Brussels, 1838) ; Natalis Briavoinne, *De l'industrie en Belgique* (1839) ; J. Lewinsky, *L'Evolution industrielle de la Belgique* (Brussels, 1911) ; L. Dechesne, *Histoire économique et sociale de la Belgique* (1932). For statistics of Belgian industry in the 1840's see Count d'Arrivabene, *Situation économique de la Belgique, exposée d'aprés les documens officiels* (1843) and Heuschling and Vandermaelin, *Statistique générale de la Belgique* (1841).

[44] Little has been written in English on John Cockerill but Continental scholars have brought to light the main facts about the career of this remarkable industrialist. See Heinrich Weber, *Beschreibung der Eisen und Maschinenfabrik zu Seraing* (Berlin, 1829) ; an article on " John Cockerill und seine Unternehmungen " in the *Journal für Gewerbetreibende*, 1829 ; an article by Nisard entitled " Souvenirs de Voyages. Le Pays de Liège " in the *Revue de Paris*, new series, XXIV, December, 1835, pp. 129-148) ; Count Antoine Gabrielle de Becdelièvre, *Biographie liègeoise* . . . (2 vols., 1836-7), II (appendix), pp. 792-8 ; an article in the *Moniteur Belge*, July 1, 1840 ; A. Lecocq, *Description de l'établissement de J. Cockerill* (Liège, 1847) ; E. Noblet and E. Sadoine, *Portefeuille de John Cockerill . . .* (4 vols., 1859-1888) ; H. Kuborn, *Histoire de Seraing* (1861) ; an article by E. Morren in the (Belgian) *Biographie Nationale*, IV (1872), cols. 230-9 ; Pierre Jacquemin, *Notice sur l'établissement Cockerill à Seraing* (Liège, 1878 : another edition, 1883) ; Pierre Jacquemin, *John Cockerill, sa vie industrielle 1790-1840* ; Ludwig Beck, *Die Geschichte des Eisens*, IV (1899), pp. 338-344 and 679-682 ; E. Mahaim, " Les débuts de l'établissement John Cockerill à Seraing " (*Vierteljahrschrift für Sozial-und Wirtschafts-Geschichte*, III, 1905, pp. 627-648) ; T. Gobert, *Les rues de Liège*, Vol. I ; T. Gobert, *Introduction du chemin de fer dans la province de Liège* (Liège, 1914) ; Heinrich Lotz, " John Cockerill in seiner Bedeutung als Ingenieur und Industrieller " (*Beiträge zur Geschichte der Technik und Industrie*, X, 1920 : Jahrbuch des Vereins deutscher Ingenieure, edited by Conrad Matschoss, pp. 103-120 : copy in the Patent Office Library in London) ; the volume entitled *Cockerill 1817-1927* issued by the Société Anonyme Cockerill in 1928 in celebration of the 110th anniversary of the founding of the firm ; and Raymond Hustin, *Les Cockerill et la cité de l'acier* (Brussels, 1944).

far afield as Berlin at the invitation of the Prussian government. In 1814 two Prussian visitors inspected the Cockerill's establishment at Liège. They were Frank and Beuth. Georg Anton Frank, an official in the Prussian Ministry of Commerce, was the leader of a small group of experts[45] who had been sent by Sack (the head of the Rhineland provisional administration in 1814-16) to report upon recent technical advances in the industrial regions on both sides of the Rhine that had been liberated from French rule by the allied armies.[46] Peter Beuth was a young Prussian official who—as a volunteer in Lützow's cavalry—had been billetted on the Cockerills at Liège and so had ample opportunities of visiting their works. The reports of Frank and Beuth led the Prussian authorities to invite John Cockerill and his brothers to Berlin. Here John Cockerill founded a factory for the manufacture of woollens by power-driven machinery and also large works for the construction of textile machinery driven by steam. John Cockerill's machine building works in the Neue Friedrichstrasse were the first in Berlin to be lit by gas. His brother William Cockerill (junior) settled in Guben in Lower Lusatia (1819) where for many years he successfully managed a large modern factory for the spinning of combed woollen yarn. The younger William Cockerill was largely responsible for the rise of Guben as a manufacturing centre. The textile factories established by the Cockerills in Berlin, Cottbus and Grünberg were eventually owned solely by John Cockerill. In 1816 John Cockerill made enquiries concerning the purchase of ironworks at Peitz near Cottbus but nothing came of the scheme.[47]

John and James Cockerill returned to Belgium. The sharp decline in the demand for their woollen machinery since the conclusion of hostilities[48] encouraged the two brothers to concentrate their attention upon the manufacture of other products

[45] Frank was an architect while his colleagues Johann Friedrich Tappert, Gottlieb Busse and Wilhelm Liepe were cloth manufacturers.

[46] For Frank's tour see W. Treue, " Eine preussische ' technologische ' Reise in die besetzten Gebieten im Jahre 1814 " (*Vierteljahrschrift für Sozial-und Wirtschafts-Geschichte*, XXVIII, 1935, pp. 15-40). In his report Frank stated that his colleague Tappert was satisfied that the machines built by the Cockerills for the spinning of wool were superior to those of their rivals.

[47] For the activities of the three Cockerill brothers in Prussia see H. von Petersdorff, *Friedrich von Motz* (2 vols. in one, 1913), p. 34 and W. Treue, *Wirtschaftszustände und Wirtschaftspolitik in Preussen 1815-25* (1927), p. 36, p. 139 and p. 215.

[48] A writer in the *Quarterly Review* (XXXI, 1824-5, p. 408 note) observed that John Cockerill " now (1825) makes 26 sets of woollen machines,

such as steam engines, pumps and hydraulic presses. In 1816 John Cockerill had an audience with the King of the Netherlands and in January 1817 William I sold the castle of Seraing (and the estate in which it stood) to John and James Cockerill for the trifling sum of 21,262 florins (45,000 francs).[49] Seraing had an admirable location from the point of view of the establishment of a new foundry and engineering works. It was close to the Cockerill's existing machine-building establishment at Liège. Its situation in the Meuse valley gave promise of excellent transport facilities by land and water. Adequate supplies of good coal and limestone were available in the vicinity. Workers were at hand since the inhabitants of the district had long been engaged in mining and in the working of metals. Seraing castle was quickly converted by the Cockerills into an engineering establishment superior to the famous Liège cannon foundry which had hitherto been regarded as the most important ironworks in the Low Countries. At first the Seraing establishment consisted of an up to date foundry (with two reverberatory and three cupola furnaces) and machine-building shops constructed on the same lines as British engineering works. Gas lighting was installed in 1819 ; a puddling plant in 1820 ; and a coke blast furnace in 1823. An early example of the work of the Cockerill's foundry was an iron bridge erected at Antwerp.[50]

The original intention appears to have been to make iron castings and to build textile machinery, steam pumps and steam engines but soon John Cockerill and his associates[51] were

where he formerly—before the peace (1815)—made 350 or 400. During the war France was open to him, and nearly one half of his supply went to that country; the remainder was sent to Saxony, Prussia and other parts of Germany. He attributes this great diminution in the demand for his machines, partly to the high import duties imposed by France, partly to Russia having prohibited all foreign cloth from entering her territories, but principally to the introduction of British cloth into Germany, of such qualities and at such prices as completely to baffle the competition of the German manufacturers "

[49] The royal decree authorising the sale of Seraing castle to the Cockerill brothers is printed by R. Hustin, *op cit.*, pp. 73-4. It has been stated that the property was probably worth about ten times what the Cockerills paid for it.

[50] It may be added that in 1822, on a visit to western Germany, John Cockerill went to Rasselstein (Neuwied) to examine the possibility of establishing a puddling plant there in association with the brothers Remy. The scheme for setting up a partnership fell through and the Remys built the ironworks themselves. Cockerill however sent some English puddlers from Seraing to help to start the new enterprise at Rasselstein.

[51] i.e. his brother James Cockerill, his nephew Conrad Gustav Pastor and the two skilled mechanics Poncelet and Wéry.

constructing many other engineering products.[52] Some years later an English observer remarked that " Mr Cockerill often boasts that he has all the new inventions over at Seraing ten days after they come out of England." Between 1818 and 1823 forty three steam engines were built to drive pumps and textile machinery.[53] The Seraing ironworks have been described as " one of the most perfect establishments in Europe."[54]

Before long John Cockerill was building steamships. In 1820 a Liège newspaper announced that the Cockerills had " just completed the construction of a steamship 75 feet long and 19 feet in width." " It was launched on the Meuse on the 9th of this month and travelled at great speed." In 1824 John Cockerill built the " Seeländer "[55] for service on the lower Rhine ; in 1825 he delivered the corvette " Atlas " (240 h.p. engines) to the Netherlands navy ; and in 1827 he constructed the " Ludwig " for the Rhine-Main shipping company.[56]

[52] G. M. Roentgen wrote: " De gieterij te Seraing van den heeren Charles James en John Cockerill is bij ver de beste in het geheele land; hier zi jn 2 reverbere-ovens, waaruit de ijzeren brug voor Antwerpen gegoten is en 3 cupola's, waaruit alle die stukken gegoten worden, die voor de stoommabinesen andere werktuigen, die aldaar vervaardigd worden, benoodigt zi jn " (Dr. M. G. de Boer, " Twee memoriën over den toestand der Britsche en Zuid-Nederlandsche ijzerindustrıe door G. M. Roentgen uit den jaren 1822 en 1823 " in the *Economisch-Historisch Jaarboek*, IX, 1923, p. 113). Later in the same memorandum Roentgen wrote: " Geen etablissement als dat van den heer Cockerill te Seraing bestaat in dit land, waar de werktuige, daartoe nodig, de enorme blaascylinders, stoommachines, pletmachines en over ge werktuigen met vereischte nauwkeurigheid en deugdzaamheid hunnen gemaakt worden, en te Seraing kan dit even goed als in Engeland gedaan worden, indien de heer Cockerill maar de nodige tekeningen en plans daarvoor worden gegeven. De heer Cockerill heeft daarbij een grot getal geoeffende werklieden om zulke werktuige te behandelen " (*ibid.*, p. 140).

[53] *Reports from the Assistant Handloom Weavers' Commissioners*, Part I, 1839 (report by J. C. Symons on Belgium), p. 157.

[54] R. J. Lemoine, *op cit.*, p. 314. John Cockerill's deliveries of steam engines included the following:

1819	2 (Jemappes and Mons)
1820	4
1821	1 (to Huart of Charleroi to work blast furnace bellows)
1822-3	2 (Tieu de Coeur)
1826-30	3 (Charleroi)

[55] H. Scrivenor, *History of the Iron Trade* (edn of 1854), p. 241.

[56] E. Gothein, *Geschichtliche Entwicklung der Rheinschiffahrt im 19en Jahrhundert* (Leipzig, 1903), p. 181. The engines and boilers of this vessel were designed by John Ericsson, the young Swedish engineer who worked for two years (1825-7) at Seraing. The results of the trials of the "Ludwig" were unsatisfactory and new engines had to be installed before the vessel was put into service (1830). Ericsson then went to England and—in

Within a few years of the establishment of the Seraing ironworks the Cockerills were exercising a considerable influence over the entire Belgian iron industry. In 1823 Lieutenant Gerhard Mortiz Roentgen (of the Netherlands navy) in a report on the ironworks of the Walloon provinces, praised the Cockerills for the liberality with which they passed on to other industrialists information concerning recent technical progress in England and elsewhere.[57]

Roentgen's visit to Seraing was a turning point in the fortunes of the Cockerills' ironworks. Roentgen was just returned from a tour in Britain where he had studied technical advances in the iron, engineering and shipbuilding industries. He was now inspecting the ironworks in the Walloon provinces. In January 1823 he reported to the Minister of Commerce that the Belgian iron and engineering industries were backward and had fallen far behind those of Britain. The United Kingdom had some 250 coke furnaces while the Belgian provinces had none at all. Roentgen criticised the vast majority of the Belgian ironmasters who still dreamed of the golden days of high wartime profits instead of adapting themselves to a world in which they had to face severe English competition. He considered that the ironmasters would be better employed in modernising their works rather than in clamouring for high duties on imported iron. He expressed his astonishment that ironmasters should give their sons a classical rather than a technical education. Roentgen declared that the introduction into the Belgian ironworks of steam power and of coke blast furnaces should be regarded as a matter of urgency.

Roentgen recommended that a big new engineering establishment should be set up with government capital and that an

association with Braithwaite—he built the "Novelty" locomotive which was entered for the Rainhill trials but failed to start. (See C. F. Dendy Marshall, "The Rainhill Locomotive Trials of 1829" in the *Transactions of the Newcomen Society*, IX, 1928-9, pp. 78-93). Ericsson subsequently emigrated to the United States (1839) where he made a name for himself as a designer of warships (e.g. the "Monitor"). He invented a screw propellor.

[57] G. M. Roentgen wrote: "Deze giererij heeft een zeer voordeelige invloed getoond op de gieterijen in de omstreken, en zelf op de meeste in die geheele landstreek; dit word ook door veele ijzergieters aldaar aanerkend; de liberaliteit, waarmede de heer Cockerill alle vorderingen, die hij maakt, of alle verbeteringen, die hij op zijn etablissement heeft ingevoerd of van Engeland heeft overgebracht, aan de overige ijzergieters mededeld, en hun zelfs behulpzaam is in het invoreen van zulke verbeteringen door het leenen van werklieden enz., is bewonderenswaardig en verdiend den dank van het gouvernement en der natie" (Dr. M. G. De Boer, "Twee me orien over den toestand der Britsche en Zuid-Nederlandsche ijzerindustrie door G. M. Roentgen uit den Jaren 1822 en 1823" in the *Economisch-Historisch Jaarboek*, IX, 1923, p. 113).

English expert should be engaged to install the most modern equipment. He thought that one of the existing Belgian ironworks might serve as the nucleus for this new undertaking. In his view only four establishments deserved serious consideration—those of Hannonent-Gendarme at Couvin, Orban at Grivegnée, Huart at Charleroi and the Cockerills at Seraing. Roentgen considered that Hannonet-Gendarme's works were unsuitable since they were located in a remote part of the province of Namur where coal was expensive while neither Orban nor Huart had the necessary technical qualifications to guide the destinies of the type of engineering works that he had in mind. The Seraing works, on the other hand, had an excellent location and John Cockerill was a man of exceptional technical skill and administrative ability. Roentgen recommended that the Cockerill's works should be extended by the erection of a coke blast furnace and rolling and slitting mills and that the well-known Scottish engineer David Mushet—of Coleford in the Forest of Dean—should be engaged to give technical advice on the reorganisation of the Seraing establishment.[58]

The Netherlands government promply accepted Roentgen's recommendations. In 1823 John Cockerill received a substantial loan to enable him to expand and reorganise the Seraing ironworks. He agreed to repay the loan in bar iron in ten years and to admit the ironmasters of the provinces of Liège and Namur "to his works to learn the true principles of the latest improvement in the art " of working iron.[59] The new capital was used to erect both a coke blast furnace[60] and rolling and slitting mills. The expert advice of G. M. Roentgen and David Mushet was made

[58] For Lieutenant G. M. Roentgen see M. G. De Boer, *Leven en Bedrijf van Gerhard Moritz Roentgen.* Roentgen was of German origin having been born in 1795 at Esens in East Frisia. His two reports on the British and Belgian iron industries (1822-3) have been reprinted (from the original manuscripts in the State Archives at The Hague) by M. G. De Boer in the *Economisch-Historisch Jaarboek*, IX, 1923, pp. 3-165. Roentgen founded important engineering and shipbuilding works on the island of Feyenoord opposite Rotterdam. Some of the skilled workers came from England and from John Cockerill's works at Seraing.

[59] H. Scrivenor, *History of the Iron Trade* (edn. of 1854), p. 241. The Cockerills had already made it a practice to allow neighbouring ironmasters to visit their works.

[60] This appears to have been Belgium's second coke-smelting blast furnace, the first having been erected shortly before at Orban's works. For Orban see H. Capitaine, *Essai biographique sur H. J. Orban* (Liège, 1858). In 1836 another blast furnace was erected at the Seraing works and on this occasion the Neilson hot blast was used for the first time in the Liège district.

available to John Cockerill. David Mushet[61] came to Seraing in 1823 and supervised the erecting of the new blast furnace. It was not an immediate success. Only after lengthy trials did it eventually work satisfactorily in 1830.[62] It had an output of ten tons of of pig-iron a day. The rolling and slitting mills, driven by three steam engines, were constructed from blueprints obtained from England by Roentgen.[63] John Cockerill's bold reorganisation of his works at this time included the acquisition of control over the Henri-Guillaume and Collard collieries. The foundry, blast furnace and machine-building works were now assured of a regular supply of coal. The collieries were modernised and new shafts were sunk within the grounds of the ironworks themselves.

The co-operation of John Cockerill, David Mushet and G. M. Roentgen—aided by government funds—had led to the establishment of one of the largest integrated enterprises in Europe where pig iron and engineering products were all made in the same works and under the same management. Men born in Lancashire, Scotland and Germany had come together to give a great impetus to the expansion of the Belgian iron industry.

There is a certain conflict of evidence concerning the extent to which John Cockerill employed skilled English workers in the early days of his engineering enterprise at Seraing. On the one hand there is the statement of Henry Maudslay that when he visited the works in 1823 he saw only a single English ironfounder there and that it was only after the British government had lifted its ban on the emigration of skilled artisans (1824) that they " have gone in flocks " to the Continent.[64] On the other hand S. Jackson informed an English parliamentary enquiry in 1833

[61] David Mushet held posts at the Clyde Iron Works and the Calder Iron Works before migrating to England where he eventually settled at Coleford in the Forest of Dean (1812). He was the first to appreciate the use that could be made of the Scottish deposits of blackband ironstone. He wrote *Papers on Iron and Steel* (1840). See an obituary notice in the *Minutes of the Proceedings of the Institute of Civil Engineers,* VI (1848); S. Smiles, *Industrial Biography* (1863), pp. 141-8; an article in the *Dictionary of National Biography,* XXXIV, pp. 429-30 and F. M. Osborn, *The Story of the Mushets* (1952). There is ample evidence of D. Mushet's visit to Seraing although—according to Mr. T. A. Seed—the surviving Mushet papers in Sheffield contain no reference to this aspect of Mushet's activities. David Mushet's younger son Robert improved the Bessemer process.

[62] R. Evrard and A. Descy, *Histoire de l'usine des Vennes . . . 1548-1948* (Liège, 1948), p. 121 and Fig. 79. As early as 1811 the Société libre d'Emulation de Liège had offered a prize for a coke-smelting blast furnace.

[63] R. J. Lemoine, *op cit.*, pp. 317-9.

[64] H. Maudslay in evidence before the *Select Committee on the Export of Tools and Machinery,* 1825, p. 35.

that when the Cockerills opened their engineering works " they employed a great number of English workmen, but I believe most of them have now returned to England." He added that John Cockerill paid Englishmen 7/- and 8/- a day but Belgian workers obtained only one or two francs a day.[65] In 1839 Grenville Withers stated that " great numbers of English workmen have been brought here (i.e. to Seraing) at various times ; but the policy has always been to get rid of them by any means, the moment their secret has been learned."[66]

John Cockerill was now in sole charge of the Seraing works since his brother James had sold his share of the establishment in 1823.[67] Despite the great extension of the Seraing works John Cockerill was unable to fulfil all the orders for machinery that he received. In 1824 it was stated that John Cockerill was importing " a vast quantity of machinery " from England because " his power of manufacturing is by no means equal to his demand."[68] A further expansion of the Seraing works would need additional capital. John Cockerill turned to William I and in 1825 the King agreed to invest a million florins in the concern and to become a partner in the enterprise.[69] At that time John Cockerill's works

[65] S. Jackson in evidence before the *Select Committee on Manufactures*, 1833, Qn. 2973 quoted by T. S. Ashton, *Iron and Steel in the Industrial Revolution* (1924), p. 204 (n).

[66] *Reports from Assistant Handloom Weavers' Commissioners*, Part I, 1839 (report by J. C. Symons on Belgium: appendix by Grenville Withers, p. 173). It may be added that many German and other foreign workers learned the new methods of ironworking and engineering at Seraing and later used the knowledge that they had acquired in their own countries. An English traveller in the Rhineland—describing Michaelis's ironworks on the Eschweiler-Stolberg railway—wrote in 1848: " The large works of John Cockerill near Liège, formed for many years a school that Germany did not possess, and hundreds of workers acquired there a skill in working rolls and steam-hammers, that has since proved to them a source of unfailing profit. Puddlers and roll-masters, instructed at Seraing, obtain (in Germany) wages nearly equal to those paid in England, if they are known to be steadily conducted " (T. C. Banfield, *Industry of the Rhine* (two volumes in one, 1846-8), Vol. II, pp. 236-7).

[67] James Cockerill settled in Aachen as a machine-builder. He appears to have retained his interest in the Liège (as distinct from the Seraing) ironworks.

[68] *First Report from the Select Committee on Artisans and Machinery, 1824*, p. 34: evidence of P. Taylor.

[69] An agreement of July 15, 1825 valued the Seraing establishment at 2,000,000 florins (or nearly 4,250,000 francs). The King of the Netherlands had provided half the capital. The contract between King William and John Cockerill (signed May 6, 1825 and approved by royal decree on May 24, 1825) is printed by Robert Demoulin, *Guillaume Ier et la transformation économique des Provinces Belges 1815-30* (1938), appendix 4, pp. 377-80.

were known as the "Koniglijk Etablissement te Seraing." William I took a close personal interest in the great engineering works and on one of his visits to Seraing he is said to have told John Cockerill : "Carry on with all your great enterprises and remember that the King of the Netherlands always has funds to spare in the service of industry." The arrangements made in 1825 survived the revolution of 1830 and did not come to an end until 1834.

By 1830 John Cockerill was making a great variety of iron products. His huge cast iron lion which was erected on the field of Waterloo was a somewhat unusual example of his work. He was at this time employing 2,500 men at the Seraing works and his weekly wages bill amounted to 70,000 francs. When Friedrich von Motz, the Prussian Finance Minister, was John Cockerill's guest for two nights in August 1827 he was greatly impressed by the vast size of the Seraing engineering works which were far more imposing than anything that he had seen on his recent tour of industrial establishments in the western provinces of Prussia. In a letter to his wife Motz wrote that three million gulden had been sunk in the machine building department alone ; that steam engines of 180 h.p. were being made ; and that the size of the undertaking was said to exceed that of any similar establishment even in Britain.[70]

John Cockerill's interests extended far beyond Liège and Seraing. He promoted a considerable number of new enterprises and erected iron works, textile factories and other establishments in various parts of Europe. Count Becdelièvre declared that "John Cockerill believed that he had a mission to extend manufactures everywhere and to fill the whole world with machinery." "To the present day (1837) he has consecrated his whole life and fortune to the attainment of this object.[71] And Nisard observed that John Cockerill had the very qualities necessary for the achievement of his ambitions—"the gift of saying little ; a knowledge of men ; the power of impartial judgment ; a disinclination to commit himself to paper coupled with the possession of a remarkable memory that retained essentials and forgot trivialities."[72]

The vast extension of John Cockerill's enterprises led to complaints in Belgium that too much power was being allowed to

[70] Herman von Petersdorff, *Friedrich von Motz* (two volumes in one, 1913), II, pp. 35-6.

[71] Le Comte de Becdelièvre, *Biographie Liègeoise* . . . (Liège, two volumes, 1836-37), Vol. II (Appendix), p. 789.

[72] Nisard, "Souvenirs de Voyages. Le Pays de Liège" (*Revue de Paris*, new series XXIV, December 1835).

fall into the hands of a single industrialist. In 1826 two citizens of Liège (named Hoto and Pacquo) were involved in a dispute with John Cockerill over a colliery concession. The point of view which they put forward in a petition to the Council of State was doubtless shared by other manufacturers in the Liège district who were alarmed at the growth of Cockerill's influence. The petitioners declared : " No one denies that Mr. Cockerill possesses great wealth and great talents. But others besides Mr. Cockerill may claim the right to exploit the national resources upon which the economic prosperity of the country is based. To justify his claims Mr. Cockerill should be in a position to argue that those whom he wishes to deprive of the fruits of their labours are not capable of conducting their affairs properly. He probably would not care to make such an allegation. Mr. Cockerill speaks of the needs of the Seraing engineering works and the desirability of linking the colliery with these works . . . but he already controls important coalmines in the district. He is at the head of several neighbouring works and he is associated with many more so that he cannot reasonably claim for his blast furnaces a monopoly of the supply of coal in the district. Mr. Cockerill's great business is becoming dangerously powerful. His insatiable complex is expanding continually and it needs more and more raw materials. It will eventually concentrate into one man's hands all the means of production. The remorseless activity of this one concern will destroy all its rivals." The petitioners claimed that if their appeal were rejected they would be " despoiled for the benefit of a man who may well suffer owing to the vast extension of his speculations."[73]

The petitioners were not far wrong, for the revolution of 1830 proved to be a serious blow to John Cockerill's fortunes. Belgium secured her political independence but only at the cost of a serious dislocation of her economy. Business languished so long as there was a danger of war between Holland and Belgium in which the Great Powers might be involved. Some years elapsed before the frontiers of the new state were finally settled since neither the Dutch nor the Belgians were willing to give up their claims to Limburg and Luxemburg. A tariff barrier now separated the Belgian manufacturers from their former markets in Holland and the Dutch colonies. Moreover Holland tried to divert to Dutch ports the considerable transit trade that Antwerp had enjoyed with the Rhenish-Westphalian industrial region.

The uncertain economic and political situation in Belguim in the early 1830s placed John Cockerill in a very difficult financial position. Although his business had had a large turnover in

[73] Quoted by Robert Demoulin, *op cit.*, p. 295.

recent years he owed large sums to the Dutch (now the Belgian) government and to private creditors. The sum of 1,800,000 francs was owing to Dubois, the well known Liège banker.[74] For two years there was serious unemployment in the Seraing ironworks. John Cockerill—like some of the other leading Liège industrialists —had in the past received substantial favours from William I of the Netherlands and he was attached to the King by ties of loyalty and friendship. It appears that he hoped to bribe General Daine and to provoke an armed rising in Liège in favour of the House of Orange.[75] Nothing came of these schemes but, in the circumstances, it was natural that Leopold I should at first have regarded John Cockerill with some suspicion.

True to his motto " Courage to the last " John Cockerill refused to admit defeat. He secured a few orders for machinery in 1831 and some more in 1832.[76] An order for a steamboat to ply on the Rhine—Cockerill had already built a similar vessel in the 1820s—gave a promise of additional employment for the ironworks. Confidence was being restored in Belgian business circles. The Société Générale, the Bank of Belgium and the Bank of Liège (founded 1835) were among the institutions which helped to finance new joint stock companies. It was as a manufacturer of armaments, rails, rolling stock and locomotives that Cockerill succeeded in re-establishing his position as the leading Belgian ironmaster. Just as he had once made himself indispensable to William I as a builder of machinery and steam engines so now he endeavoured to show Leopold I that the new Belgian State could not do without his cannon and locomotives. Before long he was supplying the Belgian army with armaments and the State railways with essential equipment. His services were

[74] Dubois himself was saved from bankruptcy by the timely financial support that he received from the Liège publishing house of Desoer. (Grégoire Dubois, founder of the Dubois bank in Liège had in 1804 married the daughter of the publisher C. J. Desoer). For the Dubois family see Paul Leuilliot, " Au Pays Liègeois. Un document d'histoire social " (*Annales* . . ., VIII (iii), July-September 1952, pp. 344-50). For the Desoer family see *Album édité à l'occasion du deuxième centenaire de la Maison Desoer 1750-1950* and an article by Jacques Stiennen in *Vie Wallon*, XXIV, 1951, pp. 157-185.

[75] H. Pirenne, *Histoire de Belgique*, VII (1932), Book 1, ch. 2, p. 60.

[76] The increase in the Belgian iron duties in 1831 gave the Belgian ironmasters substantial protection in the home market. The duty on pigiron was increased from 55 centimes per 100 kgm to 2 francs 42 centimes while the duty on bar iron was raised from 9 francs per 100 kgm to 12 francs 72 centimes. For Belgian commercial policy see E. Mahaim, " La politique commerciale de la Belgique " (in *Die Handelsbeziehungen der wichtigeren Kulturstaaten*: Schriften des Vereins für Sozialpolitik, LXIX, 1892, pp. 197-238).

recognised by the award of the Order of Leopold in December 1836.

In 1835 John Cockerill supplied some of the rails and rolling stock for the 12 mile state railway from Brussels (Allée Verte) to Malines which was opened on May 5, 1835. Robert Stephenson & Co. supplied some of the equipment and the first locomotives. On December 30, 1835 John Cockerill delivered a locomotive called " Le Belge " for this line.[77] To meet the orders which he received for railway equipment in Belgium and elsewhere John Cockerill again extended his works. He erected a second blast furnace, a copper smithy and a hammering workshop. A new factory for the construction of boilers for locomotives was opened at Sclessen on the road from Liège to Seraing. A foundry was set up at Tilleur. In 1839 when the Seraing works were turning out one locomotive every ten days J. C. Symons reported that " Mr. Cockerill's name is on all the locomotive engines on the Belgian railroads and I was told that he is the contractor for those now forming in Prussia."[78]

John Cockerill's unique position among the Belgian industrialists at this time enabled him to buy out the Belgian State which now held the share in the Seraing ironworks which had formerly belonged to the King of the Netherlands. In order to secure complete control over his establishment John Cockerill agreed to pay the government 3,500,000 fr. in twenty instalments. The contract was signed on September 7, 1834. On his return to Seraing from Brussels after the successful completion of the negotiations John Cockerill received a tumultuous welcome from his workers who wrote across the main entrance of the ironworks the proud boast : " C'est da nos tot seu."[79]

At the apex of his fortunes in the mid-1830s John Cockerill owned—or shared in the control of—a very large industrial

[77] A facsimile of John Cockerill's estimate of February 10, 1835 (written partly in French and partly in English) for constructing four locomotives for the Belgian State Railways is reproduced in *Cockerill 1817-1927* (1928), pp. 16-17. The cost of the three smaller locomotives was estimated at 27,000 fr each while the fourth cost a little over 30,000 fr. The estimate was accepted. The estimate has also been printed by R. Hustin, *op. cit.*, pp. 74-6.

[78] *Reports from the Assistant Handloom Weavers' Commissioners*, Part I, 1839 (report by J. C. Symons on Belgium), p. 157. A document printed by Symons stated that at Seraing " il s'y trouve un atelier pour la construction des locomotives: il y a en construction 82 locomotives pour la Russie, pour la Prusse et pour la Belgique: on en construit une en 10 jours " (Renseignemens sur les Ouvriers dans l'Establissement de M. Cockerill à Seraing . . .) (*ibid.*, p. 138).

[79] Walloon dialect for: " It all belongs to us ".

complex which was unique at that time. He owned or controlled about sixty separate establishments. Grouped round the main engineering works at Seraing were other establishments at Liège, Val-Benoit, Ougrée,[80] Tilleur and Sclessen as well as the Henri-Guillaume and Collard collieries. In 1839 J. C. Symons observed that " the motive steam power at the works at Seraing is 900 horse, divided among sixteen engines. The number of workmen there varies from 2,000 to 2,300 and Mr. Cockerill has also an establishment at his residence at Liège, where he employs 700 more men—all these in the production of machines from spinning machines to steam engines." At the same time Grenville Withers reported : " Seraing contains within its walls four coal-pits, two blast furnaces, rolling mills capable of making 200 tons of bar iron per week, extensive forges, and shops with 200 lathes for making locomotives, engines and machines of any description."[81] John Cockerill was also still actively interested in various branches of the textile industry as machine-builder, spinner of wool and flax, manufacturer of woollen and cotton cloths, calico printer and maker of textile cards and spindles. He had taken a leading part in the founding and running of the Banque de Belgique (1835) which had a capital of 20,000,000 francs.

In Belgium John Cockerill spun wool at Verviers[82] and flax at Liège ;[83] he manufactured printed calicoes at Andenne ; and he made textile cards and spindles at Spa. He also had substantial business interests in Prussia where his two brothers had settled, James living at Aachen and William at Guben. John Cockerill owned or shared in the control of woollen spinning mills in Berlin, Guben, and Grünberg and a cotton thread factory at Cottbus. Moreover he had a cloth factory at Przelbudz (Poland), a cotton mill in Barcelona, a warehouse in Amsterdam for the distribution of cotton goods, a plantation and a steam driven sugar manufactory at Surinam (Dutch Guiana), and a zinc mine at Stolberg (near Aachen). Some of these enterprises were part of the family

[80] John Cockerill leased the Ougrée colliery in 1827. The Société anonyme des charbonnages et hauts fourneaux d'Ougrée was established by John Cockerill in association with the Banque de Belgique in 1835.

[81] *Reports from Assistant Handloom Weavers' Commissioners*, Part I, 1839: report by Symons on Belgium, p. 157 and appendix by Grenville Withers p. 173.

[82] For the town of Verviers between 1815 and 1830 see J. Lejeur, " Histoire de la ville de Verviers. Période hollandaise et Révolution belge de 1830 " (*Bulletin de la Société verviétoise d'archéologie et d'histoire*, VII, 1906, p. 180).

[83] " Mr. Cockerill, the iron king of Liège . . . has already a very prosperous flax spinning mill at Liège of which the engine is of 90 H.P." (*Reports from Assistant Handloom Weavers' Commissioners*, Part I, 1839, (report by J. C. Symons on Belgium), p. 156).

business while others—such as the Société des Charbonnages et Hauts Fourneaux d'Ougrée and the Société des Charbonnages de Sclessin—were joint stock companies of which John Cockerill was one of the chief directors.

John Cockerill's foreign investments in 1839 included shares in the Nederland Stoomboot Maatschapij of Rotterdam and blast furnaces at Robiac in France (Gard Department). Few entrepreneurs at that time controlled so vast an industrial empire.[84] Most of Cockerill's concerns were in a flourishing condition in the mid-1830s but it was not to be expected that all the branches of so extensive an industrial complex could be uniformly successful. John Cockerill's calico print works at Andenne,[85] for example, although subsidised by the Government for some years, were eventually closed down and were later converted into a paper manufactory.[86]

[84] In 1839 J. C. Symons declared with pardonable exaggeration: " It is difficult to name any large enterprise of manufacturing industry whether in Belgium, Holland, Russia or the immense territory of the Prussian league with which Mr. Cockerill is unconnected, either as a shareholder or as the engineer from whom the machinery emanates " (*Reports from Assistant Handloom Weavers' Commissioners,* Part I, 1839; p. 157). A memorandum of the Belgian Minister of Public Works of February 7, 1839 stated that John Cockerill held the following properties in Belgium:

(*a*) Ironworks and engineering establishments at Seraing, Liège, Avroy Tilleur and Spa (valued shortly afterwards at 7 million francs);
(*b*) Collieries valued at 2,500,000 fr.
(*c*) Textile factories at Ghent, Jemappes and Brussels:
(*d*) A major share in the Saint-Léonard linen company at Liège (over one million francs); a woollen factory at Verviers and a paper mill at Andenne:
(*e*) a share in the blast furnaces at Sclessin (over 200,000 fr.); a colliery at Wandre (600,000 fr.); a steam mill at Sclessin (over 60,000 fr.); a steamship at Antwerp; the royal carpet factory at Tournai, forges at Hoyoux, the *Espérance* coalmines and ironworks at Seraing (joint stock company founded in 1836); the Société des Brasseries at Louvain; the forges at Chatelineau; and some steamships on the Meuse.

[85] J. Cockerill had established calico print works at Andenne on the Meuse in 1829 : an Englishman named Yates (who was related to J. Cockerill) was engaged to erect the machinery.

[86] James Thomson, *Notes on the Present State of Calico Printing in Belgium* (1841), pp. 5-6. Grenville Withers wrote in 1839 that the Andenne cotton printing works, which had been capable of printing a hundred pieces a day, were now closed. " A great deal of money has been sunk here, through Cockerill's foolish conduct " (*Reports from Assistant Handloom Weavers' Commissioners,* Part I (1839), appendix by Grenville Withers to Seymour's report on Belgium, p. 177). The Andenne calico printing establishement had been set up by John Cockerill in 1829. See R. Demoulin, *Guillaume Ier et la transformation économique des Provinces Belges*, 1815-1830 (1938), p. 265 and appendix vii (pp. 385-9) (letter from John Cockerill to Netscher, May 7, 1828).

The recollections of two French visitors to Seraing in the 1830's recall the profound impression that John Cockerill's great enterprise made upon his contemporaries. Nisard emphasised the significance of John Cockerill as a founder of new industrial projects in many parts of the Continent while Victor Hugo was impressed by the vast changes that Cockerill had wrought in the valley of the Meuse.

After a visit to Seraing in 1835 Nisard wrote: "This establishment is the largest in Europe. But it is only the head-quarters from which he (John Cockerill) extends his influence to all the countries that are prepared to open their doors to him. Every year he is responsible for the establishment of a machine building works, or a colliery, or a blast furnace or a cloth factory. He might be described as a Saint Bernard of industry who leaves the parent factory every year to speed the raising of new industrial establishments in every country where people believe that coal is meant to be burned and that steam engines are not come by easily.[87] "John Cockerill travels on the great highways in his coach. Here he builds furnaces and there chimney stacks. He covers fields with his tents and then when all his preparations have been made he erects the steam engines which have followed in his wake . . . and which breathe life into the great piles of bricks. And the next day the peasants hear a loud rhythmical noise coming from the factory—like the breathing of some enormous monster who, once he has begun to work, will never stop. And John Cockerill climbs back into his coach and government officials unsuspectingly sign his passport as if it referred to a consignment of wine and they do not realise that this silent man who seldom puts pen to paper is far morely likely to turn their old world upside down than many a revolutionary who has his pockets stuffed with political programmes and manifestoes."[88]

A few years later (1839) Victor Hugo gave a vivid description of a journey that he had made along the valley of the Meuse to Liège: "At this moment a singular sight suddenly presented itself. At the foot of the hills, which were scarcely perceptible, two round balls of fire glared like the eyes of tigers. By the roadside was a frightful dark chimney stack, surmounted by a huge flame, which cast a sombre hue upon the adjoining rocks, forests and ravines. Nearer the entry to the valley, hidden in the shade, was a mouth of live coal, which suddenly opened and shut, and, in the midst

[87] Nisard, "Souvenirs de Voyages: Le Pays de Liège" (*Revue de Paris*, New Series, Tome XXIV, December 1835), p. 132.

[88] Nisard, *op cit.*, p. 134. An English writer aptly remarked in 1838 that John Cockerill was "a manufacturer as Shakespeare was a poet—*nascitur non fit*" (*British and Foreign Review*, VII, 1838, pp. 549-550 and R. Demoulin, *op. cit.*, p. 230).

of the frightful noises, spouted forth a tongue of fire. It was the lighting of the furnaces."

" After passing the place called La petite Fémalle, the sight was inexpressible—was truly magnificent. All the valley seemed to be in a state of conflagration—smoke issuing from this place, and flames arising from that ; in fact we could imagine that a hostile army had ransacked the country, and that twenty districts presented, in that night of darkness, all the aspects and phases of a conflagration—some catching fire, some enveloped in smoke, and others surrounded with flames."

" This aspect of war is caused by peace—this frightful symbol of devastation is the effect of industry. The furnaces of the ironworks of Mr. Cockerill, where cannon is cast of the largest calibre, and steam-engines of the highest power are made, alone meet the eye."

" A wild and violent noise comes from this chaos of industry. I had the curiosity to approach one of these frightful places, and I could not help admiring the assiduity of the workmen, It was a prodigious spectacle to which the solemnity of the hour lent a supernatural aspect. Wheels,. saws, boilers, cylinders, scales—all those monstrous implements that are called machines, and to which steam gives a frightful and noisy life—rattle, grind, shriek, hiss ; and at times, when the blackened workmen thrust the hot iron into the water, a moaning sound is heard like that of hydras and dragons tormented in hell by demons."[89]

The two reports of the Select Committee on the Exportation of Machinery (1841) contain evidence of the relatively advanced state of the Belgian machine building industry at the time of John Cockerill's death. One witness (W. Jenkinson) declared that Belgium was Britain's most serious competitor as far as machine building was concerned.[90] Another (Grenville Withers)—modifying somewhat a view that he had expressed only a year or two previously—said that he considered Belgian textile machinery to be " as good, or nearly as good, as the best Manchester-made machines."[91] He added that Belgian engineering firms were supplying German customers with rails, locomotives and marine

[89] Victor Hugo, *The Rhine* (English translation by D. M. Aird, 1853), pp. 39-40.

[90] *First Report from the Select Committee on the Exportation of Machinery*, 1841: evidence of W. Jenkinson, Qn. 1478.

[91] *ibid.*, evidence of Grenville Withers. He referred in particular to the machinery made by John Cockerill at Seraing, by the St. Léonard company at Liège (flax spinning machinery) and by the Phoenix iron works at Ghent.

engines. Grenville Withers remarked that John Cockerill's works at Seraing had been " a wonderful nursery for machinery " and that " artisans in machine-making are becoming more dextrous every day."[92]

The second report from the Select Committee stated that " it appears that in Belgium machine-making is greatly advanced. The most noted works are at Ghent, Malines, Brussels, Tirlemont, Liège, and Verviers. There are about 8,000 mechanics in the country. The productions are steamboats, locomotives, and all descriptions of machinery for woollen and cotton (goods) and for paper-making. They are beginning to construct silk machinery. They export a great deal to Spain and other parts of the Continent as to North and South America, Egypt and Turkey. A great impulse has been given to this branch of their industry, as well as to manufacturers, through the agency of sociétés anonymes (joint stock companies) by means of which capital—the scarcity of which is universally felt on the continent—has been accumulated . . ."[93]

Although John Cockerill had re-established his business on new foundations after the revolution of 1830 he was not strong enough to escape unscathed from the storm of the commercial crisis of 1837. Belgian manufacturers—like those in the rest of western Europe—suffered from the effects of over-production, the excessive accumulation of stocks, and the uncertainty of the international situation. When the Banque de Belgique—in which he had invested heavily—suspended payments and when he failed to secure an expected order for rails for the railway from Paris to Belgium John Cockerill was unable to meet his obligations. Since his assets were valued at 26,000,000 francs the interests of his creditors—to whom 18,000,000 francs was owing—appeared to be amply safeguarded. John Cockerill authorised Gustav Pastor and Piercot to dispose gradually of all his assets except the works

[92] *ibid.*, evidence of Grenville Withers, Qns. 624, 668 and 793. But the witness considered that John Cockerill's steam engines were " very inferior to those used in this country ". In 1839 Grenville Withers had written: " Cockerill's machines are the best that are made on the Continent but . . . they are very inferior to English made machines, particularly roving frames, mule jennies and throstles for spinning cotton, worsted and flax. The best machine ever made here (i.e. in Cockerill's works) will require nearly double the power, will make double the waste, and will turn off twenty per cent less in a given time than a machine of the same number of spindles made at Manchester . . ." (*Reports from Assistant Handloom Weavers' Commissioners*, Part I, 1839: report by J. C. Symons on Belgium: appendix by Grenville Withers, pp. 173-4).

[93] *Second Report from the Select Committee on the Exportation of Machinery*, 1841, p. viii.

of Seraing and Liège so as to satisfy the demands of his creditors. Unfortunately at the height of the crisis John Cockerill was seriously injured in a road accident. When he had recovered sufficiently to return to Liège he was welcomed by great crowds. His workers again showed in no uncertain manner their affection for their employer.[94]

John Cockerill's creditors agreed to a brief postponement of payments due to them on condition that a committee of their representatives was associated with the management of the concern.[95] This committee suggested that Cockerill's works should be turned into a joint stock company and that application should be made for a state loan of a million francs.

John Cockerill, determined as ever to remain independent, conceived the characteristically grandiose plan of retrieving his fortunes by securing large orders from Russia for rails, locomotives and rolling stock. At that time there was only one short line in operation in Russia—the 27 km-railway from St. Petersburg to Tsarkoé-soélo (the summer residence of the Czar) which had been built in 1836-8.[96] Cockerill hoped to persuade the Czar to undertake the construction of a network of railways to cover his vast dominions. Despite his recent accident he undertook the long journey to Russia and secured an audience with the Czar but he failed to accomplish the object of his mission. On the return journey he was struck down by fever and died in Warsaw on June 19, 1840 at the age of fifty.[97]

John Cockerill's creditors sold some of the assets of his great concern but the heart of the enterprise—the Seraing ironworks—

[94] The following verses—addressed to John Cockerill on his return to Liège —may have few literary merits but Cockerill doubtless appreciated the warmth of the sentiments that they expressed:

Nul ne pourrait t'exprimer nos alarmes
Quand le destin cruel te frappa.
Ce jour nous fut de deuil et de larmes,
De tous un voeu vers le Ciel s'éleva.
Le Ciel fut juste, il te laisse la vie;
Marche toujours: qu'un bienfaisant génie
De paix, de calme, arrose ton sentier.

These lines are quoted by R. Hustin, *op. cit.*, p. 39.

[95] The committee consisted of Jules Nagelmackers (banker), Ferdinand Pirot (merchant), Felix van Hulst (lawyer), Victor Bellefroid (judge of the Commercial Tribunal) and D. Soyez representing the government.

[96] Subsequently extended to Pavlovsk.

[97] It was not until 1843 that the Czar undertook the construction of the two important lines from Warsaw to the Austrian frontier and from St. Petersburg to Moscow.

was reorganised as a joint stock company (with a capital of 12,500,000 francs). Half of the shares were held by the Belgian State. This company—the Société Anonyme John Cockerill—still bears the name of the founder of the concern. The first managing director under the new régime was Conrad Gustav Pastor, a nephew of John Cockerill who had for some time played a leading part in guiding the fortunes of the Seraing works. Within a few years the great engineering establishment had again been placed upon a sound financial footing. In 1846 the French minister in Brussels reported that Seraing was busily engaged in executing an Austrian order for a hundred locomotives.[98] In 1848 the first Belgian passenger steamship for the Ostend-Dover route was built at Seraing and in the following year the value of the output of machinery at the Seraing works was estimated at 18,000,000 francs.[99]

Even apart from the outstanding achievements of the Cockerills, British inventions and technical skill were of considerable importance in the development of Belgian manufactures during the period of the industrial revolution. The introduction of the steam engine for example owed much to British engineers. Among the earliest Watt engines to be erected in Belgium were one which was installed by the Perier brothers of Chaillot (Paris) at the Produits colliery (Jemappes) and another which was set up by Samuel Dobbs (an Englishman working at Eschweiler and Aachen) for Hubert Sauvage of Ensival. Woolf compound steam engines, made by Humphrey Edwards of Paris, were erected at the Escouffiaux coalmine (1817) and at the Grand-Hornu colliery (1821). These engines were popular in Belgium and in France as they consumed less coal than the Watt steam engines.[100]

In Napoleon's day Thomassin, in a report on the Ourthe Department, referred to Nicholas Dell's up-to-date rolling mills at Maseyck, Landrecies and Waldoz. In the 1820s coke-smelting furnaces were erected by Orban and by John Cockerill. Orban visited England several times to study new methods of working

[98] H. Pirenne, *op cit.*, VII (1932), p. 95.

[99] Ludwig Beck, *Die Geschichte des Eisens*, IV (1899), p. 687.

[100] Grenville Withers stated in 1841 that English steam engines were "getting into very great disrepute " on the Continent as they consumed so much fuel. In England coal was cheap and inadequate attention was paid to fuel economy. But in France and Belgium coal was usually more expensive than in England and steam engines which were economical in the use of fuel were in great demand. In England Woolf compound engines were made by Messrs. Hall of Dartford. See Grenville Withers's evidence before the *Select Committee on the Exportation of Machinery*, 1841 (*First Report*, Qn 640).

iron.[101] In 1836 the hot blast was used in a new furnace at Seraing. Thomas Bonehill erected a cannon foundry and a small coke furnace at Hourpes-sur-Sambre for a company in which the King of the Netherlands was a shareholder (1825). Subsequently he erected rolling mills at Zône (1833) and Marchienne (1835) in the Charleroi district and blast furnaces at Dohain by Verviers (1847) and Thy-le-Chateau. He is said to have supervised the erection of at least forty ironworks and engineering plants in Belgium, France and Germany. Eventually in 1855 Bonehill set up a successful engineering establishment of his own at Marchienne which had ten reverberatory (puddling) and four other furnaces.[102] Rolling mills were erected by Harold Smith for the Couillet company (1835) and by Granville for A. Goffart of Monceau-sur-Sambre (1838). Grenville Withers had an engineering establishment at Marchienne in the 1830s. A machine building plant at Ghent—established by two Scots named Duncan and Grant—was taken over in the early 1820s by Huyttenns-Kerremans who founded the famous Phoenix engineering works. These were managed by two Englishmen—first by Bell and later by Windsor—and were described in 1841 by J. E. Tennent as " certainly the most admirably arranged establishment that I ever saw—those of England not excepted."[103]

Although the most important early Belgian railways were national lines built by the Government—and Belgian firms supplied much of the equipment—nevertheless British technical knowledge and engineering skill played a part in the construction of Belgian railways. Later, when private companies began to build railways the co-operation of British capitalists and contractors was secured. In Belgium the first " railways " were constructed at collieries to transport coal in horse-drawn waggons. A line of this kind was built in 1830 at Saint-Ghislain to join

[101] G. M. Roentgen stated however that Orban did not learn very much from his investigations. He wrote: " De heer Orban is verscheideen malen in Engeland geweest met het but om de ijzerwerken aldaar te zien, doch heeft weinig kennis daarvan medegebract, en, geheel ontbloot van mechanische kundigheden, noch ijzerfabrikant zijnde, is het niet te verwonderen dat werke, ne zijne eigene plans opgericht, weinig verdineste hebben " (see *Economisch-Historisch Jaarboek*, IX, 1923, p. 126).

[102] For Thomas Bonehill see E. Stainier, *Histoire commerciale de la métallurgie dans le district de Charleroi de 1829 à 1867* (second edition, 1873) p. 17 and Ludwig Beck, *Die Geschichte des Eisens*, IV (1899), p. 343, pp. 683-5 and p. 979.

[103] J. Emerson Tennent, M.P., *Belgium* (two volumes, 1841), I, p. 67. It may be added that in 1839 J. C. Symons reported that English capitalists were contemplating the establishment of a large factory at Malines to make locomotives, steam engines and flax-spinning machinery: see *Reports from Assistant Handloom Weavers' Commissioners*, Part I, 1839, p. 157

the Grand-Hornu colliery to the Mons-Condé canal. This led to a riot on the part of the carters who had formerly carried the coal and the mansion of the managing director of the colliery was sacked.[104]

When Belgium secured her independence both the Government and a number of leading industrialists (such as John Cockerill) realised that the country would benefit greatly from the construction of a net-work of railways.[105] Belgium had an exceptionally favourable geographical location from the point of view of handling transit traffic between Antwerp and western Germany. Far-seeing German industrialists (such as Fritz Harkort) and statesmen (such as Friedrich Motz) also appreciated the advantages that would be secured by the building of a railway between Antwerp and Cologne.

The Belgian government instructed two Belgian engineers (Simonis and de Ridder) to report on the problem. In 1831 they suggested that a railway should be built to link Antwerp with Malines, Liège, Aachen and Cologne. A Belgian law of May 1st, 1834 provided for the construction by the State of a network of railways. Malines was to be the focal point. From this centre railways were to radiate to the north to Antwerp ; to the south-east to Liège, Aachen and Cologne ; to the west to Ghent and Ostend ; and to the south-west to Mons and the French frontier. The length of lines authorised by this law was 246 miles. It was decided that the first lines to be built should be those between Malines and Brussels and between Antwerp and Mons. The railways were built by the State but much of the initial capital was raised in London by the Rothschilds between 1836 and 1840.[106]

King Leopold invited George Stephenson to Belgium in 1835 to discuss the proposed network of State railways. Some of Stephenson's suggestions were embodied in a law of 1837 which authorised the construction of a further 95 miles of railways. Robert Stephenson supplied the three locomotives (" La Flèche ", " Le Stephenson " and " L'Eléphant ") which ran on the first

[104]The minutes of the board of directors of the Bois-du-Luc colliery record in 1830 a lively discussion on a proposal to build a tramway for horse-drawn vehicles (R. Hustin, *op. cit.*, p. 30).

[105]While the Belgian provinces were still united with Holland John Cockerill had—in 1829—applied unsuccessfully to King William I of the Netherlands for a concession to build a railway from Antwerp to Brussels: see Robert Demoulin, *Guillaume Ier et la transformation économique des Provinces Belges 1815-30* (1938), p. 116.

[106]Count Corti, *The Reign of the House of Rothschild* (English translation, 1928), p. 114.

Belgian railway—the short line from Brussels to Malines—when it was opened on May 5th, 1835.[107] Later in the same year Robert Stephenson delivered two further locomotives (" Rapide " and " Eclair ") for use on this line. An English locomotive was sent from Malines to Seraing and it was carefully copied.[108] In December, 1835 John Cockerill's first locomotive " Le Belge " was ready for service on the Brussels-Malines line. In the early years of the Belgian railways 29 locomotives were purchased from Robert Stephenson & Co. but by 1842 the Seraing works had provided 68 locomotives for the State lines.

When the Belgian State had built the main railway network the government granted concessions to private companies to construct secondary lines. In 1845 eight such companies were founded in London (under Belgian law) to build the following lines : the Sambre and Meuse ; the West Flanders ; the Namur-Liège ; the Charleroi-Erquilines ; the Tournai-Jourbise- Landen-Hasselt ; the Anglo-Belgian ; the Belgian Grand Junction ; and the Great Luxemburg. Over £6,000,000 was subscribed in Britain for the construction of these lines.[109]

George Stephenson visited Belgium twice in 1845 to advise the companies that had been formed to build the Sambre and Meuse Railway and the West Flanders Railway.[110] British contractors (such as Thomas Brassey ; Mackenzie, Barry & Co ; and W. P. Richards & Co.) were concerned with the construction of several of the lines. The rails, locomotives and rolling stock were usually purchased from the Société Anonyme John Cockerill and other Belgian firms[111] British railway enterprise in Belgium was not very successful. As early as 1852 most of the lines—generally still unfinished—were purchased by Belgian capitalists.

[107]In May, 1834 Tayleur & Co. (Vulcan Foundry) received an order from the Belgian Government for a locomotive. Robert Stephenson was associated with the Vulcan Foundry.

[108]Evidence of Grenville Withers in the *First Report from the Select Committee on the Exportation of Machinery*, 1841, Qn 617.

[109]L. H. Jenks, *The Migration of British Capital to 1875* (1927), pp. 150-2.

[110]Samuel Smiles, *The Life of George Stephenson* (1858), ch. 33.

[111]For the early development of Belgian railways see D. Lardner, *Railway Economy* (1850). ch. 17; Perrot, " Histoire des chemins de fer belges " (*Bulletin de la commission centrale de statistique de Belgique*, Vol. II, 1846); F. Loisel, *Annuaire special des chemins de fers belges* (Brussels, 1867); L. Avakian, " Le rythme de développement des voies ferrées en Belgique de 1835 à 1935 " (*Bulletin de l'Institut de Recherches économiques* (Louvain), III, 1935-6) and A. R. Bennett, " The West Flanders Railway Locomotives " (*The Locomotive*, XIV, p. 142 *et seq*).

No one would wish to exaggerate the part played by British—or other foreign—engineers, machine builders, merchants, contractors, and capitalists in fostering the industrial revolution in Belgium. The Belgians themselves were quick to realise that their little country possessed assets which could be turned to advantage in the machine age. They were favourably placed to handle a vast transit traffic between overseas territories and the whole of central Europe. They had adequate supplies of coal and iron.[112] They had the tradition of skilled craftsmanship in the metal and textile industries. They had good communications by road, river and canal. In Antwerp they had both a great port and a great centre of finance. They owed much to the French who opened the Scheldt and—in the period of the Consulate and Empire—did much to foster the economic development of the Belgian provinces. They owed much to William I of the Netherlands who actively pursued a policy of giving all possible support to industry. And after they gained their independence they owed much to Leopold I who realised the necessity of constructing quickly a network of railways. The Belgians therefore gained much from their own exertions. They have, however, not failed to realise the significance of the work of the Cockerills and other English entrepreneurs and skilled workers who had a share in bringing about the industrialisation of Belgium.

[112]Until about 1865 the output of iron ore in Belgium covered the home demand and there was a surplus which was exported to France and Germany. Subsequently however the Belgian iron industry came to depend almost entirely upon imported raw material: see A. Delmer, " La question du minérai de fer en Belgique " (*Annales des Mines de Belgique*, XVII, 1912, pp. 853-940).

IV. GERMANY

6. BRITISH INFLUENCE UPON THE INDUSTRIAL REVOLUTION IN GERMANY

SINCE the industrial changes of the second half of the eighteenth century turned Britain into the workshop of the world it was to this country that Continental manufacturers turned for new machinery, steam engines and skilled workers when they began to modernise their own industries. In the hundred years between 1770 and 1870 the Continent benefitted from British industrial experience and capital. Germany was no exception. But some German historians have failed to acknowledge the debt which early German industry owed to British machinery and technical skill.

The two main phases of British influence upon industrialisation on the Continent were separated by the Napoleonic Wars. In the last quarter of the eighteenth century foreigners were mainly interested in (manual and water-driven) textile machinery and steam engines to drive pumps while after 1815 Continental manufacturers wanted improved power-driven machinery to replace old fashioned appliances. And they were now installing a wider variety of machines and processes than they had done before 1800.

For many years Britain jealously guarded her inventions and skilled labour. In 1696 the export of stocking frames was forbidden and between 1750 and 1795 several Acts were passed to prohibit the export of many machines, models and drawings.[1] But occasional heavy penalties—a fine of £500 was imposed

[1] For details see Appendix (A) of the *Report from the Select Committee on the Export of Tools and Machinery*, 1825. An act of 1750 prohibited the export of tools used in the wool and silk manufactures; an Act of 1774 prohibited the export of tools in the cotton and linen manufactures; an Act of 1781 prohibited the export of tools, models and plans in the woollen, linen, cotton and silk manufactures; an Act of 1782 prohibited the export of blocks and engines used in calico, cotton and linen printing; an Act of 1785 prohibited the export of tools and utensils used in the iron and steel manufactures. An Act of 1786 repealed (in part) the Act of 1785 but prohibited another long list of tools and utensils. The Act of 1786 was a temporary one but it was renewed annually until 1795 when it was made permanent. On the other hand the export of wool-cards was allowed to the British North American colonies (Act of 1775) and elsewhere (Act of 1786). An Act of 1799 allowed Matthew Boulton to export machinery to Russia to erect a mint. Schedules of prohibited machinery appeared in the Customs Regulation Act of 1825 and again in an Act of 1833.

at Lancaster upon a German named Baden in 1785[2]—did not seriously deter foreigners from evading or defying the law.[3]

The very manufacturers who clamoured for the prohibition of the export of machinery were sometimes prepared to connive at breaches of the law. In 1787 Matthew Boulton complained bitterly when the young Freiherr vom Stein persuaded a mechanic to let him see a Boulton and Watt steam engine at Barclay and Perkins' brewery in London but shortly afterwards he entertained the intruder at Handsworth and discussed business with him.[4]

Some machinery was sold legally under Treasury license[5] but this relaxation of the law was not extended to spinning machinery.[6] In 1825 the Select Committee on the Export of Tools and Machinery proposed no change in the law but recommended that licenses should continue to be issued for the export of machinery " not likely to be prejudicial to the trade or manufactures of the United Kingdom ". Sixteen years later another Select Committee proposed the repeal of the laws prohibiting

[2] James A. Mann, *The Cotton Trade of Great Britain . . .* (1860) pp. 17-18.

[3] Britain was not the only country which tried to stop the export of machinery. For the efforts of the French authorities to prevent Jacquard looms from leaving France see the documents printed by G. Bourgin and H. Bourgin, *Le Régime de L'Industrie en France de 1814 à 1830*, I (1912), p. 147 ff, II, p. 228 ff.

[4] G. S. Ford, " The Lost Year in Stein's Life " in *On and Off the Campus* (University of Minnesota Press, 1938), pp. 161-203; J. Carswell, *The Prospector . . . R. E. Raspe* (1950).

[5] J. D. Hume told the Select Committee on the Export of Machinery, 1841 that the granting of such licenses was founded upon an undefinable but extensive constitutional power residing in the Lord High Treasurer. Huskisson had admitted in the House of Commons (on February 24, 1825) that " he had taken it upon himself to exercise a discretion which, although perhaps not strictly legal, he hoped the House would not consider criminal, in allowing the export of some articles of machinery, such as hydraulic presses and others, against the prohibition of which all mankind agreed."

[6] This was probably due to pressure from the Manchester Chamber of Commerce: see Arthur Redford, *Manchester Merchants and Foreign Trade, 1794-1858* (1934), p. 133. The Manchester Chamber of Commerce argued that " machinery cannot be classed either with raw produce or with manufactures. It differs essentially in character from both these great objects of commerce, and should be dealt with, in the arrangement of our general policy, according to its peculiar and distinctive properties. It consists of the concentrated skill of the country, embodied in a form by which we are enabled to produce our manufactures at a much lower price than we could otherwise do " (Circular letter of March 30, 1825 in the MS *Proceedings of the Manchester Chamber of Commerce* (Manchester Public Library)).

the export of machinery and this was done in 1843. The Committee reported that in 1840 British exports of machinery had amounted to nearly £600,000 (official value) of which £85,000 represented German purchases.[7]

Skilled workers too were forbidden to leave Britain by Acts of 1719 and 1750 which were not repealed until 1824. But there were practical difficulties in enforcing the laws.[8] Artisans who were really determined to emigrate usually managed to leave the country. The occasional punishment of a foreign labour recruiting agent and the prosecution of intending emigrants by their employers was no real deterrent.[9] The desire to emigrate was naturally strongest when a trade depression caused unemployment. Most emigrants went to English-speaking territories overseas but the small minority who found their way to the Continent included some highly skilled men.[10] Germany secured only a relatively small proportion of the British workers who went to the Continent. The exodus of British artisans to Germany was not as great as to France but a comparatively small number of Englishmen played a significant rôle in the early stages of the industrial revolution in Germany.[11]

[7] *First Report from the Select Committee . . . (on) the Export of Machinery, 1841*, Appendix 7.

[8] The Select Committee on Artisans and Machinery in its *Sixth Report* (May 19, 1824) stated that " it is extremely difficult, if not impossible, in this country, by any mode of executing the present laws, or by any new law, to prevent artisans, who may be so determined, from going out of the country ". The Select Committee therefore recommended that the laws should be repealed.

[9] John Martineau told the Select Committee on Artisans and Machinery, 1824, that foreign labour recruiting agents risked heavy penalties " but the punishment of the workmen is a very trivial one; it is merely that of giving bail to appear at the next Sessions, and to enter into a bond not to leave the kingdom . . ." (First Report, p. 11).

[10] Arthur Redford, *Labour Migration in England* (1926), p. 106 and table—based upon defective Custom House returns—in G. R. Porter, *The Progress of the Nation* (edn. of 1851), p. 128. Sir John Clapham remarks that the official British figures for emigration to places other than North America, New Zealand and Australia seem " quite inadequate " (*An Economic History of Modern Britain*, I, 490).

[11] The number of British artisans permanently and temporarily resident in France in the 1820s has probably been exaggerated. A Mr. Alexander told the Select Committee on Artisans and Machinery (1824) that 16,000 English artisans had gone to France in 1822 and 1823. In 1825 Alexander Galloway told the Select Committee on the Export of Tools and Machinery (1825) that he estimated the total number of English artisans in France at between 15,000 and 20,000. These statements have been quoted by later writers without comment. But a contemporary contributor to the *Quarterly Review* (XXX, 1824-5, p. 392) after making careful enquiries asserted that Galloway's estimates were " grossly exaggerated ". His own belief was that in 1824 there were about 15,000 English residents in France of whom only 1,300 or 1,400 were artisans.

The inventions which revolutionised the British textile industries were among the earliest to attract attention in Germany. In 1794 Johann Gottfried Brügelmann, having worked in Arkwright's Cromford (Derbyshire) cotton mill, installed English machinery in one of the first mechanical spinning mills—driven by waterpower—to be established in Germany. This mill was situated near Ratingen, east of Düsseldorf, and the village that developed around it was appropriately named Kromford.[12] But many years passed before large scale cotton production on modern lines developed in western Germany.[13] Even in the forties, when Banfield visited the important textile centre of the Wupper valley, only Jung's factory at Elberfeld—where the millwork was English—could be compared with a contemporary Lancashire mill.[14]

Saxony, with its old established textile industries—coarse calicoes in the Erzgebirge (Chemnitz) and muslins in the Voigtland (Plauen)—quickly showed a lively interest in the new English machines.[15] In 1791 the Saxon Government sent Baumgärtel to England to investigate recent textile inventions. On his return he tried to build a spinning machine but failed. He succeeded, however, in constructing a mechanical shuttle (1792) which—for a time—enabled the Voigtland handloom weavers to imitate Lancashire muslins with some success. Baumgärtel also set up a cloth shearing machine in 1794.

The appearance in 1796 at the Leipzig Fair of a Manchester

[12] W. Treue, " Eine preussische ' technologische ' Reise in die besetzten Gebiete . . . 1814 " (*Vierteljahrschrift fur Wirtschafts-und Sozial-Geschichte*, XXVIII (1935), p. 27). In 1802—the year of his death—J. G. Brügelmann set up a second factory at Munich which was in charge of his son Jakob Wilhelm but this venture failed and the undertaking was acquired by the Bavarian Government. R. M. R. Dehn, *The German Cotton Industry* (1913) p. 3 gives 1783 as the date of the establishment of the Kromford (Ratingen) mill.

[13] Christian Weiss—who travelled extensively in England and France—set up a modern spinning mill at Langensalza in 1807 and did well at the time of the Continental System. But in 1817 he began to change over to flax spinning.

[14] T. C. Banfield, *Industry of the Rhine* (2 vols. in one, 1846), II, p. 144. He wrote: " The mill-work is English, we believe, from Liverpool; the spinning frames . . . are from Koechlin's works at Mülhausen in France ". T. Lockett, in evidence before the *Select Committee on Copyright and Designs*, 1840 (Qn 8785) stated that it was only in 1839 that the first power-looms for calico printing were introduced into Berlin. They were built by two mechanics from Sharp, Roberts and Co. of Manchester.

[15] The first modern spinning machinery in Saxony appears to have been one (manufactured after French designs) set up at Ernsthal by Hieronymus Lange in 1782 (R. M. R. Dehn, p. 3).

merchant named Humphreys who sold large quantities of Lancashire cotton goods alarmed the Saxon cotton manufacturers. Two years later Karl Friedrich Bernhard secured from the Saxon Government the sole right to use Crompton's mule for ten years. He had worked in Manchester and had secured drawings of this machine. Three skilled British workers—Moult, Watson and Evans—set up and supervised the operation of Bernhard's new mill at Harthau. In 1799 Wöhler obtained a similar concession for the sole use of Arkwright's water frame and he placed William Whitefield of Halifax in charge of his mill at Chemnitz. Both Bernhard and Wöhler received State subsidies.[16] Mule spindles were firmly established in Saxony in the years that followed—there were over a quarter of a million of them by 1813[17]—but the attempt to introduce water frames and jennies was less successful.

Some years later (1830) a company was formed in Chemnitz to manufacture bobbinet and frames were secured from England for this purpose. English competition, however, proved to be too strong and the company was wound up in 1836.[18] Lack of skill on the part of the Saxon operatives long prevented the adoption of English power looms.[19] J. E. Tennent stated in 1841 that " the use of the power loom is so imperfect in their hands that it becomes a much dearer instrument of production than the handloom itself ".[20]

[16] Albin König, *Die sächsische Baumwollenindustrie am Ende des 18en Jahrhunderts und während der Kontinentalsperre* (1899), ch. 2; J. Kulischer, *Allgemeine Wirtschaftsgeschichte*, II (1929), p. 476 and Pierre Benaerts, *Les Origines de la grande industrie allemande* (1933), p. 360. Evans and Whitefield appear to have settled permanently in Saxony. In 1812 Evans had a spinning mill at Geyer while Whitefield was a partner in a mill at Colditz (A. König, *op. cit.*, p. 332).

[17] Spinning machines in Saxony at this time were driven almost exclusively by water power, animal power or manual power.

[18] *Second Report from Select Committee ... (on) the Exportation of Machinery*, 1841, Qn. 4611.

[19] It is stated that there had been 50 power looms at Mittweida (Saxony) as early as 1790 (R. M. R. Dehn, *op. cit.*, p. 3).

[20] *Second Report from Select Committee ... (on) the Exportation of Machinery*, 1841, Qn. 4558. The witness added: " I actually saw machines of English construction standing idle in the workshops of calico printers in Chemnitz, who stated to me that they were unable to employ them to advantage and that they found it cheaper to continue the old system of hand labour " (Qn. 4621). The Saxon hosiery industry, on the other hand, was largely mechanised in the 1820s and 1830s. In 1839 Charles Pelham Villiers told the House of Commons that Saxony's hosiery machinery was being doubled every six years and that the exports of Saxony's hosiery industry to the United States alone were greater than Britain's total hosiery exports (*The Free Trade Speeches of . . . C. P. Villiers* (2 vols., 1883), I, p. 63).

English machinery and the skill of English mechanics also contributed to the modernisation of the German woollen and linen industries. After the Napoleonic Wars the three Cockerill brothers (William, James and John)—their father William Cockerill (Snr.) had already made a name for himself as a prominent industrialist at Verviers and Liège[21]—came to Prussia. John Cockerill[22]—the youngest of the brothers—set up a mill in Berlin which contained the first power-driven machine in Germany for spinning woollen and worsted yarns and he also established " a very large manufactory "[23] for making such machinery.[24] John Cockerill's machines were installed in woollen mills set up in Lower Lusatia (Brandenburg Province) at Cottbus and at Guben—William Cockerill (Jnr.)[25] being in charge of the Guben factory in 1819—and also in Lower Silesia at

[21] For William Cockerill (Snr.) see P. Lebrun, *L'industrie de laine à Verviers pendant le xviiie siècle et le début du xixe siècle* (Liège, 1948), pp. 234-45.)

[22] For John Cockerill see *Portefeuille de John Cockerill . . .* (four volumes, 1859-88); an article in the (Belgian) *Biographie Nationale*, III (1872) col. 230; Heinrich Lotz, *John Cockerill . . .* (Beiträge zur Geschichte der Technik und Industrie, X, 1920); T. Woodcock, *William Cockerill and his Family* (reprinted from the *Haslingden Observer*, 1927: copies in the British Museum Library and the Manchester University Library); W. Treue, *Wirtschaftszustände und Wirtschaftspolitik in Preussen, 1815-1825* (1937), pp. 36, 139 and 215; and R. Hustin, *Les Cockerill et la cité de l'acier* (Brussels, 1944).

[23] The phrase was used by Maudslay in evidence before the Select Committee on Artisans and Machinery, 1824 (*First Report* p. 33).

[24] Herman von Petersdorff, *Friedrich von Motz* (two volumes in one, 1913), II, p. 34, states that John Cockerill's machine building works were in the Neue Friedrichstrasse (Berlin). P. Benaerts (p. 348) mentions a machine building establishment set up in the Köpernickerstrasse (Berlin) by Biram of Huddersfield with the help of John Cockerill. Aided by State subsidies Biram added a foundry to his works (then called the Englische Maschinenfabrik) and he supplied textile manufacturers with machinery.

[25] Few writers mention William Cockerill (Jnr.), the eldest and least well known of the three sons of William Cockerill (Snr.). Herman von Petersdorff, II, pp. 34-35 states that William Cockerill (Jnr.) managed a wool-spinning mill at Guben and that he married the daughter of Maassen who had been mainly responsible for drawing up the new Prussian tariff of 1818. This was William Cockerill's second marriage. T. Woodcock, *William Cockerill and his Family* (1927) refers to English legal documents in which William Cockerill (Jnr.) of Guben (Prussia) is mentioned as the heir of William Cockerill (Snr.). In 1827 J. G. Hoffman, accompanied by an American engineer named G. Bannister, visited William Cockerill's factory at Guben on behalf of the Prussian Ministry of Finance and reported favourably on a recently installed steam engine. Before going to Prussia William Cockerill (Jnr.) started a spinning mill in France (F. Redlich, *History of American Business Leaders*, I (Ann Arbor, Michigan, 1940), p. 42). This factory was at Sedan.

Grünberg.[26] John Cockerill received much encouragement from the Prussian Government. He secured State subsidies and was allowed to import machinery duty-free. At the first Prussian Industrial Exhibition of 1822 the King awarded him the Order of the Red Eagle (Class III). John Cockerill considered purchasing the State ironworks at Peitz (near Cottbus) but the project fell through and in 1816-17—with his brother James—he established a great engineering establishment at Seraing near Liège.[27]

In 1825 James Cockerill sold his share of these works and settled permanently in Aachen. He built machinery for Edmund Joseph Kelleter's cloth factory—where an English engineer named Dobbs was employed[28]—and for other textile manufacturers in the district.[29] At first only slow progress was made in extending the use of modern machinery in the German woollen and worsted industries. Little success attended the efforts in this direction of Charles Aldridge of Gloucestershire (1821) and William Crabtree of Liverpool (1830) who were both brought to Prussia by the Government. Friedrich Diergardt of Viersen examined woollen machinery when he visited England in about 1826 but made little headway when he tried to introduce it into Krefeld in 1820.[30] In the 1840's Thomas Jowett, William Briggs and some other weavers from Bradford were employed by the Maschinen Wollen-Weberei at Wüste Giersdorf (Lower Silesia).

[26] According to P. Benaerts (p. 363) two Englishmen named Oldroyd and Blackley, aided by John Cockerill, set up four large wool-spinning mills in the Grünberg district between 1816 and 1830.

[27] In 1822 John Cockerill visited the brothers Remy at Rasselstein (Neuwied) and considered going into partnership with them in erecting puddling works. But the authorities in Berlin would not give him all the assistance that he asked and so—beyond lending the Remys some of his English puddlers—John Cockerill went no further in the matter (F. Redlich, p. 42).

[28] Dobbs was also employed by Reuleaux of Aachen (Pierre Benaerts p. 348). Dobbs visited England with Eberhard Hoesch in 1823 to study puddling and in 1825 he supervised the initial stages of the construction of the important Hoesch ironworks at Lendersdorf by Düren. Later he supervised the erection of Caspar Diedrich Piepenstock's " Hermann " Ironworks at Hörde (1839-40) : see L. Beck, *Die Geschichte des Eisens*, IV (1899), p. 703. For Samuel Dobbs see also above, p. 134.

[29] For James Cockerill see the *Allgemeine Deutsche Biographie* IV (1876), p. 384.

[30] Pierre Benaerts, pp. 361-2. While British influence was of most significance in the Prussian woollen districts it was mainly from Alsace that modern machinery—such as Heilmann's machine—was introduced into Saxony and southern Germany. In 1839 Charles Pelham Villiers pointed out that " five or six years since the quantity of German woollen cloths exhibited for sale at the Leipzig Fair was only 50,000 ends (an end being half a piece), whereas last year the quantity exhibited was 350,000 ends." (*Free Trade Speeches of . . . C. P. Villiers. I*, p. 65).

For a time this firm drew much of its woollen yarn from Messrs. John Foster & Son Ltd. of Queensbury (Bradford).[31]

The linen industry had long been established in Germany. Hanover and Silesia were important centres of flax spinning and weaving. Before the Napoleonic Wars linen accounted for about a quarter of Prussia's exports. After 1815 the industry declined owing to its technical backwardness, undue reliance upon part-time labour, foreign competition and changing fashions. One of several steps taken by the Prussian Government to revise the industry was to send Neubauer (1816)[32] and Wedding (1824) to Britain to investigate the newest machinery. Eventually a flax-spinning machine invented by Tschredy, a Swiss, was purchased by the Prussian Government (1811) and set up in G. W. Alberti's factory in Waldenburg. In 1819 John Cockerill praised the machine and proposed to build another but his offer does not seem to have been accepted. Later the machine was improved in England and in the 1830's it was reported to have been introduced into the Kramsta factory at März-Wernersdorf (Kreis Volkenheim, Silesia). Subsequently it was mainly British machinery that was installed in a new Württemberg State linen factory established in the 1850s and in two large Bavarian linen factories at Immenstadt and Füssen (about 1850).[33]

The German jute industry was started with English capital and Scottish experts. Julius Spiegelberg, after visiting Scotland to study the industry, set up the first German jute spinning factory at Vechelde near Brunswick in 1861. Dundee jute spinners

[31] E. M. Sigsworth, " Fosters of Queensbury and Geyer of Lodz, 1848-62 " in the *Yorkshire Bulletin of Economic & Sociel Research* III (2), pp. 67-82: the article is based upon the business records of the house of Foster which have been deposited in the Brotherton Library (University of Leeds). Wüste-Giersdorf is in Lower Silesia and not in Saxony as stated in Mr. Sigsworth's article. In 1847 Jowett left Germany to take up a new post with Louis Geyer, a Saxon who was one of the pioneers in the establishement of the cotton industry in Lodz. In 1847 he began to weave a mixed cotton and worsted cloth.

[32] Neubauer was instructed to " collect all the necessary information concerning the progress made in England, Scotland and Ireland with regard to flax-spinning machinery."

[33] A. Zimmermann, *Blüte und Verfall des Leinengewebes in Schlesien* (1885), p. 281 *et seq.* Pierre Benaerts, pp. 360-1. In evidence before the Select Committee on Import Duties, 1840, J. MacGregor commented on the way in which Continental textile industries were benefitting from British capital and skill. After referring to other factories in the neighbourhood of Vienna run by Scottish and English directors and foremen he went on : " We find in France that the principal foremen at Rouen and in the cotton factories are from Lancashire ; and you find it in Belgium, in Holland and in the neighbourhood of Liège ; you find British capital going into Belgium, France and Germany to a very great amount . . . " (Qn. 1046).

trained the German workers. The necessary capital was not forthcoming in Germany but Spiegelberg was able to secure the establishment of the British and Continental Jute and Flax Works Co. Ltd. in London. The original factory—100 workers in charge of 1,000 spindles—was extended in 1869-70 when a weaving shed (with 40 looms) was added.[34]

To free German manufacturers from dependence upon foreign machinery it was necessary to develop a native machine building industry.[35] In 1819 F. A. J. Egells, a young Westphalian locksmith, was sent by the Prussian Government to England to study recent developments in machine production.[36] On his return he received a State subsidy to establish a machine-building works and an iron foundry in Berlin (1821). In 1826 Wodber's foundry was associated with Egell's enterprise. Egell's first machine was sold in 1825 to the Alberti brothers who were textile manufacturers in Waldenburg (Lower Silesia). Two of Egell's engineers—August Borsig and J. F. L. Wöhlert—later opened their own machine building works. Borsig became a famous constructor of locomotives.[37]

While Egells was still in England Friedrich Harkort was already setting up Germany's first machine building establishment at Wetter on the Ruhr (1819). He secured from England two engineers (Thomas and Godwin), a moulder (Obrey who had been trained by Maudslay), mechanics, a steam engine and various machines. Obrey soon returned to England while Thomas

[34] E. Pfuhl, *Die Jute und ihre Verarbeitung* (3 vols., 1885-91), I, pp. 4-6 ; R. Wolff, *Die Jute* . . . (1913), pp. 100-2 ; F. Bonsack, *Die Versorgung der Welt mit Jute* . . . (1929), p. 91.

[35] For the German machine-building industry see Conrad Matschoss, *Ein Jahrhundert deutsches Maschinenbaues*. (1919).

[36] The Prussian Consul in London wrote on August 18, 1820 : " Egells's hopes have to a great extent been surpassed. His visits to Manchester, Leeds, Sheffield, Birmingham (and) Gloucester have been most valuable to him and they will consequently be of advantage to his country. He has been able to acquire a thorough knowledge of everything connected with new machine-tools and of all those things which should be encouraged (in Prussia) as quickly as possible. No detail has escaped him in the various places (which he has visited). Even firms like Boulton & Watt of Soho at Birmingham, which are said to be very difficult of access, have opened their doors to us." (Quoted by Pierre Benaerts, pp. 347-8).

[37] For Egells and Borsig see Hans Dominik, " Die Anfange der Berliner Maschinenindustrie " (in the *Grossberliner Kalender*, 1915) ; Kurt Doogs, *Die Berliner Maschinenindustrie* . . . (1928) ; Franz Schnabel, *Deutsche Geschichte im 19en Jahrhundert*, III, 1934 (pp. 403-4 and P. Benaerts, p. 347. Since Egells had undertaken a prolonged study of English machinery it is difficult to accept Werner Sombart's view that " he worked according to his own ideas without imitating English models " (*Der moderne Kapitalismus*, I (ii) (4th edn., 1921), p. 868).

moved on to Bohemia. They were replaced by Richmond, Roose and Potter. Godwin stayed and was later joined by his son. Some of these men settled at Wetter while others secured posts elsewhere and became " the teachers of the new generation of machinebuilders in the Mark ",[38] Harkort erected furnaces to smelt his own iron from Siegerland ore—an early example of a " mixed enterprise " in Germany.[39]

Despite their small size—they had about 100 workers in 1830—Friedrich Harkort's works exercised a considerable influence upon the industrialisation of the Rhineland and Westphalia. A visionary and a pioneer rather than a man of business, he got little support from his partners for his more ambitious schemes and he left the firm in 1834. Not least among his troubles had been the difficulty of handling his English workers.[40]

[38] L. Beck, *Die Geschichte des Eisens*,, IV (1899), p. 346. Godwin, for example, was responsible for the erection of rolling mills at Warstein (1834-5) and Nachrod (L. Beck, IV, p. 704).

[39] Friedrich Harkort's works do not appear to have been the first " mixed enterprise " in Germany (as suggested by F. Schnabel, III, p. 280) since B. Donkin told the Select Committee on Artisans and Machinery, 1824, that in the previous year he had visited " a manufactory at Würzburg, in a suppressed monastery, established for machinery." " I found a foundry established and the iron they used with very little exception was brought from England ; all the coke they used for the melting of that iron was also brought from England, and this for the production of machinery for which there was a demand at that extravagant rate which they must necessarily charge . . . in order to get any profit at all" (*First Report*, pp. 30-1). These works were presumably the ironworks erected in the buildings of the (former) monastery of Oberzell to which Friedrich König—inventor of the steam press—referred in a letter to J. Walter. König complained that it was difficult to find skilled workers in Germany (*The History of the Times*, Vol. I (1936), p. 117 *et seq.*).

[40] L. Berger, *Der alte Harkort* (1890, fifth edn., 1926) ; Conrad Matschoss, *Ein Jahrhundert deutscher Maschinenbau* . . . (1919) and *Friedrich Harkort* . . . (Beiträge zur Geschichte der Technik und Industrie, X, 1920) ; L. Beck, IV, pp. 345-6 and F. Schnabel, III, pp. 279-82. Friedrich Harkort complained that good English workmen were not easy to get—since the demand for them in Germany exceeded the supply—and that it was difficult to maintain discipline among them. In 1821 he wrote that he longed for competent German foremen, " so that the Englishmen might all be kicked out ; but one must go easy with them since they actually talk of leaving if one fails to give them a smile " (quoted by F. Schnabel, III, p. 287). Cp. the statement in the *Quarterly Review*, XXXI, 1824-5, p. 417, that " the Englishmen abroad, though able workmen, are in general, persons of extremely bad character, continually drunk, constantly quarrelling and occasioning most serious complaints." " At Messrs. Manby's works at Charenton where some of the workmen receive £12 a week, hardly one has ever saved a farthing. They . . . never leave the cabarets till the whole of their wages are exhausted. Two men, employed from Chaillot in setting up a steam engine, drank 18 bottles of wine in three hours, and a man and a boy drank 273 in a fortnight."

English influence was also evident in other early German machine-building establishments. In Berlin John Cockerill and Biram set up factories to build textile machinery. In Hamburg in 1841 the firm of Gleichmann and Busse worked " with English iron, with English coals, (and) with English models ". " All their tools (were) English, their director (was) an Englishman and, of the 150 hands who were in their employment, 90 were likewise English . . . "[41]

Pumps and machines were first driven by power provided by human beings, animals, wind and water. The " atmospheric engines " of Savery (1706) and Newcomen (1711) aroused considerable interest on the Continent. Karl, Landgraf of Hesse-Cassel—Papin's patron—had a Savery engine erected (about 1715) to work a fountain and in 1722 he arranged for a Newcomen engine to be brought from England to Cassel.[42] James Watt's engine (1769) also quickly attracted attention in Germany and efforts were made to penetrate the closely guarded secrets of Boulton and Watt's works. In 1779 Carl Friedrich Bückling, a mining engineer, was sent by the Prussian Government to Soho.[43] On his return he built a steam engine which was set in operation on August 23rd, 1785 at a mine at Hettstedt (Burggörner) in the County of Mansfeld but it failed to work.[44] Bückling went to England again in 1786 ; bought a cast iron cylinder from Homfray of Penydarran and secured the services of George Richards, an engineer. Richards rebuilt the Burggörner machine

[41] *Second Report from the Select Committee . . . (on) the Exportation of Machinery*, 1841 : J. E. Tennent's evidence, Qns. 4436 and 4443. In 1868 the German statistician Bienengräber wrote that " whereas twenty years ago practically all our steam engines had to be imported from England, Belgium and North America our machine building establishments have now reached such a state of perfection that they not only meet the home demand but are often also busy on foreign orders " (A. Bienengräber, *Statistik des Verkehrs und Verbrauchs im Zollverein für die Jahre 1842-64* (Berlin, 1868), p. 324).

[42] Ludwig Beck, *Die Geschichte des Eisens* . . . III (1897), pp. 91-112 ; Marten Triewald, *Short Description of the Atmospheric Engine*, 1734 (English translation, Newcomen Society 1928). The first Newcomen engines to work effectively on the Continent were in Hungary (Königsberg, 1721-4), Austria (Vienna, 1724), France (Passy, 1726) and Sweden (Danemora, 1726-7).

[43] Matthew Boulton, " State(ment) of Facts," 1787 (printed by G. S. Ford, *On and Off the Campus* (1938), pp. 183-9). Boulton gives 1779 and 1786 as the dates of Bückling's visits to England. The date of Bückling's first visit has been given as 1780 (C. Matschoss, *Great Engineers* (1938), p. 117) and as 1782 (L. Beck, III, p. 541).

[44] For the Burggörner steam engine see L. Beck, III, pp. 541-3. Burggörner was a district (*Amt*) in the County of Mansfeld.

(1794) ; constructed several steam engines—with English cylinders[45]—for the Rothenburg mining authorities ; and erected a steam engine for the Prussian salt mine at Schönebeck near Magdeburg.[46]

Meanwhile Stein had undertaken a " mineralogical and technical journey " in England (November, 1786—August, 1787). He tried to secure drawings of a steam engine and he negotiated—apparently unsuccessfully—with Boulton for the purchase of an engine.[47] But von Reden acquired an English steam engine in 1787 and it was erected at the Prussian State lead-silver mine (the *Friedrichsgrube*) at Tarnowitz (Upper Silesia). It was set to work in April, 1788.[48] Ten years elapsed before the first steam engine was erected in Westphalia. This

[45] How difficult it was to get cylinders manufactured by German ironmasters at this time may be seen from the experience of Franz Dinnendahl, pioneer builder of steam engines in the Ruhr. In 1806 he was commissioned to construct a steam engine to work both a pump and a winding apparatus at the United Salzer-Neuak colliery near Essen. The task was not completed until 1809. Dinnendahl stated in a report—printed by A. von Waldthausen, *Geschichte des Steinkohlbergwerks Vereinigte Salzer und Neuak* . . . (Essen, 1902), pp. 155-7—that the delay was caused by the fact that several cylinders had to be cast at Jacobi's ironworks at Sterkrade-Oberhausen before a satisfactory one was made. For Dinnendahl see C. Matschoss, *Great Engineers* (1938), pp. 119-127.

[46] In view of Richards' record in Germany it is not possible to accept Matthew Boulton's view that " he is good for nothing " (quoted by G. S. Ford, *op. cit.*, p. 185).

[47] Stein's companions in England in 1786-7 were Count Schlabrendorf and a Clausthal engineer called Friedrich. Stein's biographers—from Pertz onwards—state that Stein was accompanied by von Reden. G. S. Ford (*op. cit.*, pp. 178-9) considers that the von Reden who visited Soho in November, 1782 and November, 1787, was Baron von Reden of Clausthal —an uncle of the more famous von Reden who was head of the Silesian Mining Office. Von Reden (Silesia) was in England in 1776 and 1789-90. He may also have been in England in 1779. On January 20 of that year Matthew Boulton warned James Watt against a German metallurgist—a baron—who was alleged to have come to England " to steal our engine." The German visitor was said to be " pimping for iron-foundry, cannon etc." (Boulton and Watt Papers in the Birmingham Public Library). There is a reference by Boulton—in a letter to John Turner, March 21, 1782—to Baron Reden (? Clausthal) who was visiting England. F. Redlich, *History of American Business Leaders*, I (Ann Arbor, 1940), writing after the appearance of Ford's essay, repeats (p. 36) the statement than von Reden of Silesia accompanied Stein to England in 1786-7.

[48] L. Beck, *op cit.*, III, p. 543 and pp. 927-8 and Hugo Koch, *Denkschrift zur Feier des hundertjährigen Bestehens des königlichen Blei- und Silbererzbergwerkes Friedrichsgrube* . . . (1884). It appears from a manuscript " List of Engines made by John Wilkinson at Bersham . . ." (Boulton and Watt Papers in the Birmingham Public Library) that von Reden of Silesia bought a steam engine for use in " a lead mine in Prussia " from John Wilkinson in 1792.

had an English cylinder and it was set up by Bückling at the Königsborn (Prussian State) salt mine at Unna.[49]

Early in 1791 the Elector of Bavaria proposed to erect a steam engine in Mannheim to pump water and to work a corn mill and a fulling mill. In June Dr. Joseph Baader came to England to place an order for an engine with Boulton and Watt.[50] He brought with him Georg von Reichenbach, a gifted young scientist, who was to be instructed in the mechanism of the engine. Reichenbach was in England for six months and a little later he came again for a year or more. During a stay of eight weeks at Soho he was regarded with much suspicion but it was difficult to get rid of him since his visit was in connection with an engine that had been ordered. Reichenbach learned a good deal about steam engines during his visit. Later he achieved eminence as a pioneer constructor of precision instruments.[51]

Efforts to construct a rotative steam engine in Germany to drive machines in factories were at first unsuccessful. In 1822, however, John Baildon, a Scot, succeeded in erecting such an engine in a State porcelain factory in Berlin.[52] The progress of power driven machinery in Germany was slow. In 1846 there were only 1,346 steam engines in Prussia and Saxony.[53]

The development of the German engineering industry was hampered by dependence upon foreign countries for iron. In the early eighteenth century—despite the prolonged effects of the ravages of the Thirty Years War—Germany's resources of iron ore, timber and water power enabled her to retain her position as the leading iron producer in Europe. But a century later the German industry could not meet the increasing demands

[49] L. Berger, *Der alte Harkort* (1890), p. 159—citing the *Westfälischer Anzeiger*, July 10, 1798—and L. Beck, *op. cit.*, IV, pp. 344-345. F. Schnabel (*op cit.*, III, p. 255) gives the date as 1788. Westphalia's second steam engine—sometimes erroneously stated to be the first in the district—was erected by Dinnendahl in 1800-1.

[50] In the Birmingham Assay Office there are three letters dated February 27, 1791, April 25, 1791 and July 4, 1791, from Dr. Joseph Baader to Messrs. Boulton & Watt concerning this engine. For Baader see also Alan Birch, " The Haigh Ironworks 1789-1856 " (*John Rylands Library Bulletin*, 1953, pp. 324-5).

[51] Sir Benjamin Thompson (Count von Rumford)—born in 1753 at North Woburn, Massachusetts—a distinguished English physicist in the Bavarian Electoral service—realised Reichenbach's capabilities and recommended him to the Elector. See Conrad Matschoss, *Great Engineers* (1938), pp. 127-40, F. Schnabel *op cit.*, III, pp. 267-8, *Dictionary of National Biography*, LVI, p. 205 and *Manchester Guardian*, March 26, 1953.

[52] Werner Sombart, *Die deutsche Volkswirtschaft im neunzehnten Jahrhundert* (edition of 1927), p. 152 and Pierre Benaerts, *op. cit.*, p. 345.

[53] Werner Sombart, *op. cit.*, pp. 152-153: these figures omit railway locomotives and engines for river craft.

for iron. By the early 1840's half of Germany's iron and iron products came from abroad.[54] The British iron industry, then the greatest in the world, contributed the lion's share of Germany's iron imports. The quality of some of the products of the German iron industry were far from satisfactory in the early nineteenth century.[55] The modernisation of Germany's old fashioned ironworks—small foundries and forges situated in remote wooded valleys and still smelting with charcoal—was an essential feature of the German industrial revolution.

The earliest improvements were made in Silesia where Frederick the Great fostered the iron industry. He set up a Mining Department under Friedrich Anton (Freiherr von) Heinitz (1769) and a special Mining Office for Silesia under Count Friedrich Wilhelm von Reden (1779). Von Reden had visited coalmines and ironworks in Britain in 1776 where he studied the smelting of iron with coke. In 1784 F. A. A. Eversmann was sent by the Prussian Government to England to investigate recent technical advances in the iron industry. He stayed for eighteen months.[56]

Attempts, inspired by von Reden, were now made to substitute coke for charcoal in existing German furnaces. When these failed William Wilkinson[57] was invited to Prussia by the

[54] Fifty-five per cent. in 1843 : see Max Sering, *Geschichte der preussisch-deutschen Eisenzölle* . . . (1882). The Zollverein's iron imports (in terms of pig iron) rose from 900,000 Zentner (cwt.) in 1839 to 4,200,000 Zentner in 1843.

[55] B. Donkin stated in 1824 : " While in Germany last year I got orders for several hundred pounds worth of things, in consequence of the badness of their cast iron : it was so bad (that) it would not answer for making the machinery wanted (*First Report from the Select Committee on Artisans and Machinery*, 1824, p. 33).

[56] Heinitz wrote in 1786 : " I sent Councillor of Mines Eversmann to examine establishments in Great Britain and Ireland. There he obtained information which has already been of value to the metal workshops of the Mark and from which they will continue to derive benefit in future " (*Mémoire sur les Produits du Règne Minéral de la Monarchie Prussienne* . . . (Berlin, 1786), p. 34). Matthew Boulton wrote in 1787 : " About three years ago a Mr. Eversman(n) was sent from Prussia to England in quest of certain Improvements, and like a faithful Ambassador he introduced himself to Mr. Wilkinsons, and other Manufactorys, without the consent of the Proprietors, particularly into some of the Iron Forges worked by Boulton and Watt's Engines, and he made very exact drawings thereof, which he took to Berlin . . . (quoted by G. S. Ford, *op. cit.*, p. 185).

[57] L. Beck, *op cit.*, III, p. 929 confuses William Wilkinson with his brother John. A letter from William Wilkinson to James Watt (printed by W. H. Chaloner in *Daedalus* (Stockholm, 1948)) shows that William Wilkinson was in Copenhagen on October 11, 1788, and was contemplating going to Germany to study " more useful ways of making bar iron." F. Redlich (*op. cit.*, p. 37)—citing H. Koch, *Denkschrift zur Feier des hundertjährigen Bestehens des Königlichen Blei- und Silberwerkes Friedrichsgrube* . . . (1884)—states that William (not John) Wilkinson was in Silesia in 1789.

Mining Department. In 1789 he smelted lead ore with coke at the furnace (*Friedrichshütte*) of the Friedrichsgrube but failed to smelt iron with coke. Von Reden accompanied him back to England where he stayed for a year. On his return von Reden renewed his efforts to smelt iron with coke. In 1791-2 Wedding successfully smelted iron with coke at Malapane (Upper Silesia) in a charcoal furnace. The blowing machine—worked by water power—had an English cylinder.[58]

Von Reden now decided to build new iron works of the most modern type at Gleiwitz (Upper Silesia). The furnace—worked by a waterwheel—was constructed in 1794-6 largely from English materials by John Baildon (a former employee at the Carron ironworks) and by two German engineers (Bogatsch and Wedding).[59] It was first used in September, 1796. In 1798-1802 Baildon and Wedding built two more coke furnaces for the Prussian State iron-works at Zabrze.[60] In 1805 Baildon constructed a coke furnace for the privately owned *Hohenlohhütte* in Upper Silesia.

An increased output of iron was necessary since this metal was now being put to new uses in Germany. In 1796, for example, the first iron bridge on the Continent was erected by Count von Burghaus at Lasser near Breslau. The cast iron parts were made by J. Baildon at Malapane.[61] In about 1815 an Englishman named Whitefield installed an iron waterwheel at the Count of Einsiedel's wool factory at Wolkenberg.[62]

[58] For the Malapane experiments see Ludwig Wachler, *Geschichte des ersten Jahrhunderts der Königlichen Eisenhütten-Werke in Malapane* . . . (Glogau, 1856) and L. Beck, III, pp. 930-1.

[59] For the Gleiwitz coke furnace see L. Beck, III, pp. 930-4. Some writers state that this was the first Continental coke furnace for iron-smelting. In fact the first such furnace had been introduced into France—at the Le Creusot State ironworks—by William Wilkinson in 1781-5 : see Dr. W. H. Chaloner, " John Wilkinson, Ironmaster " (*History Today*, May, 1951). For von Reden (Head of the Silesian Mining Office) see also Fritz Redlich, *History of American Business Leaders* (Ann Arbor, Michigan), I (1940), pp. 35-8. The title of Redlich's book is misleading since he deals with English and German business men as well as with American businessmen.

[60] The furnaces were called the *Heinitzofen* and the *Redenofen*. Zabrze was later called Hindenburg. Smelting with coke spread very slowly in Germany. As late as 1850 there was only one such furnace in the whole of the Westphalian Mining District. (L. Beck, *op. cit.*, IV, p. 983).

[61] L. Beck, III, p. 763 and F. Schnabel, III, p. 255. John Baildon settled permanently in Germany and had a distinguished career as an engineer. His son William followed his father's profession and installed gas puddling furnaces in Carinthia (Austria) at Lippitzbach in 1845 (L. Beck, IV, p. 572) and at Freudenberg in 1854 (ibid, IV, p. 856). See below, p. 197.

[62] L. Beck, IV, p. 106. I have not been able to ascertain if this is the same Whitefield as the mechanic who was in charge of Wöhler's cotton mill at Chemnitz.

After the Napoleonic Wars the Prussian Government sent several experts—for example Eckhardt, Krieger (or Krüger), Dechen and Oeynhausen—to Britain to investigate the latest methods of making iron and steel. Cort's puddling process was introduced into Germany in 1824-5 by the Remy family[63] at Rasselstein (Neuwied) and by Wilhelm and Eberhard Hoesch at Lendersdorf (Düren). Ferdinand Remy and Eberhard Hoesch had studied puddling in England. Both the Rasselstein and Lendersdorf works employed English puddlers.[64] A few years later Friedrich Harkort introduced puddling into his ironworks—his experts being MacMullen, Lewis and Swift.[65] In the early 1830's Jacob Mayer worked for a time at Sheffield before opening a small plant to make cast-steel at Nippes (Cologne). Later (1843-4) he founded a great steelworks at Bochum.[66] In 1838-9 Alfred Krupp visited England—under the name of Schropp—to study British methods of steel production.[67] At about the same time English engineers were employed by Count Hugo

[63] The Remys were (i) Friedrich Remy, (ii) his brother Christian Remy, (iii) a member of another branch of the family named Ferdinand Remy who came from Bendorf. See article by L. Beck on " Die Familie Remy . . . " in the *Annalen des Vereins für Nassauische Altertumskunde und Geschichtforschung*, Vol. XXXV (1908), pp. 1-129.

[64] F. Redlich states : " Nearly all these Englishmen came from the works of John Guest, or Richard Crawshay, or Anthony Hill or from the Homfrays. It will be remembered that it was these men who had made South Wales the centre of English puddling and rolling. That the names of all these workers are still known proves how important they were in their time. They migrated to the European continent from factory to factory ; most of them were acquainted with each other ; many were related and intermarried. In numerous cases they formed groups which worked only as units. We can trace their migration in the same way as we can trace the migration of groups of masons in the architecture of medieval cathedrals " (*History of American Business Leaders*, I (Ann Arbor, 1940), p. 41). The first English puddlers employed by the Remys were borrowed from John Cockerill's works at Seraing. At Ferdinand Remy's new ironworks at Alf on the River Mosel (1827) puddling was introduced by three Englishmen (L. Beck, IV, p. 347).

[65] F. Schnabel, III, p. 298 ; M. Sering, p. 31 ; L. Beck, IV, pp. 347-8.

[66] F. Redlich, p. 49.

[67] W. Berdrow, *Alfred Krupp* (German edition of 1943), pp. 47-8. Alfred Krupp wrote from Liverpool to his brother Hermann (January, 1839) ; " Only yesterday at a place five miles away, where I had gone for a walk with Fritz Solling, I saw, without any introduction, a new rolling mill for copper plates, which has only been working for a short time and where no one is admitted. I was properly booted and spurred and the proprietor was flattered that a couple of such good fellows should deign to inspect his Works " (W. Berdrow (ed.), *The Letters of Alfred Krupp, 1826-1887* (English translation, (1930) p. 56). Later (1851) G. R. Elkington of Birmingham purchased Krupp's machine for the mass production of spoons and forks : this was of great benefit to Krupp.

COALMINES OF UPPER SILESIA
IN THE MIDDLE OF THE NINETEENTH CENTURY

Henckel von Donnersmarck to erect an up-to-date furnace, puddling works and rolling mill at the *Laurahütte* in Upper Silesia. And it was after a visit to Scotland that Schreiber identified the Blackband iron-ore deposits in the Ruhr which proved to be of great value to German ironmasters.[68]

A generation later it was an English invention which gave the German steel manufacturers a great opportunity which they used to the full. In 1878 Sidney Gilchrist Thomas announced his discovery of a method by which phosphorous could be eliminated from pig iron in the Bessemer process. In 1879 the process was described in detail to the Iron and Steel Institute. Germany possessed large reserves of phosphoric *minette* ores in the recently annexed province of Lorraine. The English invention enabled her to turn out large quantities of basic (Thomas) steel from this ore.

Germany also profited from advances made in England in the working of non-ferrous metals. In 1824 Thomas Osler told the Select Committee on Artisans and Machinery that " some years ago, Germans resident for a short time in England for commercial purposes, paid particular attention to the brass foundry trade. They were perpetually visiting brass founders' workshops, accurately noticing the different processes . . . "[70] The information that they collected was used in the German brass foundries in the Rhineland.[71]

In the first half of the nineteenth century British capitalists showed some interest in mining in Germany. Banfield in his account of the Rhineland refers to a Mr. Bennett who directed abortive mining operations in the Westerwald about 1816 and a Mr. Williams who ran a small zinc smelting works opposite Ruhrort in the early 1840s.[72] An English company began to mine silver and cobalt in the Kinzig valley in the forties but work came to an end in 1857. Another English company which exploited the rich phosphate deposits of the German island of

[68] Friedrich Harkort had realised the existence of these deposits twenty years before but had failed to gain control over them.

[69] D. L. Burn, *The Economic History of Steelmaking 1867-1939* (1940), pp. 74-6.

[70] *Fourth Report from the Select Committee on Artisans and Machinery, 1824*, p. 315. The same witness mentioned that a German named Antie had learned the button and gilt-toy trade in Birmingham and had subsequently returned to Germany with three English artisans. Antie set up a factory near Frankfurt to make buttons and gilt-toys " after the English mode " and later he also manufactured brass nails " after our plans."

[71] It may be added that Hermann Witte introduced machinery into the needle factory established by his father at Iserlohn after he had visited up-to-date needle factories at Redditch (L. Beck, *op. cit.*, IV, p. 707).

[72] T. C. Banfield, *op. cit.*, II, pp. 49 and 113.

Deutsch-Englischer Bergwerksverein in 1850 and was purchased by a Baden firm in 1856.[73]

The middle years of the nineteenth century saw a great extension of coal-mining in the Ruhr. British enterprises[74] in this important coalfield that deserve mention include those of John Curney (Britannia Mine);[75] Collingwood, Lindsay, Wood & Co. (1850);[76] the Ruhrort Coalmining Co. (1854);[77] and the New Scotland Mining and Ironworking Company. Philip Henry Muntz of Birmingham, in association with Belgian industrialists, established the Englisch-Belgische Gesellschaft der rheinischen Bergwerke which acquired mining concessions in 1847 and founded the Dahlbusch Mine.[78]

William Thomas Mulvany[79] was one of the most successful of the many foreigners who came to the Ruhr in the fifties. An Irish engineer who had been Commissioner of Public Works in Ireland, Mulvany went to Germany in 1854 with Michael Corr van der Maeren of Brussels,[80] who held some mining concessions in the Ruhr. Following this visit Mulvany settled in Germany

[73] Pierre Benaerts, p. 350.

[74] The extent to which British and other foreign capital penetrated into the Ruhr coalfield in the early 1850s alarmed Gustav Mevissen (head of the well-known Schaafhausen Bank of Cologne) who declared : " Owing to our failure to participate in so productive an activity as the exploitation of our mines—a source of national wealth hitherto inadequately tapped owing to a lack both of spirit of enterprise and of capital—there has in recent years been an ever-increasing danger that this will fall into the hands of foreign speculators. It is well known that for some time in the Rhineland a number of coal-measures have been acquired on behalf of French and English capitalists who will profit by exploiting them. The treasures beneath the soil of our Fatherland thus helps to increase the preponderance which foreign capital already possesses elsewhere and the produce of German labour will benefit foreign shareholders. It is obviously in the supreme interests of our economy that we should retain not only these earnings but also the capital itself" (quoted by Pierre Benaerts, *op. cit.*, p. 353).

[75] Liquidated in 1856.

[76] This company at one time owned ten collieries. It was liquidated in 1860.

[77] This company opened up the Westende Mine. It was taken over by a French firm in 1870.

[78] Philip Henry Muntz had been Mayor of Birmingham in 1839-40 and in 1840-1. The partnership ended in 1849 and the assets were taken over by a company.

[79] Kurt Bloemers, *W. T. Mulvany, 1806-1885* (Essen 1922) ; Maurice Beaumont, *La grosse industrie allemande et le charbon* (1928), pp. 149, 249, 311, 411-2, 484-5 and 581 ; J. Ryan " W. T. Mulvany " (*Studies* . . . XII, 1923, p. 378). See below, pp. 179-193.

[80] Michael Corr came from Slane, Co. Meath. He took the name " van der Maeren " when he married a Flemish lady of that name. He became a leader of the Free Traders in Belgium.

and took the lead in establishing the Hibernia Company in 1856. The shares (Kuxe) were held by W. T. Mulvany, Michael Corr van der Maeren, Joseph and David Malcomson (both of " Mayfield " Portlaw), William Malcomson (of Portlaw, Waterford) and James Perry (Senior and Junior) of Dublin. The Malcolmsons were a wellknown family who were cotton manufacturers and shipbuilders. The Hibernia Mine was near Gelsenkirchen and a second mine (Shamrock) was established at Herne.[81] W. T. Mulvany was chairman of the Hibernia & Shamrock Mining Company while his younger brother (Thomas John) was manager of the two collieries. William Coulson of Durham was the chief engineer. The senior officials and a number of miners in the new collieries were Englishmen. Many of them settled permanently in the Ruhr. The last of these veterans (George Laverick) died in 1913.[82]

In 1866 W. T. Mulvany founded the Prussian Mining and Ironworks Company to take over three mines—Hansa (at Hucharde by Dortmund), Zollern (at Kirchlinde by Dortmund) and Erin (at Castrop)—and also the Vulkan ironworks at Duisburg. The capital of the company was £120,000. This was later increased to £540,000. The Hansa Mine was managed by W. T. Mulvany's son (Thomas Robert). W. T. Mulvany helped to found two important employers' associations in the Rhenish-Westphalian industrial district.[83] He played a prominent part in the move to export Ruhr coal from Dutch and Belgian ports and in agitating vigorously for improved transport facilities and lower rail freight charges for coal. In 1860 W. T. Mulvany and his son accompanied a Prussian Coal Enquiry Commission on a two months tour of inspection of English and Scottish coalfields.

In March, 1873, Mulvany ran into financial difficulties and the Shamrock and Hibernia mines were taken over by two Berlin banks which formed a new German company to manage the collieries.[84] The brothers Mulvany were members of the board

[81] The shareholders were the same as for the Hibernia Mine with the addition of P. C. Roney of Dublin (a railway director).

[82] It was stated that Mulvany paid his English miners ten shillings a day at a time when German miners were earning from two shillings to half a crown a day. Another of Mulvany's Irishmen who deserves mention is James Tool who is said to have introduced horse-racing into Dusseldorf.

[83] These were (i) the *Verein fur die bergbaulichen Interessen im Oberbergamtsbezirk Dortmund*, 1858 and (ii) the *Verein zur Wahrung der gemeinsamen wirtschaftlichen Interessen in Rheinland und Westfalen*, 1871. W. T. Mulvany was also a leading member of the *Eisen-und-Stahl Verein*.

[84] H. Fürstenberg (editor), *Carl Fürstenberg. Die Lebensgeschichte eines deutschen Bankiers* . . . (1931), p. 122.

of directors of the new company. In 1877 the Prussian Mining and Ironworks Company was reorganised as the Westfälischer Grubenverein which was soon afterwards (1882) purchased by Friedrich Grillo.

When the German railway network was constructed—an essential feature of the German industrial revolution—British materials, machinery and expert knowledge were needed. After the opening of the Stockton and Darlington railway in September, 1825 German officials and engineers, such as the Prussian mining engineers Carl von Oeynhausen and Heinrich von Decken, came to Britain to examine the new means of transport with the same zeal that they had previously shown when investigating textile machinery, ironworks and steam engines.[85] The first German railway was a four mile line opened in December, 1835 between Nürnberg and Fürth in Bavaria. Camille von Denis, the engineer, had investigated railways in England and America. The first two locomotives to run on this railway—*The Eagle* (1835) and *The Arrow* (1838)—were built by Robert Stephenson.[86] In 1838 two short lines

[85] As early as 1826 the Prussian officials Peter Beuth and Karl Friedrich Schinkel visited England to study railway—and other industrial—developments (Alfred von Wolzogen, *Aus* (*K.F.*) *Schinkel's Nachlass* . . . (3 vols., 1862-3), Vol. III and H. von Petersdorff, II, p. 313). A report by the two Prussian mining engineers Carl von Oeynhausen and Heinrich von Dechen on English Railways (1826-7) appeared in the *Archiv für Bergbau und Hüttenwesen,* Vol. XIX (1829). This report has been summarised in a paper read to the Newcomen Society in London by E. A. Forward on October 14, 1953. King Ludwig of Bavaria sent Klenze, an architect to England—and also to France and Belgium—on a similar errand (H. von Treitschke, *History of Germany in the 19th Century,* VI (English trans., 1919), p. 108). Joseph von Baader, one of the leading advocates of railways in Bavaria, had lived in England for eight years (1787-95), had introduced Reichenbach to the Soho works (1791) and had written a book about English machinery (1789). As early as 1814 von Baader had suggested the building of a railway (horse traction) between Nürnberg and Fürth (E. Koch, *Geschichte der deutschen Eisenbahnpolitik* (Sammlung Göschen, 1911), p. 35). In 1815 von Baader tried to interest Boulton and Watt in a " new mode of applying the power of steam-engines of any construction to the conveyance of carriages upon railways, in a much more advantageous manner than has been effectuated till now . . ." (Joseph von Baader to Boulton & Watt, September 2, 1815, in the Boulton & Watt Papers in the Birmingham Public Library). Von Baader favoured a pulley system worked by stationary engines (F. Schnabel, III, p. 269). In Baden it was Newhouse, an Englishman who had settled in Mannheim, who was the first to propose (in 1833) that a railway should be built between Mannheim and Basel (A. Böhtlingk, *Carl Friedrich Nebenius* (1899), p. 88).

[86] In 1841 it was stated that all the locomotives on the Leipzig-Dresden railway had been built in England : see *First Report from the Select Committee . . . (on) the Exportation of Machinery,* 1841, Qn. 1142. For the history of German railways see A. von Mayer, *Geschischte und Geographie der deutscher Eisenbahnen* (1891).

were opened in Prussia (Berlin-Zehlendorf[87] and Düsseldorf-Eckrath)[88] and one—Germany's first nationalised railway—in Brunswick (Brunswick-Wolfenbüttel). Meanwhile ambitious plans were being made in Saxony to link Dresden and Leipzig by rail. James Walker, an English engineer, earned a £1,000 fee for his advice on the route to be followed by this line. The short Leipzig-Althen section (4½ miles) was opened in April, 1837 and the line was completed in April, 1839. Its first locomotive (*The Comet*), the first engine driver and the carriage builder all came from England. Stephenson's gauge was adopted on this and later German railways.[89] For some years Germany depended upon Britain for many of her locomotives and engine drivers.[90] By the end of 1845 German railways had bought 237 locomotives from England—168 being supplied by Robert Stephenson (Newcastle) and Sharp & Roberts (Manchester)—and thirty more were on order.[91]

The German engineering industry, however, made rapid progress and before long its output of locomotives, coaches, waggons, rails and so forth covered a high proportion of the needs of the growing German railway system. But German railway engineering establishments continued to depend largely upon British ironworks for their iron and steel. Beck estimated that between 1835 and 1850 Germany purchased from abroad iron worth £16,000,000 for the construction and fitting out of her railways.[92] In 1847 it was reported of the sixteen principal German firms engaged in building railway coaches and waggons

[87] Part of the Berlin-Potsdam line.

[88] Part of the Berg-Mark (Düsseldorf-Elberfeld) line.

[89] The Baden lines, originally broad gauge, were eventually converted to the standard gauge.

[90] " In Germany in those days the Englishman was as common a figure on the footplate as in the factory. And whenever a new line was built in Germany the engineers first went to England to examine the railways there " (F. Schnabel, III, p. 403).

[91] D. Lardner, *Railway Economy* (1850), p. 482. At the same time the German railways bought 57 locomotives from the United States of America (Messrs. W. Norris of Philadelphia); 25 from France (Meyer and Co. of Mülhausen in Alsace) ; and 43 from Belgium. Up to the end of 1845 German factories had delivered 125 locomotives to the German railways.

[92] L. Beck, IV, p. 693. See the Earl of Bessborough (editor), *Lady Charlotte Guest . . . 1833-52* (1950) for an extract from Lady Guest's diary of October 10, 1842, concerning a visit to Goldschmidt's warehouse at Mainz where large quantities of Welsh and Staffordshire iron were kept in bond (pp. 141-2).

five obtained all or some of their iron from England, two others imported English steel (*Federstahl*) and another used English lead.[93]

English influence on the introduction of steam navigation on German rivers was of less significance. Nevertheless the first two wooden steamships to cross the North Sea and to sail from Rotterdam up the Rhine to German territory were British vessels—the *Defiance* which reached Cologne in June, 1816 and the *Caledonia* (owned by James Watt Jnr.) which arrived at Cologne in October, 1817.[94] Jacobi, Huyssen and Haniel—owners of the well-known *Gutehoffnung* ironworks at Sterkrade-Oberhausen (Ruhr)—were in touch with Watt and they sent Wilhem Lueg to England to investigate recent progress in steam navigation.[95] Eventually this firm established at Ruhrort a large yard for the building of river craft. The first steam tug to haul coal barges on the Rhine was also of English construction. It was purchased by Matthias Stinnes in 1843.[96] The first regular steamship service on the lower Elbe (between Cuxhaven and Hamburg)

[93] von Weise, " . . . Eisenbahn-Wagenbau in Deutschland " (*Zeitschrift des Vereins für deutsche Statistik*, I, 1847, pp. 920-1.

[94] *The Times* reported on June 24, 1816 : " A letter from Cologne of the 12(th) of June says—' Today we had the entirely novel spectacle of a steamboat entering our port . . . ' " A correspondent of the *Glasgow Chronicle* in a letter dated June 16 wrote from Cologne : " Today, about noon, we enjoyed a sight equally novel and entertaining, a pretty large vessel without a mast ascending the Rhine, and proceeding with astonishing rapidity, arrive before this city. All the vessels stationed on the Rhine in this neighbourhood were in a moment covered with spectators, to see the arrival of this vessel, which is a steamboat coming from London and bound for Frankfurt . . . " (quoted by John Kennedy, *The History of Steam Navigation* (third ed., 1905), p. 30). Most writers give June 12 (not 16) as the date of the arrival of the first steamboat at Cologne. There has been much confusion between the voyages of the *Defiance* in 1816 and the *Caledonia* in 1817. Some writers—probably following J. P. Muirhead, *Life of James Watt* . . . (1859), pp. 429-30—ignore the *Defiance's* voyage of 1816 and state that James Watt (Jnr.) was the first person to ascend the Rhine in a steamship. Others (e.g. C. Eckert, *Rheinschiffahrt im 19en Jahrhundert* (1900), p. 198 and E. Gothein, *Geschichtliche Entwicklung der Rheinschiffahrt* (1903), p. 176) realise that the first ascent of the Rhine by a steamship was in 1816 but state that it was in this year that James Watt (Jnr.) made his voyage. L. Beck (IV, p. 149) and J. Kennedy (pp. 29-30) correctly differentiate between the voyages of 1816 and 1817 though Beck appears to be in error in suggesting that James Watt (Snr.)—then over eighty years of age—went up the Rhine in 1817.

[95] P. Benaerts, p. 348.

For Matthias Stinnes see P. Neubauer, *Matthias Stinnes und sein Haus* . . . (1909).

was started in June, 1816 with a vessel built in Scotland (the *Lady of the Lake*).[97]

British capital and skill also played some part in the early development in Germany of public utilities such as gas and water. The Munich gasworks—one of the earliest in Germany—were erected by Joseph von Baader who had investigated gas-lighting in England.[98] In 1825 Barlow and Manby founded the Imperial Continental Gas Association and in the following year it supplied gas in Berlin and Hanover. Subsequently gasworks were set up in other German towns such as Aachen, Magdeburg and Frankfurt am Main. Forty years later it had 13 establishments and a subsidiary company in Austria. In 1852 Sir Charles Fox promoted a Berlin waterworks company.[99]

Germany also benefited from Britain's industrial superiority in the early nineteenth century since some neglected German inventions were developed in Britain and were later of service to the Germany economy. The career of Friedrich König may serve as an example. König was a journeyman printer in Leipzig who invented a steam printing press which, in his own words, " bears the same sort of relationship to the old press as the spinning machine bears to the spinning wheel." Receiving no encouragement at home König went to London where he secured capital to build a steam printing press (1810). He improved this machine by using rotating cylinders. The proprietors of the *Times* decided to adopt the new machine and their issue of November 29, 1814 was the first newspaper in the world to be printed in this way. König returned to Germany where he eventually established himself successfully as a manufacturer of steam presses.[100]

British influence was felt on commercial as well as upon industrial developments in Germany. Young men from the main German centres of commerce and shipping were often sent to

[97] L. Beck, IV, p. 149.

[98] F. Schnabel, III, p. 269.

[99] L. H. Jenks, *The Migration of British Capital to 1875* (1927), p. 186 ; Werner Sombart, *Der moderne Kapitalismus* III (ii) (edn. of 1928), p. 1001. This great gas company was still a flourishing concern in 1914. By that time it had disposed of most of its German properties to municipalities (e.g. Frankfurt am Main in 1909) but it still supplied Hanover with gas. A. Sartorius von Waltershausen points out that in the middle of the nineteenth century Germany's imports of coal from Britain were largely used for the manufacture of gas (p. 167).

[100] T. Gobel, *Friedrich König und die Erfindung der Schnellpresse* (1883) ; Franz Schnabel, 111, p. 283.

London for part of their training.[101] English merchants and shippers were familiar figures in the chief German ports.[102] In the eighteenth century John Parish—followed by his sons John and Richard in 1797—had amassed a fortune as one of the leading merchants of Hamburg. Between 1815 and 1870 English shipping dominated Hamburg and many agents of British firms were established in the city. In 1847 McCulloch estimated that the total annual commerce of Hamburg and Altona was £20,000,000 and stated that "the largest portion of this immense trade is in our hands."[103] As late as 1870 there were plenty of middle-aged business men in Hamburg who visited London regularly but had never set foot in Berlin.[104]

Moreover English credit played a not unimportant role in some of the main centres of German commerce in the middle years of the nineteenth century.[105] The extent to which Hamburg merchants relied upon the credit afforded by London houses was seen during the business crisis of 1857. In the early 1850s the "open credits" granted by English houses to Hamburg firms were much extended and they "afforded the chief support to the system of accommodation pursued by Hamburg merchants." When London houses such as Hoare, Buxton & Co., H. Sillem, Son & Co., and A. Hintz & Co., suspended payment the Hamburg firms dependent upon them for credit quickly collapsed.[106]

An essential preliminary to the industrial revolution in

[101]For example August von der Heydt (a future Prussian Minister of Commerce) went from Elberfeld as a young man (1823) to enter the service of the London firm of Jameson & Aders (merchants and insurance brokers at 25 Laurence Putney Lane). F. Harkort was in touch with Jameson & Aders when he went to England to secure men and machinery for his machine building enterprise at Wetter. Karl Ludwig von Bruck (who, like von der Heydt, came from Elberfeld) went to London as a young man (1820) in the hope of securing a post under the East India Company. He later helped to found the Austrian Lloyd shipping company of Trieste and he became Austrian Minister of Commerce.

[102]William Richmond, in evidence before the *Select Committee on Manufactures, Commerce and Shipping* (1833) stated: ". . . I know no town in England that has increased more, or where there has been a greater mass of happiness and comfort generated than in the town of Memel through the means of English trade and capital" (Qn. 7320).

[103]J. R. McCulloch, *Dictionary of Commerce* (ed. of 1847), I, p. 622.

[104]Percy Ernst Schramm, *Deutschland und Übersee* (1950), p. 112.

[105]" The bills on London became to a degree currency in German market centres, stimulating enterprise and, at several removes, production" (H. L. Jenks, p. 191).

[106]Reports by Colonel G. L. Hodges, British Consul at Hamburg, November 21, 1857 to January 28, 1858 in *Report from the Select Committee on the Bank Acts*, 1858, Appendix 20, pp. 434-4. For the commercial crisis of 1857 in Hamburg see books and articles listed by Hans Rosenberg, *Die Weltwirtschaftskrisis von 1857* (1934), p. 128 note i.

Germany was that the antiquated social and administrative structure of the various federal States should be recast to meet the needs of a new age. It was necessary also for the Germans to become accustomed to new ideas concerning the working of the economic system. British ideas and practises exercised a powerful influence upon those who were responsible for bringing about these changes in Germany. In the last quarter of the eighteenth century many of Germany's future statesmen and civil servants were trained in Universities which—as far as economics and public administration were concerned—were dominated by the ideas of Adam Smith.

The first attempt in Germany to assess the significance of *The Wealth of Nations* (1776) was by J. G. H. Feder, a Göttingen professor[107] who wrote two articles on the book in the *Göttinger Gelehrte Anzeiger* in 1777.[108] C. J. Kraus, an outstanding colleague of Kant at Königsberg University, soon became the leading exponent of Adam Smith's views in Germany and he strongly influenced many future Prussian officials. At Halle University L. H. von Jakob lectured on Adam Smith. Stein, Hardenberg, Vinke,[109] Sack,[110] and Motz[111] all studied at Göttingen. Beuth[112] was a student at Halle. Theodor von Schön,[113] Schrotter,[114] Auerswald,[115] and Boyen[116] were at Königsberg University.

Among the prominent Prussian reformers whose knowledge of

[107]Göttingen, the University of the Electorate of Hanover, naturally had close connections with Britain in the eighteenth century and had many English students. See W. Treue, " Adam Smith in Deutschland . . ." (in the Hans Rothfels Festschrift).

[108]A German translation of *The Wealth of Nations*, Vol. I, had already appeared in 1776.

[109]Freiherr von Vincke was Senior President of the Province of Westphalia, 1816-44. In 1796 he said that he always began his day's work by reading a chapter of *The Wealth of Nations.*

[110]Johann August Sack was Senior President of the Rhineland Province (1814-16) and of Pomerania (1816-31).

[111]Friedrich von Motz was the Prussian Minister of Finance between 1825 and 1830.

[112]Peter Beuth was Director of the Department for Industry, Commerce and Public Works in the Prussian Ministry of Finance. He retired in 1845. When he visited Scotland in 1823 he wrote that he considered himself fortunate to have seen Adam Smith's grave at Edinburgh.

[113]Theodor von Schön was Senior President of West Prussia (1816-24) and of East and West Prussia combined (1824-42).

[114]Freiherr von Schrotter was one of Stein's closest colleagues in 1807-8.

[115]Hans Jakob von Auerswald was von Schön's predecessor as Senior President of East Prussia.

[116]Boyen founded the Prussian militia (Landwehr).

British ideas was based not merely upon books but upon visits to England mention may be made of Hardenberg, Stein, Vincke, von Schön[117] and Beuth.[118] The men who recast the political, social and economic structure of Prussia after Jena owed much to British influences—though of course they also copied reforms introduced by the French into Western Germany, during the Napoleonic Wars.

Subsequently Ricardo and other classical economists found many followers in Germany. And it was an Englishman—John Prince Smith—who spread the Free Trade gospel in Germany. Though not a popular political leader he exercised some influence over those responsible for the fiscal policy of the Zollverein and was justified in claiming some of the credit for the German Free Traders' successes in the 1860s.[119]

In one respect Germany did not follow England's example. The Germans never accepted the view, prevalent in Britain during much of the nineteenth century, that industrialists and merchants should, as far as possible, be left to their own devices. Far from embracing *laissez-faire* doctrines the Germans held that the State should give the fullest support to manufacturers and traders. The Prussian Finance Minister von Rother, for example, declared in an official report on the activities official Overseas Trading Corporation (*Seehandlung*) that " little advance will be made by accepting the common belief that the State should stand aloof from the natural development of manufacturers and commerce and should certainly not itself engage in industrial enterprise." "I have shown how false is the familiar cry that a civil servant cannot compare with the private citizen when it comes to running an industrial undertaking successfully."[120]

In Prussia the State had its own salt mines, collieries, iron-works and armament factories. There was a Royal Bank and there were nationalised railways. The *Seehandlung* undertook many

[117]Theodor von Schön was in England in 1789 and he later declared that " it was England that taught me statesmanship ".

[118]Beuth visited England in 1823 and in 1826.

[119]See below ch. 7.

[120]Quoted by B. Brockhage, *Zur Entwicklung des preussisch-deutschen Kapitalexports* (*Erster Teil*) (Leipzig, 1910), p. 27. In a report of 1844-5 Rother mentioned the following industrial enterprises in which the Seehandlung had an interest—paper factories at Berlin and Hohenofen; machine-building works in Berlin and Breslau; worsted weaving sheds at Wüste-Giersdorf (Lower Silesia); cotton spinning and weaving establishments at Eisersdorf; iron and steelworks (cast iron products) at Bergthal various cornmills; flax spinning mills at Erdmannsdorf and Landshut; sea-going vessels and also rivercraft on the Spree, Havel and Elbe (see B. Brockhage, *op cit.*, p. 76).

commercial and industrial activities—including the fitting out of vessels for distant voyages to bring Prussian products to new markets. Progressive industrialists were assisted by subsidies and by licenses to import machinery duty free. The Government sent many experts abroad to study foreign inventions. When J. E. Tennent was in Prussia in about 1840 he " found at Berlin the most enterprising and systematic exertions made on the part of the Government to obtain a command of the manufacture of machinery. I found no expense spared for that purpose, and the exertions quite astonished me."[121] And smaller German States, as far as their means allowed, gave similar encouragement to manufacturers and traders.

This aspect of the work of the German Governments in fostering industrial progress may be illustrated by examing the career of Peter Beuth who for twenty-seven years played a leading part in the activities of the Prussian Department for Industry, Commerce and Public Works. As a volunteer in the Waterloo campaign Beuth was quartered on the Cockerills at Liège and he invited John Cockerill to set up modern textile mills and machine-building works in Berlin. In 1816 Beuth established the Industrial Institute (*Gewerbeinstitut*)[122] in Berlin to train engineers—particularly machine-builders.[123] He acted as Director himself. The Institute drew its pupils from Berlin and from newly founded provincial technical schools. Scholarships were offered to attract promising young technicians to the Institute.[124] Through the Prussian Consul in London and the agents of the *Seehandlung* Beuth purchased many new machines. A model of each machine was made for the Institute and the original was then presented to a German manufacturer. In this way Beuth assembled a collection of machine models comparable with any other on the Continent.

In the same building as the Institute were the offices of a Technical Industrial Committee (*Deputation*) of civil servants and industrialists which was responsible for sending experts abroad to

[121] *Second Report from the Select Committee . . . (on) the Exportation of Machinery*, 1841, Qn. 4464.

[122] The first pupils were admitted in 1821. The name *Gewerbeinstitut* dates from 1827. In 1866 it was changed to *Gewerbeakademie*.

[123] The Berlin Building Academy (*Bauakademie*)—closely associated with the Academy for Fine Arts since Schadow was Director of both institutions between 1816 and 1824—trained architects and engineers for service in Statebuilding and public works projects. In 1879 the Building and Industrial Academies were combined to form the Charlottenburg Technical College.

[124] One of the earliest students (1823) was August Borsig who—after serving in Egells' machine works—set up his own work for the building of railway locomotives (L. Beck, IV, p. 698).

study machinery and also for making recommendation on applications for patents.

A third organisation which had its headquarters in the same building as the Industrial Institute was the Association for the Promotion of Industrial Knowledge in Prussia (*Verein zur Beförderung des Gewerbefleisses in Preussen*)—modelled on the Society of Arts in England—which had 367 members[125] when it was founded by Beuth in 1816.

Through these three organisations—and by his work as head of the Department for Industry, Commerce and Public Works—Beuth probably did more than anyone else in Germany to spread information conerning British (and other foreign) machinery and technical processes in the early nineteenth century. The Industrial Exhibition held in Berlin in 1844 was a fitting climax to a career devoted to his country's industrial expansion.[126]

Seven years later the products of some 1,700 exhibitors from the Zollverein were shown at the Crystal Palace.[127] By the middle of the nineteenth century Germany, though still in certain respects behind Belgium and France as an industrial state, was already taking her place as one of the leading manufacturing countries of the Continent. But even in 1851 the extent to which her manufacturers were still content to imitate foreigners rather than to stand upon their own feet was commented upon by Germans themselves.[128]

[125] 110 civil servants and 257 industrialists.

[126] For Beuth see F. Schnabel, III, pp. 308-13; C. Matschoss, *Preussens Gewerbeförderung und ihre grossen Männer 1821-1921* (1921); R. von Delbrück, *Lebenserinnerungen* . . . (2 vols., 1905), I, pp. 134-142 and J. E. Tennent's evidence before the Select Committee on the Exportation of Machinery, 1841 (*Second Report*, Qn 4464 etc.). The Industrial Exhibition of 1844 attracted 3,040 exhibitors.

[127] Alfred Krupp, for example, showed a steel block weighing 2,150 kgm, axles for railway coaches and a six-pounder: he secured a Council Medal. Other German exhibitors of iron and steel goods were Lehrkind, Falkenroth & Co. (of Haspe), Boing, Rohr & Lefsky; Huth & Co. (of Hagen), Peter Harkort & Son (of Wetter), L. Lohmann (of Witten), and D. Piepenstock (of Hörde).

[128] At the time of the Great Exhibition in London a correspondent wrote to the *Allgemeine Zeitung*: " I cannot deny that German industry has no peculiar character. In the Exhibition (from which alone we judge) it appears as if every national characteristic were carefully avoided. Everywhere German industry appears to lean on some foreign industry and to imitate it . . . Here one beholds the supporting hand of France, there that of England " (*Economist*, June 28, 1851, quoted by Sir John Clapham, *op. cit*., II, p. 20 who comments: " This is not a complete or final verdict on the German industry of 1850-1. But . . . there is truth in it ").

7. PRINCE SMITH AND FREE TRADE IN GERMANY[1]

WHILE the career of List who inspired the German protectionists in the nineteenth century is well known, the work of his rival Prince Smith has been neglected by students of free-trade developments on the Continent. Yet Prince Smith's career was by no means without interest. An Englishman, educated at Eton, he became a naturalized Prussian citizen. A teacher in a remote Baltic port, he became a respected citizen of Berlin. Without a University training or substantial industrial or commercial experience he became the leader of the German free-traders who included among their numbers professional economists and practical business men. But the credit for initiating and maintaining the low tariff policy of the Zollverein in the middle years of the nineteenth century went to Prussian officials rather than to Prince Smith and when—in the late 1870's—Bismarck adopted a policy of protection the labours of the free-trade pioneers were soon forgotten.

John Prince Smith was born in London in 1809. His father was a barrister whose interests lay not only in the law but also in administration and in political economy.[2] In 1817 he went to Demerara as second fiscal and John accompanied him. In 1820 John returned to England and went to Eton. His schooling ended on his father's death two years later (1822). At the age of thirteen he was apprenticed to Messrs. Daniel of Mincing Lane where he stayed for six years. There followed two years of irregular employment as banker's clerk, parliamentary reporter and journalist.

In 1830 Prince Smith went to Hamburg to serve on the staff of an English newspaper. Soon afterwards (April 1831) he became

[1] John Prince Smith's collected works (*Gesammelte Schriften*) were edited in three volumes by Michaelis and Braun in 1871-8 with a biography by O. Wolff. His only English work was a translation of C. H. Hagen's *System of Political Economy* (1844). See also M. Schippel, *Grundzüge der Handelspolitik* (Berlin, 1902), ch. 3; J. Becker, *Das deutsche Manchestertum* (Karlsruhe, 1907), ch. 3; W. Lotz, *Die Ideen der deutschen Handelspolitik* . . . (1892), ch. 1; W. H. Dawson, *Protection in Germany* (1904), pp. 23-5; article by Lippert in the *Handwörterbuch der Staatswissenschaften*, 1st edn, 1893, v, 280-2, and 2nd edn, vi, 246-7, and article in the *Dictionary of National Biography*, LIII, p. 86.

[2] Two of his pamphlets were *Elements of the Science of Money* . . . (1813) and *Advice for the Petitioners against the Corn Bill* (1815). For the elder John Prince Smith see the *Dictionary of National Biography*, LIII, pp. 85-86.

modern language master at Cowle's Gymnasium in the small East Prussian port of Elbing. Here, as at other Baltic ports, the merchants had close contacts with English traders to whom they sold corn and timber and from whom they bought manufactured goods. Elbing merchants favoured low import duties so that they could import English manufactures as cheaply as possible. Politically the merchants of the Baltic ports were progressive and had little sympathy with the feudal notions of the junkers who lived on the great estates of the hinterland. But on economic matters the Baltic merchants saw eye to eye with the Prussian squirearchy which—led by von Bülow-Cummerow—favoured free trade.

The economic situation of the Prussian Baltic ports when Prince Smith settled in Elbing was similar to what it was sixteen years later when Cobden visited Stettin. Cobden wrote in August 1847 :

" The protective duties of the Zollverein are particularly injurious to the Baltic provinces of Prussia, which export wheat, timber and other raw produce. The manufacturing districts of Rhenish Prussia are entirely cut off and detached from this part of the kingdom : they receive their imports and send out their exports by the Rhine, not through a Prussian port ; thus the protective system stands in the way of the increase of the foreign trade in the Prussian ports, and stops the growth of the mercantile marine without even offering the compensation of an artificial trade in manufactures. In fact, owing to her peculiar geographical position, the maritime prosperity of Prussia is more completely sacrificed than any other State by the protective system."[3]

The Old Etonian, who had hardly yet mastered the German language, found a congenial field for political activity in the Elbing Wednesday Club which was frequented by merchants of liberal political views. Soon he secured an influential position in the society. In 1837, when seven Göttingen professors were dismissed for protesting against the abolition of the Hanoverian constitution, Prince Smith induced the Wednesday Club to express its sympathy to Professor Albrecht (a native of Elbing). Moreover Prince Smith sent a copy of the address to the Prussian Minister of the Interior and, not unnaturally, received a sharp rebuke for his pains.

Meanwhile, Prince Smith was also actively engaged as a journalist and advocated free trade in articles appearing in the *Elbinger Anzeiger*. In 1840 he gave up teaching to devote himself to political and literary work. A series of pamphlets—the most

[3] John Morley, *The Life of Richard Cobden* (2 vols. 1881), I, pp. 449-50.

important of which was *Über Handelsfeindseligkeit* (Königsberg, 1843)—established his position as the leading free-trade advocate in Germany. Two familiar free-trade arguments used by Prince Smith deserve mention. First, he thought that Prussia should adopt free trade whatever her neighbours did. He denounced tariff wars and reprisals since (in his view) they hurt those who imposed them more than those against whom they were directed. "If England increases the price of the bread of its citizens why should Prussia as a reprisal raise the cost of the cotton goods consumed by its people?" Secondly, Prince Smith argued that world free trade would lead to universal peace.

In the previous quarter of a century there had been some increases in the Prussian tariff. The tariff of 1818—which had been adopted by the Zollverein (1834)—had levied much lower import duties than those of any other European Great Power. Raw materials had been admitted free, manufactured goods paid only 10% *ad valorem* while tropical products (*Kolonialwaren*) paid from 20 to 30%. Transit dues were usually 1*s.* 6*d.* a (Prussian) hundredweight.

By the 1840's, however, these rates had been considerably increased. The demands of the Rhenish and south German manufacturers had led to increases in import duties—the most important being a twenty-shilling per ton duty on pig-iron.[4] Moreover, since Zollverein duties were levied on weight or quantity (and not by value) recent price-falls had caused rates (which in 1818 had equalled 10% *ad valorem*) to be greatly increased in the 1830s.[5] Prince Smith and his followers wanted to abolish these recent—deliberate and fortuitous—tariff increases and to check the demands of Friedrich List and his fellow-protectionists for still higher import duties.

The triumph of the free-trade movement in Britain in 1846 was naturally a great encouragement to Prince Smith. He took the initiative in drawing up an address to Sir Robert Peel which was signed by the leading merchants of Elbing (July 1846). The letter praised Peel for the three outstanding measures of his administration—the income tax, the Bank Act and the reform of the tariff. It appealed to continental countries to follow Britain's example and adopt free trade. Peel was congratulated on breaking a monopoly that was supported by a party which put class

[4] This was in 1844. Belgian pig-iron paid only 10s. per ton duty.

[5] Dr. John Bowring told the Select Committee on Import Duties in 1840 that the original intention of the Prussian tariff as regards manufactures was to impose a maximum duty of 10%, 'but effect has not been given to that intention, for on a great number of articles the duty is from 60 to 100 per cent.' (Qn. 834). Bowring agreed that this was 'in consequence of taking the duty by weight' (Qn. 835).

interests before national welfare. The address claimed that Prussian statesmen had long been working for free trade and had successfully resisted many protectionist demands.

Peel's reply declared that the protectionists had no hope of victory since it had been proved that free trade would benefit the whole nation. Under protection the national finances for revenue fell as smuggling increased while the cost of trying to suppress smuggling was considerable. Peel thought that commerce would flourish and revenue improve if customs duties were levied solely for revenue. He believed that world free trade would fulfil the intentions of the Almighty who had given to different countries various climates, soils and crops. The maximum international exchange of goods would benefit everybody.[6] The Elbing declaration and Peel's reply gave the free-trade agitation in Germany a standing which it had not hitherto enjoyed. So far the movement had been confined to limited academic and official circles and to some of the merchants at the ports. Now free trade became a national issue.

Prince Smith settled in Berlin in 1846 to direct the movement from the Prussian capital.[7] He married Auguste Sommerbrod, the daughter of a well-known banker. The lady had ample means and so Prince Smith was able to devote all his time to the free-trade crusade. He became a respected burger of Berlin and represented the " Academic Constituency " of Unter den Linden in the City Council (March 1848).

He felt that free trade should be promoted not merely by articles and pamphlets but by an active propaganda society run on the same lines as the English Anti-Corn Law League. In December 1846 a small group of industrialists, merchants and intellectuals met in the Berlin Bourse to consider founding such a society. A larger meeting was held in March 1847 when Prince Smith proposed the establishment of a Free Trade League. Other speakers, however, wanted a society in which people holding different fiscal views could discuss economic problems. The meeting set up a Scientific Society for Trade and Industry and about eighty people joined it. Soon, however, the title of Free Trade Union was adopted. Similar societies were set up in such

[6] The Elbing address and Peel's reply are printed in Prince Smith's collected works (III, 260 ff.). C. S. Parker states that Peel's answer ' was regarded by his opponents as a symptom of disordered brain. " The Elbing letter ", wrote Lockhart to Croker, " *sent furieusement l'apoplexie* " '. (C. S. Parker, *Sir Robert Peel* (3 vols. 1891-9), III, 459.)

[7] When Prince Smith migrated from Elbing to Berlin he hoped to become commercial editor of a new liberal review. But the post went to a protectionist—Gustav von Höfken.

leading commercial centres as Frankfurt-am-Main, Hamburg, Rostock and Stettin. Free trade newspapers were founded—for example, the *Freihandelszeitung* (Leipzig), the *Volkswirt* (Frankfurt-am-Main), the *Deutscher Freihafen* (Hamburg) and the *Rostocker Zeitung*.

Prince Smith sought political allies for his agitation. He might have attempted co-operation with the reactionary junkers who were interested in low import duties on foreign manufactures and luxuries. Bismarck's view was typical of his class: " We pay high prices for cheap English iron to support the Silesian miner." " Our red wine from Bordeaux (the national drink of the north Germans) is made expensive to help the sour wines of the Ahr and Nahe " (1849). The Liberals on the other hand—except in the ports—were generally protectionists. Moritz Mohl, the leading south German Liberal, was a strong protectionist as were many influential Liberals in the industrial Rhineland such as Mevissen and Hansemann. Nevertheless, Prince Smith embarked on a campaign to convert the Liberals to free trade and his first success in this direction was when he and Julius Faucher won the support of the left-wing Berlin paper, the *Abendpost*. Eventually, he succeeded in " identifying economic with political and parliamentary Liberalism."[8]

Despite his desire to secure political allies Prince Smith resolutely refused to compromise his free-trade views. He advocated immediate and complete free trade. He rejected the view that—in fairness to industrialists whose manufactures had long enjoyed protection—a change to free trade should be made gradually. He often said that this argument was no better than that used by the man who claimed that the most humane way to cut off a dog's tail was by instalments.

Prince Smith tried to link the German free-traders with the international free-trade movement. In several countries free-trade societies had been formed as a result of the success of the British Anti-Corn Law League. Cobden visited the Continent for fourteen months in 1846-7, his journey being a triumphal progress. He visited leading statesmen and spoke at many free-trade functions. In the summer of 1847 he saw in Berlin the chief Prussian officials (Eichhorn and Dieterici) who had played a leading part in founding the Zollverein, and he was entertained to dinner by 180 free-traders. He declined to address another free-trade gathering since he felt that he should in no way intervene in Prussian domestic concerns.[9]

[8] W. H. Dawson, *Protection in Germany* (1904), p. 24.

[9] John Morley, *The Life of Richard Cobden* (2 vols. 1881), I, pp. 446-8.

In the following month Prince Smith and Dr. Asher represented the Berlin free-traders at the Brussels Free Trade Congress.[10] There were 170 delegates from most of the European countries. The English visitors included Dr. Bowring, Colonel Perronet Thompson and James Wilson.[11] Resolutions in favour of free trade were passed but, owing to the outbreak of revolutions shortly afterwards, this first international free-trade conference had little practical success.

Despite the uncertainties of the years 1848-50 Prince Smith continued to devote his energies to the free-trade cause. He had three immediate aims—first, to affiliate local free-trade societies into a central association ; secondly, to establish a permanent information and statistical bureau ; and thirdly, to raise a fund for propaganda purposes. In May, 1849, with the support of the Hamburg and Stettin free-traders, Prince Smith set up a Central Association for Free Trade in Berlin. By 1851 some thirty societies were affiliated to this body. But it survived for only a few years. A bureau was also established to provide journalists with information on free-trade topics, but this venture was a costly failure.

In the early 1850s the German free-traders had some success in influencing those responsible for the economic policy of the Zollverein, but their movement still lacked any wide measure of popular support. They were pleased with developments in the Zollverein where the free-trade elements were strengthened by the adhesion of Hanover (1851-4)[12] and by the failure of Bruck's plan for the establishment of an Austro-German customs union on a protectionist basis (1853).[13]

Moreover, Prince Smith appears to have been in close touch with Manteuffel (the Prussian Minister President in the 1850's) and he may have played some part behind the scenes in securing in 1856 the appointment of a Prussian departmental committee

[10] For the proceedings of this conference see *Congrès des Economistes réunis à Bruxelles par les soins de l'association belge pour la liberté commerciale. Session de 1847. Séances de 16, 17 et 18 Sept.* (Brussels, 1847). See also article on ' Economistes (congrès des)' in Coquelin and Guillaumin, *Dictionnaire de l'Economie Politique* (2 vols. 1854), I, pp. 671-2.

[11] James Wilson was the editor of *The Economist*.

[12] The treaty was signed in September 1851 but only came into effect on 1 January, 1854.

[13] The Austro-Prussian Commercial Treaty of February 1853 shelved the issue, for it merely provided for further discussions in the future on the question of an Austro-Zollverein union.

of civil servants to consider the reform of the Zollverein tariff on free-trade lines.[14]

On the other hand Prince Smith's agitation made little headway as a popular movement. Even the fervour of the enthusiasts waned. The Hamburg Free Trade League, once in the forefront of the movement, almost ceased to function in 1856-7.[15] The result was, as the *Bremer Handelsblatt* observed (23 May, 1857), that often well-meant Government reforms failed owing to the ignorance of the masses.

The weakness of the free-traders was due to various causes. They were a heterogeneous group which included such diverse elements as Prussian land-owners, Hanoverian farmers, Hanseatic merchants and some Rhenish and Saxon industrialists. Their spokesmen included some business men, but most free-trade propaganda came from journalists and intellectuals—doctrinaires rather than men of affairs. The officials responsible for Zollverein affairs—Delbrück, Pommer Esche and Philipsborn—though free-traders themselves held aloof from any attempt to gain popular support for their policy.

The free-traders were divided among themselves. There were extremists and moderates. Every free-trade group had its own axe to grind. Thus the treaty which brought Hanover into the Zollverein was supported by most free-traders—since it rebuffed protectionist Austria—but was opposed by Hamburg free-traders who disliked the appearance of Zollverein officials on the other side of the Elbe.

Another weakness of the free-traders was their failure to find a popular rallying cry. The British free-traders by concentrating their attack on the Corn Laws had been able to represent their campaign as a crusade to raise the workers' standard of living. But the German free-traders could hardly be expected to set the Spree on fire by denouncing pig-iron duties or Rhine tolls.

Prince Smith frequently regretted the failure of free-traders to convert the workers to their cause. One might have expected the Silesian weavers to complain of the yarn duties or the Solingen

[14] The committee was set up as the result of an instruction given by Frederick William IV to his Finance Minister, von Bodelschwingh. Representatives of the Ministries of Foreign Affairs, Finance, Commerce and Agriculture sat on the committee. See E. Franz, ' Die Entstehungsgeschichte des preussisch-französischen Vertrages vom 29 März 1862 ' in the *Vierteljahrschrift für Sozial- und Wirtschafts-Geschichte* (1932), XXV, 2-4.

[15] For the Hamburg Free Trade League see E. Baasch, ' Der Verein für Handelsfreiheit in Hamburg ' in the *Zeitschrift des Vereins für hamburgische Geschichte* (1920), XXIV.

smiths to grumble at the pig-iron duties, but these workers were domestic craftsmen rather than factory hands and were not yet politically minded. The Socialists—the only group which seriously canvassed working-class support—gave Prince Smith no encouragement. They argued that if free trade reduced living costs then employers would cut wages. They thought that if Germany adopted free trade her industries would be crushed by powerful British rivals.[16]

The subsequent revival of the German free-traders was due mainly to Prince Smith's skill in linking the free-trade issue with other progressive movements which had a more popular appeal—at any rate with the educated middle classes—than his own agitation. The first of these movements was one started by Dr. Böhmert (editor of the *Bremer Handelsblatt*) in 1857 when he appealed for the establishment of an association to foster various projects dear to the hearts of liberal economists—such as free trade, industrial freedom, the abolition of transit dues and the reduction of river tolls.

The second was a movement to alleviate working-class distress. Some of the German representatives at an international welfare congress (*Wohltätigkeitskongress*) held at Frankfurt-am-Main in 1857 considered that industrial freedom rather than charity would cure poverty. The influential Berlin Central Association for the Welfare of the Working Classes sympathized with this point of view.

Thirdly, there was Schultz-Delitzsch's well-known co-operative movement. Supporters of these progressive groups joined with free-traders to establish an Economic Congress.[17] This *Volkswirtschaftlicher Kongress* linked the free-traders with more influential German liberal reformers. The first Congress met at Gotha in 1858. Subsequent meetings were held annually in various towns.

The significance of the Economic Congress has been summed up as follows :

"Whoever hoped to be regarded in wide circles of the population as an expert economist and a progressive thinker on economic problems joined the Congress and sought to make himself heard

[16] See leading article in the *Neue Rheinische Zeitung*, 1 August 1848, reprinted by M. Schippel, op. cit. pp. 345-6.

[17] At this time the German free-traders resumed contact with the international free-trade movement. In 1857 Hertz and Wickmann of Hamburg attended a meeting of the International Association for Tariff Reform at Brussels.

at its meetings. The majority of the members were deputies in parliamentary bodies (who influenced new legislation) and their appearance at the Congress gained them the support of electors. The wealthy middle class saw that its interests were being furthered by the Congress and therefore gave it every support. The Federal Governments and both senior and junior civil servants could not disregard the decisions of the Congress. Even opponents of the principles for which the Congress stood were often forced to take part in its deliberations in the hope of having some attention paid to their point of view ".[18]

A committee on tariff reform appointed at the first meeting of the Economic Congress recommended the abolition of transit dues. The Congress of 1859 proposed the removal of the "general import duty"—a fixed impost upon all imports not specifically mentioned in the Zollverein tariff. It suggested also the abolition of all duties on foodstuffs and other agricultural products as well as duties on most industrial raw materials.

In 1860 the Economic Congress boldly went to Cologne—the heart of the protectionist Rhineland—to discuss the highly controversial pig-iron duties. Since anyone could attend the Congress by paying a small fee, representatives of the protectionists were present at the Cologne meeting. The free-traders were succesful and secured the adoption by the Congress of plans for a thorough reform of the Zollverein tariff. The Congress recommended the abolition of differential import duties and differential dues on shipping ; the removal of all duties levied for protective purposes in favour of moderate duties levied for revenue only ; the abolition of all export and transit dues ; and the establishment of a uniform tariff applicable to goods from all foreign countries. This programme, which embodied views expressed by Prince Smith for the past thirty years, was virtually adopted by the Prussian Government and was carried out by the Zollverein in the 1860s.

The tactics employed in the Rhineland in 1860 were repeated in south Germany in 1861—but with less success. Just as the Economic Congress had gone to Cologne to denounce the pig-iron duties so it went to Stuttgart to condemn the cotton-yarn duties. But here Dr. Kerstorf, veteran champion of the cotton interests, appeared and made a vigorous speech in defence of protection for the cotton industry. After a lively debate the

[18] E. Leser, 'Freihandelsschule' in the *Handwörterbuch der Staatswissenschaften* (Jena 1892), III, 670.

Congress passed on to its next business without making any proposal concerning the duties on cotton yarn.[19]

In the various free-trade activities of the Economic Congress Prince Smith played a leading part. He was for some years chairman of its Standing Committee which handled the business of the Congress between the annual conferences. He led the free-trade attack on the pig-iron duties with a trenchant article in 1859[20] which was followed by a paper on " The World-Political Importance of Free Trade " at the Cologne Congress of 1860. His influence was strengthened by his election two years later to the Prussian lower house where he represented Stettin. When Germany was united in 1870 he was elected by Anhalt-Zerbst to the first Reichstag.

Prince Smith died in 1874. He lived to see his task accomplished and free trade established. The various reforms of the Zollverein tariff by which this was brought about were due as much to political necessity as to economic conviction.[21] The simplicity of the Prussian tariff of 1818 was due largely to the need for devising a customs system suited to the peculiar geographical arrangement of Prussia's scattered territories. The maintenance of low import duties in the early 1850's was the obvious method of defeating the attempt of protectionist Austria to enter and to dominate the Zollverein. The sweeping tariff reductions of the 1860s were, at any rate in part, the natural Prussian reaction to the surprising change in French fiscal policy first announced by Napoleon III in his letter to Fould of 5 January, 1860. Three weeks later the Anglo-French commercial treaty was signed, and it was clearly in Prussia's interest to secure for the Zollverein concessions similar to those which Cobden had gained for Britain. The Franco-Prussian commercial treaty of 29th March,

[19] It was in this year (1861) that another organization was formed which the free-traders used, with some success, as a platform from which to put forward their views. This was the General German Commercial Conference (*Allgemeiner deutscher Handelstag*) which was a union of German and Austrian chambers of commerce.

[20] ' Der eiserne Hebel des Volkswohlstandes ' in the *Deutscher Botschafter* (1859).

[21] See, for example, Bismarck's comment on the Franco-Prussian commercial treaty of 1862—the turning-point in the Zollverein's change to free trade. He told the Reichstag in 1879: ' In the further struggle with Austria that threatened in 1865 and which took place in 1866, the restraint of France would certainly not have continued up to the point to which happily for us it did if I had not cultivated relationships with her in every way open to me.' Bismarck clearly viewed the matter much more from a political than from an economic standpoint.

1862 (which came into force in 1865) provided for the reduction of over 160 Zollverein duties.

A fundamental obstacle to tariff changes between 1834 and 1867 was the fact that unanimity was required for all decisions reached by the Zollverein general conference. Reforms could be achieved only slowly and by hard bargaining. Sometimes the free-traders secured a reduction in an import duty only by placating the protectionists with an increase in some other duty. Before 1867 the Zollverein was not placed on a permanent basis. The treaties between Prussia and the other members of the Customs Union were renewed in 1841, 1853 and 1865. Changes in the structure or the tariff of the Zollverein which could not be secured in any other way could be achieved by embodying them in the treaties of renewal. It was by threatening to refuse to renew the Zollverein that Prussia forced recalcitrant fellow-members in 1853 to accept the September treaty with Hanover and in 1865 to accept the sweeping tariff changes brought about by the Franco-Prussian Commercial Treaty of 1862. The free-trade victory was thus won only at the cost of a serious crisis in Zollverein affairs.[22]

There is here a sharp contrast between the triumph of the free-traders in Britain and in Germany. In Britain Corn Law Repeal was a political issue which was fought out in public debate inside and outside parliament. The popular agitators of the Anti-Corn Law League played an all-important part in the struggle. In Germany, on the other hand, the issue was settled by hard private bargaining between ministers of state and civil servants of Prussia and other Zollverein members. The popular free-trade agitation—culminating in the spirited debates of the Cologne meeting of the Economic Congress—was almost insignificant when compared with the activities of the British Anti-Corn Law League. It has been pointed out that " Free Trade never became in Germany a popular cry and a party policy in the English sense, nor did its success depend at any time in any degree whatever upon the attitude of the great body of the people ".[23] Prince Smith never became an influential demagogue like Cobden

[22] A year later (1866) the old Zollverein came legally to an end owing to the Seven Weeks War. The new Zollverein of 1867 (in which the whole of the North German Federation was a single member) had no *liberum veto* in its Customs Council and Customs Parliament. Here decisions were by majority vote. This made it much simpler to secure tariff changes. Import duties on wine (1868) and sugar (1869) were reduced. After the unification of Germany the pig-iron duties were first reduced (1873) and then abolished (1 January 1877).

[23] W. H. Dawson, *Protection in Germany* (1904), p. 26.

or Bright. His role, however, was by no means without significance, for he did influence some of those in whose hands lay the power to alter the economic destinies of Prussia and the Zollverein in the middle years of the nineteenth century.

The short-lived free-trade epoch in Germany coincided with a considerable expansion of industry and commerce as well as a rise in the standard of living of many workers. In the year of Prince Smith's death Treitschke wrote :

"The transformation of our national economy has given to the working class a great increase of wages, without parallel in German history. Therewith they secured, as aforetime the English working classes, the possibility of permanently improving their standard of life, and of approximating more nearly to the habits of the middle classes ".[24]

Prince Smith could have wished for no better epitaph. Happily, he probably never realized how ephemeral was his success. Within only a few years of his death rapid political and economic changes in Germany brought about a complete reversal of the policy to which he had given a life of political agitation.

[24] Quoted by W. H. Dawson, *op. cit.* pp. 31-2. This seems a sounder judgement than the view expressed by Bismarck in a speech to the Reichstag on November 29, 1881: ' I had the impression that under the Free Trade system, introduced in 1865, we fell into a condition of decline, which was indeed staved off for a time by the new blood which came with the five milliards' (i.e. the French indemnity) (*ibid.* p. 47).

8. WILLIAM THOMAS MULVANY: AN IRISH PIONEER IN THE RUHR.[1]

ONE of the major factors which retarded the industrialisation of Ireland in the nineteenth century was lack of capital.[2] Since adequate funds were not forthcoming from private sources the Government had to provide money both to encourage industrial enterprise and to build public works—such as canals, railways and harbours—which in England were constructed by private enterprise. As the Irish did not have enough capital for their own needs they seldom had any to spare for investment elsewhere and they were concerned only to a very minor extent with the migration of capital overseas which was a characteristic feature of the English economy in the nineteenth century. It is therefore surprising to find that Irish capital and managerial skill played a not insignificant rôle in the industrial expansion of the Ruhr in the fifties and sixties of the nineteenth century.

In this connection the career of William Thomas Mulvany is of considerable importance. Yet his achievements appear to have been forgotten in his native country and no biography of him has appeared in English.

William Thomas Mulvany was a member of a Dublin family still remembered for its artistic achievements. His father (Thomas James) and his uncle (John George) were two of the fourteen foundation members of the Royal Hibernian Academy which was established in 1823. Thomas James Mulvany became Professor of Perspective and subsequently (1841) Director of the Academy. One of W. T. Mulvany's brothers (George

[1] See Kurt Bloemers, *W. T. Mulvany, 1806-85* (Essen, 1922). The Mulvany papers which Bloemers used are now in the Rheinisch-Westfalischen Wirtschaftsarchiv in Cologne. See also: *Die Jubelfeier des Herrn Presidenten W. T. Mulvany zu Düsseldorf am 17en März, dem fünfundzwanzigsten Jahrestag der Aufnahme seiner Tätigkeit in Deutschland* (1880); obituary notices in the *Irish Times*, November 5, 1885 and the *Düsseldorfer Anzeiger*, October 31, 1885; report by T. R. Mulvany in Appendix II of the *Second Report of the Royal Commission on Depression of Trade and Industry* (Cmd 4715 of 1886); and Annabella Catherine Mulvany (editor), *Letters from Professor T. J. Mulvany to W. T. Mulvany . . . 1825-1845* . . . (1907). Miss Mulvany's book includes pictures of W. T. Mulvany as a child and a young man.

[2] The lack of capital in Ireland in the middle years of the nineteenth century should not, however, be exaggerated. Robert Kane, writing in 1845, stated that over £2,000,000 of Irish capital was transferred every year to England to buy British Government stock and that "the property in steam vessels belonging to Dublin is only exceeded in amount by that of London, and is actually greater than the united steam property of Bristol, Hull and Liverpool" (*The Industrial Resources of Ireland* (1845), p. 409).

Field) succeeded his father as Director of the Royal Hibernian Academy and later became the first Keeper of the National Gallery of Ireland.[3] Another brother (John Skipton) was an architect. W. T. Mulvany was born on March 11th, 1806 at Sandymount, Dublin, and was educated at Dr. Wall's school in Hume Street. Owing to the influence of his headmaster he became a Protestant. He entered Trinity College, Dublin, as a medical student but soon decided to be a surveyor. At the age of nineteen he secured an appointment as a student-surveyor in the Irish Ordnance Survey—his first assignment being to Coleraine—and he was subsequently promoted to the post of Assistant Boundary Surveyor.

Soon after his marriage to Alicia Winslow in 1832 Mulvany received an appointment as a Civil Engineer under the Board of Public Works.[4] In 1835 he settled at Limerick where for some years he played an important part in drawing up ambitious projects for the regulation of the River Shannon. He skilfully combined schemes to assist transport by improving the navigation of the river with plans to further agriculture in the valley by arterial drainage.

After careful surveys had been made[5] Mulvany assisted in preparing the Shannon Navigation Bill which was passed in 1839. In the same year he was appointed one of the two District Engineers who were responsible for carrying out the scheme. One of his younger brothers (Thomas John Mulvany) assisted him in this work.

Owing in no small measure to Mulvany's administrative gifts and technical skill considerable progress was made in the next few years in carrying out the Shannon scheme despite delays caused by floods in 1839 and by opposition from smallholders, fishermen and owners of watermills who complained that inadequate attention was being paid to their interests. By 1848 the scheme had cost over £533,000.[6]

In 1841 Mulvany was selected by Fox Burgoyne to prepare

[3] For T. W. Mulvany's father and uncle see article on Thomas James Mulvany in the *Dictionary of National Biography*, XXXIV, p. 285.

[4] For some years W. T. Mulvany worked in close association with Sir John Fox Burgoyne, chairman of the Public Works Board between 1831 and 1835 (see *Dictionary of National Biography*, VII, p. 342) and Sir Harry David Jones, Commissioner of the Irish Boundary Survey (1836) and chairman of the Public Works Board between 1845 and 1850 (see *Dictionary of National Biography*, XXX, p. 105).

[5] See the *Fifth Report of the Commissioners for the Improvement of the River Shannon* (H.M. Stationery Office, Dublin, 1839).

[6] C. E. Trevelyan, *The Irish Crisis* (1848), p. 20 and Robert Kane, *The Industrial Resources of Ireland* (2nd ed. 1845) pp. 272 and 354.

certain Irish drainage and fishery Bills for presentation to Parliament and in 1842 he was appointed a Drainage Commissioner and Inspector of Fisheries. His headquarters were now in Dublin. The reports of the Board of Public Works contain evidence of the vigour with which Mulvany carried out his new duties. The improvements which he made in the Shannon fisheries—by constructing stake-weirs for example—deserve mention.

Mulvany was promoted to the position of one of the three Commissioners of Public Works—at a salary of £1,000 a year—in September, 1846. He undertook his new duties at the critical period of the potato famine when his Department was responsible for public relief works employing some 97,000 persons.[7] In the following year the distress was even more serious. It was stated that in 1847 " the Board of Works became the centre of a colossal organisation : 5,000 separate works had to be reported upon : 12,000 subordinate officers had to be superintended. Their letters averaged upwards of 800 a day . . . "[8] In March, 1847 no less than 734,000 persons were employed upon relief works. In addition the Board of Works co-operated closely with the two official Relief Commissions and the Poor Law Commissioners as well as with charitable organisations engaged in distributing relief and promoting projects to alleviate unemployment.[9]

The Board of Works—and other public and private organisations—were criticised for abuses that undoubtedly occurred in the carrying out of public works at the time of the potato famine. But it was the first time that such a remedy had been attempted upon so vast a scale under exceptionally difficult conditions and it may be doubted whether the critics would have done much better if they had shared the responsibility that Mulvany and his colleagues shouldered so courageously.

Mulvany strongly advocated the improvement of communications which were unusually backward in Ireland. In this way he hoped both to foster economic expansion and to provide employment. As early as 1839 he had reported in favour of building a canal to join the Shannon and the Erne.[10] At the

[7] This was the figure for August 1846: see C. E. Trevelyan, *op. cit.*, p. 48.

[8] C. E. Trevelyan, *op. cit.*, pp. 58-9.

[9] See, for example, Mulvany's letter of May 29, 1847 to the Central Relief Committee of the Society of Friends enclosing an application for assistance for fishery purposes (*Transactions of the Central Relief Committee of the Society of Friends during the Famine in Ireland* (Dublin, 1852), Appendix XVII).

[10] W. T. Mulvany, *Report . . . on . . . the Country between the Rivers Shannon and Erne with a view to the formation of a proposed Junction between these Rivers* (H.M. Stationery Office, Dublin, 1839).

time of the potato famine a considerable number of relief works for which he was responsible were road improvements. And he supported schemes for the construction of State railways.[11]

After the potato famine the emergency relief works were wound up but the normal activities of Mulvany's Department continued to expand. In 1849 the Board of Works was responsible for the improvement of inland navigation, roads, bridges, piers, harbours, public buildings, asylums, educational establishments (the colleges at Maynooth, Belfast, Cork and Galway), drainage (239,922 acres) and fisheries. In addition loans amounting to £1,420,000 had been made to proprietors for the improvement of their land.[12]

Soon afterwards Mulvany retired on a pension. "It is a suggestive commentary on our system that long experience and abilities of high order, which should have been devoted to the amelioration of this country and the development of its resources, were more highly prized and rewarded in a foreign land."[13]

After a long period of service in various Government Departments in Ireland Mulvany embarked upon a new career as an industrialist in the Ruhr. In the middle of the nineteenth century this district was by no means so important a manufacturing region as it later became.[14] In 1850 the towns of Dortmund, Duisberg, and Essen each had a population of only about 7,000 ; Krupp of Essen was employing only some 700 men and the output of the Dortmund Mining District amounted to only 1,665,662 tons of coal and 11,490 tons of pig iron. But the formation of the German customs union, the improvement of communications,[15] the discovery of "blackband" iron ore near

[11] At the end of 1846 only 123 miles of railways had been completed in Ireland and only 164 were in course of construction. The construction of a network of railways—to be financed by Government grants or loans—had been advocated by a Royal Commission in 1836, by the Devon Commission (1845) and by Lord George Bentinck in 1847. For Bentinck's scheme see Benjamin Disraeli, *Lord George Bentinck* (1851), ch. 19 and 20. The Government rejected Bentinck's scheme but subsequently voted a loan of £600,000 to build three Irish railways.

[12] See *17th Report from the Board of Public Works, Ireland*, 1849 and James Caird, *The Plantation Scheme* . . . (1850), ch. 11.

[13] *Irish Times*, November 5, 1885.

[14] For the development of the Ruhr industrial area in the nineteenth century, see Norman J. G. Pounds, *The Ruhr: a Study in Historical and Economic Geography* (London, 1952).

[15] Communications in the Rhineland and Westphalia had been improved by the introduction of steam tugs on the Rhine; the construction of the inland port of Ruhrort; and the opening (in 1848) of both the Cologne-Minden and the Berg-Mark railways.

THE RUHR IN THE MIDDLE OF THE NINETEENTH CENTURY

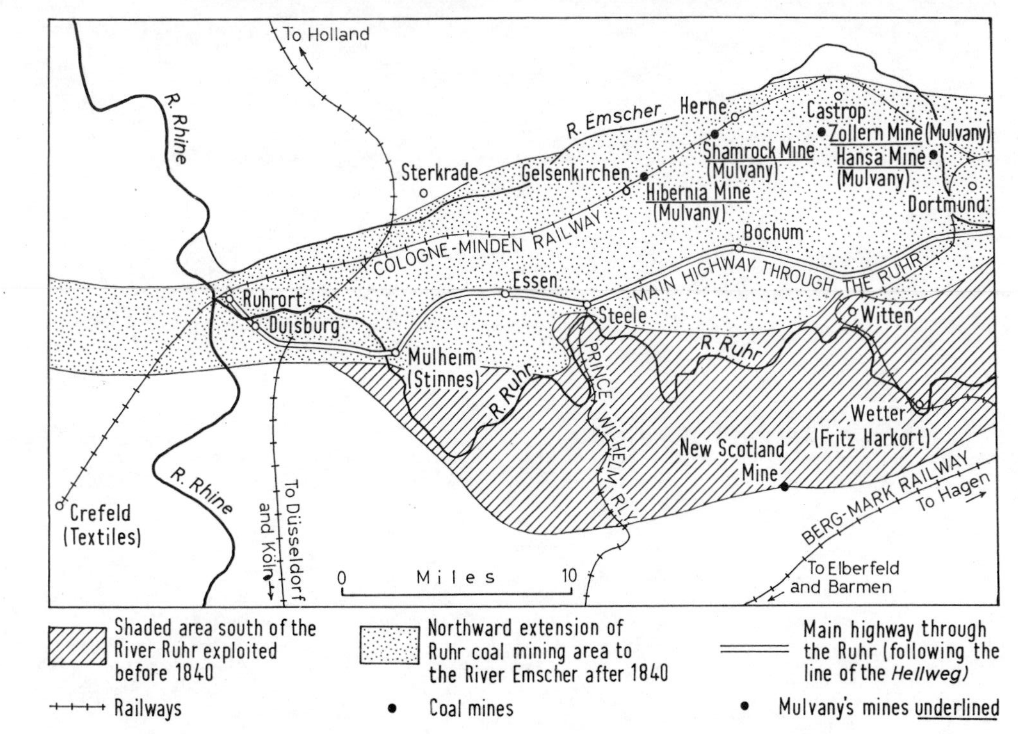

Essen, and the reform of Prussian mining legislation[16] had paved the way for the greatly increased activity of the Ruhr coalfield in the 1850's.

This expansion was to the north of the old collieries in and adjacent to the Ruhr valley. It was the deeper seams north of the *Hellweg* and south of the River Emscher—the area between Duisberg, Gelsenkirchen, Dortmund and Hamm—that were to produce the coal upon which the prosperity of the whole Rhenish-Westphalian industrial region depended in the later years of the nineteenth century.

In 1853 Michael Corr van der Maeren—who had been born in Ireland but had settled in Belgium where he became a leading Free Trader—visited Ireland to raise capital to exploit the mining concession called Ludwigsglück[17] which he had acquired in the Gelsenkirchen district.[18] He secured the support of William Perry of Obelisk Park, Dublin, and Mr. Malcomson of Portlaw, Waterford, and the three investors invited Mulvany to take

[16] A Prussian Law of May 12, 1851, reduced the coal tax on the right bank of the Rhine from ten to five per cent. (on gross receipts): a further reduction took place in 1860. A second Law of May 12, 1851 removed many former restrictions imposed by the Government on the day to day working of coalmines and left private coalowners reasonably free to manage their collieries as they pleased.

[17] In 1857 the *Neu Christiansglück* concession was added to the *Ludwigsglück* concession: the two together covered just over 200 hectares.

[18] A number of foreign—mainly British, French, Belgian and Dutch—capitalists embarked upon coalmining ventures in the Rhenish-Westphalian industrial area at this time. L. H. Jenks, *The Migration of British Capital to 1875* (1927) states that at least 19 British mining companies were founded in the 1850's " to engage in mining along the Rhine " (p. 390, note 74). Two of the most important companies founded with British capital were the Ruhrort Mining Company (which established the Westende Mine in 1854) and the New Scotland Mining and Ironworking Company (Neu Schottland mine founded in 1857). Gustav von Mevissen—the well-known Cologne industrialist who was the principal director of the Schaafhausen Bank and the Rhenish Railway—was alarmed at the extent to which foreign interests were penetrating into the Rhenish-Westphalian industrial district in the 1850s. He declared: " Owing to our failure to participate in so productive an activity as the exploitation of our mines—a source of national wealth hitherto inadequately tapped because of a lack both of a spirit of enterprise and of capital—there has in recent years been an ever increasing danger that this will fall into the hands of foreign speculators. It is well known that for some time a number of coal measures in the Rhineland have been acquired on behalf of French and English capitalists who will profit by exploiting them. The treasures beneath the soil of our Fatherland thus help to increase the preponderance which foreign capitalists already possess elsewhere and the fruits of German labour will benefit foreign stockholders. It is evidently in the supreme interest of our economy to retain not only the earnings but also the capital itself " (quoted by Pierre Benaerts, *Les origines de la grande industrie allemande* (1933), p. 353).

charge of the proposed undertaking. After visiting Gelsenkirchen and Herne in 1854 Mulvany agreed to do so.

Twenty-five years later Mulvany, recalling his first visit to the Ruhr, declared : " When I visited the Head Mining Office I examined a geological map and I realised by investigations on the spot what wonderful rich deposits lay beneath the soil. I saw how inadequate were your railways and canals in those days and I appreciated what a heavy burden your existing transport facilities had to bear. I said : ' These people do not know their own wealth ' ".[19]

In 1856 van der Maeren and his Irish friends decided to establish the Hibernia Mine near Gelsenkirchen. Work began on St. Patrick's Day and on March 21st a formal agreement was reached by the partners concerning the number of shares to be held by each of them. The capital of the *Gewerkschaft*—a partnership with unlimited liability—was divided into 128 mining shares (called *Kuxen*). Joseph Malcomson of Mayfield (described as a shipowner) held 40 shares. William Malcomson of Portlaw and David Malcomson of Mayfield held eight shares each. J. Perry (Senior) and J. Perry (Junior) of Kingston also had eight shares each while Mulvany and van der Maeren held sixteen shares each. Mulvany was not only a shareholder but the salaried manager of the colliery. His brother (Thomas John) and his son (Thomas Robert) were associated with him for many years in the Ruhr.[20] Perrot, an Irish bank manager, was appointed accountant of the enterprise in 1858.

Many difficulties had to be faced in sinking shafts, installing machinery and making other preparations to start production. The coal lay at a greater depth than that to which German engineers and coalminers in the Ruhr were accustomed. Mulvany secured the services of William Coulson—an experienced colliery engineer from the Durham coalfield—and other skilled English ironworkers. Coulson used the " tubbing " method of lining shafts with iron casings. German mining engineers, who had formerly built brick shafts, eventually adopted the " tubbing " method. There were no good roads in the Gelsenkirchen district at this time and the machinery, engines, pumps, cast-iron pipes and so forth (which were imported from England) had to be transported over rough footpaths.

Mulvany overcame these obstacles and opened the first shaft of the Hibernia Mine in the middle of 1858. A second shaft was completed in 1861. Meanwhile the Irishmen responsible

[19] *Die Jubelfeier des Herrn Presidenten W. T. Mulvany* . . . (1880), p. 30.

[20] After working with his brother for twenty-three years in Germany Thomas John Mulvany emigrated to New Zealand where he died in 1892.

for establishing the Hibernia Mine were planning a second venture.[21] This was the Shamrock Mine near Herne. The first shaft was opened in 1860 and the second in 1862. By 1872 the output of the Hibernia and Shamrock mines together amounted to 338,000 tons. In the seventies the Hibernia and Shamrock company was one of the three great mining firms which dominated the Ruhr. The other two were the Harpen Mining Company of Dortmund (*Harpener Bergbau AG.* founded in 1856) and the Gelsenkirchen Mining Company (*Gelsenkirchener Bergwerks AG*, founded by Grillo and Kirdorf in 1873).

Although some English engineers and miners were engaged in the initial stages of establishing the Hibernia and Shamrock mines[22]—a few of them settled permanently in the Ruhr[23]—German workers were soon employed in considerable numbers. Mulvany took a paternal interest in the welfare of his workers. He built a number of cottages for them at the Hibernia Mine. He opposed trade unions—then in their infancy in the Ruhr—and claimed that employers "had done a thousand times more for the workers than paper laws or Socialist agitators".[24]

As early as 1860 Mulvany's position as one of the leading mining experts in the Ruhr was officially recognized when he was invited to accompany a Prussian Coal Commission to Britain in 1866. Mulvany and his son showed the members of the Commission round industrial establishments and docks in London and over some of the English and Scottish coalfields.

Not content with running two of the most efficient collieries in the Ruhr, Mulvany extended his interests by opening up the Erin colliery at Castrop. This mine, which was managed by his son, was one of Mulvany's less successful ventures since it suffered from extensive flooding and the output could seldom be regarded as satisfactory.[25] In 1859 Mulvany sank much of his capital in the purchase of two collieries near Dortmund which were in financial difficulties—the Hansa Mine at Hucharde[26]

[21] P. C. Roney was a shareholder in the Shamrock Mine but not in the Hibernia Mine.

[22] Mulvany's English miners were paid up to ten shillings a day at a time when German miners in the Ruhr were earning only 2/- to 2/6d. a day.

[23] The last survivor of these English pioneers was George Laverick who died in Germany in 1913.

[24] Quoted by Kurt Bloemers, p. 119. See also Mulvany's denunciation of strikes in his pamphlet: *Der Strike der Bergleute im Essener Revier* . . . (Düsseldorf, 1872).

[25] The Erin mine was closed in 1877 but was reopened in 1885 after it had been acquired by Friedrich Grillo.

[26] The Hansa mine had been established by the *Dortmunder Bergbau-und Hüttengesellschaft* in 1856.

and the Zollern Mine at Kirchlinde.[27] In 1866 Mulvany set up a mixed coal and iron concern by linking the Erin, Hansa and Zollern mines with the Vulkan Ironworks (Duisburg). The Prussian Mining and Ironworks Company was founded with a capital of £120,000 to run this enterprise.[28]

The companies in which Mulvany was interested came to grief in the financial crisis that followed the boom after the Franco-Prussian war. In 1873 the Hibernia and Shamrock mines were sold for over £800,000 to two Berlin banks[29] which promoted a new German company to take them over. Mulvany retained his post as chairman of the company.[30] He and his colleague Leo Graff successfully guided the firm through the difficult period of the slump in the seventies. Then the exploitation of the rich *Dickebank* and *Sonnenschein* seams in the northern portion of the Shamrock concession in 1880 assured the future of the undertaking for many years to come.[31]

In 1877 the Prussian Mining and Ironworks Company was turned into the *Westfälischer Grubenverein* which was purchased in 1882 by a consortium led by Friedrich Grillo.[32] The last vestiges of Irish capital investment in the Ruhr had now disappeared but the Mulvany family continued for many years to take an active part in the industrial life of the Rhineland and Westphalia. Mulvany lived to see an immense expansion of coal production in the Ruhr for the output of the Dortmund Mining District rose from a little over four million tons in 1858 to nearly 23½ million tons in 1884.

Mulvany's services to the Ruhr were not confined to founding

[27] The Zollern mine had been founded by the *Steinkohlenbergbau A.G. Zollern* in 1857.

[28] Owing to the inadequate transport facilities between the Hansa and Zollern mines Mulvany built a light railway between the two collieries: horse traction was used. It may be added that the capital of the Prussian Mining and Ironworks Company was later raised to £540,000.

[29] The banks were the *Handelsgesellschaft* and S. Bleichroder. The new company was the *Preussische Bergwerks-und Hütten-Action Gesellschaft*.

[30] For the Hibernia and Shamrock mines after they were taken over by a German company see: *Festschrift aus Anlass des fünfundzwanzigjährigen Bestehens der Bergwerkgesellschaft Hibernia 1873-98* (1898). The Prussian State made an unsuccessful attempt to acquire a controlling interest in the Hibernia Company in 1904-6 but succeeded in doing so in 1917.

[31] See Paul Steller, *Führende Männer des rheinisch-westfälischen Wirtschaft* (1930), p. 37. In 1887 the Hibernia Company acquired the Wilhelmina Viktoria mine.

[32] F. Grillo had established his reputation in the Ruhr in 1873 when he founded the *Gelsenkirchener Bergwerks A.G.* the nucleus of which was the *Rheinelbe* and *Alma* mines (managing director: Emil Kirdorf).

and managing several progressive and efficient collieries. The pioneers who survive the cut-throat competition of the early years of expansion in a rapidly growing industrial region are generally ruthless individualists who pursue their own interests with little regard for the welfare of their neighbours. They seldom appreciate the necessity of working together for the prosperity of the industrial district in which their enterprises are situated. But Mulvany—probably because of his long experience of public service in Ireland—took a wider view from the first. He realised more quickly than many of his fellow Ruhr industrialists that only by united action on the part of the great firms could the problems confronting the district be solved. For many years he worked unceasingly to persuade the coal-owners, ironmasters and others that some measure of co-operation was essential for the future prosperity of the Rhenish-Westphalian industrial area.

He had been in Germany for only two years when—towards the end of 1858—he took a leading part in setting up at Essen the Ruhr Mineowners Association (*Verein für die bergbaulichen Interessen im Oberbergamtsbezirk Dortmund*).[33] Mulvany was one of the most active members of this association. The first chairman was Dr. Friedrich Hammacher and the first secretary was Dr. Gustav Natorp. This association—which was usually called the *Bergbauverein*—was founded shortly after the financial crisis of 1857. At that time coal prices were falling. They dropped by more than half between 1858 and 1863.[34] The mineowners were in difficulties not only on this account but because their output was increasing so rapidly that coal stocks were accumulating at the pithead. Transport facilities were inadequate—there was a shortage of railway wagons[35]—and the existing markets were unable to absorb all the coal that was

[33] The Bergbauverein replaced a moribund mineowners association called the *Mark Gewerkenverein* which was wound up in June 1859. For the *Bergbauverein* see its journal (*Glückauf*) and Ernst Jungst, *Festschrift zur Feier des funfzigjährigen Bestehens des Vereins fur die bergbaulichen Interessen im Oberbergamtsbezirk Dortmund . . . 1858-1908* (1908). Mulvany's long services to the *Bergbauverein* were recognized in 1880 when—on the occasion of the twenty-fifth anniversary of his arrival in Germany—he was elected an honorary member of the association. It is interesting to note that Thomas—a former British consul who had secured an appointment on the staff of the Dahlbusch Mine—was also associated with the establishment of the *Bergbauverein*.

[34] For details of Ruhr coal prices at this time see Maurice Baumont, *La grosse industrie allemande et le charbon* (1928), p. 327.

[35] The shortage of wagons was particularly acute in the autumn when potatoes and beet were being transported by rail.

produced. A somewhat similar crisis occurred in the Ruhr shortly after the Franco-Prussian war.[36]

Two main remedies were suggested by the Bergbauverein. The first was to extend the market for Ruhr coal at home and abroad by persuading the railways to reduce their freight rates and by securing the provision of additional transport facilities by rail and inland waterways. Mulvany strongly supported this policy and visited Antwerp with Dr. Natorp to investigate the possibility of exporting Ruhr coal from that port.[37] Eventually the *Bergbauverein* set up a Coal Export Committee (March, 1876)[38] of which Mulvany was chairman. In the following year an independent Westphalian Coal Export Association (*Westfälischer Kohlen Ausfuhr Verein*) was set up and Mulvany was also chairman of this organization. The Coal Export Association embarked upon a propaganda campaign to persuade customers that the quality of Ruhr coal was equal to that of English coal. It tried to secure better facilities for landing and storing Ruhr coal in German river harbours and seaports. It put pressure on German railways to secure cheaper freights.

When the Export Association was wound up in 1894—the founding of the Rhenish-Westphalian Coal Syndicate in 1893 having rendered the older organization superfluous—a fair measure of success had been achieved. As early as 1861 the first large consignment of Ruhr coal had been sent to Rotterdam to be exported overseas. By 1868 the statistician Bienengräber was able to report that Ruhr coal was being sent regularly to Bremen and Hamburg (for use on transatlantic steamers and for export) and to Holland.[39] At the time of Mulvany's death (1885) Ruhr coal was being sold in Russia, Switzerland and Italy. In the last years of his life Mulvany was trying to extend the sale of Ruhr coal as far afield as China.

A second remedy for overproduction which received some

[36] See W. T. Mulvany, *Praktische Vorschläge zur Beseitigung der Transportnot* (Düsseldorf, 1896) and Wilhelm Beumer, *Fünfundzwanzig Jahre Tätigkeit des Vereins zur Wahrung der gemeinsamen wirtschaftlichen Interessen in Rheinland und Westfalen* (Düsseldorf, 1896), pp. 11-17.

[37] Maurice Baumont, *op. cit.*, p. 311.

[38] In January of the previous year (1875) 29 Ruhr collieries had set up a joint export association. This organization was replaced by the Coal Export Committee of the *Bergbauverein.*

[39] A. Bienengräber, *Statistik des Verkehrs und Verbrauchs im Zollverein für die Jahre 1842-64* (1868), p. 260. He mentioned that owing to the repeal of the Dutch import duty on coal the export of coal from Prussia to Holland had increased from 9,433,898 *Zentner* (cwt.) in 1860 to 14,901,055 *Zentner* in 1864. Bienengräber added that " many gasworks which formerly used only English coal now use only Ruhr coal " (p. 260). Mulvany agreed, in return for a substantial tariff concession to send 200 tons of coal a day on the (British financed) Dutch-Rhenish Railway Companies lines.

support from members of the *Bergbauverein* when prices again fell in the mid-seventies was to restrict output. Agreements made by most of the Ruhr collieries during the slump of 1878-80 to curtail production failed. Output actually rose by ten per cent in 1880 and by another five per cent in 1881. In the first half of 1886, however, a slight reduction in output was secured. Mulvany viewed this policy with some misgivings since he realized the practical difficulties of enforcing agreements to restrict output especially when not all the mineowners had joined in the scheme.

The *Bergbauverein* also considered the possibility of securing some advantage for Ruhr coal in the home market by advocating the imposition of an import duty upon English coal. Mulvany had been a Free Trader for many years but he changed his views at the time of the controversy on the German iron duties in the early 1870's[40] He now suggested that an import duty of sixpence a ton should be levied upon foreign coal. After some hesitation the executive committee of the *Bergbauverein* came round to this point of view. But the Government refused to impose a duty upon imported coal.[41]

Mulvany saw the need for a larger organization than the Ruhr Mineowners Association which would embrace as many of the industrialists of the Rhineland and Westphalia as possible. In 1871 he took the lead in founding such a body—the Association for the Protection of the common economic Interests of the Rhineland and Westphalia (*Verein zur Wahrung der gemeinsamen wirtschaftlichen Interessen in Rheinland und Westfalen*).[42] For many years Mulvany was the President of this organization. To him and to the energetic secretary (A. H. Bueck) much of its early success was due. At first the Association devoted itself largely to putting pressure on the railways and on the Government to secure improvements in the transport facilities of the Rhineland and Westphalia. Eventually the industrialists of the district came to use the conferences of the Association as a means of arriving at an agreed policy on many problems of common interest. Fiscal policy, factory reforms and company law were among the more

[40] See W. T. Mulvany, *Deutschlands Handelspolitik und deren Wirkung auf den deutschen Nationalwohlstand* (Düsseldorf, 1876).

[41] The *Bergbauverein* was also unsuccessful at this time in its efforts to secure the abolition of the mining tax on coal. This tax was not abolished until 1895.

[42] See Wilhelm Beumer, *Fünfundzwanzig Jahre Tätigkeit des Vereins zur Wahrung der gemeinsamen wirtschaftlichen Interessen in Rheinland und Westfalen* (Düsseldorf, 1896). The Association was popularly known as " the association with the long name ". See J. Winschuch, *Der Verein mit dem langen Namen* (Berlin, 1932).

important topics that were discussed.[43] The association also developed into a sort of informal clearing house for the activities of numerous specialized employers organizations in the Rhenish-Westphalian industrial region.

Mulvany was farsighted enough to appreciate the economic advantages that could be secured by linking independent firms together in cartels. He saw that by joining mining and other companies great savings could be effected and increased efficiency could be achieved. In 1880 Mulvany and his son wrote a pamphlet advocating the amalgamation of a number of collieries in the eastern Ruhr. These were the *Westfälischer Grubenverein* (the Hansa, Zollern and Erin mines) and the Viktor, Adolf von Hansemann, Graf Schwerin and Westhausen companies.[44] Nothing came of this suggestion at the time though subsequently the formation of cartels was a characteristic feature of the development of the German coalmining industry.[45]

Of all the causes that Mulvany championed during his eventful career in Germany—employers' associations, cartels, protective duties, bimetallism—none appeared to him to be more important than the transport problem. The man who had once planned a canal between the Shannon and the Erne and had advocated the construction of networks of railways in Ireland now devoted his energies to trying to improve the transport facilities of the Ruhr. He considered cheap and efficient communications were indispensable to a great industrial country and he favoured State ownership and management of all the main forms of transport.

When Mulvany first came to the Ruhr the district was served by three railways. The Cologne-Minden line ran through the northern part of the coalfield that was just being opened up. It linked Oberhausen with Gelsenkirchen, Herne and Dortmund. The Berg-Mark Railway ran from the great textile centre of Elberfeld-Barmen in the Wupper valley to Witten and Dortmund. The Prince Wilhelm Railway—a branch line from the Berg-Mark Railway to Steele—was of minor significance.

[43] Other organizations in which Mulvany was interested were the *Verein Deutscher Eisen-und Stahlindustrieller* of Berlin (1874), the Düsseldorf Produce Exchange (1875) and the Central Association of German Industrialists of Berlin (*Verein deutscher Eisen- und Stahlindustrieller*, 1876.)

[44] See W. T. Mulvany and T. R. Mulvany, *Amalgamation von Kohlenbergwerken im östlichen Teile des Oberbergamtsbezirks Dortmund* (1882).

[45] For German coal cartels see Curt Goldschmidt, *Über die Konzentration im deutschen Kohlenbergbau* (1912) and A. H. Stockder, *Regulating an Industry ; the Rhenish-Westphalian Coal Syndicate* (Columbia University Press, 1932).

These railways charged different rates for the carriage of coal[46] and showed little sympathy with the demands of the coalowners for a more efficient and cheaper service. Some improvement occurred when the virtual monopoly of the Cologne-Minden and Berg-Mark lines was broken with the extension of the Rhenish Railway from the left bank of the Rhine to the Ruhr. In 1874 the line from Osterath (Krefeld) across the Rhine to Ruhrort and Oberhausen was completed. Gustav von Mevissen, the chairman of the Rhenish Railway Company, had a greater understanding than the directors of the Cologne-Minden Railway of the needs of the Ruhr industrialists.

In May 1860 Mulvany wrote a pamphlet advocating a uniform " One Pfennig Tariff " for coal.[47] This was one silver Pfennig per *Zentner* (hundredweight) per German mile (league) and was the equivalent of 2.2 Pfennigs per ton-kilometre in the Mark currency later adopted by the united Reich. Mulvany argued that the cost of transporting fuel and raw materials—which was then substantially higher than in Britain—seriously hampered Germany's industrial development. The Association of North German Railways had recently agreed to carry up to 500,000 cwt of Ruhr coal to Magdeburg[48] and further east at the " One Pfennig Tariff." But this concession was at first limited to special coal trains travelling long distances and there were supplementary charges.[49] Gradually more and more special cheap coal trains were run and by the late 1860s the principal German railways were applying the " one Pfennig Tariff " to most of their regular goods trains.[50]

[46] When the Ruhr lines were first opened the Cologne-Minden Railway charged from 3.7 to 4.4 pfennigs per ton-kilometre for coal while the Berg-Mark Railway charged the high rate of 6.2 pfennigs. The Prussian Minister of Commerce von der Heydt tried to nationalize the Cologne-Minden Railway in the 1850s but he failed and in 1866 this line passed completely under the control of private owners.

[47] W. T. Mulvany, *Denkschrift über den Pfennigtarif* (Stuttgart, 1860). It was little short of ridiculous that in 1859 the cost of sending coal from the Ruhr to Magdeburg should have been equal to the price at which English coal was selling in that town: see M. Baumont, *op. cit.*, p. 413.

[48] The first consignment of Ruhr coal (from the United Salzer and Neuak Mine at Essen) had been sent to Magdeburg in February 1858.

[49] i.e. two Thalers per 100 *Zentner* loading fee and two Thalers " zonal fee " (*Streckenzuschlag*). The zonal fee was soon abolished.

[50] A. Bienengräber remarked in 1868 that the introduction of the " One Pfennig Tariff " had been of " immense importance " (*unendlicher Wichtigkeit*) for the extension of markets for German coal at home and abroad *Statistik des Verkehrs und Verbrauchs im Zollverein . . . 1842-64* (1868), p. 260. On April 7, 1863 Dr. F. Hammacher, chairman of the *Bergbauverein*, received a presentation from the Ruhr coalowners in recognition of his untiring efforts to secure the introduction of the " One Pfennig Tariff ".

After the Franco-Prussian war the German railways were faced with rising costs. The Prussian Ministry of Finance, fearing a loss of revenue from the State lines, favoured a general increase in freight charges. In 1874 a twenty per cent increase was authorized. Most of the railways availed themselves of this permission though the cost of sending Ruhr coal to Hamburg and Bremen was increased by only eleven per cent. Mulvany vigorously attacked the raising of freight charges. He claimed that the reduction made in the 1860s had contributed substantially to Germany's economic prosperity and he argued that any increase would be a retrograde step.[51] In 1877 the twenty per cent increase in freights was dropped though a supplementary loading fee was reintroduced.[52]

Mulvany also pressed for improvements in the inland waterways of northern Germany,[53] Holland and Belgium and for an extension of Germany's inland habour facilities.[54] He achieved little in his lifetime though eventually the Dortmund-Ems and Rhine-Herne canals were of great benefit to the Ruhr.

August von der Heydt (the Prussian Minister of Commerce)—after having with difficulty secured the introduction of the " One Pfennig Tariff " on the Silesian lines so as to bring coal more cheaply from Upper Silesia to Berlin—supported the efforts of the Ruhr industrialists to obtain a similar concession from the North German Railways. The opposition of the Government of Hanover (where the lines were owned by the State) proved a serious stumbling block and it was not until 1860 that the " One Pfennig Tariff " was introduced even on a limited scale (see A. Bergengrün, *Staatsminister August Freiherr von der Heydt* (1908), ch. 7).

[51] See W. T. Mulvany, *Deutschlands Eisenbahn-Tarif-Frage* (January, 1874), *Für und Gegen die Eisenbahn-Tarif-Erhöhung* (April, 1874); and *Memorandum über die Folgen der Erhöhung der Eisenbahn Tarife* (December, 1874).

[52] See W. T. Mulvany, *Deutschlands Verkehrswesen. Eisenbahn-Tarif-Reform* . . . (1877) and *Denkschrift über Reform der Eisenbahn-Gütertarife* . . . (1879). Mulvany's son pointed out that his father " got prohibitive freights reduced to—next to America and Belgium—the lowest in the world ". " Formerly he used to hold up English railway freights to German railway managers as an example of what could be done; now the tables are completely turned " (Report by T. R. Mulvany in the *Second Report of the Royal Commission on Depression of Trade and Industry*, 1886, Appendix Part II, p. 172). It may be added that before 1871 freights on German railways were generally calculated according to the value of the goods carried. Between 1871 and 1877 freights were usually calculated according to the amount of wagon-space which they occupied. After 1877 a new method of calculating freights—a compromise between the two principles previously adopted—was introduced.

[53] See, for example, W. T. Mulvany, *Deutschlands Wasserstrassen* (1881) and *Fluss-See-Dampfschiffe* (1884). Mulvany's proposals for the construction of steamers which would link German inland harbours with foreign ports led to the establishment of regular voyages between Cologne and London.

[54] See, for example, W. T. Mulvany, *Düsseldorfer Eisenbahn- und Hafen-Frage* . . . (1882): a later edition was issued by T. R. Mulvany in 1889.

Mulvany died on 30th October, 1885. He had lived to see the Ruhr develop from relatively small beginnings to be the largest coalfield and industrial centre not only in Germany but on the Continent. He had introduced important improvements in the technique of coalmining and he had shown the Ruhr coalowners and other industrialists how to combine effectively to promote their common interests. He had worked unceasingly to improve transport facilities and to widen the markets for Ruhr coal at home and abroad.

This brief survey of Mulvany's career and achievements may be concluded with a tribute that T. R. Mulvany paid to his father's memory. T. R. Mulvany was the British Consul at Düsseldorf and in December, 1885, in the course of a report upon the effects of the "Great Depression" on the Rhenish-Westphalian industrial region, he wrote :

"I am proud to say, and all our countrymen will, I am sure, be pleased to hear that to a considerable extent the development of this great district is here generally admitted to be owing to the initiative talent of my own father, the late William Thomas Mulvany, formerly Commissioner of Public Works in Ireland, latterly chairman of the Hibernia and Shamrock Mining Company of Herne in Westphalia, as also of the great association for the protection and promotion of the general interests of the industry of Westphalia and the Rhenish provinces, which last-mentioned institute he, with a German friend, in 1871 formed in connection with the leading industrial men of all branches of industry in the provinces and of their railway companies. This association . . . under my father's able leadership . . . worked wonders during the trying years of, and subsequent to, the crisis ; it gained immense influence with the Parliament and Government, and all the economic reforms of the day are mainly to be attributed to the wise use made of this influence in conjunction with the *Verein für (die) bergbaulichen Interessen des Obergamtsbezirk Dortmund* of which my father was a member and Dr. Hammacher chairman. The reduction of railway freights, the purchase of the railways by the State, the introduction of a moderate import duty on iron, the improvement of navigation, the proposed great canal from the Rhine to the North Sea ports and Elbe . . . are all mainly due to the influence of my father . . . He was admitted by all to be the coalmining pioneer of Westphalia where he introduced the English system of mining and shaft-sinking in 1855 . . . "[55]

[55] Report of T. R. Mulvany, British Consul at Düsseldorf, December 24, 1885 in the *Second Report of the Royal Commission on Depression of Trade and Industry* (1886), Appendix Part II, p. 171.

V. CENTRAL EUROPE

9. BRITISH INFLUENCE ON THE INDUSTRIAL REVOLUTION IN THE HABSBURG DOMINIONS, HOLLAND AND SWITZERLAND

HABSBURG DOMINIONS

BRITISH influence on the development of the industrial revolution in the Habsburg dominions was of greatest significance in textiles, iron, machine building and transport. In the manufacture of textiles the achievements of John Thornton were of outstanding importance. In 1800 an Austrian bank—the *Kommerz Leih- und Wechsel-Bank*—sent Freiherr von Glave-Kolbielski to England and Germany to secure foreign textile machinery and the services of skilled workers. Two English mechanics named John Thornton and John Lever agreed to supply Kolbielski with machines for spinning cotton, wool and flax. Despite an official report that Thornton's machines were no better than those already in use in Bohemia the *Kommerzleih-und Wechsel-Bank* placed Thornton in charge of the Yarn Manufacturing Company of Pottendorf (Lower Austria) in 1801. This became one of the largest cotton mills on the Continent in the early years of the nineteenth century. In 1811 it had 38,800 spindles and employed 1,800 operatives. By 1828 the number of spindles had increased to 47,460. Largely owing to the success of Thornton's establishment the spinning and weaving of cotton became more sharply differentiated in Lower Austria than in Bohemia. In the former region specialised factories for spinning and weaving developed while in the latter province the two processes were often carried out in the same establishment.[1]

John Thornton also influenced the expansion of the Austrian linen industry. At the request of Thaddäus Edler von Berger and Eduard Schultz he designed and constructed flax spinning machines which were installed in 1838 in the works of the Pottendorf Linen Yarn Manufacturing Company. By 1845 this establishment had 8,000 spindles and it was by far the largest flax spinning mill in the Habsburg dominions.[2]

[1] Johann Slokar, *Geschichte der österreichischen Industrie . . . unter Kaiser Franz I* (Vienna, 1914), pp. 182-5, 274, 280 and 283. In 1822 John Thornton took out a patent for an improved spinning machine. The name Thornton appears also in lists of cotton spinning establishments in Lower Austria in 1841—Jonathan Thornton at Ebenfurth, C. Thornton at Munschendorf, and Joseph Thornton at Unter-Eggendorf and Unter-Waltersdorf. All these establishments were in the Wiener Wald district (*ibid.*, p. 286).

[2] J. Slokar, *op cit.*, p. 381.

Meanwhile Rowland and Osborne had established a factory at Georgeswalde (Kreis Leitmeritz) in Bohemia for the manufacture of cotton and linen cloth. In 1824 Thomas Busby of Wiener-Neustadt secured a licence for the preparation and spinning of silk-waste by new machinery. In the early 1840s several Englishmen were engaged in the Austrian textile industries. John Thornton now had his own cotton mill at Ebenfurth in the Wiener Wald district. In 1843 this establishment had 78 machines carrying 15,000 spindles and employed 400 operatives. The output of yarn in 1843 was a little over 500,000 (Vienna) lbs. At the same time in Bohemia L. Thomas ran a small mechanical worsted spinning mill at Graslitz while C. Thomas owned a cotton mill at Normy. John Brady had a cotton factory at Ingrowitz in Moravia.

In the Vorarlberg in the 1840s there were two joint stock companies engaged in cotton spinning which had been formed with English capital. Peter Kennedy (Edwin Chadwick's brother-in-law) had established a cotton spinning mill at Feldkirch. In 1843 this firm—Escher, Kennedy & Co.—had 15,000 spindles, employed 290 operatives and produced over 500,000 (Vienna) lbs of yarn and twist. John Douglas had founded both a spinning and a weaving establishment in the village of Thüringen. An English cotton manufacturer stated that, in his opinion, John Douglas's cotton mill was " better than the average as it includes all our best machines, and some improvements which we might advantageously copy from them ".[3] In 1843 the Thüringen cotton spinning mill—then run by Escher, Kennedy and Douglas—had over 9,000 spindles, employed over 200. operatives and produced 380,000 (Vienna) lbs. of yarn and twist.[4]

Norman Douglas, grandson of the founder of the Thüringen cotton mill, wrote :

" I cannot . . . say when this business was founded. It may have been in the late thirties, for he died October, 1870, aged sixty-six at Banchory, N.B., where he ought to have died, and there lies entombed in our vault. His object in thus exiling himself and family for a whole lifetime was to earn enough money to pay back some heavy mortgages on his ancestral estate, for which he had an idolatrous affection. This much I happen to

[3] *First Report on the Commissioners appointed to enquire as to the best means of establishing an efficient Constabulary Force* . . . (Parliamentary Papers, 1839, XIX) : evidence of Samuel Robinson, pp. 78-9.

[4] J. Slokar, *op cit*., pp. 286, 293, 306, 311, 350 and 407. See also references to Peter Kennedy in the *First Report of the Commissioners appointed to enquire as to the best means of establishing an efficient Constabulary Force* . . . 1839, pp. 78-9.

know: that in 1856 already, by working these mills, he was able to repay £36,000 towards the cost of them, and £24,000 towards redeeming the mortgages. So he set himself to his grim task; and a grim task it must have been to master the immense technical and commercial details of such an undertaking, and all in a foreign language; to import (among other little difficulties) every scrap of machinery from Lancashire with no railway nearer, I fancy, than Zürich. He worked with single aim and lived to reap his reward, although the losses due to the American Civil War, and the Austro-German one, were such that the whole enterprise nearly came to grief".[5]

In many factories owned by Austrians machinery from England was installed and English managers and foremen were employed. Johann Josef Leichtenberger—one of the most important manufacturers of cotton cloth in Bohemia—opened a large machine-spinning establisment at Wernstadtl in 1797. Here were installed the first English water-frames and mule-jennies to be seen in Bohemia. It was soon realised that they were more efficient than the machinery formerly imported from Saxony. In 1803 the Emperor expressed his thanks to Leichtenberger—and also to Prince Charles of Auersperg and the Count of Rottenhan—for introducing modern British textile machinery into the Habsburg dominions.[6] When the manufacture of bobbinet was introduced into Prague—by Nottrot and Breitfeld—English machines, worked by English operatives, were used. In 1840 John MacGregor, one of the few British officials who was well-informed about Austrian economic affairs, stated that in the cotton mills around Vienna "the directors and foremen . . . are chiefly Englishmen or Scotsmen from the cotton manufactories of Glasgow and Manchester".[7]

In the smelting of iron and the construction of machinery and steam-engines British influence also made itself felt in the Habsburg territories. In 1774 it was reported that an Englishman named Collins had established himself in Vienna as a master cutler and that he was employing several of his countrymen in his workshop.[8] In 1806 Tylor and Royce received permission

[5] Norman Douglas, *Together* (1923), p. 63.

[6] J. Slokar, *op cit*., pp. 187, 289, 290, 304. By 1799 English machinery had also been installed in cotton mills at Kosmanos and Neureichstadt.

[7] *Report from the Select Committee on Import Duties*, 1840; evidence of J. MacGregor, Qn. 1046.

[8] William Eden to Sir John Fielding, January 31, 1774 in R. A. Roberts *Calendar of Home Office Papers, 1773-5* (1899), No. 482. Eden stated that Collins was reported to be in England looking for more skilled cutlers and suggested that he should be found and arrested.

to set up a factory for the construction of textile machinery and two years later Tylor and Tuton superintended the fitting out of a tool manufactory at Count Radetzky's ironworks at Neumarktl.[9] One of the earliest steam-engines to be built in Austria was constructed in 1815 at the Stiepanau ironworks in Moravia which had been leased by John Baildon.[10] He was a Scottish engineer who had made a name for himself by erecting coke-furnaces for smelting iron in Upper Silesia. Five years later Edward Thomas and James Thomas established at Reichenberg the first works in Austria for the construction of steam-engines. In 1830, in association with Bracegirdle, they set up an establishment at Altharzdorf (by Reichenberg) for the construction of various types of textile machinery. By the end of 1841 Edward Thomas had built 35 steam-engines (434 h.p.) and many textile machines.

Other British machine builders in the Austrian dominions in the 1830's who deserve mention are L. Thomas at Graslitz, R. Holmes at Neudeck, David Evans and Joseph Lee at Prague (1834), James Park at Beraun, and Williams (in partnership with Völkert) at Reichenberg. All these works were in Bohemia.[11] In the 1840s William Baildon, son of John Baildon,[12] erected furnaces in Carinthia at Lippitzbach (1845) and at Freudenberg (1854).[13] The former were gas-puddling furnaces. In 1846 Edward Thomas owned ironworks at Gratzen (Budweiser Kreis) in Bohemia. The output of these works in that year was 2364 (Vienna) cwt. of pig iron and 832 (Vienna) cwt. of cast iron. Edward Thomas was one of the first ironmasters to introduce the puddling process into Bohemia.[14] In Vienna M. Fletcher and J. Punshon established a factory in 1833 for the construction of steam-engines. Later these works were leased to W. Norris

[9] L. Beck states in his *Geschichte des Eisens* . . . Vol. IV (1899), p. 366, that an Englishman named Dutton erected important works at Neumarktl about 1812 for making steel by the cementation process.

[10] J. Slokar, *op cit*., pp. 189, 486, 611-2. The first two steam-engines to be built in the Habsburg territories were erected for instructional purposes at the Prague polytechnic (1806) and upon Count Bouquoy's estate at Rothenhaus (1810). In 1815 an engine " to move a vehicle " was built by Johann Bozek at the Prague polytechnic.

[11] J. Slokar, *op cit*., p. 615.

[12] John Baildon had set up a coke-furnace at the *Hohenlohehütte* in the Prussian province of Upper Silesia in 1805: see above p. 151.

[13] L. Beck, *Geschichte des Eisens*, IV, p. 572 *et seq*. and p. 856.

[14] J. Slokar, *op cit*., p. 451 and p. 458.

of Philadelphia who built locomotives in them. British machinery was installed in many Austrian engineering establishments. The Vienna workshops of the Vienna-Gloggnitz railway were fitted out with the most modern English machines. The works were described as " an establishment which served as a model for the whole of Austria ".[15] Some English capital was invested in Austrian railways particularly during the period of reconstruction after the war against Prussia in 1866. Thomas Brassey —in association with Klein & Schwarz—secured contracts for the building of the Crown Prince Rudolf Railway (1867) and the Vorarlberg Railway (1870).[16]

HOLLAND

English influence on the industrial revolution in Holland was particularly marked in the 1830's after the loss of the Belgian provinces.[17] The Dutch did not wish to see the export of cotton and woollen cloth to Java fall entirely into the hands of English and Belgian manufacturers. The initiative in this matter was taken by van den Bosch (Governor of the Dutch East Indies) in 1830. King William I supported his plans and both the Dutch Government and the influential State overseas trading corporation (the *Handelsmaatschappij*) made strenuous efforts to found a modern cotton industry in Holland. Their efforts met with considerable success particularly in the Twente industrial district in the south east of the province of Overyssel. Here—in the small manufacturing towns of Enschede, Lonnaker, Oldenzaal, Almelo, Hengelo and Goor—a relatively moribund rural textile industry was revived.[18]

A young Englishman named Thomas Ainsworth played an important part in this revival of the Twente cotton industry. He

[15] J. Slokar, *op cit*., p. 617 and p. 621. See also Carl Pfaff in *Entwicklung von Industrie und Gewerbe in Osterreich . . . 1848-88* (Jubilee Industrial Exhibition, Vienna, 1888), p. 270.

[16] L. H. Jenks, *The Migration of British Capital to 1875* (1927), p. 420.

[17] See N. W. Posthumus, " Bijdragen tot de Geschiednis der Nederlandsche Grootindustrie " No. 2 and No. 3 in the *Economisch-Historisch Jaarboek*, XI, 1925, pp. 168-244 and XII, 1926, pp. 179-215.

[18] For the Dutch rural domestic industries in the seventeenth and eighteenth centuries see Z. W. Sneller, " La naissance de l'industrie rurale dans les Pays-Bays aux XVIIe et XVIIIe siecles " in *Annales d'Histoire Economique et Sociale*, I, 1929, pp. 193-202.

had been associated with the *Handelsmaatschappij* since 1830 and he had introduced an improved winding spool onto the looms of L. A. Möfke's machine weaving establishment at Almelo. In a memorandum submitted to Willem de Clercq in 1832[19]—the covering letter was dated July 14th—Ainsworth put forward his views on the establishment of a new " manufactory of calicoes ". He rejected the idea of introducing steam-driven machinery. " To establish power looms where labour is low as in this country, would be an undeniable absurdity ". He criticised a project for bringing Belgian weavers into the country because some of them might be " persons of immoral character ". Ainsworth suggested that 100 pairs of looms should be imported and that four skilled English operatives—a foreman, a weavers' joiner, a heald-knitter and a sizer—should be brought over to Holland to instruct Dutch workers in the art of the hand-weaving of calicoes. He estimated the initial cost of the enterprise at £55,000. After visiting England to secure machinery and a few skilled operatives Ainsworth established a training centre for weavers at Goor in the Twente district. In September, 1833, it was reported that this centre had recently been opened. An Englishman named Thomas Walsh had set up the looms. The institute appears to have been a success and many weavers were trained there. Moreover fifteen weaving sheds, subsidiary to the main establishment at Goor, were founded at Borculo, Denekamp, Dleden, Diepenheim, Enter, Haaksbergen, Hengelo, Holten, Kampen, Losser, Neede, Oldenzaal, Rijssen, Vollenhoven and Westervlier.[20]

At the same time Thomas Wilson—an Englishman who had been living in the Netherlands for some years—established a factory at Harlem for the weaving, bleaching, printing and finishing of cotton cloth. He visited England to study recent textile inventions and it was here that he secured the machinery and tools that he needed for his enterprise. In August, 1833, he was reported to have returned safely to Harlem with his family and in November the factory was ready to start production. The most modern powerlooms and other machinery were installed. In the summer of 1834 Wilson again visited Manchester. In September 1834 he was stated to have 155 looms in his factory.

19 " Notice on the Formation of an Establishment for weaving cloth goods " (1832) in the *Economisch-Historisch Jaarboek*, XI, 1925, pp. 176-9. The covering letter is on pp. 175-6.

20 *Economisch-Historisch Jaarboek*, XII, 1926, p. 180 and p. 200. For Thomas Ainsworth (who was born at Bolton-le-Moors in 1795) see also an article in the *Niew Nederlandsch Biografisch Woordenboek* Vol. I (Leiden, 1911), col. 49 and H. Smissaert, *Bijdragentot de Geschied der ontwikkeling v.d. Katoeunijverheid* (The Hague, 1906).

Official reports in the 1830's paid tribute to the rapid progress of Wilson's establishment.

It may be added that British capitalists and engineers were largely responsible for the building of the important Dutch—Rhenish railway from Amsterdam to the German frontier at Emmerich.[21] The line was planned as early as 1838—as a rival to the projected Antwerp—Cologne railway. The section between Amsterdam and Utrecht was opened in 1843 but then the scheme languished. Two years later a company called the *Nederl.Rhijn-Spoorweg-Maatschappij* was formed to complete the project. Most of the new capital was raised by a group of London bankers led by John Masterman (junior). The line was built by the well known English contractor Thomas Brassey. Construction, however, was not begun until 1853 and the railway was only completed in 1856.[22]

SWITZERLAND [23]

The development of Switzerland as an industrial country of some importance is at first sight somewhat surprising. The country was without coal and iron[24] which were the basic materials upon which the early economic prosperity of England and Germany were based. Switzerland had no seaports, no mercantile marine and no overseas possessions. She was situated far from large centres of population where the goods might be sold.

[21] As early as 1826 a Scottish projector (J. A. Stevenson of Leith) had suggested to King William I of the Netherlands the introduction of steam-propelled carriages on the Dutch highways. But nothing came of this scheme. For Stevenson's letter to the King (September 19, 1826) see Robert Demoulin, *Guillaume Ier et la transformation économique des Provinces Belges* (1938), appendix 5, pp. 381-2.

[22] See J. H. Jonckers Nieboer, *Geschiednis der nederlandsche spoorwegen* (Haarlem, 1907) ; Ernst Baasch, *Holländische Wirtschaftsgeschichte* (1927) ; the centenary volume *100 Jaar Spoorwegen in Nederland* (Utrecht, 1930) ; the Admiralty's Geographical Handbook on *The Netherlands* (1944), p. 558 ; and L. H. Jenks, *The Migration of British Capital to 1875* (1927), p. 144.

[23] For industrial developments in modern Switzerland see T. Geering and R. Hotz, *Wirtschaftskunde der Schweiz* (1910) ; William E. Rappard, *La révolution industrielle . . . en Suisse* (Berne, 1914) and H. Nabholz, L. von Muralt, R. Feller and E. Bonjour, *Geschichte der Schweiz*, Vol. II (Zürich, 1938), Book iv, ch. 9, and Book vi, ch. 11.

[24] Small deposits of iron ore were found in the Swiss Jura at Mühltal (Oberhasli) and Gonzen (Sargans). For the modern Swiss steel industry see *The Swiss Iron and Steel Industry* (British Iron and Steel Federation, 1953).

The division of the country into small cantons each of which had a considerable measure of control over its own economic affairs hampered the development of a national economic policy.

On the other hand Switzerland commanded important trade routes in central Europe and the Swiss derived considerable profit from the transit trade that they controlled. Switzerland's great timber resources were the basis of important manufactures and fast-flowing Alpine streams were an invaluable source of power.[25] The Swiss escaped the devastations caused in many other parts of Western Europe during the Thirty Years War and the long drawn out conflicts of the eighteenth century. Switzerland's geographical position enabled her to benefit from inventions and other technical advances in the neighbouring countries of France, Germany and Italy. She provided an asylum for numerous religious and political refugees who introduced new skilled crafts. The Swiss were a hardworking and thrifty race and they developed an excellent system of primary, secondary and technical education.

John Bowring in a report on Switzerland in 1836[26] remarked that a well informed-Swiss had told him that the success of his countrymen in industry was due to : "(a) Free trade, which enables us to buy all that we want in the cheapest markets without import duty worth mentioning, (b) our light taxes which affect but very slightly the working classes, (c) the low price of labour . . . , (d) efficient capitals and the low rate of interest (3 to 3½ per cent.) resulting from the simplicity and efficiency of the laws relating to mortgages and credit, (e) the intelligence, prudence and economy of our manufacturers, who, although they do not hastily and without reflection undertake new enterprises, pursue their object with energy and perseverence, (f) the aptitude of our population for manufacturing occupation, and their laborious habits of which the higher classes set the example ".

The commercial relations between England and Switzerland[27]

[25] As early as June 18, 1798 Johann Conrad Escher told the Swiss Grand Council : " In the waterfalls of its many streams Helvetia possesses sources of power of incalculable value. If we are able to harness this source of power to industry our achievements will be prodigious and will be greater than those of other nations however many steam engines they may possess." (Quoted by William E. Rappard, *op cit*., p. 159).

[26] John Bowring, *Report on the Commerce and Manufactures of Switzerland*, (Parliamentary Papers, XLV, 1836), p. 60. A German translation entitled *Bericht an das englische Parlament über den Handel, die Fabriken und Gewerbe der Schweiz* was published at Zürich in 1837.

[27] For the economic relations between England and Switzerland see William Waldvogel, *Les relations économiques entre la Grande Bretagne et la Suisse* . . . (Neuveville, 1922).

may be traced back to the middle years of the sixteenth century when English Protestant refugees and students settled, either temporarily or permanently, in such centres as Zürich and Geneva.[28] Some of these Protestants combined business activities with theological studies. In Geneva in 1555-59 several English refugees were described as merchants, weavers and tailors. At Zürich William Petersen and John Burcher made longbows from Swiss wood and exported them to England.

Richard Hilles has been described as " the first Anglo-Swiss trader ".[29] His correspondence between 1540 and 1579 has survived so that it is possible to trace his business activities in outline. On returning to London, after a period of exile in Zürich, Hilles went into business as a wool merchant. He maintained contact with his Protestant friends in Switzerland and he acted as an agent to supply them with money, cloth and other necessities. He settled on the Continent again in 1539—this time at Strassburg—and continued to sell English woollen cloth to Swiss merchants. John Burcher, who was still at Zürich, acted as Hilles' agent for many business transactions. The two men were associated in exporting Swiss timber down the Rhine to England where it was used for ship's masts and bows. Richard Hilles returned to England in about 1548. His business affairs on the Continent were then handled by John Burcher and later by his son Barnabas Hilles.

In the eighteenth century important contacts of a financial nature developed between England and Switzerland.[30] In 1710 the city of Berne lent Queen Anne £150,000 repayable in ten years. Six per cent interest was charged on the loan. Berne subsequently placed several other foreign loans and, with the interest, the city was able to pay for the erection of a number of fine public buildings. Two Berne banks—Malacrida & Co. and Müller & Co.—had close contacts with the City of London at this time. In the middle years of the eighteenth century the city of Berne

[28] For English Protestant refugees in Switzerland in the sixteenth century see J. C. Mörikofer, *Geschichte der evangelischen Flüchtlinge in der Schweiz* (1876) T. Heyer, *Notice sur la colonie anglaise établie à Genève de 1555 à 1560* (Geneva, 1855) ; Charles Martin, *Les Protestants anglais refugiés à Genève* (1915) ; Alfred Stern, *Briefe englischer Flüchtlinge in der Schweiz*, (Göttingen, 1874) ; T. Vetter, *Englische Flüchtlinge in Zürich während der letzten Hälfte des 16en Jahrhunderts* (Zürich 1893); T. Vetter, *Relations between England and Zürich during the Reformation* (Zürich, 1904).

[29] A. Latt, " The first Anglo-Swiss Trader " (in the *Revue Anglo-Suisse*, 1920, Nos. vi and vii).

[30] J. Landmann, " Die auswärtigen Kapitalanlagen aus dem Berner Staatsschatz im 18en Jahrhundert " (*Jahrbuch für schweizer Geschichte*, 1903).

invested some of its funds in Bank of England shares. Berne had a permanent agent in London to handle the loans made by the city in England. In 1790 Berne funds in London amounted to over £440,000. At the same time the city of Zürich held £50,000 of Bank of England stock. Citizens of Geneva had also invested money in London. When Switzerland was overrun by the French in 1798 the British Government impounded Swiss funds lying in London. It was not until 1816 that this money was returned to its owners.

The English inventions of the eighteenth century which revolutionised the textile industries do not at first appear to have aroused any great interest in Switzerland. But in about 1785 English cotton cloth, made by power-driven machinery, began to compete successfully on the Continent with the hand-made fabrics of eastern Switzerland.[31] The weavers of Appenzell and Zürich began to use imported machine-made Lancashire cotton yarn and twist instead of hand-spun Swiss yarn. It was becoming clear that the Swiss spinners would have to adopt machinery. In 1788 Tronchin (Minister of the Republic of Geneva in Paris) forwarded to Puerari (Secretary of State) a memorandum written by Aimé Argand who had lived for some time in England.[32] Argand observed that raw cotton from the Levant passed through Geneva in transit for Zürich where it was spun by hand. He suggested that, since the raw material was available, a machine-spinning industry should be established in Geneva. He pointed out that John Milne and his three sons had successfully introduced Arkwright's water-frame into France and he proposed that these skilled entrepreneurs should be invited to Geneva to set up cotton spinning machines. Argand's proposal was rejected on the grounds that the Milnes were asking too much for their services and were also demanding exclusive privileges.

A few years later another attempt was made to introduce machine spinning into the Swiss cotton industry. Marc Antoine Pellis[33] went to Bordeaux in 1794 where he came into contact

[31] For the development of the Swiss cotton industry see A. Jenny-Trümpy, *Handel und Industrie des Kantons Glarus* (Glarus, two volumes 1898-1902); A. Jenny-Trümpy, *Die Schweizerische Baumwollindustrie* (Bern 1909); and A. Jenny-Trümpy's article on " Baumwollindustrie " in the *Handworterbuch der schweizerischen Volkswirtschaft* (ed N. Reichesberg), vol. III, p. 864 *et seq.*

[32] Aimé Argand (1755-1803) was the inventor of an improved oil lamp with a new form of wick and a glass chimney. It was first patented in England. For Argand's memorandum see W. E. Rappard, *op. cit.*, pp. 127-131 and W. Waldvogel, *op. cit.*, pp. 47-50.

[33] His real name was Marc Antoine Samuel Henri Comod.

with two English skilled operatives named John Heywood and James Longworth who had assisted in the introduction of modern textile machinery into France. In October, 1798 Pellis suggested to Finsler (Minister of Finance) that Heywood and Longworth should be persuaded to settle in Switzerland. The Swiss cotton industry was now in a critical position owing to the occupation of the country by French troops, the loss of foreign markets owing to the war, and the British threat to ban the export of cotton yarn. In November, 1799 Pellis was back in Switzerland and he laid before the Directory of the Republic his plans for the establishment of cotton spinning machinery.

It was owing to Pellis's efforts that the Machine Spinning Cotton Company (*Gesellschaft der mechanischen Baumwollspinnerei*) was set up at St. Gall in February, 1801.[34] Its 4,000 spindles were operated by some 120 workers. The government granted the company the sole right (*privilegium exclusivum*) for seven years to construct four types of textile machines. These were (i) mule-jennies, (ii) drawing machines (*tirage*), (iii) spinning machines (*grosse filature*), and (iv) carding machines. Heywood[35] and Longworth, who had come to St. Gall to supervise the establishment of the new enterprise, were granted patents for a number of textile machines. Pellis's company was not a commercial success and it was finally wound up in 1825. But it was important as being the first firm to introduce modern cotton machinery into Switzerland.

The year in which Pellis's pioneer enterprise was set up saw also the founding of a second machine spinning establishment in Switzerland. Three firms at Winterthur—J. H. Ziegler, J. J. Haggenmacher & Son and J. R. Sulzer & Co.—secured the services of a skilled English mechanic named Travies[36] and set up a joint-stock company to operate a cotton spinning mill on the banks of the River Töss. This enterprise survived until 1840.

In 1805 the newly-founded firm of Escher, Wyss & Co. set

[34] This was the first joint-stock company (société anonyme) to be established in the canton of St. Gall. For this company see H. Wartmann, *Industrie und Handel des Kantons St. Gallen auf Ende 1866* (St. Gall, 1875).

[35] This may be the same John Heywood who later established himself in Alsace—first in Strassburg and then in the valley of the River Breusch—as a cotton manufacturer and constructor of so-called " Schirmeck looms." See above, p. 27.

[36] Travies was also in touch with the well-known Swiss industrialists J. C. Fischer and J. C. Escher: see J. C. Fischer, *Tagebücher* (edn. of 1951), p. 777.

up the " New Mill " (Neumühle) at Zürich. This establishment developed into one of the largest of its kind in Switzerland and had 15,000 spindles in 1830. The firm also established large works for the construction of textile machinery. Johann (Hans) Caspar Escher,[37] the founder and guiding spirit of the company, visited England on several occasions. In articles published in Zürich in 1815-16 he gave an account of his travels and showed how he had secured information concerning recent progress in Britain in the construction of textile machinery.[38] In the 1820s J. C. Escher gave a leading Manchester engineering firm—Messrs. Fairbairn & Lillie—an order for millgearing and water-machinery for his cotton factory which was already one of the largest on the Continent.[39] Subsequently the firm of Escher, Wyss & Co. built Dyer roving frames and other English machines under licence and sold them not only in Switzerland but also in Germany and Italy. In the late 1850s an Englishman named Jackson was placed in charge of the shipbuilding department of Escher, Wyss & Co. He improved the oscillating marine engine and played an important part in securing for Escher, Wyss & Co. the high reputation that they long enjoyed as constructors of river and lake steamers.

By 1814 it was estimated that there were some 700 cotton spinning machines in Switzerland. About half of them were in the canton of Zürich. These machines were driven by water-power or by oxen and not by steam. In the period of reconstruction that followed the collapse of the Continental System[40] the Swiss weaving establishments to a great extent ceased to be dependent upon Lancashire yarn and secured a considerable proportion of their yarn from Swiss machine-spinning mills.

[37] For Johann Caspar Escher (1775-1859) see article in the *Schweizer Lexikon*. He should not be confused with his uncle Johann Conrad Escher.

[38] Johann Caspar Escher, " Briefe aus England " in the *Züricherbeiträge*, 1815-16, Nos. i to iii.

[39] For William Fairbairn see Samuel Smiles, *Industrial Biography* (1863) ch. 16 and an article in the *Dictionary of National Biography*, XVIII, p. 123.

[40] For the effects of the Continental System on Swiss industry see Bernard de Cerenville, *Le système continental et la Suisse* (Lausanne, 1906) and E. F. Heckscher, *The Continental System* (1922), pp. 306-310. For Geneva (then incorporated into the French Empire) see E. Chapuisat, *Le commerce et l'industrie à Genève pendant la domination française* (Geneva and Paris, 1908). Heckscher wrote: " What really caused suffering during this period was not the general state of trade, but the hopeless struggle that hand-spinning was carrying on against machine spinning, hastened, as it was by the importation of yarn and also by the increasing necessity to fall back on the short-stapled Levantine cotton : for this quality did not admit of the spinning of fine numbers of yarn, which otherwise constituted the only chance left to hand-spinning " (*op. cit.*, p. 308).

A Lancashire spinner told a parliamentary committee in 1833 : " To Switzerland we now send less weight of yarn than formerly : it is almost entirely confined to the higher ranges, say from 70 upwards and to some throstle yarns. The lower and middle numbers of mule twist the Swiss produce cheaper than we can send them ".[41]

The mechanisation of the weaving branch of the Swiss cotton industry came rather later than the introduction of spinning machinery. As early as 1815 Johann Caspar Escher warned his countrymen that the power looms he had recently inspected in Manchester and Glasgow were far more efficient than the handlooms still in use in Switzerland. In the 1820s Jacquard looms were introduced from France. In 1826 Heer & Co. of Rheineck employed two English engineers to build ten bobbinet (*tulle*) looms. At first the firm tried to keep the knowledge of the new weaving machines to themselves but in November 1827 —in return for 300 louis d'or—Heer & Co. agreed to pass on information about the looms to other Swiss weaving establishments and machine-builders. Early in 1828 the machine building firm of Michael Weniger & Co. of St. Gall succeeded in smuggling a similar bobbinet loom direct from England. This machine was copied and sold in Switzerland. The bobbinet industry however, was never established on a large scale. In the late 1820s power looms for general use (i.e. not confined to bobbinet) were also introduced into Switzerland and this led to acts of violence on the part of some of the handloom weavers of the Zürich " Oberland ".[42] The last of these " Luddite " risings—the " fires of Uster "—took place on November 22nd, 1832.[43] This " Luddite " movement appears to have slowed down somewhat the introduction of power looms into the Swiss cotton industry. In 1842 Kaspar Honneger of Rüti invented a loom which

[41] *First Report . . . into Employment of Children in Factories* (Parliamentary Papers, 1833, XX), Part i, p. 120 and William E. Rappard, *op. cit.*, p. 152.

[42] The activities of the Zürich " Luddites " in the late 1820's merged into the movement for political reforms. The connection between the two movements may be seen from the famous demonstration at Uster in the autumn of 1830. When one of the orators had appealed to the crowd to support a petition demanding political and constitutional reforms he asked if anything should be added to the petition. The crowd cried : " Down with power looms " and an appropriate new clause was added to the petition. The fact that the cantonal constitutional reforms of the following year (1831) did not alleviate the distress of the Zürich handloom weavers led to an outbreak of incendiarism at Uster in November, 1842.

[43] For the grievances of the Swiss handloom weavers at this time see Jakob Stutz's poem " Der Brand von Uster " (1836), in *Gemälde aus dem Volksleben* (7 vols. 1830-53).

was based upon existing English machines. The machine building works which he established (*Ateliers de Construction Rüti*) eventually specialised in the construction of automatic looms for silk weaving. It may be added that the introduction of machine-spinning and machine-weaving in Switzerland was fostered not only by English experts who worked in Swiss factories but by young Swiss operatives and mechanics who learned their trade in Lancashire. J. C. Fischer, in the diary of his visit to England in 1825, stated that when he visited Johann Georg Bodmer—a Zürich engineer then living in Manchester—he found that he was helping four young Swiss mechanics who were studying English cotton spinning machinery.[44]

The influence of British technical advances in the metal and engineering industries on the modernising of these manufactures in Switzerland may be seen by an examination of the activities of J. C. Fischer, J. J. Sulzer and Charles Brown. Johann Conrad Fischer[45] was both an inventor of note and one of Switzerland's leading industrialists in the first half of the nineteenth century. Born in 1773 at Schaffhausen Fischer followed in his father's footsteps as a coppersmith. On completing

[44] J. C. Fischer, *Tagebücher* (edn. of 1951), p. 262. Bodmer invented a machine to cast toothed wheels : see W. Waldvogel, *op. cit.*, p. 150. For J. G. Bodmer (1786-1864) see articles in the *Transactions of the Newcomen Society*, Vol. VI (1925-6) pp. 86-110 and the *Journal of the Royal Society*, Vol. 101 (No. 4905), August 7, 1953, p. 681 *et seq.* Bodmer was an inventor and a consulting civil engineer. He has been described as " one of the greatest engineers of all time." He first visited England in 1816 and inspected many textile mills and ironworks in various parts of the country. His second stay in England was in 1824-9 when—in partnership with Novelli—he started a cotton mill at Egston near Bolton-le-Moors. He again lived in England (Lancashire and London) between 1833 and 1848. He installed rubber manufacturing machinery at the Chorlton Mills (Manchester) in about 1840. On the Continent Bodmer was at various times active in France (Alsace), Germany (Baden), Switzerland and Austria. He did much to make recent advances in engineering known on the Continent.

[45] For Johann Conrad Fischer see Karl Schib (ed.), *Johann Conrad Fischer 1773-1854 : Tagebücher* (Georg Fischer AG., Schaffhausen, 1951) ; Rudolf Gnade, *The Metallurgist Johann Conrad Fischer 1773-1854 and his relations with Britain* (Georg Fischer AG., Schaffhausen, 1947) ; Otto Vogel, " Johann Conrad Fischer und die englische Tempergiesserei " in *Stahl und Eisen*, 1920, pp. 869-72 ; Berthold Schudel, *Johann Conrad Fischer, ein schweizer Pioneer der Stahlindustrie* (Schaffhausen, 1921) ; and F. M. Feldhaus, " Zwei technologische Reisen nach England 1814 und 1825 . . ." (*Geschichtsblätter fur Technik und Gewerbe*, V, 1918). There are a number of references to J. C. Fischer in L. Beck, *Geschichte des Eisens*, Vol. IV (1899). For the industrial development of Schaffhausen see Hermann Pfister, *Entwicklung der Industrie der Stadt Schaffhausen* (1901).

his apprenticeship he worked for a year in an engineering establishment in London (1794-5).[46] He moved the family works to Mühlental near Schaffhausen in 1802.

At about this time he invented a method of making crucible cast steel. The process had been discovered many years before by Benjamin Huntsman but the secret had been successfully kept and Fischer had to invent the process for himself. Fischer's cast steel was shown at an industrial exhibition at Bern in 1804 and it was the first steel of this kind to be manufactured on the Continent. A German visitor reported in 1810 that Fischer's steel was of high quality and that the inventor had recently extended his works.[47] Fischer also invented copper and nickel steel alloys.[48]

By 1814 Fischer's steelworks were already so well known that they were visited by the Czar Alexander I who tried unsuccessfully to persuade the inventor to settle in Russia. But Fischer was soon extending his industrial interests beyond the narrow confines of his native land. He set up steelworks and engineering workshops in France (La Roche by Voujeaucourt[49]) and Austria (Hainfeld, Traisen and Salzburg).[50]

Johann Conrad Fischer toured the English manufacturing districts on several occasions. Apart from his stay in 1794-5 he visited England in 1814, 1825, 1826, 1827, 1845, 1846 and 1851. His diaries throw valuable light on the development of English manufactures in the first half of the nineteenth century. Much that Fischer saw in England he applied in his own workshops in Schaffhausen. The journey of 1845 was undertaken to study English railways. Fischer strongly advised his fellow

[46] His great uncle (also a coppersmith) had worked in England for eleven years and his father had also visited that country.

[47] P. A. Nemnich, *Tagebuch einer der Kultur und Industrie gewidmeten Reise*, VIII (1811), p. 69 *et seq* ; an article in the *Morgenblatt für gebildete Stände*, March 23, 1808 ; J. C. L. Blumhof, *Versuch einer Encyklopedie der Eisenhüttenkunde* (Giessen, 1817), p. 507 ; and Karl Schib's introduction to Johann Conrad Fischer, *Tagebücher* (edn. of 1951), p. xv.

[48] Fischer called his copper-steel alloy " yellow steel " and his nickel-steel alloy " meteor steel." For these alloys see L. Beck, *op. cit.*, Vol. IV, p. 132 and p. 783.

[49] These works were built for Frédéric Japy.

[50] The Hainfeld (Wiener Wald) steelworks were founded by Georg Fischer (1804-1888), who was J. C. Fischer's youngest son, in 1826. Over 80 workers were employed. Georg Fischer was awarded medals at the Austrian industrial exhibitions of 1835 and 1845 : see Johann Slokar, *Geschichte der österreichischen Industrie* . . . (Vienna, 1914), p. 489. Georg Fischer later moved his works to Traisen, Wilhelm Fischer (1803-1882) ran the ironworks at Salzburg.

countrymen—" particularly artists, craftsmen and manufacturers " —to follow his example and to study on the spot the technical advances that were being made year after year in the leading industrial country in the world[51]. Fischer knew well a number of English scientists and manufacturers such as Michael Faraday, Matthew Robinson Boulton, James Watt (junior), William Murdock, William Fairbairn and Benjamin Gott. It was fitting that towards the close of a long and active life Fischer should have visited England for the last time at the age of 78 as one of the exhibitors at the Great Exhibition of 1851.

J. J. Sulzer[52] of Winterthur, like J. C. Fischer, was a Swiss manufacturer who was strongly influenced by industrial developments in England. He too travelled frequently in England and recorded his impressions in a journal. Sulzer was interested in the manufacture of gas, the improvement of the steam engine and Bodmer's machine for the making of toothed wheels. When Bodmer's machine was exhibited in Paris in 1855 Sulzer sent his son Heinrich to Manchester to study the way in which it was manufactured. J. J. Sulzer and his son visited several English ironworks and steelworks and also investigated recent improvements in the building of steam engines which were economical to use from the point of view of fuel consumption. On a visit to Leeds Heinrich Sulzer also learned something of recent progress in England in the manufacture of armaments. This knowledge was later used by the firm of Sulzer when they modernised the rifles and artillery which they supplied to the Swiss army.

In 1851 Gottlieb Hirzel, J. J. Sulzer's brother-in-law, was employed in London by the well known machine building firm of Maudslay, Son & Field. Here he met the 24-year-old Charles Brown[53] whose exceptional abilities as an engineer were already being realised. Hirzel suggested to Sulzer that Brown should be given an appointment at the Sulzer workshops at Winterthur. For twenty years Brown worked for the firm of Sulzer and he was largely responsible for the great progress made by the firm in the third quarter of the nineteenth century. He extended the firm's engineering workshops and introduced new and up to date machine tools. He greatly improved the steam engine of that day from the point of view of fuel economy.

[51] Johann Conrad Fischer, *Tagebücher* (edn. of 1951), p. 214.

[52] After his marriage he was known as Sulzer-Hirzel. He was born in 1806 and he died in 1883. It has been seen that early in the nineteenth century the firm of Sulzer had co-operated with two other Winterthur firms to establish a modern cotton spinning mill. See C. Matschoss, *Geschichte der Firma Gebr. Sulzer.*

[53] For Charles Brown see A. Hirzel, *Fils de leurs oeuvres* (Neuchatel).

Charles Brown left the firm of Sulzer in 1871 to become the manager of an important Winterthur locomotive construction works (1871-84). In the late 1880s he was engaged by the firm of Armstrong to supervise the erection of an armaments factory and shipbuilding yard at Pozzuoli near Naples. On his return to Switzerland in 1891 Charles Brown and his sons established works at Baden (in Aargau canton) for the manufacture of electrical equipment such as dynamos, power stations, and electric railway installations. The firm (Brown-Boveri et Cie) employed only 180 men in 1893 but it eventually employed over 5,000 workers. The factories were greatly extended in 1900 when the firm began to build steam turbines (invented by Parsons) under licence.

These examples of English enterprise in Holland, Austria and Switzerland show how the industrial revolution in these countries was fostered by English technical knowledge. It was, however, in France, Belgium and Germany that British influence was of fundamental importance.

CONCLUSION

BRITAIN AND INDUSTRIAL EUROPE IN THE 1870S

In the 1870s there were signs of a change in the economic relationship between Great Britain and the industrial states of the Continent. It has been seen that for over a hundred years before the Franco-Prussian war British technical knowledge had, in various ways, contributed to the industrial development of important manufacturing regions on the European mainland. British entrepreneurs, contractors, managers, foremen and skilled workers had played their part in promoting the expansion on modern lines of textiles, engineering and transport in France, Germany, Belgium, Switzerland and elsewhere.

By 1875, however, the position was very different from what it had been in the second half of the eighteenth century. Although Great Britain's output of coal, iron and steel, engineering products and textiles was still very impressive there is reason to suppose that the annual rate of increase in the output of the industry of the United Kingdom was showing signs of slowing down.[1] Moreover, Great Britain's output expressed as a proportion of world output was also declining. In the 1870s Great Britain was, of course, still the leading industrial country in the world but new competitors were arising. An examination of the catalogues and the juries' reports of various international industrial exhibitions held between 1850 and 1880 shows how the range and the quality of the manufactures of Germany, France, Belgium, Switzerland and the United States were steadily improving in this period. Industrial output on the Continent was expanding rapidly, particularly in Germany, and foreign goods were making an unwelcome appearance in overseas markets in which British merchants had once enjoyed a virtual monopoly. In some branches of manufacture the Germans, Belgians, French and Swiss could now compete successfully with their British rivals. In these countries the " infant industries " of an earlier generation were now growing to lusty manhood.[2]

[1] See Walther Hoffmann, *Wachstum und Wachstumsformen der englischen Industriewirtschaft von 1700 bis zur Gegenwart* (Jena, 1940) and an article by Professor Hoffmann on " The Growth of Industrial Production in Great Britain . . ." in *The Economic History Review*, second series, Vol. II, No. 2, 1949, pp. 162-180. See also Carl Snyder, " Measures of the Growth of British Industry " in *Economica*, new series, Vol. I, 1934, pp. 421-435.

[2] For evidence in the late 1860s of the rapid progress of certain industries on the Continent see the *Report of the Select Committee on Scientific Instruction* (Parliamentary Papers, 1867-68, Vol. XV). See also H. L. Beales, "The 'Great Depression' in Trade and Industry" in *The Economic*

In the circumstances Britain's rôle as the schoolmaster of industrial Europe was coming to an end. In the more advanced manufacturing regions on the Continent—such as the Ruhr, the Nord Department and the Sambre-Meuse valleys—the services of British foremen, skilled operatives, mining and marine engineers, and locomotive drivers were no longer required. Men trained in the excellent technical colleges of the Continent (such as Charlottenburg and Zürich) could now do the work without foreign help. It has been remarked that in the steel industry in the early 1870s " in all likelihood England learned more than she taught "[3] And in some of the newer branches of manufacture, such as the chemical and electrical industries, Continental and American firms were now sometimes ahead of the average British firm. The rise of the dyestuffs and optical industries in Germany illustrates this point. So does the development of the electric steel furnace in the United States and Sweden and of electric welding in the United States. In place of the former stream of visitors from the Continent to the United Kingdom there were now deputations of British chambers of commerce who crossed the Channel to inspect factories on the mainland. And English experts were reading foreign technical journals such as *Stahl und Eisen* with as much profit as Continental readers had once gained from studying the *Journal of the Society of Arts*.

Countries which had once relied upon Britain for technical knowledge were now passing on their own skill to less advanced countries. The important part played by Ludwig Knoop in establishing a modern cotton spinning industry in Russia in the middle of the nineteenth century may serve as an example.[4]

History Review, Vol. V, No. 1, pp. 65-75 and W. W. Rostow, *British Economy of the nineteenth Century* (1948). The revival of Protection in the leading industrial countries on the Continent in the seventies and eighties fostered the development of certain branches of industry.

[3] D. L. Burn, *The Economic History of Steelmaking 1867-1939* (1940), pp. 43-44.

[4] Ludwig Knoop (born 1821), son of a Bremen shopkeeper, served for a year as a clerk in Manchester with the firm of De Jersey. In 1839 he was sent to Moscow as an assistant to the Russian representative of this firm. The turning point in Knoop's career came when C. W. Morosoff, a leading Moscow cotton yarn merchant, entrusted him with the task of establishing an up-to-date cotton mill in Moscow on the English model. He succeeded in this enterprise with the result that one after another of the Moscow cotton yarn merchants availed themselves of Knoop's services to erect cotton spinning mills with modern machinery. At the end of his career Knoop had set up 122 spinning mills in Russia. There was a little verse about him which ran :

No church without a Pope,
No mill without a Knoop.

See G. von Schultze-Gaevernitz, *Volkswirtschaftliche Studien aus Russland* (1899), pp. 91-92.

German, French, Belgian and Swiss engineers and skilled workers were to be found in Russia, the Habsburg dominions, the Balkans, the Ottoman empire and elsewhere.

Industrial Europe moreover no longer needed the assistance that formerly came from British investors. Indeed the more advanced manufacturing countries on the Continent were now themselves lenders rather than borrowers though of course by no means on the same scale as the United Kingdom.[5] In the middle years of the nineteenth century much German capital had been sunk in American railways[6] and after the unification of the Reich a number of German banks considerably extended the range of their foreign interests both on the Continent and overseas. British investors were putting their money into colonial and American rather than into European enterprises. It has been estimated that on the eve of the first World War only about five per cent of Britain's overseas capital was invested on the Continent. The shift in the direction of the overseas investments of the United Kingdom had begun in the early 'sixties. The world economic crisis of 1857 had caused some British capitalists to regard Continental investments with some suspicion, while India—in the period of reconstruction after the suppression of the Mutiny—offered new opportunities for investment in public works such as railways, harbour works, dams and irrigation projects.[7] And it

[5] It has been estimated that in 1914 the amount of British capital invested overseas was about £4,000 millions. French overseas capital investments amounted to approximately £1,800 millions and German to about £1,200 millions : see J. A. Hobson, *The Evolution of Modern Capitalism* (edition of 1930), p. 462. See also Sir George Paish, " Great Britain's Capital Investments . . ." (*Journal of the Royal Statistical Society*, LXXIV (ii), January, 1911, pp. 186-7) ; C. K. Hobson, *The Export of Capital* (1914); H. Feis, *Europe the World's Banker* 1870-1914 (Yale University Press, 1930); A. H. Imlah, " British Balance of Payments and Export of Capital; 1816-1913 " (*Economic History Review*, second series, V (ii), 1952, p. 208) ; and A. K. Cairncross, *Home and Foreign Investment, 1870-1913* : *Studies in Capital Accumulation* (1953). For Germany's exports of capital see Karl Helfferich, *Deutschlands Volkswohlstand* 1888-1913 (fifth edn., 1915), p. 111.

[6] Professor F. E. Hyde has observed that by the 1870s " German interests were already very strong in Oregon, and the bondholders' committee in Frankfurt (am Main) by means of some 11,000,000 dollars invested in the Oregon & California Railway, controlled practically all the transportation in the country west of the Cascade Mountains—a territory through which the Northern Pacific desired to run. Henry Villard, who was the agent of the German bondholders, had by a judicious purchase of the stock of the Oregon and California Railway made himself President of this company in 1876 " (F. E. Hyde, " British Capital and American Enterprise in the North West," *Economic History Review*, VI (1935-6), p. 202).

[7] For British capital investment in the second quarter of the nineteenth century see D. Thorner, *Investment in Empire* : *British Railway and Steam Shipping Enterprise in India* (University of Pennsylvania Press, 1950).

has been pointed out that during the " Great Depression " of 1873-96 the slackening of home demand caused some capital from both the United Kingdom and the Continent to find " a refuge in foreign investment in non-capitalist or semi-capitalist countries."[8]

Although it was non-capitalist agrarian regions in the Americas, in Africa and in Asia that attracted British capital and technical skill in the last quarter of the nineteenth century the needs of Continental countries were by no means wholly neglected by British investors. This may be briefly illustrated from British capital investments first in Spanish and Swedish iron ore mining and secondly in the opening up of Germany's newly acquired overseas possessions.

With the introduction of the Bessemer process in the late 1850s there was a considerable growth in the British steel industry. A time came when this expansion outran the supplies of the raw material—hematite non-phosphoric iron ore—which were available in Britain (Cumberland). And this type of ore was needed so long as the Bessemer converter or the Siemens-Martin open-hearth furnace were used. To ensure for themselves a future supply of such ores British steel firms began to develop some of the hitherto neglected (non-phosphoric) iron ore mines on the Continent.[9] The most important of these mines lay in northern Spain and in central Sweden. The experience of British capitalists who had invested in Spanish government bonds had not been a happy one[10]—Spain had had the melancholy distinction of

[8] H. Rosenberg, " Political and Social Consequences of the Great Depression of 1873-96 in Central Europe " (*Economic History Review*, XIII, 1943, p. 60).

[9] Another solution of the problem would of course have been to have changed over from the manufacture of " acid steel " to " basic steel." Acid steel was made in the original Bessemer-Mushet converters and Siemens-Martin open-hearth furnaces. Basic steel was made in these furnaces when they were lined with a " basic " material as suggested by Sidney Gilchrist Thomas and Percy Gilchrist in the late 1870s. Only non-phosphoric ores (such as hematite) could be used in the original Bessemer converters but phosphoric ores (such as Lorraine *minette*) could be used when the converter was lined with dolomite instead of silica bricks. In Germany and the United States the change from " acid " (original Bessemer) to " basic " (Thomas) steel took place quickly but in Britain it took place more slowly. In 1928 the official *Survey of Metal Industries* (Committee on Industry and Trade) reported that before 1914 " many engineers in this country were so strongly prejudiced in favour of acid open-hearth steel that they insisted on having it even when basic steel would have done just as well " (p. 4).

[10] Lord Macaulay once told his banker : " Active Spanish bonds profess to pay interest now, and do not. Deferred Spanish bonds profess to pay interest at some future time, and will not. Passive Spanish bonds profess

being the first country whose persistent defaults had led to the formation of a bondholders' committee (1827)—but British investments in the mining of non-ferrous Spanish ores had been more profitable. Lead was mined by the Linares Lead Mining Company (1852) and the Fortuna Company (1854) while copper was mined both by the Tharsis Sulphur and Copper Company (1866) and by the well-known Rio Tinto Company (1873). It has been estimated that British capital investments in copper, lead, quicksilver and vanadium mines in Spain amounted to about £7,500,000 in 1900. Most of this money (£6,500,000) was invested in copper mines. The visit to Bilbao in 1870 of Sir Isaac Lowthian Bell, the great Middlesbrough ironmaster, may be regarded as the first step in the opening up of this important iron ore district by British capital and engineering skill. Non-phosphoric iron ore from both Santander and Bilbao had indeed been used to in England since the 1860s but only in small quantities. In 1871 four British companies were set up to mine Spanish iron ore, the most important being the Bilbao Iron Ore Company. In 1872 another eight British mining companies were established in Spain. The Carlist risings of 1872 and 1873 seriously dislocated the Bilbao iron ore industry since the province of Vizcaya was overrun by the insurgents. The government held on to Bilbao itself—which withstood a siege from June 1873 to May 1874—but it was not until May 1876 that order was again restored throughout northern Spain. The sharp decline in Bilbao's iron ore exports at this time led some British mining companies to try and tap the iron ore resources of Santander and southern Spain. Nevertheless even during the civil war British capital continued to be invested in Bilbao mining enterprises. It was in 1873 that the Orconera Iron Ore Company was founded. Altogether ten new British companies were founded in 1873-5 to open up Spanish iron ore mines. No new mining companies were established in the next five years (1875-80) but in the 1880s several fresh ventures were launched of which the most important was the Luchana Mining Company of 1886. Between 1893 and 1901 twenty-three more British mining companies were set up to operate in Spain.[11] In 1906 Spanish exports of iron ore to the United Kingdom reached

to pay interest neither now, nor at any future time. I think that you might buy a large amount of passive Spanish bonds for a very small sum " (Sir George Otto Trevelyan, *Life and Letters of Lord Macaulay* (edition of 1908), Vol. II, p. 418).

[11] In 1894 a writer in the *Journal of the Iron and Steel Institute* (Part I, p. 64) declared : " Twenty-five years ago our ships, bridges and boilers and railway tracks were made of iron derived almost entirely from British ores. Now almost all these are made of steel derived from Spanish ores." For British owned mining railways in Spain see G. L. Boag, *The Railways of Spain* (1923), p. 7.

their peak (9,272,000 tons). Exports subsequently declined[12] for by this time the best iron ore had been removed from Spain. Altogether 64 British limited liability joint stock companies were floated between 1871 and 1914 to mine iron ore in Spain. In this period about 150,000,000 tons of iron ore were sent to Britain from Spain and perhaps half of this total came from mines owned or operated by British firms. British and other foreign capital did much to develop the iron ore districts of Spain between 1870 and 1914. Spaniards themselves, encouraged by this British activity, opened new iron ore mines ; participated profitably in the transport of the ore to the United Kingdom and elsewhere (for example Messrs Sota & Aznar); and occasionally even developed large-scale smelting concerns in Spain itself (for example the Ibarra brothers).[13]

Towards the end of the nineteenth century the basic (Thomas) process at last became more popular in this country and British steelmakers began to turn to northern Sweden for new supplies of phosphoric ores. These ores could bear high transport costs since they were exceptionally rich in metallic iron. After about 1868 some iron ore from Lapland reached Britain through the port of Lulea in the Gulf of Bothnia. But this harbour was open for only a few months in the year. The problem of securing iron ore from Lapland could be solved only by building a line to the ice-free Norwegian port of Narvik. In the early 1880s three British firms were established to exploit the Lapland iron ore mines by means of this new route. One was a railway company (the Swedish and Norwegian Railway Company) ; another was a shipping concern (the Anglo-Scandinavian Steamship Company) ; while the third was a smelting firm (the Magnetic Iron Mountain Smelting Company). British steelmakers, however, were unfortunately discouraged by early difficulties in smelting Lapland iron ore and in 1891 the assets of the Swedish and Norwegian Railway Company were sold to the Swedish Government. Soon afterwards British capital ceased to play an active part in the exploitation of Lapland iron ore.[14]

[12] Total exports of iron ore from Spain were 8,907,000 tons in 1913 ; 3,827,000 tons in 1924 ; and only 1,857,000 tons in 1926. See *Survey of Metal Industries* (Committee of Industry and Trade, 1928, p. 104).

[13] In the 1920's it was estimated that Spain had the capacity to produce about 600,000 tons of pig iron annually and the same quantity of crude steel.

[14] See M. W. Flinn, *British Overseas Investment in Iron Ore Mining 1870-1914* (University of Manchester M.A. typescript thesis). Exports of Swedish iron ore to the United Kingdom were small. They rose from 52,000 tons in 1892-5 (annual average) to 780,000 tons in 1913. But exports of Swedish iron ore to Germany and Holland (most of the exports to Holland going on to Germany) were much larger. They amounted to over five million tons in 1913 and to over seven million tons in 1925.

Although British capital no longer played any significant part in the development of German industries after 1871 it did find its way into the overseas possessions of the Reich. There were two reasons for this. First, there were a number of British financial houses which had far longer experience than their German rivals of making investments in undeveloped territories. In the nineteenth century the export of British capital had been of considerable significance in the opening up of economically backward regions. German colonies presented problems with which British investors were not unfamiliar. Secondly, in the 1860s and 1870s British traders and financiers had been active in various territories which eventually came under German rule. Their activities continued even after the hoisting of the German flag. In the Cameroons in 1914 the well-known Liverpool firm of John Holt maintained nearly fifty trading stations. In German South West Africa the South West Africa Company was founded in 1892 to exploit the rich mineral resources of the Otavi region. After initial difficulties had been overcome, Anglo-German subsidiary companies of this concern successfully mined copper and zinc at Tsumeb, Asis, Guchab and Gross-Otavi. A second British privileged company—the South African Territories Company—was set up in 1895. Its activities were however confined to the selling and leasing of plots of land to settlers. The exploitation of the guano resources of this colony was largely in British hands while the Colmanskop Mines Ltd. of Cape Town was one of the earliest diamond mining firms in the territory. In German East Africa a number of British companies were founded during the rubber boom of 1910. They had a capital of nearly £1,000,000 and their object was to grow rubber and other tropical products. In the South Seas the Pacific Phosphate Company of London exploited the rich phosphate deposits of the German island of Nauru. Communications by submarine cables between Germany and her colonies were largely in the hands of British firms. A British company owned and operated the telegraph line between Abercorn (Rhodesia) and Ujiji (German East Africa). The German colonists depended for their news almost entirely upon Reuters which was a British-owned newsagency.[15]

There has been some controversy concerning the relationship between advanced and backward industrial countries. When citizens in an advanced industrial state establish and operate manufacturing enterprises in a backward country there are frequently complaints that the former country is "exploiting" the latter. As national feeling grows in backward countries

[15] See W. O. Henderson, "British Economic Activity in the German Colonies" in *The Economic History Review*, XV, 1945, pp. 56-66.

politicians are quick to rouse the passions of the mob by denouncing foreign investors who are alleged to wax fat at the expense of the poverty-stricken citizens of underdeveloped countries.

It is useless to generalise on this question. There have in the past been many different kinds of relationships between highly industrialised and non-capitalist countries. The benefits which two countries linked in this way derive from their association cannot be precisely evaluated. It may be conjectured that sometimes a fair balance is struck and the arrangements benefit both countries. The citizens of a highly industrialised country secure interest on their overseas investments or draw salaries or wages for exercising their skill abroad. On the other hand a backward industrial country may require new branches of industry that it would not have had—at the time—but for the exertions of men from the more advanced industrial state. But on other occasions the benefits of such transactions may have been distributed in a less equitable manner. When foreigners control for their own advantage the exploitation of an irreplaceable capital asset—such as a mineral ore or petrol—the advantage may well be with the advanced industrial state. But when governments or firms repudiate foreign loans they may, in effect, secure valuable capital assets—such as public works, factory buildings or machinery—for far less than they are really worth. Investing money abroad may be a risky business. In the nineteenth century some Englishmen found it highly profitable to transfer their capital and technical skill to foreign countries. But other British investors lost their savings in foreign ventures and so contributed to building up the industrial wealth of foreign countries without securing any proper return for the money they had spent in this way.

SELECT BIBLIOGRAPHY[1]

This is a list of some general works on topics of major imporance. It does not include monographs of a specialised character ; official reports ; articles in learned journals ; or papers read to academic or professional organisations. References to material of this kind will be found in the footnotes to the text.

Bibliographies

Europe

Dolléans, E., and Crozier, M. : *Mouvements ouvriers et socialistes, chronologie et bibliographie : Angleterre, France, Allemagne 1750-1918*, 1950.

Grandin, A. : *Bibliographie générale des sciences juridiques, politiques, économiques, et sociales de 1800 à 1925* (three volumes, 1926 and supplements).

Haussherr, H. : Bibliography to *Wirtschaftsgeschichte der Neuzeit*, third edition, 1960, pp. 467-503.

Leuilliot, Paul: Bibliography to H. Heaton, *Histoire économique de l'Europe*, Vol. II *De 1750 à nos jours*, 1960, pp. 467-503.

Great Britain

Ashton, T. S. : *The Industrial Revolution : A Study in Bibliography*, 1937.

Beales, H. L., and Cole, G. D. H. : *A Select List of Books on Economic and Social History*, 1927.

Chaloner, W. H. : Bibliography to Arthur Redford, *The Economic History of England 1760-1860*, 1960.

Peddie, R. A. : *Railway Literature 1556-1830*, 1931.

Power, Eileen : *The Industrial Revolution 1750-1850. A Select Bibliography*, 1927.

Williams, J. B., : *A Guide to the Printed Materials for English Social and Economic History*, two volumes, 1926.

France

Fohlen, Claude : ' Recent Research in the Economic History of Modern France,' *Journal of Economic History*, December, 1958.

Fohlen, Claude : ' Recherches récentes sur l'économie française au XIXe siècle ' (*Vierteljahrschrift für Sozial- und Wirtschaftsgeschichte*, Vol. 49, 1962, pp. 214-225).

Leuilliot, Paul : ' The Industrial Revolution in France,' *Journal of Economic History*, June, 1957.

Leuilliot, Paul : ' Recent French Writings on the Social and Economic History of Modern France,' *Economic History Review*, second series, Vol. v, 1953.

Schnerb, Robert: Bibliographies to H. Sée, *Histoire économique de la France*, Vol. II. *Les temps modernes*, edition of 1951, pp. xxii-xlix and 369-464.

Germany

Dahlmann, F. C., and Waitz, G. : *Quellenkunde der deutschen Geschichte*, 9th edition by H. Haering, 1931, Book vii, section 4, and Book viii, section 2.

Franz, G. : *Bücherkunde zur deutschen Geschichte*, 1951.

Austria

Barcza, Imre : *Bibliographie der mitteleuropäischen Zollunionsfrage*, 1917.

Charmatz, R. : *Wegweiser durch die Literatur der österreichischen Geschichte*, 1912.

Slokar, J. : Bibliography to *Geschichte der österreichischen Industrie und ihrer Förderung unter Kaiser Franz I*, 1914.

Switzerland

Rappard, W. E. : Bibliography to *La révolution industrielle . . . en Suisse*, 1914, pp. 317-338.

Holland

Baasch, E. : Bibliography to *Holländische Wirtschaftsgeschichte*, 1927, pp. 592-65.

Belgium

Pirenne, H. (and others) : *Bibliographie de l'histoire de Belgique*, 1931.

Spain

Alonso, B. S. : *Fuentes de la Historia Española e Hispano Americana*, second edition, 1927.

Italy

Caroselli, M. R. : ' Gli studi italiani dell'ultimo seculo sulla vita economica italiana dal 1861 al 1961, in *L'economica italiana dal 1861 al 1961*, pp. 716-915.

Mori, Giorgio : ' La storia dell'industria italiana contemporanea nei saggi, nelle ricerche e nelle publicazioni giubiliari di questo dopoguerra,' *Annali, Istituto Feltrinelli*, 1959, pp. 264-366.

See also bibliographical articles published in the *Economic History Review*, the *Journal of Economic History*, and the *Revue Historique*; lists of books in the Admiralty's *Geographical Handbooks*; and the various volumes of the *Géographie Universelle* the *Handwörterbuch der Staatswissenschaften* and the *Bibliographie der Sozialwissenschaften.*

General

Europe

Bairoch, P. : *Révolution industrielle et sous-développement*, 1963.

Barbagallo, C. : *Le origine de la grande industria contemporanea en 1750-1950*, two volumes, 1929-30.

Beckerath, H. von : *Der moderne Industrialismus*, 1930.

Blanqui, A. : *Cours d'économie industrielle*, three volumes, 1837-9.

Clapham, J. H.: *Economic Development of France and Germany*, 1929 ; new edition 1961.

Guillaumin, G. A. : *Dictionnaire du commerce et des marchandises*, two volumes, 1841.

Haussherr, H. : *Wirtschaftsgeschichte der Neuzeit*, third edition, 1960.

Heaton, H. : *Economic History of Europe*, 1936; new edition, 1948.

Henderson, W. O. : *The Industrial Revolution on the Continent*, 1961.

Henderson, W. O. : *The Genesis of the Common Market*, 1962.

Hobson, J. A. : *The Evolution of Modern Capitalism*, 1894, new edition, 1926.

Hoffmann, W. G. : *The Growth of Industrial Economies*, German edition, 1931; English translation by W. O. Henderson and W. H. Chaloner, 1958.

Kulischer, J. : *Allgemeine Wirtschaftsgeschichte*, Vol. II. *Die Neuzeit*, 1929.

Kuske, B. : *Die Bedeutung Europas für Entwicklung der Weltwirtschaft*, 1924.

Luxemburg, Rosa : *The Accumulation of Capital.* German edition, 1913; English translation, 1951.

Luzatto, G. : *Storia economica dell'età moderna e contemporanea*, Vol. II. *L'età contemporanea*, 1952.

McCulloch, J. : *A Dictionary of Commerce*, two volumes, edition of 1846.

Ritter, U. P. : *Die Rolle des Staates in der Frühstadien der Industrialisierung . . .*, 1961.

Singer, C. (and others) : *A History of Technology*, Vol. IV. *The Industrial Revolution*, 1958.

Sombart, W. : *Der moderne Kapitalismus*, fourth edition, three volumes, 1921-8: English summary—F. L. Nussbaum, *A History of the Economic Institutions of Modern Europe*, 1935.

Timm, A. : *Kleine Geschichte der Technologie*, 1964.

Treue, W. : *Wirtschaftsgeschichte der Neuzeit 1700-1960*, 1962.

Ure, A. : *A Dictionary of Arts, Manufactures and Mines*, second edition, 1840.

Usher, A. P. : *An Economic History of Europe since 1750*, 1937.

Wolf, A. : *A History of Science, Technology, and Philosophy in the* 16*th and* 17*th Centuries*, 1935.

Wolf, A. : *A History of Science, Technology, and Philosophy in the 18th Century*, 1938.

Wrigley, E. A. : *Industrial Growth and Population Change*, 1961.

Great Britain

Ashton, T. S. : *Economic Fluctuations in England 1700-1800*, 1959.

Ashton, T. S. : *An Economic History of England: the Eighteenth Century*, 1955.

Ashton, T. S. : *The Industrial Revolution*, 1948.

Beales, H. L. : *The Industrial Revolution*, 1928; new edition, 1958.

Chambers, J. D. : *The Workshop of the World: British Economic History from 1820 to 1880*, 1961.

Chaloner, W. H., and Musson, A. E. : *Industry and Technology*, 1963.

Clapham, J. H. : *An Economic History of Modern Britain*, three volumes, 1926-38.

Court, W. H. B. : *A concise Economic History of Britain from 1750 to Recent Times*, 1954.

Crouzet, F. : *L'économie britannique et le blocus continental*, 1806-13, two volumes, 1958.

Gayer, Rostow and Schwarz : *The Growth and Fluctuations of the British Economy 1790-1850*, two volumes, 1953.

Hamilton, H. : *The Industrial Revolution in Scotland*, 1932.

Hoffmann, W. G. : *British Industry 1700-1950*, German edition, 1940; English translation by W. O. Henderson and W. H. Chaloner, 1955.

Jenks, L. H. : *The Migration of British Capital to 1875*, 1927.

Jones, G. P., and Pool, A. G. : *A Hundred Years of Economic Development in Great Britain*, 1939.

Mantoux, Paul : *The Industrial Revolution of the Eighteenth Century in England*, 1928; revised edition, 1961.

Moffitt, L. W. : *England on the Eve of the Industrial Revolution . . .*, 1925, and 1963.

Pressnell, L. S. (ed.) : *Studies in the Industrial Revolution presented to T. S. Ashton*, 1960.

Rostow, W. W. : *British Economy in the Nineteenth Century*, 1948.

Rousseaux, P. : *Les mouvements de fond le l'économie anglaise 1800-1913*, 1938.

Schlote, W. : *British Overseas Trade . . .*, German edition, 1938; English translation by W. O. Henderson and W. H. Chaloner, 1952.

Smelser, N. J. : *Social Change in the Industrial Revolution . . . 1770-1840*, 1959.

Zweig, K. : ' Strukturwandlungen und Konjunkturschwingungen im englischen Aussenhandel der Vorkriegszeit,' *Weltwirtschaftliches Archiv*, Vol. xxx, 1926, Part 2.

France

Bourgin, G. and H. : *Le régime de l'industrie en France de 1814 à 1830*, documents, three volumes, 1912-41.

Cameron, Rondo : *France and the Economic Development of Europe 1800-1914*, 1961.

Chaptal, le Comte : *De l'industrie françoise*, two volumes, 1819.

Clough, S. B. : *France: A History of National Economics 1789-1939*, 1939.

Dunham, A. L. : *The Industrial Revolution in France 1815-48*, 1955.

Fohlen, Claude : ' La rivoluzione industriale in Francia . . .,' *Studi Storici*, II, 1961, pp. 517-47.

Gille, B. : *Recherches sur la formation de la grande entreprise capitaliste 1815-48*, 1959.

Hayem, J. (ed.): *Mémoires et documents pour servir à l'histoire du commerce et de l'industrie en France*, twelve volumes, 1911-29.

Levasseur, E. : *Histoire des classes ouvrières et de l'industrie en France de 1789 à 1870*, two volumes, edition of 1903.

Martin, G. : *La grande industrie en France sous le Règne de Louis XV*, 1900.

Palmade, G. P. : *Capitalisme et capitalistes français au xix*[e] *siècle*, 1961.

Priouret, R. : *Origines du patronat français*, 1963.

Sée, H. : *La France économique et sociale au xviii*[e] *siècle*, second edition, 1933; English translation, 1927.

Sée, H. : *Histoire économique de la France*, Vol. II. *Les temps modernes 1789-1914*, new edition, 1951.

Germany

Benaerts, P. : *Les origines de la grande industrie allemande*, 1933.

Eisenhart, Rothe: E. von Ritthaler, A *Vorgeschichte und Begründung des deutschen Zollvereins*, documents, three volumes, 1934.

Henderson, W. O. : *The Zollverein*, 1939; new edition, 1959.

Henderson, W. O. : *The State and the Industrial Revolution in Prussia 1740-1870*, 1958.

Henderson, W. O. : *Studies in the Economic Policy of Frederick the Great*, 1963.

Hoffmann, W. G. : 'The Take-Off in Germany' in W. W. Rostow (ed.), *The Economics of Take-Off into sustained Growth.*

Jantke, C. : '*Industrialisierung im Deutschland des Iqen Jahrhundert . . .*' *Studium Generale*, XVI, No. 10, pp. 585-96.

Krüger, Horst : *Zur Geschichte der Manufakturen und der Manufakturarbeiter in Preussen*, 1958.

Lütge, F. : *Deutsche Sozial-und Wirtschafts-Geschichte*, second edition, 1960.

Mottek, Hans and others : *Studien zur Geschichte der industriellen Revolution in Deutschland*, 1960.

Sombart, Werner : *Die deutsche Volkswirtschaft im neunzehnten Jahrhundert*, 8th edition, 1954.

Treue, W. : *Wirtschaftszustände und Wirtschaftspolitik in Preussen 1815-25*, 1937.

Reuter, O. : *Die Manufaktur im fränkischen Raum*, 1961.

Schnabel, F. : *Deutsche Geschichte im neunzehnten Jahrhundert*, Vol. III. *Erfahrungswissenschaften und Technik*, 1934. New edition, 1950.

Waltershausen, Sartorius von : *Deutsche Wirtschaftsgeschichte 1815-1914*, second edition, 1923.

Weber, W. : *Der Deutsche Zollverein*, 1869.

Italy

Barbagallo, C. (ed.): *Cent'anni di vita italiana 1848-1948*, two volumes 1948-50.

Clough, S. B. : *The Economic History of Modern Italy*, 1964.

Bonnefons-Crapone: *L'Italie au travail*, Paris, no date.

Corbino, E. : *Annali dell'Economia italiana*, five volumes, 1933-8.

Greenfield, K. R. : *Economics and Liberalism in the Risorgimento . . .*, 1934, ch. 4.

Lémonon, E. : *L'Italie économique et sociale 1861-1912*, 1913.

Martiis, C. de : *Saggio storico sull'industria italiana*, 1885.

Messeri, A. : *Cinquant'anni di vita economico-finanziaria in Italia*, 1912.

Milone, F. : *La localizzazione delle industrie in Italia*, 1937.

Morandi, R. : *Storia della grande industrie in Italia*, 1931.

Pino-Branca, A. : *Cinquant'anni de economia sociale in Italia*, 1922.

Sachs, I. : *L'Italie, ses finances et son développement économique 1859-84*, 1885.

Zaja, E. : *L'Italia economica*, 1912.

Cinquant'anni di storia italiana (three volumes) includes articles on the economic development of Italy.

Holland and Belgium
Baasch, E. : *Holländische Wirtschaftsgeschichte*, 1927.
Briavoine, H. : *De l'industrie en Belgique*, 1839.
Colenbrander, H. T. : *Gedenkstukken der algemeene geschiednis van Nederland van 1795 tot 1840*, documents, ten volumes, 1905-22.
Dechesne, L. : *Histoire économique et sociale de la Belgique*, 1932.
Demoulin, R. : *Guillaume Ier et la transformation économique des provinces belges 1815-30*, 1938.
Austria
Slokar, J. : *Geschichte der österreichischen Industrie und ihrer Förderung unter Kaiser Franz I*, 1914.
Entwicklung von Industrie und the Gewerbe in Österreich in den Jahren 1848-88 (issued by the Commission for the Jubilee Industrial Exhibition in Vienna, 1888).
Hungary
Földeab, A de Navay de : *La Hongrie: son rôle économique*, 1911.
Vautier, G. : *La Hongrie économique*, 1893.
Wirth, Max. : *Ungarn und seine Bodenschätze*, 1889.
Sweden
Drachmann, P. : *The Industrial Development . . . of the three Scandinavian Countries*, 1915.
Fridlizius, G. : ' Swedish Exports 1850-1960 . . .,' *Economy and History*, Vol. VI, 1963.
Heckscher, E. F. : *An Economic History of Sweden*, 1954.
Hedlund und Nyström, T. : ' The Swedish Crisis of the 1850s,' *Economy and History*, Vol. VI, 1963.
Sönderlund, E. F. : ' The Impact of the British Industrial Revolution on the Swedish Iron Industry,' L. S. Presnell, ed., *Studies in the Industrial Revolution presented to T. S. Ashton*, 1960.
Sönderlund, E. F. (and others) : *Swedish Timber Exports 1850-1950*, 1952.
Stora Kopparberg, Six Hundred Years of Industrial Enterprise, third edition, 1960.
Switzerland
Bodmer, W. : *Die Entwicklung der schweizerischen Textilwirtschaft im Rahmen der übrigen Industrien und Wirtschaftszweige*, 1960.
Rappard, W. E. : *La révolution industrielle et les origines de la protection légale du travail en Suisse*, 1914.

MINING AND METALLURGY

General
Jars, Gabriel : *Voyages métallurgiques . . .*, three volumes, 1774-8.

Percy, J. : *Metallurgy* . . ., four volumes, 1861-80.

Pounds, N. J. G., and Parker, W. N. : *Coal and Steel in Western Europe*, 1957.

Villain, G. : *Le fer, la houille et la métallurgie à la fin du xixe siècle*, 1901.

Coal

Archer, M. : *Sketch of the History of the Coal Trade of Northumberland and Durham*, 1897.

Ashton, T. S., and Sykes, J. : *The Coal Industry of the Eighteenth Century*, 1929; new edition, 1964.

Bald, R. : *General View of the Coal Trade of Scotland*, 1808.

Baumont, M. : *La grosse industrie allemande et le charbon*, 1928.

Baumont, M. : *La grosse industrie allemande et le lignite*, 1928.

Burat, A. : *Le matérial des houillères en France et en Belgique* . . ., two volumes, 1861-5.

Dunn, M. : *An Historical . . . View of the Coal Trade of the North of England*, 1844.

Galloway, R. L. : *A History of Coal Mining in Great Britain*, 1882.

Galloway, R. L. : *Annals of Coal Mining* . . ., two volumes, 1898-1904.

Gras, L. J. : *Histoire économique générale des mines de la Loire*, two volumes, 1922.

Gruner and Bousquet : *Atlas générale des houillères*, 1911.

Jevons, W. S. : *The Coal Question*, 1865; new edition, 1965.

Nef, J. U. : *The Rise of the British Coal Industry*, two volumes, 1932.

Schneider, E. : *Le charbon*, 1945.

Stillich, O. : *Nationalökonomische Forschungen auf dem Gebiet der grossindustriellen Unternehmungen*, Vol. II, *Steinkohlenindustrie*, 1906.

Vaillemin, E. : *Le bassin houiller du Pas-de-Calais*, three volumes, 1878-9.

Wibail, A. : ' L'évolution économique de l'industrie charbonière belge de 1813 à 1913,' *Bulletin de l'institut des Sciences Economiques*, November, 1934.

Iron, Steel, and Engineering

Ansiaux, M. : *L'industrie armurière Liègeoise*, 1899.

Ashton, T. S. : *Iron and Steel in the Industrial Revolution*, 1924; new edition with bibliographical note by W. H. Chaloner, 1963.

Beck, L. : *Die Geschichte des Eisens*, five volumes, 1884-1903.

Boesch and Schib : *Beiträge zur Geschichte der schweizerischen Eisengiesserei*, 1960.

Bourgin, G. and H. : *L'Industrie sidérurgie en France au début de la Révolution*, 1920.

Chaloner, W. H. : 'Les frères John et William Wilkinson et leurs rapports avec le métallurgie française 1775-86,' in *Le fer à travers les ages*, report on conference held at Nancy in October, 1955, and published as a supplement to *Annales de l'Est*, 1956.
Engel, E. : *Die Zeitalter des Dampfes*, 1881.
Gille, B. : *Les origines de la grande industrie métallurgique en France*, 1948.
Hemardinquer, J. J. : 'Une dynastie de mécaniciens anglais en France : James, John et Juliana Collier (1791-1847)', *Revue d'Histoire des Sciences*, IV, 1965, pp. 193-208.
Hottinger, G. : *L'ancienne industrie du fer en Lorraine*, 1927.
Johannsen, O. : *Geschichte des Eisens*, 1925.
Leducq, J. : *Du développement de la production du fer dans le nord-ouest de la France*, 1884.
Levainville, J. : *L'industrie du fer en France*, 1932.
Le Play, Frédéric : 'Mémoire sur la fabrication et le commerce des fers à acier dans le nord de l'Europe . . .,' *Annales des Mines*, 4th series, Vol. IX, 1846, pp. 113-306.
Pelouze, E. : *L'art du maître des forges*, 1827.
Rickard, T. A. : *Man and Metals, A History of Mining*, two volumes, 1932.
Scrivenor, H. : *History of the Iron Trade*, edition of 1854.
Stillich, O. : *Nationalökonomische Forschungen auf dem Gebiet des grossindustriellen Unternehmungen*, Vol. I, *Eisen und Stahlindustrie*, 1904.
La sidérurgie française, 1864-1914, Comité desForges, 1914.

TEXTILES

General

Houte, F-X van : *L'evolution de l'industrie textile en Belgique et dans le monde de 1800 à 1939*, 1949.
Kisch, H. : 'The Textile Industries in Silesia and the Rhineland . . .,' *Journal of Economic History*, December, 1959.

Cotton

Baines, E. : *History of the Cotton Manufacture of Great Britain*, 1835.
Beaumont, G. : *Étude sur des industries du coton, du lin et de la soie . . . dans la région Nord*, 1860.
Demmering, G. : *Die Glauchaue-Meeraner Textilindustrie*, Würzburg, 1928.
Fohlen, Claude : *L'industrie textile au temps du Second Empire*, 1956.
Henderson, W. O. : *The Lancashire Cotton Famine 1861-5*, 1934.
Herkner, H. : *Die oberelsässische Baumwollindustrie . . .*, 1887.

Jenny-Trümpy, J. : *Die schweizerische Baumwollindustrie*, 1909
Klein, J. : *Die Baumwollindustrie im Breuschtal*, 1905.
König, A. : *Die sächsische Baumwollindustrie am Ende des vorigen Jahrhunderts und während der Kontinentalsperre*, 1899.
Lecomte, H. : *Le coton*, 1900.
Lévy, R. : *Histoire économique de l'industrie cotonnière en France*, 1912.
Lochmüller, W. : *Zur Entwicklung der Baumwollindustrie in Deutschland*, 1906.
Mann, J. A. : *The Cotton Industry of Great Britain*, 1860.
Pupin, R. : *Le coton*, 1906-7.
Reybaud, M. R. L. : *Le coton*, 1867.
Rotschild, H. : *Die süddeutsche Baumwollindustrie*, 1922.
Sambeth, H. : *Die Betriebe und das Personal der württembergischen Textilindustrie*, 1904.
Schulze-Gaevernitz, G. von : *The Cotton Trade in England and on the Continent*, 1895.
Wadsworth, A. P., and Mann, J. de L. : *The Cotton Trade and Industrial Lancashire 1600-1780*, 1931; new edition, 1964.

Woollens and Worsteds

Alcan, M. : *Traité du travail des laines*, two volumes, 1866.
Bischoff, J. : *A . . . History of the Woollen and Worsted Manufactures . . .*, two volumes, 1842.
Burnley, J. : *History of Wool and Woolcombing*, 1889.
Clapham, J. H. : *The Woollen and Worsted Industries*, 1907.
Dechesne, L. : *L'évolution économique . . . de l'industrie de la laine en Angleterre*, 1900.
Kisch, H. : 'Growth Deterrents of a Medieval Heritage : The Aachen-area Woolen Trades before 1790,' *The Journal of Economic History*, Vol. XXIX, December, 1964, No. 4.
Lipson, E. : *The History of the Woollen and Worsted Industries*, 1921.
Reybaud, M. R. L. : *La laine*, 1867.
Rondot, N. : *Rapport . . . sur l'industrie lainière de la Belgique en 1837*, 1849.
Sigsworth, E. M. : *Black Dyke Mills*, 1958 ; includes chapters on the development of the Yorkshire woollen industry.
Schmidt, F. : *Die Entwicklung der Cottbuser Tuchindustrie*, 1928.
Senkel, W. : *Wollproduktion und Wollhandel im neunzehnten Jahrhundert*, 1901.

Lace

Felkin, W. : *History of Machine Wrought Hosiery and Lace Manufactures*, 1845, and 1867.

Herron, W. : *L'industrie des tulles et des dentelles mécaniques dans le Département du Pas-de-Calais 1815-1900*, 1900.

Silk

Beauguis, A. : *Histoire économique de la soie*, 1910.
Milz, H. : *Die Kölner Grossgewebe von 1750-1835*, 1962.
Schmoller and Hintze : *Die preussische Seidenindustrie im 18en Jahrhundert, Acta Borussica*, three volumes, 1892.

Linen

Warden, A. J. : *The Linen Trade*, 1865, and 1867.
Zimmermann, A. : *Blüte und Verfall des Leinengewebes in Schlesien*, 1885.

Jute

Bonsack, F. : *Die Versorgung der Welt mit Jute . . .*, 1929.
Pfuhl, E. : *Die Jute und ihre Verarbeitung*, three volumes, 1885-91.
Wolff, R. : *Die Jute*, 1913.

TRANSPORT AND PUBLIC WORKS

General

Biedenkapp, G. : *Die Entwicklung der modernen Verkehrsmittel*, 1911.
Borght, van der : *Das Verkehrswesen*, 1894.
Huber, F. C. : *Die geschichtliche Entwicklung des modernen Verkehrs*, 1893.
Jackman, W. T. : *The Development of Transportation in Modern England*, 1916; new edition with introductory guide to recent published work on the history of British transport by W. H. Chaloner, 1962.
Kirkaldy, A. W., and Evans, A. D. : *The History and Economics of Transport*, third edition, 1924.
Lotz, W. : *Verkehrsentwicklung in Deutschland, 1800-1900*, 1900.
Teubert, O. : *Die Binnenschiffahrt*, 1912.

Roads

Cavaillès, H. : *La route française . . .*, 1946.
Grabo, W. : *Die ostpreussischen Strassen . . .*, 1910.
Hartung, G. : *Die bayerischen Landstrassen . . .*, 1902.
Hilpert, J. : *Le messagiste*, 1840.
Sälter, F. : *Entwicklung . . . der Chaussee-und Wegebaues in der Provinz Westfalen 1815-44*, 1917.
Schellenberg, A. : *Die Entwicklung des Landstrassenwesens im Gebiet der jetzigen Regierungsbezirks Merseburg*, 1929.

Stark, W. : *Die Strasse*, 1958.
Thimme, P. : *Strassenbau und Strassenpolitik in Deutschland zur Zeit der Gründung des Zollvereins, 1825-35*, 1931.
Vollheim, S. : *Staatsstrassen und Verkehrspolitik in Kurhessen von 1815 bis 1840*, 1931.

Inland Waterways

Bonneaud, P. : *Navigation à Roanne sur la Loire et les canaux*, 1944.
Clapp, E. J. : *The Navigable Rhine*, 1911.
Cozza, L., and della Berta, J. C. : *Navigatión Intérienne Italienne*, 1905.
Demangeon and Febvre : *Le Rhin . . .*, 1935.
Dutens, J. M. : *Histoire de la navigation intérieure de la France . . .*, 1829.
Eckert, C. : *Rheinschiffahrt im neunzehnten Jahrhundert*, 1900.
Gothein, E. : *Geschichtliche Entwicklung der Rheinschiffahrt im neunzehnten Jahrhundert*, 1903.
Grangez, E. : *Précis historique . . . des voies navigables de la France*, 1855.
Kriele, M. : *Die Regulierung der Elbschiffahrt 1819-21*, 1895.
Lindley, W. H. : *Report on the Waterways of France, Belgium, Germany and Holland*, Royal Commission on Canals and Waterways, Vol. VI, Cd. 4841 of 1909.
Monsier, E. : *De l'état actuel de la navigation de la Seine . . .*, 1832.
Riese, F. K. : *Entwicklung der Oderschiffahrt*, 1914.
Rivet, F. : *La navigation à vapeur sur la Saône et le Rhône 1783-1863*, 1962.
Say, Jean-Baptiste : *Des canaux de navigation dans l'état actuel de la France*, 1818.
Schmidt, W. : *Die Binnenschiffahrt Deutschlands*, 1937.
Suppán, C. V.: *Die Donau und ihre Schiffahrt*, 1917.
Willan, T. S. : *River Navigation in England 1600-1750*, 1936 ; new edition, 1964.

French Railways

Audiganne, A. : *Les chemins de fer . . .*, two volumes, 1858-62.
Chevalier, M. : *Des chemins de fer en France*, 1838.
Dauzet, P. : *Le siècle des chemins de fer en France 1821-1938*, 1948.
Doukas, K. A. : *The French Railways and the State*, 1945.
Goy, G. : *Hommes et choses du P.L.M.*, 1911.
Gras, L. : *Histoire des premiers chemins de fer français*, 1924.
Jouffroy, C. M. : *Une étape de la construction des grandes lignes de chemins de fer en France. La ligne de Paris à la frontière d'Allemagne 1825-52*, three volumes, 1932-3.

Kauffmann, R. von : *Eisenbahnpolitik Frankreichs*, two volumes, 1896; French translation, 1900.
Lefèvre, A. : *Sous le Second Empire : chemins de fer et politique*, 1951.
Legoyte, A. : *Le livre des chemins de fer . . .*, 1845.
Peyret, H. : *Histoire des chemins de fer en France . . .*, 1949.
Picard, A. : *Les chemins de fer en France*, six volumes, 1884-5.
Wallon, M. : *Le Saint-Simonisme et les chemins de fer*, 1908.

Belgian Railways

Avakian, L. : ' Le rythme de développement des voies ferrées en Belgique de 1835 á 1935 ' (*Bulletin de l'Institut de Recherches Économiques*, Vol. VII, 1935-6.)

German Railways

Fricke, A. : *Die Anfänge des Eisenbahnwesens in Preussen*, 1912.
Hoeltzel, M. : *Aus der Frühzeit der Eisenbahnen*, 1935.
Jakob, O. : *Die Kgl. württembergischen Eisenbahnen . . .*, 1895.
Kech, E. : *Die Gründung der Grossh. badischen Staatseisenbahnen*, 1905.
Kech, E. : *Geschichte der deutschen Eisenbahponlitik*, 1911.
Klomfass, H. : *Die Entwicklung des Staatseisenbahnsystems in Preussen*, 1900.
Kumpmann, K. : *Die Entstehung der rheinischen Eisenbahngesellschaft 1830-44*, 1910.
Leyen, A. von der : *Die Eisenbahnpolitik des Fürsten Bismarck*, 1914.
Leinhardy, H. : *Die Anfänge der Eisenbahnen rechts des Rheins*, 1883.
Marggraf, H. : *Die Kgl. Bayerischen Staatsbahnen . . .*, 1894.
Mayer, A. von : *Geschichte und Geographie der deutschen Eisenbahnen . . .*, two volumes, 1891.
Metzelin, E. : *Die Lokomotive feiert mit. Das* 100-*jährige Bestehen der deutschen Eisenbahnen*, 1935.
Morlock, G. von : *Die Kgl. Württembergischen Staatseisenbahnen*, 1890.
Müller, K. : *Die badischen Eisenbahnen*, 1948.
Scheyrer, F. : *Geschichte der Main-Neckarbahn*, 1902.
Schreiber, J. F. : *Die preussische Eisenbahnen in ihrem Verhältniss zum Staat 1834-74*, 1874.
Schulze, F. : *Die ersten deutschen Eisenbahnen*, 1917.
Supper, O. : *Die Entwicklung des Eisenbahnwesens im Königreich Württemberg*, 1895.
Ulbricht, G. : *Geschichte der Kgl. Sächsischen Staatsbahnen*, 1889.

Hundert Jahre deutsche Eisenbahnen, Reichsverkehrsministerium, 1935 : second edition 1938.

Festschrift über die Tätigkeit des Vereins Deutscher Eisenbahnverwaltungen in den ersten 50 Jahren seines Bestehens 1846-96, 1896.

Hundert Jahre Eisenbahn Berlin-Potsdam 1838-1938, Reichsbahndirektion Berlin, 1938.

Hundert Jahre Eisenbahndirektion Wuppertal 1850-1950, 1950.

Berlin und seine Eisenbahnen 1846-96, two volumes, 1896.

Public Works

Chapman, J. M., and Brian: *The Life and Times of Baron Haussmann, Paris in the Second Empire*, 1957.

Girard, L. : *La politique des travaux publics du second Empire*, 1957.

Leonard, C. M. : *Lyons transformed: Public Works of the Second Empire*, 1961.

McKay, D. C. : *The National Workshops . . .*, 1933.

Treisereve, E. : *Les travaux publics en Belgique et les chemins de fer en France*, 1839.

MACHINERY AND FACTORIES

Babbage, C. : *On the Economy of Machinery and Manufactures*, 1832; fourth edition, 1835.

Ballot, C. : *L'introduction du machinisme dans l'industrie française*, 1923.

Beck, L. : *Beiträge zur Geschichte des Maschinenbaues*, second edition, 1900.

Beckmann, J. : *A History of Inventions*, five volumes, 1797-1814.

Brunet, P. : 'Transformations techniques et conditions de développement de l'industrie en France à la fin du xviiie siècle,' *Comité des travaux historiques. Bulletin de la section des sciences économiques*, 1932.

Dickinson, H. W. : *A Short History of the Steam Engine*, 1938; new edition with introduction by A. E. Musson, 1963.

Doogs, K. : *Die Berliner Maschinenindustrie*, 1928.

Eude, E. : *Histoire documentaire de la mécanique française . . .*, 1902.

Froriep, O. : *Zur Geschichte der Maschinenindustrie . . .*, 1918.

Lohren, A. : *Die Kamm-Maschinen . . .*, 1875.

McCloy, S. T. : *French Inventions of the Eighteenth Century*, 1952.

Matschoss, C. : *Männer der Technik*, 1937.

Matschoss, C. : *Grosse Ingenieure*, 1937: English translation, *Great Engineers*, 1938.

Matschoss, C. : *Geschichte der Dampfmaschine*, 1901.
Matschoss, C. : *Ein Jahrhundert deutsches Maschinenbaues, 1819-1919*.
Matschoss, C. : *Preussens Gewerbeforderung und ihre grossen Männer*, 1921.
Matschoss, C. : *Friedrich der Grosse als Beförderer des Gewerbefleisses*, 1912.
Passy, F. : *Les machines et leur influence sur le développement de l'humanité*, 1866.
Turgan, J. F. : *Les grandes usines*, 18 volumes, 1866-88.
Vierendeel, A. : *Esquisse d'une histoire de la technique*, two volumes, 1921.

INDUSTRIAL BIOGRAPHIES AND MEMOIRS

France

Allemagne, H-R : *Prosper Enfantin et les grandes Entreprises du xixe siècle*, 1935.
Bouvier, J. : *Les Rothschild*, 1960.
Brandt, A. : ' Une famille de fabricants mulhousins au début du xixe siècle : Jean Koechlin et ses fils,' *Annales*, 1951, pp. 319-30.
Chaloner, W. H. and Henderson, W. O. : ' Aaron Manby, Builder of the first Iron Steamship ' and ' The Manbys and the Industrial Revolution in France 1819-94,' *Transactions of the Newcomen Society*, Vol. XXIX, 1953-5, and Vol. XXX, 1955-7.
Chevalier, J. : ' François-Ignace de Wendel,' *Annuaire de la Société d'Histoire et d'Archéologie de la Lorraine*, Vol. XLVII 1938, pp. 181-206.
Duchon, P. (ed.) : *Mémoire de Laffitte 1767-1844*, 1932.
Ernouf, P. : *Paulin Talabot . . . 1799-1885*, 1886.
Fohlen, Claude: *Une affaire de famille au xixe siècle : Mequillet et Noblot*, 1955.
Grandet, H. : *Monographie d'un établissement métallurgie sis à la fois en France et en Allemagne*, 1909.
Hemardinquer, J. J. : ' Une dynastie de mécaniciens anglais en France: James, John et Juliana Collier, 1791-1847 ' (*Revue d'Histoires des Sciences*, 1965, pp. 193-208).
Jackson, W. F. : *James Jackson et ses fils*, 1893.
Joinville, P. de : *Le réveil économique de Bordeaux sous la Restauratlon. L'armateur Balguerie-Stuttemberg et son oeuvre*, 1914.
Lambert-Dansette, J. : *Essai sur les origines d'évolution d'une bourgeoisie. Quelques familles du patronat textile de Lille-Armentières 1789-1914*, 1954.
Laronze, G. : *Le baron Haussmann*, 1932.

Laurent de Villedeuil, P. C. : *Oeuvres de Emile et Isaac Pereire* (four volumes, 1913-20.)

Mossmann, X. : *Un industriel alsacien. Vie de Engel-Dolfus*, 1887.

Pigeire, J. : *La vie et l'oeuvre de Chaptal 1765-1832*, 1932.

Reid, S. J. : *Memoirs of Sir Edward Blount*, 1902.

Rémond, A. : *John Holker*, 1946.

Rouff, M. : 'Tubeuf, un grand industriel français au xviiie siècle,' *Mémoires et documents pour servir à l'histoire du commerce et de l'industrie*, Vol. vii, 1922.

Roy, J. A. : *Histoire de la famille Schneider et du Creusot*, 1962.

Samuel-Lajeunesse, R. : *Grands mineurs français*, 1948.

Sédillot, R. : *Deux cent cinquante ans d'industrie en Lorraine. La maison de Wendel de 1704 à nos jours*, 1958.

Thuillier, André : *Un grand chef d'industrie aux xixe siècle. Emile Martin 1794-1871*, Nevers, 1964.

Thuillier, Guy : *Georges Dufaud et les débuts du grand capitalisme dans la métallurgie en Nevers au xixe siècle*, 1959.

Wolff, Otto : *Ouvrard, Speculator of Genius 1770-1846*, 1962.

Motte-Bussuet : un homme, une famille, une firme 1843-1943, Tourcoing, 1944.

Germany

Auerbach, F. : *Ernst Abbe . . .*, second edition, 1922.

Beck, L. : *Die Familie Remy und die Industrie am Mittelrhein*, 1906.

Berdrow, W. : *Alfred Krupp und sein Geschlecht*, two volumes, second edition 1943; with appendix by F. G. Kraft.

Bergengrün, A. : *David Hansemann*, 1901.

Bergengrün, A. : *Staatsminister August von der Heydt*, 1908.

Bertram, W. : *Jacob Mayer, der Erfinder des Stahlformgusses*, 1938.

Bloemers, Kurt : *W. T. Mulvany*, 1806-1885, 1922.

Caspary, A. : *Ludolf Camphausens Leben*, 1902: second edition 1919.

Däbritz, W. : *David Hansemann und Adolph von Hansemann*, 1954.

Däbritz, W. : *F. Grillo als Wirtschaftsführer*, 1926.

Däbritz, W. : *Unternehmugsgestalten aus dem rheinisch-westfälischen Industriebezirk*, 1929.

Ehrenberg, R. : *Grosse Vermögen*, Vol. i, *Fugger, Rothschild, Krupp*, 1902, Vol. ii, *Das Haus Parish in Hamburg*, 1904, and 1925.

Ehrenberg, W. : *Biographen der verschiedenen Krupp*, 1907.

Fürstenberg, H. (ed.) : *Carl Fürstenberg. Die Lebensgeschichte eines deutschen Bankiers*, 1931.

Goebel, T. : *Friedrich König und die Erfindung der Schnellpresse*, second edition, 1906.

Hansen, J. : *Gustav von Mevissen* . . . 1815-99, two volumes, 1906.
Hardegen, F., and Smidt Käthi : *H. H. Meyer, der Gründer des Nord-Deutschen Lloyds* . . ., *1809-98*, 1920.
Hashagen, J. : *Geschichte der Familie Hoesch*, two volumes, 1911.
Hellwig, F. : *Carl Freiherr von Stumm-Halberg 1826-1901*, 1936.
Jungnickel, F. : *Staatsminister Albert von Maybach*, 1910.
Kellen, T. : *Friedrich Grillo* . . ., 1913.
Kelleter, H. L. : *Geschichte der Familie Haniels* . . ., 1924.
Klass, G. von : *Krupps: the Story of an Industrial Empire*, 1954.
Koepper, G. : *Die Kruppwerke* . . ., 1922.
Krause, Max: *A. Borsig, Berlin 1837-1902*, 1902.
Macco, H. F. : *Geschichte* . . . *der Familie Pastor*, 1905.
Matschoss, C. : ' Franz Dinnendahl . . .,' *Zeitschrift des Vereins Deutscher Ingenieure*, 1903.
Matschoss, C. : ' Friedrich Harkort . . .,' *Beiträge zur Geschichte der Technik und Industrie*, Vol. x, 1920.
Neubaur, P. : *Matthias Stinnes und sein Haus* . . ., 1909.
Pachter, F. : *August Borsig*, 1953.
Philipps, O. : *Johann und Georg Egerstorff* . . ., 1936.
Pinner, F. : *Deutsche Wirtschaftsführer*, 1924.
Ritter, H. : *Alte rheinische Fabrikantenfamilien*, 1920.
Schnee, H. : *Rothschild. Geschichte einer Finanzdynastie*, 1961.
Schramm, P. E. : *Neun Generationen*, two volumes, 1963-4: a history of the Schramm family in Hamburg.
Schwann, M. : ' Ludolf Camphausen als Wirtschaftspolitiker,' *Veröffentlichungen des Archivs für rheinische Wirtschaftsgeschichte*, Vols. III, IV and V, 1915.
Spamer, O. : *Der Kaufmann zu allen Zeiten*, Vol. III, 1869; appeared under pen name Franz Otto.
Spethmann, H. : *F. Haniel. Sein Leben und seine Werke*, 1956.
Steller, Paul : *Führende Männer des rheinisch-westfälischen Wirtschaftslebens*, 1930.
Treue, W. : *Egestorff*, 1956.
Der bayerische Unternehmer, special number of *Bayerland*, 1960
Rheinisch-Westfälische Wirtschaftsbiographien, seven volumes. 1932-60.

Austria

Charmatz, R. : *Minister Freiherr von Bruck* . . ., 1916.

Belgium

Lotz, H. : *John Cockerill in seiner Bedeutung als Ingenieur und Industrieller 1790-1840*, 1920.

Switzerland

Fischer, J. C. : *Tagebücher*, edited by K. Schib, 1951.

Switzerland

Gagliardi, E. : *Alfred Escher . . .*, 1919.

Gnade and Schib : *Johann Conrad Fischer 1773-1854*, 1954.

Henderson, W. O. : 'J. C. Fischer. A Swiss Industrial Pioneer,' *Zeitschrift für die gesamte Staatswissenschaft*, Vol. CXIX, Heft ii, April, 1963, pp. 360-76.

Peter, Charlotte : 'Hans Caspar Escher 1775-1859,' *Schweizer Pioniere der Wirtschaft und Technik*, Vol. VI, 1956, pp. 9-30.

Schweizer Pioniere der Wirtschaft und Technik, fourteen volumes, 1955 onwards.

INDUSTRIAL UNDERTAKINGS[1]

Adelmann, G. : 'Die Gründung der Aktiengesellschaft Gladbacher Spinnerei und Weberei,' in *Spiegel der Geschichte : Festgabe für Max Braubach zum 10. April, 1964*, Münster, Westfalen, 1964.

André, J. (ed.) : *Histoire de l'industrie dans la vallée de Masevaux*, 1952.

Böhmert, W. : *Die Hamburg-Amerika Linie und der Norddeutsche Lloyd*, 1909.

Chevalier, J. : *Le Creusot . . .*, new edition, 1946.

Däbritz, W. : *Bochumer Verein für Bergbau und Gusstahlfabrikation in Bochum . . .*, 1934.

Däbritz, W., and Metzeltien, E. : *100 Jahr Hanomag . . .*, 1934.

Ehlers, W. : *50 Jahr Norddeutscher Lloyd*, 1907.

Eichborn, K. von : *Das Soll und Haben von Eichborn und Co. in 200 Jahren*, second edition, 1928.

Evrard and Descy : *Histoire de l'usine des Vennes . . . 1548-1948.* Liège, 1948.

Gignou, C. J. : *Histoire d'une entreprise française: Pechiney*, 1955.

Hieke, E. : *G. L. Gaiser, Hamburg-Westafrika, 100 Jahre Handel mit Nigeria*, 1949.

Hieke and Schramm : *Zur Geschichte des deutschen Handels mit Ostafrika. Das hamburgische Haus Wm. Oswald & Co.*, 1939.

[1] For French business archives see B. Gille, 'Les archives d'entreprises,' *Revue Historique*, Vol. IX, May, 1949, pp. 45-62. *Etat sommaire des archives d'entreprises conservées aux Archives Nationales . . .*, 1957, B. Gille, R. Gourmelon and C. Pris, *Répertoire numérique des archives de la Compagnie du Nord conservées aux Archives Nationales*, 1961. For German business archives see the report of the second conference of German business archivists held at Dortmund in 1964. For lists of German business histories see F. Redlich, *The Beginning and Development of German Business History*, supplement to the *Bulletin of the Business Historical Society*, September, 1952, the list of the Schacht collection in the Reichsbank issued by the Bücherei des Reichsbankdirektorium in 1936 and entitled *Katalog der Fest-und Denkschriften wirtschaftlicher Betriebe*, and H. Corsten, *Hundert Jahre deutscher Wirtschaft in Fest-und Denkschriften: eine Bibliographie*, 1937. For German chambers of commerce see *Bibliographie zur Geschichte der deutschen Industrie- und Handelshammern.*

Joiville, P. de : *Le réveil économique de Bordeaux. L'armateur Balgueris-Stuttenberg et son oeuvre*, 1914.

Jungbaum, O. : *Die Gründung und Weiterentwicklung der Königshütte*, 1902.

Meerwein, G. : *Die Entwicklung der Chemnitzer bzw. Sächsischer Baumwollspinnerei*, 1914.

Mony, A. : *Histoire d'une mine: Commentry*, 1911.

Müller, O. (ed.) : *Festschrift zum Jubiläum der Grube Heinitz*, 1897.

Neubauer, P. : *Der Norddeutsche Lloyd, 50 Jahre der Entwicklung 1857-1907*, 1907.

Palewski, J. P. : *Histoire des chefs d'entreprise*, 1928.

Schmidt, H. : *Von Leinen zur Seide. Die Geschichte der Firma A. Delius und Söhne 1722-1925*, 1926.

Siemens, G. : *Geschichte des Hauses Siemens*, three volumes, 1947-51.

Treue, W. : *Die Geschichte der Ilseder Hütte*, 1960.

110e anniversaire de la fondation des usines Cockerill 1817-1927, Brussels, 1928.

Hundert Jahre Nuenkircher Eisenwerke Gebrüder Stumm, 1906.

Hundertfünfzig Jahre Georg Fischer Werke 1802-1952, by F. Aschinger. Schaffhausen, 1952.

Zschopauer Baumwollspinnerei A.G. (vormals Georg Bodemer) . . ., Chemnitz, 1919.

Industrial Regions and Towns

1. *France*

Alsace-Lorraine

Hottenger, G. : *La Lorraine économique au lendemain de la Révolution*, 1924.

Kahan-Rabecq, M. : *L'Alsace économique et sociale sous le régime de Louis-Philippe*, two volumes, 1939.

Leuilliot, Paul: *L'Alsace au début du xixe siècle . . ., 1815-30*, three volumes, 1959-61.

Somme, A. : *La Lorraine métallurgique*, 1930.

Histoire documentaire de l'industrie à Mulhouse, Société Industrielle de Mulhouse, two volumes, 1902.

Amiens

Calonne, L. M. A. de : *Histoire de la ville d'Amiens*, two volumes, 1899-1900.

Dauphiné

Léon, Pierre : *La naissance de la grande industrie en Dauphiné*, two volumes, 1954.

Nord and Pas-de-Calais

Fohlen, Claude: ' Esquisse d'une évolution industrielle : Roubaix aux xixe siècle,' *Revue du Nord*, 1953.

Gossez, A. M. : *Le Départment du Nord sous la deuxième République 1848-52 . . .*, 1904.

Leuridan, T. : *Histoire de Roubaix*, five volumes, 1859-64 ; see Vol. v.

Vaillemin, E. : *Le bassin houiller du Pas-de-Calais . .*, two volumes, 1880-2.

Normandy

Dardel, P. : *Le trafic maritime de Rouen aux xviie et xviiie siècles*, Rouen, 1945.

Debon, P. : *Essai historique sur Louviers*, 1836.

Lesguilliez, A. : *Notice historique sur la ville de Darnétal*, 1835.

Pompon-Levainville, J. R. : *Rouen, étude d'une agglomération urbaine*, 1913.

Vidalenc, J. : *Le Département de l'Eure . . . 1814-48*, 1952.

Paris

Maury, F. : *Le port de Paris . . .*, 1904.

Pinkney, D. : *Napoleon III and the Rebuilding of Paris*, 1958.

Lyons and Saint-Étienne

Beaulieu, C. : *Histoire du commerce et l'industrie et les fabriques de Lyon*, 1838.

Chaulanges, H., and Page, J. : *La région de Lyon et de Saint-Étienne . . .*, four volumes, 1831-8.

Labasse, J. : *Le commerce des soies à Lyon sous Napoléon et la crise de 1811*, 1957.

Perrin, M. : *Saint Étienne et sa région économique*, 1937.

Poriset, E. : *Histoire de la fabrique lyonnaise*, 1901.

Saint-Quentin

Picard, C. : *Saint-Quentin: de son commerce et ses industries*, two volumes, 1865-7.

Saône-et-Loire

Un siècle de vie économique de Saône-et-Loire 1843-1943, 1943.

Sedan

Pregnon, M. : *Histoire du pays et de la ville de Sedan*, three volumes, 1856.

2. *Belgium*

Demoulin, R. : *Guillaume 1er et la transformation économique des provinces belges 1815-30*, 1938.

Stainer, E. : *Histoire commerciale de Charleroi et dans le district de Charleroi de 1829 à 1867*, second edition 1873.

3. *Germany*

General

Braun, G. : *Deutschland . . .*, 1916, and 1936.
Dickinson, R. E. : *Germany*, 1953.
Partsch, J. : *Central Europe*, 1903; German edition entitled *Mitteleuropa*, 1904.

Bavaria

Eheberg, K. F. : *Die industrielle Entwicklung Bayerns seit 1800*, 1879.
Kahls, A. : *Geschichte der Bayerischen Industrie*, 1926.
Zorn, W. : *Grundzüge der Handels- und Industriegeschichte Bayerisch-Schwabens 1648-70*, 1961.
Zorn, W. : *Kleine Wirtschafts- und Sozialgeschichte Bayerns 1806-1933*, 1962.
1815-1915, Hundert Jahre technische Erfindungen und Schöpfungen Bayerns, Jahrhundertschrift des Polytechnischen Vereins in Bayern, 1922.

Berlin

Arendt, Faden and Gandert (ed.) : *Die Geschichte der Stadt Berlin*, 1937.
Hirschfeld, P. : *Berlins Grossindustrie*, three volumes, 1897.
Rachel, H. : *Das Berliner Wirtschaftsleben im Zeitalter des Frühkapitalismus*, 1931.
Rachel, Papritz and Wallich : *Berliner Grosskaufleute und Kapitalisten*, three volumes, 1934-8.
Wiedfeldt, O. : *Statistische Studien zur Entwicklusgngeschichte der Berliner Industrie von 1720 bis 1890*, 1898.

Frankfurt am Main

Dietz, A. : *Frankfurter Handelsgeschichte*, four volumes, 1910-25.
Schwemer, R. : *Geschichte der Freien Stadt Frankfurt am Main, 1814-66*, three volumes in four parts, 1910-18.

Hanover

Aschenbrenner, K. : *Die hannoversche Maschinenindustrie seit ihrer Entstehung im Anfang der dreissiger Jahre bis zum Jahre 1874*, 1921.
Ericke, W. : *Die Entwicklung der Stadt Hannover zu einem Centrum moderner Maschinenindustrie*, 1924.
Hartmann, R. : *Geschichte Hannovers von den ältesten Zeiten bis auf die Gegenwart*, 1886.

Rhineland and Westphalia (including the Ruhr)[1]

Banfield, T. C. : *Industry of the Rhine*, two volumes in one, 1846-8.

Däbritz, W. : *Entstehung und Aufbau des rheinisch-westfälischen Industriebezirks, Beiträge zur Geschichte der Technik und Industrie*, edited by C. Matschoss, Vol. xv, 1925, pp. 13-107.

Darpe, F. : *Geschichte der Stadt Bochum*, Vol. II, 1893.

Evermann, A. F. A. : *Die Eisen- und Stahlerzeugung auf den Wasserwerken zwischen Lahn und Lippe*, 1804.

Gebhardt, G. : *Ruhrbergbau Geschichte, Aufbau und Verflechtung seiner Gesellschaften und Organisationen*, Essen, 1957.

Hocker, N. : *Die Grossindustrie Rheinlands und Westfalens*, 1867.

Jahn, R. : *Essener Geschichte*, 1952, and 1957.

Jüngst, E. : *Festschrift zur Feier des fünfzigjuhrigen Bestehens des Vereins für die bergbaulichen Interessen im Oberbergamtsbezirk Dortmund in Essen 1858-1908*, Essen, 1908.

Hansen, J. (ed.) : *Die Rheinprovinz 1815-1915*, 1917.

Kempken, F. : *Die wirtschaftliche Entwicklung der Stadt Oberhausen*, 1917.

Kuske, B. : *Die Volkswirtschaft des Rheinlands . . .*, 1925.

Kuske, B. : *Wirtschaftsgeschichte Westfalens . . .*, second edition, 1949.

Lehmann, H. : *Duisburgs Grosshandel und Spedition vom Ende des 18^en Jahrhunderts bis 1905*, 1958.

Matschoss, C. : *Aus der Geschichte des rheinisch-westfälischen Industriegebiets*, 1922.

Meister, A. (ed.) : *Die Grafschaft Mark*, two volumes, 1909.

Pieper, H. : *Der Westfälische Hellweg . . .*, 1928.

Pounds, N. J. G. : *The Ruhr*, 1952.

Ribbek, K. : *Geschichte der Stadt Essen*, 1915.

Schmidt, C. : *Le Grand-Duché de Berg 1806-13*, 1905.

Spethmann, H. : *Das Ruhrgebiet*, three volumes, 1933-8.

Schwann, M. : *Geschichte der Kölner Handelskammer*, Vol. I, 1906.

Thun, A. : *Die Industrie am Niederrhein und ihre Arbeiter*, two volumes, 1881.

Trende, A. : *Aus der Werdezeit der Provinz Westfalen*, 1933.

Villefosse, A. M. H. de : *De la richesse minérale : considérations sur les mines, usines, et salines des differénts états, et particulièrement du royaume de Westphalie . . .*, three volumes 1810-19 and a supplementary volume of plates by A. le Coq, 1838.

[1] For literature on the Ruhr see the bibliography in M. Baumont, *La grosse industrie allemande et le charbon* (1928); pp. 688-91. Several Ruhr colliery and iron and steel firms have issued jubilee or centenary volumes, e.g. *Phoenix 1855-1912; Harpenbergbau 1855-1905; Gutehoffnungshütte 1810-1910; Concordia 1850-1950; Zeche Langenbrahm 1772-1922; Thyssen-Bergbau am Niederrhein 1871-1921.*

Voye, E. : *Geschichte der Industrie im märkischen Sauerland*, four volumes, 1908-13.

Waldthausen, A. von : *Geschichte des Steinkohlenbergwerks Vereinigte Sälzer und Neuak . . .*, 1902.

Wiedenfeld, K. : *Ein Jahrhundert rheinischer Montanindustrie 1815-1915*, 1916.

Wirth, M. : *Die Industrie der Grafschaft Mark und die französische Gesetzgebung 1793-1813*, 1914.

L'économie de la Ruhr, Institut Nationale de la statistique et des études économiques, 1947.

100 Jahre Industrie- und Handelskammer Dortmund. Umrisse der Geschichte einer Ruhrhandelskammer 1863-1963, Dortmund, 1963.

Articles in journals concerned with the provinces of Westphalia and the Rhineland, e.g. *Beiträge zur Geschichte Dortmunds und der Grafschaft Mark*, *Rheinische Vierteljahrsblätter*, and *Rheinisches Archiv*.

Rheinisch-Westfälische Wirtschaftsbiographien, seven volumes, 1932-60.

Saar

Hasslacher, A. : *Das Industriegebiet an der Saar und seine hauptsächlichen Industriezweige*, 1879.

Hasslacher, A. : ' Les houillères et les usines sidérurgiques de la Saar ', *Revue universelle des Mines*, second series, Vol. VII, 1880, pp. 457-85.

Hasslacher, A. : *Literatur über das Industriegebiet an der Saar*, second edition, 1910.

Hellwig, F. : *Die Anfänge der Handelskammer zu Saarbrücken 1864-70*, 1934.

Hellwig, F. : *Die Saarwirtschaft und ihre Organisationen*, 1939.

Kellman, J. : *Deutsche Arbeit. Die Grossindustrie des Saargebiets*, 1911.

Kloevenkorn (ed.) : *Das Saargebiet*, 1921.

Müller, O. (ed.) : *Festschrift zum 50-jährigen Jubiläum der Grube Heinitz*, 1897.

Nutzinger, Böhmer and Johannsen : *50 Jahr Röchling Völkingen . . .*, 1931.

Ruppersberg, A. : *Geschichte des Saargebiets*, 1923.

Die Steinkohlenbergbau im Preussischen Staate in der Umgebung von Saarbrücken : I Four studies (published separately between 1884 and 1890) by R. Nasse, B. Jordan, R. Remy, and A. Brandt. II Six studies issued in 1904 by Z. Prietze, A. Ceppla, R. Mütter, and M. Hohensee.

Saxony

Forberger, R. : *Die Manufaktur in Sachsen vom Ende des 16. bis zum Anfang des 19. Jahrhunderts*, 1958.

Forberger, R. : 'Zur Aufnahme der maschinellen Fertigung durch sächsische Manufakturen. Ein Beiträg zur Geschichte der Fabriken in Sachsen,' *Jahrbuch für Wirtschaftsgeschichte*, 1960, Part I.

Forberger, R. : 'Beiträge zur statistischen Erfassung der gewerblichen Produktion Sachsens in der Frühzeit des Kapitalismus,' *Jahrbuch für Wirtschaftsgeschichte*, 1962, Part IV.

Gebauer, H. : *Die Volkswirtschaft im Königreich Sachsen*, three volumes, 1889-91.

Kroker, E. : *Handelsgeschichte der Stadt Leipzig*, 1925.

Silesia

Fechner, H. : *Wirtschaftsgeschichte der Preussischen Provinz Schlesien zur Zeit ihrer provinziellen Selbstständigkeit 1741-1806*, 1908.

Felsch, G. : *Die Wirtschaftspolitik des preussischen Staates* **bei** *der Gründung der oberschlesischen Kohlen- und Eisenindustrie 1741-1871*, 1920.

Frahn, C. : *Die Textilindustrie im Wirtschaftsleben Schlesiens 1802-1902*, 1905.

Jungbaum, O. : *Die Gründung und Weiterentwicklung der Königshütte*, 1902.

Voltz, H. (ed.) : *Der Bergbau im Osten des Königreichs Preussen. Festschrift zum xiien Allgemeinen deutschen Bergmannstag: Handbuch des oberschlesischen Industriebezirks*, 1913.

Zimmermann, A. : *Blüte und Verfall des Leinengewebes in Schlesien*, 1892.

Württemberg

Vischer, L. : *Die industrielle Entwicklung im Königreich Württemberg . . .*, 1875.

Rural and Craft Industries

Schmoller, G. : *Zur Geschichte der deutschen Kleingewerbe im 19en Jahrhundert*, 1870.

Tarlé, E. V. : *L'industrie dans les campagnes à la fin de l'ancien régime*, 1910.

Ports and Shipping

General

Reinhard, E. : *Die wichtigsten Seehandelsstädte*, 1901.

Sargent, A. J. : *Seaports and Hinterlands*, 1938.
Weidenfeld, C. : *Die nordwesteuropäischen Welthäfen*, 1903.

Amsterdam

Brugmans, H. : 'De ontwikkelingsgang van Amsterdam,' *Catalogues der Historische Teutoonstellung*, Amsterdam, 1925, Part I Introduction.

Antwerp

Desprez, J. : 'Le port d'Anvers . . .,' *Bulletin de la Société d'études géographiques*, Vol. VIII, 1938, pp. 182-229.

Bordeaux

Devienne, J. B. : *Histoire de la ville de Bordeaux*, 1862.
Joinville, P. de : *Le réveil économique de Bordeaux sous la Restauration. L'armateur Balguerie-Stuttenberg et son oeuvre*, 1914.
Melvezin, T. : *Histoire du commerce de Bordeaux*, four volumes, 1892.

Bremen

Lörner, A. : *Bremen im Welthandel*, second edition, 1927.
Rauers, F. : *Bremer Handelsgeschichte im 19*[en] *Jahrhundert*, 1913.
Veröffentlichungen aus dem Staatsarchiv der Freien Hansestadt Bremen, Vols. I to XXXII, 1928-64.
Die Freie Stadt Bremen, Weser-Gilde, 1922.

Greiz

Beck, F. : *Die wirtschaftliche Entwicklung in der Stadt Greiz während des 19. Jahrhunderts: Ein Beitrag zur Geschichte der Industrialisierung in Deutschland*, Weimar, 1955.

Hamburg

Alemann, E. F. : *Hamburgs Schiffahrt und Handel nach dem La Plata*, 1915.
Baasch, E. : *Forschungen zur hamburgischen Handelsgeschichte*, two volumes, 1889-98.
Baasch, E. : *Geschichte Hamburgs 1814-1918*, two volumes 1924-5.
Büsch, J. G. : *Versuch einer Geschichte der Hamburgischen Handlung*, 1797.
Articles in the *Zeitschrift des Vereins für Hamburgische Geschichte*.

Le Havre

'Le Havre maritime,' *Mémoires et documents pour servir à l'histoire du commerce et de l'industrie*, Vol. VI, 1921.

Marseilles

Busquet, R. : *Histoire de Marseille*, 1945.

Fouque : *Histoire raisonné du commerce de Marseille . . .*, two volumes, 1843.

Giraud, H. : *Les origines et l'évolution de la navigation à vapeur à Marseille 1829-1900*, 1929.

Guiral, P. : ' Le monde vu de Marseille autour de 1820', *Provence Historique*, December, 1956.

Guiral, P. : *Marseille et l'Algérie 1830-41*, 1956.

Guiral, P. : ' Marseille et l'Algérie de 1848 à 1870,' *Revue Africaine*, 1956.

Julliany, J. : *Essai sur le commerce de Marseille*, second edition, 1842.

Masson, P. : *Marseille et la colonisation française*, 1912.

Nantes

Guépin, A. : *Histoire de Nantes*, 1839.

COMMERCIAL AND FISCAL POLICY

Ashley, P. : *Modern Tariff History*, 1904.

Bloch, C. : *Etudes sur l'histoire économique de la France 1760-89:* see pp. 241-269 for an account of the Anglo-French commercial treaty of 1786.

Brinkmann, C. : *Die preussische Handelspolitik vor dem Zollverein*, . . . 1922.

Brodnitz, G. : *Bismarcks nationalökonomische Anschaungen*, 1902.

Curien, G. : ' Rhythmes du monde. Les accords économiques internationaux depuis 1860,' *Annales*, 1946, pp. 219-234.

Dunham, A. L. : *The Anglo-French Treaty of Commerce of 1860 . . .*, 1930.

Ehrman, J. : *The British Government and Commercial Negotiations with Europe 1783-93*, 1962.

Girault, A. : *The Colonial Tariff Policy of France*, 1916.

Haight, F. A. : *A History of French Commercial Policies*, 1941.

Haumer, F. : *Die Handelspolitik der Niederlande 1830-1930*, 1936.

Hirst, M. E. : *Life of Friedrich List*, 1909.

Lambi, I. N. : *Free Trade and Protection in Germany 1868-1879. Vierteljahrschrift für Sozial-und Wirtschaftsgeschichte*, Supplement 44, 1963.

Lenz, F. : *Friedrich List. Der Mann und das Werk*, 1936.

List, F. : *The National System of Political Economy*, German edition, 1841; English translation, 1928.

Nitzsche, M. : *Die handelspolitische Reaktion in Deutschland*, 1905.

Posthumus, N. W. (ed.) : *Documenten betreffende de Buitenlandsche Handelspolitiek van Nederland in de negentiende eeuw*, eight volumes, 1919-31.
Schneider, O. : *Bismarck und die preussisch-deutsche Handelspolitik 1862-76*, 1910.
Sering, M. : *Geschichte der preussisch-deutschen Eisenzölle . . .* 1882.
Smith, John Prince: *Gesammelte Schriften*, three volumes, 1877.
Truchy, H. : *Les relations économiques internationales*, 1948.
Wright, H. R. C. : *Free Trade and Protection in the Netherlands 1816-30*, 1955.
Zimmermann, A. : *Geschichte der preussisch-deutschen Handelspolitik*, 1892.
Zimmermann, A. : *Die Handelspolitik des Deutschen Reiches*, third edition, 1901.

Overseas Commerce

Arnauné, A. : *Le commerce extérieure et les tarifs de douane*, 1911.
Bedemann, A. : *Die Rheinisch-westindische Compagnie*, 1915.
Böhmert, W. : *Die Hamburg-Amerika-Linie und der Norddeutsche Lloyd*, 1909.
Colin, A. : *La navigation commerciale aux xix*e *siècle*, 1911.
Levasseur, E. : *Histoire de commerce de la France*, two volumes, 1911-12.
Schramm, P. E. : *Deutschland und Übersee*, 1950.
Schrader, Paul : *Die Geschichte der Kgl. Seehandlung* . . , 1911.
Die Entwicklung des Schweizerischen Aussenhandels in den Jahren 1866-1912, Swiss Customs Department, Berne, 1913.

The Industrial Workers

Aguet, J. P. : *Les grèves sous la Monarchie de Juillet 1830-47*, 1954.
Anton, G. K. : *Geschichte der preussischen Fabrikgesetzgebung . . .* 1891 ; new edition 1953.
Blanc, Louis : *L'Organisation du travail*, 1839 : new edition edited by J. A. R. Marriott, 1913.
Buret, Eugène : *De la misère des classes laborieuses en Angleterre et en France* . . ., 2 vols., 1840.
Chaumel, G. : *Histoire des cheminots et de leur syndicats*, 1948.
Chavellier, E. : *Les salaires au xix*e *siècle*, 1887.
Dlugoborski, Wand Popiolek, K. : ' A study of the Growth of Industry and the History of the Working Classes in Silesia, *Annales Silesia*, Vol. I, 1960.
Dautry, R. : *Compagnonnage* . . ., 1951.

Dohler, W. : *Die ökonomische Lage der Zwickauer Bergarbeiter im vorigen Jahrhundert*, 1963.

Dolléans, E. : *Histoire du mouvement ouvrier*, two volumes, 1936-48.

Du Cellier, F. : *Histoire des classes laborieuses en France*, 1860.

Duveau, G. : *Le vie ouvrière en France sous le second Empire*, 1946.

Engels, F. : *The Condition of the Working Class in England.* German edition, 1845 ; first English translation, 1887; new English translation by W. O. Henderson and W. H. Chaloner, 1958.

Fischer, W. : 'Soziale Unterschichten im Zeitalter der Frühindustrialisierung,' *International Review of Social History*, 1963, pp 415-35.

Fischer, W. : ' Das deutsche Handwerk in den Frühphasen der Industrialisiering' in *Zeitschrift für die gesamte Staatswissenschaft*, 1964.

Goldschmidt, E. F. : *Die deutsche Handwerkerbewegung bis zum Siege der Gewerbefreiheit*, 1916.

Kuczynski, J. : *Die Geschichte der Lage der Arbeiter unter dem Kapitalismus*, several volumes, 1961 onwards.

Larogue, P. : *Les rapports entre patrons et ouvriers. Leur évolution en France depuis le xviii*e *siècle*, 1938.

Perdiguier, A. : *Mémoires d'un compagnon*, two volumes, 1854-5 : new edition edited by D. Halévy, 1914.

Maritch, S. : *Histoire du mouvement social sous le second Empire à Lyon*, 1930.

Mönckmeier, W. : *Die deutsche Überseewanderung*, 1912.

Montreuil, J. : *Histoire du mouvement ouvrier en France*, 1946.

Rigandrias-Weiss, H. : *Les enquêtes ouvrières en France entre 1830 et 1848*, 1936.

Rude, F. : *Le mouvement ouvrier à Lyon*, 1944.

Syrup, F., and Neulok, O. : *Hundert Jahr Staatliche Sozialpolitik 1839 bis 1939*, 1957.

Teuteberg, H. J. : *Geschichte der industriellen Mitbestimmung in Deutschland*, 1961.

Thomas, Emile : *Histoire des ateliers nationaux*, 1848: new edition, edited by J. A. R. Marriott, 1913.

Villermé, L. R. : *Tableau de l'état physique et moral des ouvriers employés dans les manufactures de coton, de laine et de soie*, two volumes, 1840.

Weill, G. : *Histoire du mouvement social en France*, 1904.

Wendel, H. C. M. : *The Evolution of Industrial Freedom in Prussia 1845-9*, New York, 1921.

Statistics

Behre, O. : *Geschichte der Statistik im Brandenburg-Preussen Staat bis zur Gründung des Königlichen Statistischen Bureaus*, 1905.

Bienengräber, A. : *Statistik des Verkehrs und Verbrauchs im Zollverein für die Jahre 1842-64*, 1867-8.

Dieterici, C. F. W. : *Statistik und Übersicht der wichtigsten Gegenstände des Verkehrs und Verbrauchs im preussischen Staat und im Zollverein 1838-57*, six volumes, 1938-57.

Dieterici, C. F. W. : *Der Volkswohlstand im preussischen Staate*, 1846.

Dieterici, C. F. W. : *Handbuch der Statistik des preussischen Staates*, 1861.

Ferber, C. W. : *Beiträge zur Kenntnis des gewerblichen und kommerziellen Zustände der preussischen Monarchie*, 1829. A supplementary volume entitled *Neue Beiträge . . .*, appeared in 1832.

Hermes, Gertrude : ' Statistische Studien zur wirtschaftlicen und gesellschaftlichen Struktur des zollvereinten Deutschlands,' *Archiv für Sozialwissenschaften und Sozialpolitik*, Vol. XLIII, 1930, p. 121.

Hoffmann, J. G. : *Die Stellung des Bevölkerungs- Geburts- Ehe- und Sterblichkeitsverhältnisse im Preussischen Staate 1820-34*, 1843.

Hoffmann, W. G., and Müller, J. H. : *Das Deutsche Volkseinkommen 1851-1957*, 1959.

Moreau de Jonnès, A. : *Statistique de l'industrie de la France*, 1856.

Mulhall, M. G. : *The Dictionary of Statistics*, fourth edition, 1899.

Pénot, A. : *Statistique générale du département de Haut-Rhin*, 1831.

Viebahn, G. von : *Statistik des zollvereinten und nördlichen Deutschlands*, three volumes, 1858-68.

Villeneuve-Bargemont, J. : *Statistique du département des Bouches-du-Rhôn*, four volumes, 1821-9.

Voigtel, F. G. : *Versuch einer Statistik des preussischen Staates*, 1857.

For this third edition, additions have been made to the bibliography, overleaf.

P. Bairoch, *Le tiers-monde dans l'impasse*, 1971.

A. Birch, ' Foreign Observers of the British Iron Industry during the eighteenth century ', *Journal of Economic History*, Vol. xv, 1955, 23-33.

A. Brandt, ' Apports anglais a l'industrialisation de l'Alsace au XIXe siecle ', *Bulletin de la Société industrielle de Mulhouse*, No. 726, 1967.

A. Brandt, ' Travailleurs anglais dans le Haut Rhin dans la première moité du XIXe siecle', *Actes du 92e Congrès National des Sociétés Savantes, Strasbourg et Calmar, 1967*, Vol. II (Le commerce et l'industrie), Paris, 1970, 297-312.

M. W. Flinn, ' Samuel Schröderstierna's "Notes on the English Iron Industry " (1749) ', *Edgar Allen News*, August 1954.

M. W. Flinn, ' The Travel Diaries of Swedish Engineers of the Eighteenth Century as Sources of Technological History ', *Transactions of the Newcomen Society*, Vol. XXXI, 1957-9, 95-109.

C. Fohlen, *Qu'est-ce qui la révolution industrielle*, 1971.

J. J. Hermandinquer, ' Une dynastie de mécaniciens anglais en France: James, John et Juliana Collier (1791-1947) ', *Revue d'Histoire des Sciences et de leurs applications*, cahier no. 4 *Documents pour l'histoire des techniques* 1965, 193-208.

G. Thuillier, *Georges Dufaud et les débuts du grand capitalisme métallurgique en Nivernais*, 1959.

INDEX